LIVING PHILOSOPHY

LIVING PHILOSOPHY

Philip Lawton and Marie-Louise Bishop

Canfield Press ⊕ San Francisco
A department of Harper & Row, Publishers, Inc.
New York   Hagerstown   London

Living Philosophy
Copyright © 1977 by Philip Lawton and Marie-Louise Bishop

Design: Janet Bollow
Interior and cover illustrations: Patrick Maloney
Copy editor: Judith Chaffin
Editors: Ann Ludwig, Eva Marie Strock

Composition by Computer Typesetting Services. Printed and bound by Kingsport Press.

Library of Congress Catalog in Publication Data

Lawton, Philip, 1947–
  Living Philosophy.

  Bibliography
  Includes index.
  I. Philosophy, Modern.   2. Philosophers, Modern—Biography.   2. Bishop, Marie-Louise, joint author.
  II. Title.
  B791.L38   190   76–44914
  ISBN 0–06–384800–7

77 78 79 80   10 9 8 7 6 5 4 3 2 1

CREDITS

For Jean Ladrière
and Henry Rago,
our teachers.

The title of this textbook—*Living Philosophy*—may already have suggested our objectives and our concerns. We have written the book to meet the widely recognized need for an introduction to philosophy that will speak to its readers' practical experience and engage their lively interest without compromising the discipline's integrity. Most of the textbooks and anthologies currently available err one way or the other: They are too technical and so too difficult, or they are too popular and so insufficiently rigorous. By stressing the contributions of modern and contemporary Western philosophers and by focusing on recent Western experience, we have tried to find the middle ground in content. By philosophically examining issues immediately concerning students and by preparing Inquiries that encourage their active participation, we've also tried to find a middle ground in method.

Living Philosophy is organized around themes rather than historical periods or academic specialties. Its style is informal. We have generally avoided using technical terms, but where we have introduced them, we have taken care to define them in context.

This approach does not, however, betray any scorn for the history of philosophy, for specialization, or for technical language. On the contrary, we are sharply aware of the fact that although every philosopher begins anew, no philosopher begins as for the first time. We recognize too that in our times specialization alone has allowed professional philosophers to deal cogently and critically with complex philosophical questions, making considerable regional progress in many areas. And we know very well that the traditional terms of technical philosophy, as well as some neologisms, are useful tools for research and investigation—tools that may have to be cleaned and oiled and sharpened and sometimes redesigned but whose value for professional philosophers is inestimable.

For all that, *Living Philosophy* intends to introduce students to the philosophical life, not by teaching them magisterially, but by involving them actively in philosophical debate. Those students who go on to follow advanced courses in the discipline will have every opportunity to study the history of philosophy, to specialize, and to master the technical language; those students who do not will still emerge from their introductory course with a clear idea of what philosophy is and an informed opinion of its value. Most important, these students will come to appreciate the involvement of philosophical thought in everyday life: They will learn, many of them for the first time, what it is to evaluate philosophical arguments, and they will learn too to recognize what difference it makes if one view or another is right.

In our opinion, the following features combine to make *Living Philosophy* a good working textbook:

Chapter Surveys.   Each chapter is preceded by an outline, or survey, denoting the topics and posing the questions that the chapter will address. Given their format, these outlines may serve not only to offer students a prospect of the chapters but also to provide them with review and study questions. The questions also appear at the appropriate points in the margins of the text so students can easily follow the chapters' development.

Biographical Sketches.   Each chapter is also preceded by a 500-word essay on a prominent modern or contemporary philosopher whose work relates to the chapter's concerns. Apart from their intrinsic interest, these sketches may serve students as starting points for research papers.

Viewpoints.   Each chapter is punctuated by a number of Viewpoints, brief excerpts from philosophical and literary works relevant to the questions under discussion. These excerpts are boxed to set them off from the text proper. Some Viewpoints expand and illustrate points we've made in the text—the passages from philosophical essays by presenting arguments and the

excerpts from fictional works by making philosophical ideas and insights concrete or by suggesting the philosophical dimensions of lived situations. Other Viewpoints counter our arguments. Hopefully these passages will spur students to read essays and novels on their own; certainly, the passages will make students aware of the diversity of philosophical perspectives and styles. The Viewpoints' juxtaposition may also provoke lively class discussions.

Summaries.   Each chapter is followed by a concise summary that may serve both to anticipate and to recall the main points made. Students would of course be well advised to read both the chapter survey and the summary before *and* after reading the chapter itself.

Suggestions for Further Reading.   Each chapter is also followed by an annotated listing of recommended works.

Inquiries.   The two Inquiries that conclude each chapter unit are self-contained, problem-centered essays suitable for general class discussion, for small-group seminars, or for individual "reaction papers." Teaching philosophy is an art. There is not a "right" and a "wrong" way to use these essays and exercises; rather, to adopt a pragmatic view, whatever works for the individual professor and his or her class is the right way. However they are used, the Inquiries are designed to involve students in philosophical argumentation. Their primary instructional objective is not of course to stimulate consensus on the 'questions; it is the more modest one of allowing students to discover for themselves the complexity of the issues under consideration. Our own teaching experience has convinced us that a high level of student involvement and participation is crucial to the success of an introductory philosophy course. These Inquiries may contribute significantly to the course by stimulating such involvement and encouraging such participation.

Glossary-Index. We have also provided a glossary-index in which technical terms defined in context are set off in boldfaced type to assist students who may be unclear about them.

Living Philosophy is flexible enough to be used effectively in one- or two-semester courses. Based on a sixteen-week semester system, the following remarks may suggest possible applications. The professor can easily establish a plan suitable for a trimester or quarter system or for summer and evening school sessions.

In a sixteen-week, three credit-hour course, the professor may develop programs that high-light certain areas. For instance, a course stressing topics and problems in social and political philosophy might include the careful study of Chapter 1 (persons); Chapter 3 (communication); Chapter 4 (value); Chapter 5 (freedom); Chapter 7 (work); and Chapter 10 (environment). A course focusing on existential themes and problems might stress Chapters 2, 4, 6 (religion), 7, 8 (play and art), and 9 (death). A course emphasizing the philosophy of culture might center on Chapters 2 (myth and science), 3, 7 to 10, and the appendix on Eastern thought.

In addition, many Inquiries may accompany chapters other than those with which we have chosen to place them. For example, the Inquiry essay on abortion following Chapter 1 might equally well be used in connection with Chapter 4; the essays following Chapter 10 might also be introduced after Chapter 5; and the Inquiry on religious language following Chapter 3 might be moved to Chapter 6. Other variations will suggest themselves.

In a thirty-two-week, six credit-hour course, we would simply recommend that the professor follow the first contents, variously allowing two to three weeks for each chapter (including one or both Inquiries). The chapters are largely independent of one another, however, so the professor may indeed reorder them to suit his or her preference. For instance, Chapter 3, "Communication: From Rituals to Reasoning," might serve well as the first reading assignment since it presents logical principles for philosophical argumentation. Of course, professors teaching two-semester courses in philosophy or the humanities will want to supplement this textbook by using films and novels or an anthology of primary sources.

We have offered more detailed recommendations for the use of *Living Philosophy* in the instructor's manual; our present purpose is merely to indicate some possibilities. We would like to call attention to the second contents included here, however. Cast in familiar terms, it may suggest other ways in which the professor may prefer to organize a course covering the principal areas of traditional philosophic inquiry.

At the conclusion of this project, it is difficult to establish precisely who did what. The endeavor was a philosophical dialogue in every sense, and our correspondence would fill another volume quite as large. Canfield Press identified the similarity in our goals for an introductory text, and Philip Lawton's prospectus was revised and expanded in the course of his extended conversations with Marie-Louise Bishop. The coauthors consulted with one another on the development of every chapter. Marie-Louise Bishop wrote Chapters 1, 2, 4, and 6. Philip

Lawton wrote the biographical sketches and Chapters 7 to 10. Conferring with Marie-Louise Bishop, James Royse of San Francisco State University wrote the first draft of Chapter 3. Working with Philip Lawton, Richard Gillis of Norwalk, Connecticut, wrote the first draft of Chapter 5. In close association with Marie-Louise Bishop and Philip Lawton, Margaret Fleming and Olivia Byrne drafted the appendix on Eastern thought in its initial form. Finally, Marjorie Pavesich expertly edited the entire text.

At Canfield Press, Jack Jennings, Roger Williams, and Wayne Oler encouraged the book's development, and Ann Ludwig did everything possible to expedite its completion. Her keen interest, sound editorial judgment, and unfailing optimism made writing it a pleasure. Eva Marie Strock directed production. Her creativity and technical skill are evident on every page. We are deeply grateful to the entire staff at Canfield Press for their enthusiasm and ability.

In Massachusetts, John Dunn consistently offered support and encouragement. Stephen Weisner, John Kikoski, and Richard Parkin read large parts of the manuscript at various stages and offered thoughtful suggestions for its improvement, as did Philip N. Lawton, Sr. Dena Lange Lawton has been infinitely patient; without her faith, this book might never have seen the light of day.

In California, David Cole Gordon read portions of the manuscript and shared his professional experience, critical insight, and enthusiasm. Frank C. C. Young of the Cañada College faculty offered his expertise in Eastern philosophy and made suggestions for the text's improvement. Donald Palmer of the College of Marin made a considerable contribution to the later parts of Chapter 2. Alfred V. Boursy and Richard B. Bishop offered inspiration and support through their lifelong dedication to teaching, research, and the scholarly tradition. They unselfishly shared family visits, typewriters, books, and ideas. Ken A. Collinsworth urged the dream to become reality.

We are also grateful to the following reviewers whose critical remarks on earlier drafts of these chapters spared us many mistakes and made *Living Philosophy* better than it would have been otherwise: Raziel Abelson, New York University; Timothy Chadsey, Rochester Community College; Roger Eastman, Reedley College; James L. Edwards, Nassau Community College; H. Phillips Hamlin, University of Tennessee; Bernard J. Mahoney, Houston Community College; Stanley V. McDaniel, California State College, Sonoma; Harvey Solganick, Eastfield College; Jacob Needleman, San Francisco State University; Patrick Pidgeon, San Diego Mesa College; Steven Sanders, Bridgewater State College; Anita Silvers, San Francisco State University; Robert D. Sweeney, John Carroll University; and Jean Thompson, El Centro College. We accept full responsibility for any errors that may have escaped our notice.

Philip Lawton
Arlington, Massachusetts

Marie-Louise Bishop
Redwood City, California

AUTHOR PROFILES

Philip Lawton majored in philosophy at John Carroll University, Cleveland, and the College of the Holy Cross, Worcester, Massachusetts. He then earned a bachelor's degree, licentiate degree, and doctorate "avec grande distinction" (the latter in June 1973) from the Higher Institute of Philosophy at the Catholic University of Louvain in Belgium. Dr. Lawton began his teaching career at St. Francis College in Biddeford, Maine, as an instructor of philosophy. From 1973 to 1976 he was Assistant Professor of Philosophy and Western Civilization at Springfield Technical Community College in Massachusetts. Dr. Lawton is presently a free-lance writer and editor, living with his wife Dena Lange and son Philip in Massachusetts. His scholarly articles have appeared in such journals as *Tijdschrift voor Filosofie* and *Philosophy Today*.

Marie-Louise Bishop majored in English, with history and philosophy as related fields, at Regis College, Weston, Massachusetts. She then obtained a master's of art degree in English, with related field in philosophy, from the University of Michigan in 1967. Pursuing her interest in interdisciplinary studies, Ms. Bishop earned a second master's degree, in theology and literature, from the Divinity School of the University of Chicago. Ms. Bishop was admitted to candidacy for the Ph.D. degree at the University of Chicago in 1975, but her dissertation—on Marianne Moore's poetry as a reflection of the American religious tradition—has been put aside temporarily for *Living Philosophy*. She has been on the faculty at Cañada College since 1971, teaching primarily philosophy, as well as English, American civilization, religious studies, and women's studies (Ms. Bishop very recently became coordinator for the Women's Reentry to Education Program at Cañada College).

CONTENTS

SUBJECT CONTENTS

Note: In the following contents we have frequently specified chapter *sections* that are immediately relevant to the subject under consideration. Although chapter sections may of course be read in isolation as indicated here, we caution the reader that each chapter has a certain structural unity; thus, taking parts out of context without having first surveyed the whole might lead to misconstructions. However, the Inquiries are entirely self-contained.

Philosophy of Art

Socrates
c. 470–399 B.C.

". . . the unexamined life is not worth living."

The war was over. Defeated and torn by internal dissension, Athens had finally surrendered to Spartan domination. The next five years were turbulent; the Athenian resistance movement eventually succeeded in restoring the city-state's traditional democratic government, but the people's confidence in democracy itself had been shaken by the experience. So had their faith in the old moral order and the old religious myths. It was during this distressing time of change and reconstruction that Socrates was charged as an evil-doer whose teaching corrupted the youth of the city because he did not believe in the gods of the state but had other new gods of his own.

In his defense—as his companion Plato presented it in Apology—Socrates tried to explain his philosophical activity to the judges. A friend of his had once asked the god Apollo's oracle at Delphi if there lived any man wiser than Socrates, and the prophet had answered no: Socrates was the wisest man. When his friend reported this to him, however, Socrates was confused. What could the god mean? How could he interpret this riddle? For Socrates knew he had no wisdom.

Socrates reflected, then, that if he could only find someone wiser than himself, he could prove Apollo's oracle wrong. Accordingly, he went to those who had a reputation for wisdom—politicians, poets, artisans, and others—to ask them questions. Socrates discovered, however, that he was in fact wiser than they were because although they thought they knew something, he knew that

he knew nothing. Still, he continued to inquire.

"This inquisition," Socrates went on, has led to my having many enemies. . . . And I am called wise, for my hearers always imagine that I myself possess the wisdom which I find wanting in others; but the truth is, O men of Athens, that God only is wise; and by his answer he intends to show that the wisdom of men is worth little or nothing; he is not speaking of Socrates, he is only using my name by way of illustration, as if he said, He, O men, is the wisest, who, like Socrates, knows that his wisdom is in truth worth nothing. And so I go about the world

obedient to the god, and search and make enquiry into the wisdom of any one, whether citizen or stranger, who appears to be wise.

Socrates' philosophical mission, however, was not only to show that people's opinions were usually unjustified but also to reach truth by establishing logically satisfactory definitions of such ethical ideas and ideals as courage, justice, piety, and beauty. He never wrote any textbooks; his method was to ask questions in a living philosophical dialogue with others. It was only when people saw that their own opinions were confused, Socrates held, that they too would start to search for truth, and so become philosophers: "lovers of wisdom."

Socrates also argued at his trial that Athens would harm itself by condemning him to death. "For if you kill me," he warned, "you will not easily find a successor to me, who, if I may use such a ludicrous figure of speech, am a sort of gadfly, given to the State by God; and the State is a great and noble steed who is tardy in his motions owning to his very size, and requires to be stirred into life." His critical questions, Socrates suggested, were intended not to undermine religious belief, nor to corrupt the young, but rather to benefit Athens by stinging its citizens into pursuing truth and excellence. However, Socrates' speech succeeded only in provoking the judges, and when he refused to give up philosophizing, the court condemned him to death by poison.

INTRODUCTION

If you're like many other students, you probably don't know just what to expect from an introductory philosophy course. You may have some idea what philosophy is, but you probably have some doubts and some misgivings about it too. For instance, chances are that you picture philosophers as bearded young men with flashing eyes or bearded old men with books and pipes. They're always men, and they always wonder about things ordinary people never give a second thought—or a first thought! They debate nonsensical riddles, they play word games, and they propose elaborate, impractical schemes for perfecting society; they go round and round, contradicting one another from one generation to the next, and they never reach any sound and lasting conclusions.

Chances are too that although you're interested in learning first-hand what people *do* when they philosophize, you don't imagine it really has much to do with you. Philosophy doesn't speak to the way most people think and live in the United States in this last part of the twentieth century, and, in particular, it doesn't address the hopes, fears, beliefs, and doubts that concern you personally.

In short, philosophy, you might suspect, has noting to do with everyday life. It's too difficult for ordinary people, and it is too abstract for their ordinary world and too remote from their ordinary concerns. Philosophical riddles are not your problem, and your problems are not philosophical.

One of our purposes in making this textbook available is to show you that, very much to the contrary, philosophy may be meaningful and important to your life. In fact, you may find during the course of your studies that many of the questions that vex philosophers have already occurred to you. In the following chapters, among other things we'll examine the notion of "persons," and we'll inquire into the nature of freedom in political society; we'll investigate valuation; we'll scrutinize religious experience; we'll discuss the ways people use language; we'll consider the meaning of work, and play, and death; and we'll look into the attitudes people adopt toward their physical environment. Clearly, these questions, and many others like them, are not of interest to academic philosophers alone. They're important to anyone who wants to arrive at a more critical appreciation of human reality and human possibilities.

But what exactly *is* "philosophy"? Literally, the word means "the love of wisdom," but beyond that philosophy isn't easily defined. Professional philosophers—the many teachers and writers who have devoted their lives to the discipline of philosophical inquiry—disagree with one another over the method, the nature, the limits, and the very goals of their own work. We'll see that disagreement, even over principles, is not incidental to philosophy but essential to it. For the moment, we'd like to propose, at least tentatively, one view of philosophy and its aims, a view that has its place among others in contemporary thought.

In this view, philosophy represents an effort to think critically (which is not to say "negatively") about ourselves and our experience—our values, our ways of seeing things and our ways of thinking and talking about them, our relations to other persons, and our relations to the natural world. So understood and pursued with intellectual honesty, philosophical reflection may allow us to attain a sharper awareness of the dimensions of the human condition, the wealth of human experience, and the range of human possibilities: *our* condition, *our* experience, and *our* possibilities.

In general, to understand human existence is to understand ourselves as persons in our "relatedness" to the world, to others, and perhaps to the divine, or whatever ultimate reality is. For persons, "to be" is "to be in relation to" something or somebody else. It is, for instance, to be physically in the world, where work postpones death; it is, moreover, to have that world in common with other persons, other selves, whose freedom may limit ours but in whose midst we first discover ourselves, our freedom, and our limits. In addition, to be persons *may* mean to be "creatures," that is, to have been created, not by the random and fateful play of natural forces, but by God— although even if so it would mean to have been created so radically independent that atheism is also a human possibility. In our view then, to philosophize is to attempt to get clear about our relational presence to the world, to others, and (again, perhaps) to the divine, however it is understood. Moreover, to philosophize is to recognize not only the stances we *do* take as persons but the positions we *might* adopt as well.

To the rather limited extent that such labels are valuable, this approach to philosophy might be considered more or less "existential": It focuses on experience. As we've already indicated, however, there are other approaches, certainly no less legitimate. Of these, today the most important by far is "linguistic analysis" or "ordinary language philosophy." As these tags suggest, this latter approach focuses not on experience but on language.

Neither existential philosophy nor linguistic analysis is a "school of thought"; no such unity prevails within either movement. Philosophers who agree with one another in recognizing existential problems may differ significantly in their viewpoints, their reasoning, and their conclusions. Similarly, philosophers who agree that certain problems of language are properly philosophical may very well disagree over their analyses of them. Generally, however, existential philosophy and linguistic analysis represent two predominant trends in recent thought.

In the analysts' view, philosophy, correctly understood, aims at the logical clarification of concepts through the careful scrutiny of the words we use and the ways in which we use them. In some cases, such analysis may reveal that what we mistook for a perplexing philosophical problem is merely a confusion about language; in every case, it will make a problem's resolution more apparent by defining its terms more clearly.

Existential philosophy, which has enjoyed some popularity in Germany, Belgium, and France, and ordinary language philosophy, which is more popular in English-speaking countries, are frequently seen as hostile camps. But they are not mutually exclusive; we would prefer to stress their complementarity. Both movements, after all, are concerned with problems of meaning: The one inquires into the meaning of experience, and the other, the meaning of expressions. In writing this textbook we have largely adopted an existential approach, but we have also introduced the analyses of ordinary language philosophers whose distinctions may clarify problems.

We suggested earlier that disagreement, not only over details but over principles as well, is essential to philosophy. This is so because philosophy is essentially a critical discipline. Whether it centers on lived relations or on the conceptual and linguistic framework in terms of which we organize and interpret our experience, philosophical thinking is critical thinking. In other words, philosophers are not naïve; they don't want to be taken in or duped by impressions (appearances) or expressions (words). Moreover, philosophers criticize one another's ideas and arguments—their assumptions, their logic, and their conclusions. Thus, the popular image of the solitary philosopher musing in an armchair by the midnight fire in his study is as misleading as the caricatures we sketched in opening the introduction. Obviously, philosophical reflection is best carried on in quiet surroundings, but morning comes and the philosophical life is also a life of dialogue with others. Their mutual criticism may not ensure that philosophers will reach the truth, but it does at least serve to minimize the probability of error. What is more, it may compel philosophers to approach a given problem from more than one perspective, enabling them to recognize and appreciate its different aspects.

This idea, that philosophy is essentially a critical discipline, has immediate practical consequences for you. It means that your reading of this text—more accurately, your *use* of it—should be more active than your study of other textbooks in other courses. In the following chapters we have presented certain logical principles and procedures that govern philosophical debate; we've also introduced many points of information, a good number of names, and some words that may be new to you. In addressing ourselves to various problems, we've tried to bring out as many aspects and viewpoints as possible. But in every chapter we have also developed arguments that reflect our own philosophical perspective and our own experience. If you read these chapters thoughtfully and attentively, you may very well find that your orientation and your experience are different. You may see things that escaped us; you may question our commitments, and our arguments, and our conclusions. In short, you may have objections to make. Make them! Make them in the margins; make them in your notebook and your journal; above all, make them in the classroom. We've written this textbook not so much to inform or to instruct as to introduce you to the philosophical life by inviting you to participate in philosophical dialogue.

To what end? What good is philosophy, and what's the point of dialogue? Why spend time and why expend energy debating philosophical issues?

Admittedly, philosophy is not for everybody at all times. It presupposes a commitment to reason, presupposes, that is, a value choice and a decision which cannot themselves be based on reason because they are prerational. It is entirely possible not to make this first commitment to reason, to decide instead that critical objectivity is a ridiculous posture and dialogue a waste of time. It is entirely possible to decide that every individual has his or her "own" truth and his or her "own" values, and that's an end to it. It's possible, that is, to remain silent and to prefer flight or violence to reason. But if you *argue* your position, if you attempt to justify it, then you've already acknowledged the value of reason itself, and you're already philosophizing. What good is philosophy? What good is argument? You'll have to decide for yourself. But we can explain why *we* think philosophical dialogue is worthwhile.

First, you philosophical inquiries may contribute significantly to your intellectual formation simply by affording you the chance to evaluate arguments, your own and others', in a more or less formal classroom or seminar situation. Your active participation in an introductory philosophy course will include identifying presuppositions, weighing evidence, analyzing logical forms, and assessing consequences. The critical skills you develop in this course will serve you well in other areas.

Second, your philosophical studies may help you find your bearings in these confusing times. Moral uncertainties, social tensions, political disorders, economic convulsions, the experience of rapid change, and the desperate sense that we're running out of time combine to make contemporary life in a pluralistic society extraordinarily difficult. Philosophical reflection and dialogue will not make your life any easier, but it may at least bring you to know yourself better—to understand your experience, to establish your values, and to appreciate your relations to those with whom you share the world. And self-knowledge, understood in these terms, may give you a greater measure of control over your own life.

There's an urgent need today not only for specialists and technicians but also for generalists, for critical thinkers who know themselves and understand their world, for men and women who can dispel confusion and define options. We won't promise more than philosophy, and especially a first course in philosophy, can give. Critical thinking is a discipline, self-knowledge is a continuing affair, and "getting an education" is hard work that never ends. We would like to suggest, however, that your involvement in philosophical reflection and debate may enrich your life and equip you to enrich others', at least in some small measure.

A few words about a few words. In writing this textbook we have tried to avoid using sexist terms, notably the generic terms "man," "mankind," and the like, by choosing instead such neutral words as "individuals," "persons," and "people." The choice of these plural forms wherever possible has also allowed us generally to avoid such cumbersome expressions such as "he or she" and "his or her." In all too many cases, however, we have not succeeded in eliminating phrases that might well be construed as sexist. In the chapter on work, for instance, we have discussed "contemporary images of man"; in the chapter on play and art, we have considered *Homo ludens,* "man at play"; and in the chapter on the future and the environment, we have examined scientific and religious ideas about "man and nature." It *doesn't* "go without saying" that such traditional and seemingly innocent uses of "man" include men and women alike; that's just the point. Moreover, the problem is more than merely a quibble about words, because language both shapes and reflects perceptions, attitudes, and ways of thinking. Although we have sometimes had to use the term "man," then, we don't mean to reinforce stereotypes or to endorse discrimination, however subtle their forms. Our intention throughout has been to understand persons in their relatedness to the world and one another.

It is dangerous to show man too often that he is equal to beasts, without showing him his greatness. It is also dangerous to show him too frequently his greatness without his baseness. It is yet more dangerous to leave him ignorant of both. But, it is very desirable to show him the two together.

BLAISE PASCAL

It is my conviction that a part of modern living is to face the paradox that, viewed from one perspective, man is a complex machine. . . . On the other hand, in another dimension of his existence, man is subjectively free; his personal choice and responsibility account for his own life; he is in fact the architect of himself. . . . If in response to this you say, "But these views cannot both be true," my answer is, "This is a deep paradox with which we must learn to live."

CARL ROGERS

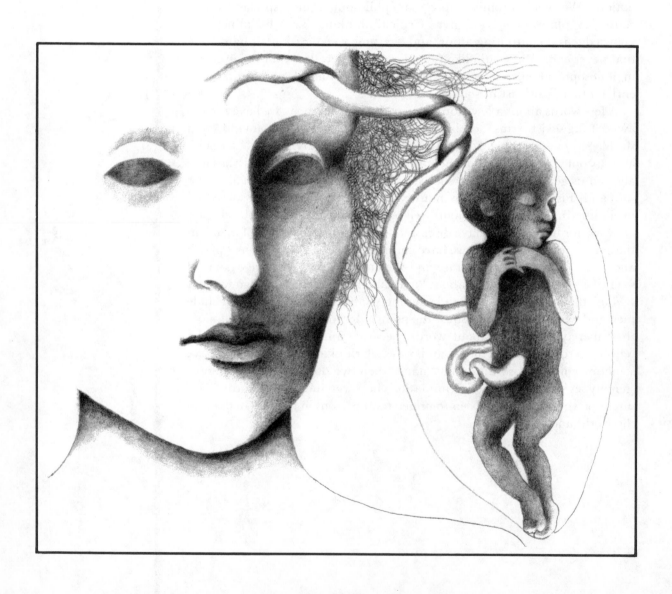

Chapter 1

THE IDEA OF A PERSON
Reflections on Being Human

Chapter Survey

The Problem of the Self

From what situation does the question "Who am I?" emerge?

What related philosophical issues are involved in this question?

Descartes and His Critics

In what sense is the person a "thinking substance"?

How did Hume and Ryle reply to Descartes?

Other Options besides Descartes' Position

Are we simply our behavior?

Can we be explained as products of will?

How is consciousness a "relation"?

The Problem of Other Selves

What is the argument from analogy?

How do Wittgenstein and Malcolm respond to the problem of other minds?

Is A. J. Ayer's defense of the argument from analogy adequate?

What is P. F. Strawson's concept of the "person"?

Our Relations to Others

How is the body essential to communication?

Why do Scheler and Schütz think philosophers must begin with the idea of "we"?

Do we relate to others primarily through conflict?

Can we relate to others through respect?

René Descartes
1596–1650

". . . that the soul, which is incorporeal, can move the body . . . is one of those things, known by themselves, which we obscure when we want to explain."

René Descartes was dissatisfied with the courses he'd studied in school and at the university despite his academic success. Apart from mathematics, all the knowledge he'd acquired seemed like so many opinions, not truths, so when he finished his formal education, he decided that for a while, at least, he'd abandon the scholarly life. He later explained by saying:

> *Resolving myself no longer to seek any other science than that which might be found in myself, or in the great book of the world, I spent the rest of my youth travelling, to see courts and armies, to frequent people of diverse humors and conditions, to collect diverse experiences, to prove myself in the encounters fortune proposed to me, and everywhere so to reflect on the things which presented themselves that I could draw some profit from them.*

One November night during his travels, Descartes had a series of dreams in which he had a revelation and found his vocation. The revelation was actually an intuition into the fundamental agreement between the laws of nature and the laws of mathematics. It would eventually lead Descartes to seek a new and more certain basis for philosophical thought, a basis as certain as mathematics itself.

Reduced to its simplest terms, Descartes' primary philosophical effort was directed toward the establishment of a firm foundation for all knowledge. He'd

long been aware of the differences of opinion that divided scholars not only in his own century but in earlier times too. He also recognized that he couldn't even count on his own senses, on his own eyes and ears, for absolutely certain knowledge. How often have you awakened,

confused and frightened, from a bad dream? How do you know you're not always dreaming? How do you know that the book you're reading right now really exists and that you haven't just dreamed it up or imagined it? Descartes was sensitive to such questions, questions that are, perhaps, an insult to common sense but that apparently can't be answered. How do you know? How can you be sure? He decided systematically to doubt everything, including the existence of the external world—including, indeed, his own existence—in the hope of finding one proposition so clear and evident that it couldn't be doubted.

"I noticed," Descartes wrote,

> *that while I was trying to think everything false, it must needs be that I who was thinking this, was something. And observing that this truth, I am thinking, therefore I exist, was so solid and secure that the most extravagant suppositions of the sceptics could not overthrow it, I judged that I need not scruple to accept it as the first principle of philosophy that I was seeking.*

This first principle implied a certain dualism, a split between mind and body, that some contemporary philosophers have contested. Nonetheless, Descartes' philosophical ideas have played an immensely important role in the development of modern thought. During the course of his life, Descartes wrote such celebrated works as the Discourse on Method, the Meditations, and the Principles of Philosophy. He also published some noteworthy studies of geometry and optics, and as his fame increased, he corresponded with some of the leading scholars and public figures of his age.

In 1649, Queen Christine of Sweden called Descartes to Stockholm to serve as her academic adviser. Since philosophy is an arduous discipline requiring energy and alertness, she decided that the best time to meet with him would be every morning at dawn. For the frail philosopher who had never risen before noon, this regimen was entirely too much. He contracted pneumonia and died.

THE IDEA OF A PERSON

The Problem of the Self

"Who am I" as an individual? As a human being? If we introspect honestly, which is by no means easy to do, we will be forced to confront our confusion over this question. Philosophers have puzzled over the issue of "Who" (or perhaps "What") am I?" for centuries.

Many people are uncertain what to do with their lives, what they want to become, and how to establish their value priorities. All these issues are concerned with the basic question "Who am I?" This is not simply an "adolescent identity crisis." More and more frequently we hear of people in mid-life realizing they have never "gotten it together." They've fallen into the rut of a job they're unhappy with and a life style they feel stifles their individuality and capacities. Suddenly they wake up one morning to find they don't really know who they are, only what they *do,* and maybe where they're supposed to fit in the complex of social institutions.

If we look briefly at some topics and themes in literature and the arts in the last century and a half, we see that this concern with the meaning of life and our particular place in it has become an all-consuming passion. In Thomas Hardy's novel *Jude the Obscure,* Jude was "obscure" both in the sense of being unrecognized by others and in the sense of being a puzzle to himself. The central character in Gustave Flaubert's *Madame Bovary* awoke to the painful awareness of being stifled by her marriage and social situation, and she became even more disillusioned in her quest to find what she thought she needed and wanted. More recently, contemporary novelists like Ralph Ellison proclaim,

I am a man of substance, of flesh and bone, fiber and liquids—and I might even be said to possess a mind. I am invisible, understand, simply because people refuse to see me. Like the bodiless heads you see sometimes in circus sideshows, it is as

though I have been surrounded by mirrors of hard, distorting glass. When they approach me they see only my surroundings, themselves, or figments of their imagination—indeed, everything and anything except me.

But what is "me"? What is this "self," and how are related questions about our mental, biological, environmental, economic, and social constitutions important to framing our answer? Many people are under the impression that philosophers attempt to deal with such questions by means of abstract theories and fancy language and tricks of reasoning rather than by basing their answers firmly in ordinary everyday experience. The "theories" of philosophers, however, originate nowhere if not within some life situation the philosopher shares with all of us. When philosophers consider what it means to be a human being, in both the individual and the collective sense, they do not set out to provide a universal solution to each person's *unique* predicament. They try to describe the human situation and to provide suggestions for dealing with it. They try to identify the paths already explored and the advantages and disadvantages along various routes. In short, the philosophic views presented in this chapter are an attempt to provide some perspective on the question of what being human is all about. The fifth century B.C. Greek philosopher Socrates said that the unexamined life is not worth living. It is the continuing awareness of this need to examine one's life that motivates the search each of us shares with human beings like Descartes, Hume, William James, or Sartre, who happen also to have been or to be philosophers.

History provides a wealth of instances to demonstrate that the question "Who am I?" is important for society as well as for the individual. Two major instances are slavery and genocide. The fourth century B.C. philosopher Aristotle thought that some people were slaves "by nature." These people, he argued, were not capable of governing themselves. Perhaps he would also have included in this category mentally retarded or mentally deficient individuals. Aristotle did not think, as the Nazis did in the twentieth century, that some people were inferior because of race; rather, some individuals, he believed, should be laborers or servants because they were incapable of anything more. Whenever we have regarded others as less than individual human selves, for whatever reasons, we have treated them like things and not like people. Thus the slave is exploited, and the Jew sent to the gas chamber.

It now seems obvious that "Who am I?" is a question with broad implications. Exploring this question necessitates exploring related philosophic questions, considering the matters of, for example, human mental capacity, physical constitution, social situation, and environment and whether or not we have free choice. We may not ordinarily think of our thinking process itself as related to who we are. We don't usually consider our biological makeup as our "self" either. Even less frequently do we wonder how our thoughts and our physical activity are related to the complete entity called "me." On the most distant fringe of the awareness of each of us hovers perhaps some dim feeling that maybe our family, our schooling, our friendships, and our social institutions have some bearing on *who* we are.

This chapter will emphasize these related questions to illuminate what it means to be human. It will begin with an examination of the seventeenth century French philosopher René Descartes' position because his view has so profoundly affected how modern thinkers have dealt with what the self is. Then the discussion picks up where Descartes left off. For this, we must consider the views of modern philosophers who argue that Descartes made a great mistake in his answer to the question "Who am I?" and in the way he posed the problem of the human self. In an attempt to correct Descartes' view, other positions have been proposed. Among them are arguments that there is not a substantial "self" anyway; that human beings can't be spoken of in mental or "immaterial" terms because they are in fact purely material;

Viewpoint

But then, even in the most insignificant details of our daily life, none of us can be said to constitute a material whole, which is identical for everyone, and need only be turned up like a page in an account-book or the record of a will; our social personality is created by the thoughts of other people. Even the simple set which we describe as "seeing some one we know" is, to some extent, an intellectual process. We pack the physical outline of the creature we see with all the ideas we have already formed about him, and in the complete picture of him which we compose in our minds those ideas have certainly the principal place. In the end they come to fill out so completely the curve of his cheeks, to follow so exactly the line of his nose, they blend so harmoniously in the sound of his voice that these seem to be no more than a transparent envelope, so that each time we see the face or hear the voice it is our own ideas of him which we recognise and to which we listen.

MARCEL PROUST, Swann's Way. From *Remembrance of Things Past*, trans. C. K. Scott Moncrieff that we are products of our will; that we *ourselves* create whatever it is we are; and that the entire philosophic discussion is based on massive linguistic confusion in the first place.

Once we begin to realize the complexity of the question of the self, we will be forced to ask about other people. Can we experience other minds or beings? Can we know what someone else is really thinking or feeling? If so, how can we possibly prove it? And, if there are others that we can experience, how are we related to them? We'll take up these questions after looking carefully at some of the major attempts to answer the question "Who am I?"

Descartes and His Critics

I may decide, along with some philosophers, that the best way to discover who or what I am and to find out what I can know is to scrutinize all the beliefs I take for granted; that is, I may decide to doubt what I believe I know and see if there are, finally, any beliefs I cannot doubt. For instance, I may doubt "knowledge" based on sense experience because I remember how my senses have deceived me in the past. Maybe I didn't see or hear what I thought I did. Perhaps I am not the size and shape I think I am. Maybe others don't appear as I think they do. Maybe they are all illusions. Perhaps I am not really sitting here reading this book. A god may be deceiving me into thinking all the things I think. But wait! I am aware that I can doubt all these things. I cannot doubt that I doubt. Therefore, in some sense, I must exist as a thinking thing or being. Well, of course, after this sequence of reasoning we are left with much that we still do not know, but at least we have a starting point. And we'll come back to the problems generated by this philosophical position. But it is an example of how one philosopher—René Descartes—began his answer to the questions "Who am I?" and "What can I know?"

It is the mark of great minds that they take great risks in attempting to formulate new responses to old questions. Descartes took an immense risk in his answer to the question of the self. He took the fact that we wonder about and even doubt what the "I" is to be the most characteristic aspect of who we are as well as the key to what we can know. In *Meditations* (1641) Descartes reflected in depth on this question and came to the conclusion that

In what sense is the person a "thinking substance"?

> *I know that I exist, and I inquire what I am, I whom I know to exist. But what then am I? A thing which thinks. What is a thing that thinks? It is a thing which doubts, understands, [conceives], affirms, denies, wills, refuses, which also imagines and feels.*

These reflections are based on Descartes' famous dictum, "I think, therefore I am."

Descartes emphasized our thinking capacity as that which we most certainly know (and even if we doubt this, we can't doubt that we doubt it!), but he was sensible enough to recognize that we also have physical bodies. Our bodies, however, can be located in space, are extended, and therefore are operated on by the same mechanical laws that apply to all other objects in space. Mind is characterized by thought, and the body is characterized by "extension." The two are essentially different.

But if Descartes began by claiming that we know ourselves as a thinking substance, how did he arrive at a certainty that things outside our mind exist? If we know the "I" as a thinking thing, how do we also come to know it as a material body? Descartes used an argument based on the perceptions we have. Our perceptions have to come from someplace. If we simply think them up in our own heads, then we can also think them away, but that's something we've never been able to do. Suppose God were the direct source of our perceptions and were not trying to deceive us. We should, then, see God in all things. This doesn't seem to be the case for most of us either. The only other possibility is that an external material world outside of our thinking self is the source of our perceptions.

Descartes decided an external world is the source of our perceptions. He also said we can have scientific knowledge of it. He argued that God would not deceive us about the regularities in nature. After all, God by definition is good and therefore can't be a deceiver. Philosophers have challenged this argument, and you too may find it difficult to accept. But it is typical of philosophers in Descartes' time to try to reconcile scientific advances with theological beliefs inherited from the Middle Ages.

More important for our investigation of philosophical views of the person than Descartes' view of the external world is his dualism. Descartes saw reality in terms of two entities, each equally real, that can't be reduced to each other. Mind and body, the two entities, are the basic constituents of what exists. In philosophical language, they are "substances." Descartes thought that everything, including cats, trees, and balls of wax, could be understood in terms of mind or body or both. The pressing dilemma that arises from such a view is how these two entities, mind and body, interact. Descartes was aware that mental and bodily states influence one another. (I do sometimes break out in a cold sweat because I am anxious about an exam.) But the question is how? Descartes never satisfactorily resolved the issue, and it has been a source of philosophical debate ever since.

Does the statement "I think, therefore I am" exhaust the possible answers to the question of the self? Did Descartes have enough evidence to say he was a "thinking thing" whose existence was "guaranteed" by God? Does our experience really give us knowledge of God or of substance? Can we perceive either one? Philosophers who followed Descartes began to ask these questions because scientific advances led them to a sharper focus on perception of the natural world and observing capacity. What people are capable of perceiving became the standard for what they could know.

How did Hume and Ryle reply to Descartes?

But "What do we really perceive?" asked the British philosopher David Hume. Hume also tried to understand human nature. And in *An Enquiry Concerning Human Understanding* (1748), he reveals that he also took doubt, the skeptical attitude, seriously. The results of his skepticism seem to indicate we cannot know as much as Descartes supposed. Hume, like philosophers before him, was interested in perceptions and how these relate to both who we are and what we know. When considering what perceptions are and where they come from, Hume could not accept either God or matter as being anything more than an assumption. Descartes had investigated three options for where perceptions might originate: within our own minds, from God, and from the external world. His resolution finally was that God wouldn't deceive us: The external world exists independently of our minds and is the source of our perceptions. Hume had very serious doubts about our ability to know this external world. We believe in it, but we cannot prove anything about it. He recognized that Descartes had not resolved the difficulty of how the mind, which is unlike the body, can know the material world. And Descartes' invoking the hypothesis of God did not clearly resolve the dilemma. Hume didn't feel he could accept the existence of the material or the spiritual order without looking very carefully at his own experience of his mind at work trying to know these things.

Viewpoint

As I said at the beginning of this tale, I divided each soul into three—two horses and a charioteer; and one of the horses was good and the other bad. . . . The right-hand horse is upright and cleanly made; he has a lofty neck and an aquiline nose; his colour is white, and his eyes dark; he is a lover of honour and modesty and temperance, and the follower of true glory; he needs no touch of the whip, but is guided by word and admonition only. The other is a crooked lumbering animal, put together anyhow; he has a short thick neck; he is flat-faced and of a dark colour, with grey eyes and blood-red complexion; the mate of insolence and pride, shag-eared and deaf, hardly yielding to whip and spur.

PLATO, Phaedrus

What Hume discovered when he "introspected" was that he couldn't find his "self" in the sense of some thing or substance that he could identify as "I." What he did find was a bundle of sensations. He was, purely and simply, what he experienced.

Introspect for a minute. What do you perceive? Aren't you aware of the pressure of the chair you're sitting in, your hunger, restlessness, effort at concentration on the philosophy assignment? You're aware of these sensations, Hume said, and not of any "self" holding them together.

What's responsible for our sense of "self" then? For Hume, our sense of a continuity we identify as our "self" is at least in part related to our understanding of the connection between events in terms of what causes them. Hume claimed we've fallen victim to sleights of hand in our own mental process. Our ideas are really "copies" or imitations of sense perceptions that Hume called "impressions." The reason we mistake the conglomeration of impressions for a continuous and substantial "self" is our confusion about cause and effect. Hume said we think we perceive a self for three reasons: because our experiences are close to each other in a temporal succession; because they are close to each other in space (contiguous); and because we see what appear to be the cause and the effect as connected or joined repeatedly. And since our experiences seem connected and to be caused by other experiences, we assume our selves are connected also. We conclude that this is *necessarily* the case.

Let's say you are walking in the woods and fall over a tree stump. Fifteen minutes later your ankle begins to ache, and you decide that tripping over the stump caused it. But couldn't there be other factors whose relation to your painful ankle are unclear to you? Perhaps you're sensitive to dampness or have a long-forgotten muscle injury aggravated by a long walk. We can't assume causal relation, Hume argued, only on the basis of *observing* succession, contiguity, and constant conjunction.

Hume attempted to find out what the necessary connection *was*. He was unable to claim any experience of the connection between what he perceived as a cause and what he observed as an effect. Since he could discover no *necessary* principle relating phenomena to one another, he said we couldn't know if there was a substantial or underlying "self" holding perceptions and sensations together. Instead of providing the basis for the existence of an "I" as it did with Descartes, thought undid the possibility of knowing an "I" for Hume. We certainly do not perceive anything about God, so we cannot use God as a guarantor of the validity of our perceptions.

The contemporary British philosopher Gilbert Ryle also argues against adopting Descartes' position as the "official doctrine." Descartes held that we have both mind and body, which, although connected, are separate enough to allow the mind to continue to exist after the body dies. Ryle argues, however, that Descartes made a logical mistake, not a perceptual one. He maintains that the traditional account of human beings is erroneous because it suffers from a "category mistake": It improperly attempts to analyze the mind in the same way—employing the same categories—as we analyze the body. It makes use of terms such as "mental causes," "mental states," and "mental processes," which suggest parallels with physical causes, states, and processes. Thus we're led to believe that minds exist just as physical·objects do.

What is a category mistake? In *The Concept of Mind*, Ryle proposes a series of illustrations intended to explain his idea. One example of a category mistake is that made by a visitor to Oxford who, having seen a certain number of libraries, museums, playing fields, laboratories, and lecture halls, asks, "But where is the university?" His mistake is to think of the university as something alongside the libraries, playing fields, and classrooms, whereas the university is not another building but the way all these institutions are organized. The visitor's mistake is to put the university into the same category as that of the various buildings that make it up.

Ryle says we're making the same sort of mistake when, after recognizing that people engage in various activities, we inquire about the self, the person, or the mind. Descartes' "thinking substance" would be comparable to the false idea of the university as something existing apart from its labs and lecture halls. Thus the mind becomes "the ghost in the machine" of the body.

This incorrect reasoning leads us to postulate a "two-world" theory according to which our private mental lives run parallel to our public physical lives. Focusing on intelligent behavior, Ryle explains, "To do something thinking what one is doing is, according to this legend, always to do two things; namely, to consider certain appropriate propositions, or prescriptions, and to put into practice what these propositions or prescriptions enjoin. It is to do a bit of theory and then to do a bit of practice."

Ryle does not mean to deny that mental processes occur. He maintains, however, that, properly understood, the phrase "there occur mental processes" differs logically from the phrase "there occur physical processes." Despite their grammatical similarity, the phrases don't mean the same sort of thing. Therefore, Ryle says, "it makes no sense to conjoin or disjoin the two."

In opposition to the two-world theory, Ryle argues that "when we describe people as exercising qualities of mind, we are not referring to occult episodes of which their overt acts and utterances are effects; we are referring to those overt acts and utterances themselves." In his view, overt or public intelligent performances—like cooking a meal, playing chess, or telling a joke—are not clues to the workings of people's minds: "they are those workings."

We have problems in trying to answer our questions about the "self" if we agree with either Hume or Ryle. Ultimately, Hume would say we cannot know for sure anything about inner experience, the external world, or God. We may assume we are thinking beings, in Descartes' sense, but we can't prove it. Human beings are rational; but reason is severely limited. All so-called knowledge, including scientific knowledge, must be taken with a grain of salt. And Ryle holds that mental phenomena are not to be explained by resorting to some nonmaterial "thing" or "inner source": To speak of "inner" and "outer" experiences is to presuppose a false dichotomy.

Other Options besides Descartes' Position

But let's return to Descartes' dualism. Even though it seems logical when we think about it, there's an unresolved problem in saying that our body is not mental and our mind is not physical. How do we account for the fact that

Viewpoint

Man's basic drive is for unification, to be one in mind and body, to be one with the world, to be one with others and to resolve the subject-object bifurcation that divides him from others since his birth. This drive for unification is also the mainspring of man's behavior, which is characterized by his search for happiness and ultimate reality. Much of his activity is unconscious in that man is not aware of the real object of his quest, except insofar as he feels incomplete, alienated, restless and unhappy. . . .

Again it must be emphasized that the chief characteristic of the mind during these unification states is that it is thoughtless, contentless and, in effect, there is no mind operating at all. The mind and body have coalesced and man is one with himself—even if only for a nanosecond. He is no longer divided, standing back and looking at himself as an object. This characteristic but basic misuse of man's thinking apparatus is the seminal and root cause of his distress and unhappiness, because he not only regards everything he sees out there as separate from himself, but he regards his body as separate from his mind. Once he has tasted these unification experiences, he finds them so profoundly satisfying that he becomes a recidivist and constantly seeks to renew them and to find even deeper and more satisfying experiences.

DAVID COLE GORDON, Self-Love

such different entities as our bodies and our thoughts somehow seem related? When we have a cold it's hard to "think straight." How many times have you read about recoveries from near-fatal illnesses and accidents because of the patient's will to live? Our experience seems to indicate that we are a whole being and not two separate substances.

The most direct resolution of Cartesian dualism is to claim that there aren't two factors at all. We feel whole because we *are* only one thing. The debate then occurs over what that one thing is. Some argue that it's matter, and others, spirit. The first position holds that there is no such thing as mind in any abstract sense at all. "Mind" is only matter. To be exact, it is "gray" matter: the brain.

Are we simply our behavior?

Watson, Lashley, and other "behaviorists," notably the contemporary proponent of this view, B. F. Skinner, develop their view of human behavior from work originally done with animals. They observed the activities of individuals in particular situations and concluded that it's not at all necessary to have the concept of a "self" to understand human behavior. There is no specific pattern or organization to the so-called human mind. It is simply the result of external forces (stimuli) that function according to scientifically discoverable laws. Environmental influences form the individual. What we see is all there is.

Skinner argues that as a practical matter empirical psychology need not pay attention to mental events at all; it should be concerned only with observable behavior. Observable behavior is best understood by means of causal laws manifested in phenomena like stimulus, response, and reinforcement. It follows that mastering these basic principles can result in a scientifically designed Utopia, like Skinner's Walden Two. We could set up a controlled society, rewarding desirable behavior and punishing undesirable behavior.

Skinner does not deny the existence of minds. Indeed, he remarks, "Nothing is changed because we look at it, talk about it, or analyze it in a new way." But he argues that public consequences, not private intentions, shape our behavior. Success and gratification reinforce certain patterns of action; failure discourages us from repeating other moves. "Purpose" and "intention" are irrelevant. In *Beyond Freedom and Dignity* he explains that "in operant conditioning the purpose of a skilled movement of the hand is to be found in the consequences which follow it. A pianist neither acquires nor executes the behavior of playing a scale smoothly because of a prior intention of doing so. Smoothly played scales are reinforcing for many reasons and they select skilled movements."

But this means that the outcome of any act is equal to the purpose of that act; what results is what was meant to be. How then do we account for the experiences in our lives when we fail to accomplish what we set out to do? Or when we "accomplish" something we never intended or desired? Simply to respond that we weren't doing what we thought we were seems to avoid the question entirely. Did something go wrong with the conditioning process? What about the factor of willing? Could it be that what occurs is not merely conformity to causal scientific laws? Perhaps events are influenced by something nonmaterial.

The position implied by these questions is exactly opposite to the behavioral materialism that claims matter is the only reality. In this position, the nonmaterial is most fundamental. The material world is not primary, but the characteristics of activity and dynamism that it possesses are. How, then, might a "nonmaterialist" answer the question of the self?

The nineteenth century philosopher Arthur Schopenhauer's answer implies a pessimistic view of human beings. As soon as something we desire or "will" is achieved, there is always something more that we are driven to desire, and so we are never satisfied. We are like addicts in our selfish desires and need to have more and more. Schopenhauer's position is that we are the product of the wills that we have visibly manifested. We are determined by the desires we pursue; in fact, we are those desires.

Can we be explained as products of will?

The individual is not the only entity subject to the drive of the will. The entire social order including all beings and things is so subject. Violence, war, and conflict are due to the constant struggle of all things to pursue this drive. Everything that is, is a manifestation of "blind will" struggling and battling with other wills. There is no way out. This view is much like Sigmund Freud's view that we are largely determined by unconscious motivations. The only hope for a resolution, for freedom, is to cease being a slave to will. We have to want not to will in order to break the vicious circle. But Schopenhauer believed not willing was next to impossible. His answer to our question is that the essence of the person is thus not reason as most famous philosophers believed. We delude ourselves into thinking we can control something just because we can rationally evaluate it. Reason is on the surface; our ever unsatisfied desires and ego-centered will are our true essence. Schopenhauer casts doubt on the belief of many philosophers and thinkers in the seventeenth century that human beings could make progress socially, scientifically, and artistically through the development of reason.

Friedrich Nietzsche, a later nineteenth century philosopher, was intrigued with Schopenhauer's ideas. He did not maintain that the world is "blind will," always painful and never capable of giving satisfaction, but he did talk about life in terms of the "will to power." All individuals act, in essence, to attain more power, although they differ in their ideas of what will give them power. People believe that money, politics, "influence," or even the creation of guilt feelings in others are sources of power. But this kind of strong-arming is not true power according to Nietzsche; it is only an illusion.

Nietzsche used the term "superman," or "overman," to designate the kind of person who can obtain real power. This person masters his own destiny, his own passions, and he lives according to chosen ideals. An example of a person with power is not someone like Adolf Hitler, but a person like Mahatma Gandhi. Making use of his own abilities, the superman tries to creatively change the stagnation that contents most people. Supermen are rare because very few people are capable of overcoming the negative and painful things in life.

If in spite of great difficulty other forms of life in nature can evolve into higher forms, Nietzsche thought human beings could do the same if they

Viewpoint

. . . *Life is to be lived, not controlled; and humanity is won by continuing to play in the face of certain defeat. Our fate is to become one, and yet many—This is not prophecy, but description. Thus one of the greatest jokes in the world is the spectacle of the whites busy escaping blackness and becoming blacker every day, and the black striving toward whiteness, becoming quite dull and gray. None of us seems to know who he is or where he is going. . . .*

Perhaps to lose a sense of where *you are implies the danger of losing a sense of* who *you are. That must be it, I thought—to lose your direction is to lose your face. So here he comes to ask his direction from the lost, the invisible. Very well, I've learned to live without direction. Let him ask. . . . Nevertheless, the very disarmament has brought me to a decision. The hibernation is over. I must shake off the old skin and come up for breath. . . .*

In going underground, I whipped it all except the mind, the mind. *And the* mind *that has conceived a plan of living must never lose sight of the chaos against which that pattern was conceived. That goes for societies as well as for individuals. Thus, having tried to give pattern to the chaos which lives within the pattern of your certainties, I must come out, I must emerge. . . . I'm shaking off the old skin and I'll leave it here in the hold. I'm coming out, no less invisible without it, but coming out nevertheless. And I suppose it's damn well time. Even hibernations can be overdone, come to think of it. Perhaps that's my greatest social crime, I've overstayed my hibernation, since there's a possibility that even an invisible man has a socially responsible role to play.*

RALPH ELLISON, Invisible Man

really wanted to. Perhaps we could modify the evolutionary development of higher forms of human life by using our reason and learning to channel our passions into creative activity. Such an evolutionary development is not a simple process of progress and growth. A specific effort to create superior individuals is demanded. Supermen are not just the haphazard result of biological and social forces. Rather, through the will to power they themselves become who they are; they create their own life and values. The answer to the question "Who am I?" is that I may be a remote hope that things can be better. But it is more likely that I am a mass of willful, selfish desires.

The American philosopher William James proposed another option that turned the Cartesian position around entirely. Like Hume, James argued that we don't experience our life as purely mental, but as the complete experience we have of it. Unlike Hume, James proposed our experience to consist, not of bundles of discrete and separate things and sensations we experience, but of "fields," or relations, that can't be further reduced to bits and pieces. James argued, as Ryle did later, that mind is not a "thing." The linguistic concerns of Ryle's generation did not, however, provide the basis for James' position. James stated that consciousness is a relation between mind and object, and therefore not a "thing." For James, there really is no mind apart from its relation to objects. Try to think a thought that doesn't refer to something, whether physical or mental. Is it possible? James didn't think so. And like Schopenhauer and Nietzsche, James was aware that will, desire, or appetite are formative for the individual, but unlike these philosophers, James refused to conclude for the existence of a purely subjective realm.

How is consciousness a "relation"?

What, then, is James' attempted description of the human psyche? In the 1880s when he was writing *Principles of Psychology,* the relationship between mind and body was one of his principal concerns. The manner in which he approached the study of this interaction was crucial for the conclusions he drew. James did not begin with doubt, as Descartes had, or with introspective examination of separate sensations, as Hume had. His medical and scientific training had developed in him a healthy respect for observation and experience. He recognized, however, that these tools should be used critically. Two assumptions bothered him in the traditional empirical approach: that "experience" was limited to the senses; and that experience was "atomistic" (meaning that it could be broken down into the simpler and smaller parts of which it was supposed to be composed). James raised questions such as "Do we really experience discrete sensations?" "Do we experience pure red, blue, hot, cold?" "Does this kind of fragmentation into separate sensations account for my experience as a whole?"

James wanted to adopt a "radical" rather than a traditional empirical stance. He thought we should begin with a description of exactly how we experience things as a whole before making any assumptions about the basic elements experience might be divided into. It just may be that we can't reduce experience to any basic elements. If we think of how we are aware of things, including imagined creatures, mystical states, mathematical abstractions, rough surfaces, and bright colors, we see that we never experience the separate parts of an object, person, or idea. We're aware of these elements intertwined with one another, a phenomenon James called the "stream of consciousness." We recognize one thing because of its relation to another: silence with respect to sound, a you because of an I, pain in contrast to comfort, joy as opposed to sorrow.

A particular experience, however, is not repeatable in precisely the same way once it has occurred. The experience of waking up *this* morning as opposed to yesterday or tomorrow morning is unique. The possibility of novelty and newness can exist despite the interdependence of one thing with another. What we can experience isn't of necessity set up or determined in advance. New relationships and combinations of things are always possible. What does this view of experience imply about the individual person? Is it possible to speak of an independent subject or object, independent mind or body? Can we speak of an independent self, material object, or other self? James would say we can know only what we experience, and we only experience things in relation to one another. Something would be an "object" only for, or only if there were, a "subject." A boot is defined in relation to a foot, a lover in relation to a beloved. Distinctions between subjects and objects and distinctions between independent minds or bodies are useful tools for discussion, but they are interpretations or hypotheses about what we know more directly. We don't experience our body or our consciousness or this book in a completely isolated manner. If we ask what constitutes "experience," the response is the mutual interdependence of all its parts. If we ask "Does consciousness exist?" (as James did in one of his most famous essays), we reply that it does not exist as some "thing," rather as a process or relationship.

Using this insight as a guide, James presents his view on the "self" in Chapter 10 of *The Principles of Psychology*. He says there:

> *We see then that we are dealing with a fluctuating material. The same object being sometimes treated as a part of me, at other times as simply mind, and then again as if I had nothing to do with it at all.* In its widest possible sense, *however,* a man's Self is the sum total of all that he CAN call *his, not only his body and his psychic powers, but his clothes and his house, his wife and children, his ancestors and friends, his reputation and works, his lands and*

horses, and yacht and bank account. All these things give him the same emotions.
If they wax and prosper, he feels triumphant; if they dwindle and die away, he
feels cast down. . . .

He continues to explain that the self has four main constituents: the
material self (the body); the social self (the recognition of mates); the
spiritual self (one's inner or subjective being, psychic faculties or dispositions); and the pure ego (the bare principle of personal identity). These
combined aspects of the self arouse the feelings of self-complacency and self-
dissatisfaction, which, in turn, prompt the actions of self-seeking and self-
preservation. His conclusion is that the consciousness of the "self" involves a
stream of thought. The "I" that knows feelings, things, and thoughts is not
an aggregate of separate perceptions, or an "unchanging metaphysical
entity like the Soul," or a principle. Rather, James says, it is a *thought,*
different in each moment but related to all of them. James' answer to our
question, then, is: I am my experience, or more precisely, I am the ongoing
organization of my experience.

So far we've focused on answers to the question "Who am I?" But each
answer also implies ideas about what we can or cannot know about other
persons.

The Problem of Other Selves

Suppose for a moment we (unlike James) hold the view that the self is a
mental substance; that is, that it is totally "self-contained." If we do, we are
confronted with the formidable problem of explaining how we can *know* that
people and things outside of our own self exist. This has been referred to as
the problem of other selves, or other minds.

Descartes was aware of this inherent difficulty in his dualistic mind-body
position. He attempted to overcome it by arguing that we know others
through analogy with our own experience and ideas. Take, for example, the   *What is the argument from*
perception of pain. We usually associate the occurrence of pain in ourselves   *analogy?*
with particular physical states in our body and certain behavior patterns
that accompany these states. We personally feel the experience of being in
pain, and we can observe changes in our physical body as well as in the way
we act. Perhaps we frown, moan, curse, or become pale or flushed. We
associate our mental and physical states with one another.

Not only can we observe our own bodies and behavior, but we can also see
physical beings like ourselves. We see that the other body looks pale, hear
sounds of distress and discomfort, and observe contorted facial expressions.

How do Wittgenstein and Malcolm respond to the problem of other minds?

In our own experience these physical characteristics have been associated with the feeling we identified as "pain." Our conclusion is, by analogy, that the other body is in "pain." We have not felt the other's pain; we can't get inside the other self to know whether what is felt is the same as our own experience. All we can do is infer that there is more to the other body than simply the physical states and behaviors that I can observe. But can we infer this? Can it be that I can't tell anything about consciousness or "inner states" by observing behavior? Maybe there is no consciousness as such separate from the behavior. Perhaps all I can study are physical states of another. Let's look at the assumption made by arguers from analogy.

In all the questions raised about the "other," what remains the constant reference point? Philosophers like Cornell University's Norman Malcolm object to the analogy argument in part because it is so egocentric. If we define what *is* exclusively on the basis of how we alone experience it to be, is there any way we can possibly be proved wrong? Not likely. The argument doesn't appear to allow for anything but our own point of view. Furthermore, if we argue by analogy, how can we possibly verify whether *our* assessment of someone else's inner state has the same relationship to his or her observable actions as our own inner state has to *our* action? If there are only observable actions, then we won't need analogies because there'll be no "inner" state that the actions relate to or reflect. In addition to these problems, if all we can rely on is our own individual case, how can we ever be sure the others' behavior doesn't differ from our own when they are in pain? Maybe the relationship between their feeling and their behavior was one in which pain manifested itself by smiling.

But why is there such confusion? Malcolm, following the twentieth century philosopher Ludwig Wittgenstein, says the problem of other minds is due first to confusion about the language we use to describe our experience. Second, it is due to supposing that our own experience should be the criterion used to verify what counts as knowledge of other minds. The two problems are related, and we'll investigate them more carefully.

Let's take the "pain" example again. We use the word as a symbol to indicate a particular sensation we experience. But we had a sensation we suspect was identical to this one some time in the past. We call it the "same" sensation of "pain" because comparison of the two suggests that they are the same. But for us to call it pain, more than a seeming identity is necessary. Perhaps my memory is hazy about what I thought I felt before. Wouldn't there have to be some standard to establish whether or not our perceptions are right? And how could we know they were "right" except by reference to more of our own impressions?

Wittgenstein says that beginning with individual experience as we've described is hopeless. If we begin with the isolated individual, nothing beyond oneself, not even oneself, can be understood. It would be impossible to establish a criterion to test our perceptions since we could never find anything outside our own experience to compare our experience to.

But it is clear that we do communicate, that we do understand one another and are sometimes aware of how other people feel. It is precisely the richness and complexity of language and behavior that is the basis for communication. Introspection into my own mental states will not yield a criterion that will tell me what I am experiencing or what you are experiencing. Rather I should simply "look and see" that you cry, you hold your elbow, and you glare at the door you hadn't perceived. It is true that I will never know your pain in the same way I know my own. But my observation of your behavior is enough for communication to have taken place without invoking the immaterial self that our language leads us to suppose is lurking behind all behavior.

Viewpoint

"I am sorry," I said.

"Oh, you just think you are sorry. Or glad. You aren't really."

"If you think you are sorry, who in the hell can tell you that you aren't?" I demanded, for I was a brass-bound Idealist then, as I have stated, and was not going to call for a plebiscite on whether I was sorry or not.

"That sounds all right," she said, "but it isn't. I don't know why—oh, yes, I do—if you've never been sorry or glad then you haven't got any way to know the next time whether you are or not."

"All right," I said, "But can I tell you this: something is happening inside me which I choose to call sorry?"

"You can say it, but you don't know." Then, snatching her hand from under my hand, "Oh, you start to feel sorry or glad or something but it just doesn't come to anything."

"You mean like a little green apple that's got a worm in it and falls off the tree before it ever gets ripe?"

She laughed, and answered, "Yes, like little green apples with worms in them."

"Well," I said, "here's a little green apple with a worm in it: I'm sorry."

ROBERT PENN WARREN, All the King's Men

Furthermore, these statements are true if we look at how we use the word "pain." To discover our own "private" pain we use a language with mutually agreed-on *public* rules. There is no private language, as some have supposed, in which words refer only to what we assume they refer to. If I say I'm in pain, it is generally understood, and this is because we are born into and grow up in a context of others with whom we communicate and for whom the term "pain" has meaning. If this were not true, no one would ever know what anyone was talking about. Everything would be relative; we would be totally unable even to perceive anything about an "other." Language is, thus, intimately connected with life as human beings experience it.

Two contemporary English philosophers, A. J. Ayer and P. F. Strawson, follow in Wittgenstein's tradition. While attempting to further refine Wittgenstein's views, however, they raised fundamental questions about his approach. Both Ayer and Strawson are concerned with the meaning of the term "person." But Ayer defends the argument from analogy, while Strawson proposes an intermediate position between the behavioral and the analogical. The central point in their debate is the one that divides those who are Cartesian from those who are not. Is it necessary to have an idea of what a person is in order to understand an individual mind or consciousness? Supporters of a Cartesian-inspired view, like Ayer, would argue that we can make sense of individual consciousness without having to depend on the idea of a person to which consciousness belongs. For Strawson, this is impossible. The person, he agrees, is not a mental substance, but the person is a "self" understood as an integrated mind and body in a social context. The idea of the person is presupposed by the idea of consciousness, because we can't speak of consciousness apart from the person whose consciousness it is. What this means is that I can't speak of what my next-door neighbor Mary thinks, feels, or does without speaking of the concrete individual who is my neighbor. And I must be able to ascribe mental and physical characteristics to this individual. I know Mary partly through observation of her behavior and partly by her avowals.

Is A. J. Ayer's defense of the argument from analogy adequate?

Ayer defends a version of the argument by analogy for the existence of other minds. He says it is possible for states of consciousness to be distinct from "their physical causes and . . . the physical manifestations" without having to establish that there is a "mental substance" to which they belong. He gives the hypothetical example of a child kept from contact with any other human being who is cared for by machines and entertained by automata. The child hears language from a voice broadcast over a loudspeaker. This voice speaks as if the automata (but not the "inanimate objects" in the room) are conscious. As a result of interacting with the automata, the child learns the concept of a person. He can then apply it not only to himself but to other things as well, including, in this instance, to the automata who obviously aren't persons. Such a hypothetical case, argues Ayer, shows that we can ascribe experiences to our "self" and be wrong in ascribing such experience to others. This means that there's at least the possibility that my consciousness is the *only* one and that other "people" are not necessarily primary for my own awareness of self-identity.

Basically Ayer is pointing out that anytime we know anything by *inference,* our own experience or the experiences of others included, we can't expect absolute certainty. We never have all the evidence we need. Anytime we reason inductively, from particular things to general ideas or universals, there's a chance that we can be mistaken. The most we can expect is that sometimes our conclusions can be tested more directly than other times. There doesn't seem to be an answer to whether I'm justified in feeling certain that my conclusions about other consciousnesses are right or not. The doubt can't be absolutely dispelled on either side of the argument, so it only makes sense for us to rely on what seems to be the case in our own experience when we can test our conclusions and find them as "correct" as they can be.

Strawson thinks such an argument is circular and really doesn't get us anywhere. It amounts to saying that we don't have adequate criteria to check our experiences so we can't check them because the criteria are inadequate. In other words, if our evidence is insufficient, insufficient evidence must suffice. To avoid this merry-go-round in our heads, Strawson says we must be able to ascribe consciousness to others who aren't our "self."He attempts to prove in his book *Individuals* that the concept of a "person" is "primitive"; that is, we must presuppose some idea of a person that we do not analyze into separate parts like body and mind. If we begin with this dualism of mind and body, as the Cartesian position does, then we have to assume what we're trying to prove: namely, that for me to be able to identify experiences as belonging to *my* "self," I have to be able to identify others as having them also. Furthermore, I can't be clear whether "I" "own" the experience of my body if the "I" is split into mind and body. As Strawson says in "Persons":

To put it briefly: one can ascribe states of consciousness to one's self only if one can ascribe them to others; one can ascribe them to others only if one can identify other subjects of experience; and one cannot identify others if one can identify them only as subjects of experience, possessors of states of consciousness.

Only if we begin with the nonreductionistic idea of a "person" can we free ourselves of this dilemma, Strawson feels. The word "I" makes sense and has a reference because the I is "a person among others." The person is neither

What is P. F. Strawson's concept of the "person"?

"an animated body" nor "an embodied anima." The concept of person is necessary before either of these because neither can be considered an "I" without there being an individual ("person" or "act"). Action is more than mere physical movement (the body). It also implies some purpose or intention (the mind). We can never understand how we act or how we act on one another unless we have the primitive concept of "person," which is neither pure consciousness (the thinking I) nor pure matter (the physical body), but *both* before we can think of it as one or the other. We control our bodies as well as feel them. We also know other objects put limits on what we can do with our bodies. We can't manipulate our body through a brick wall, for example. This "resistance," as Stuart Hampshire called it when arguing a position similar to Strawson's, defines my situation as "an object among other objects."

Our Relations to Others

The question of the existence of other minds and the attempts to explain how we might know them have led us to an examination of our human situation. We have moved from the consideration of the "I" as an individual self to the "I" that is defined in terms of being human, one among many, the social self. Once we see the attempted explanation of self-identity, we discover that we're forced to consider human identity at the same time. This means we have to think about ourselves in relationship to others.

It is just because we *can* share experiences and make ourselves understood despite our differences that consciousness has been a primary concern of philosophers. They ask, *is* there something common in our human experience? One proposal is that all persons are aware that they are aware, even if their awarenesses are of different things. Descartes' insistence that we begin with the thinking self, or consciousness, might still prove fruitful. And some modern philosophers, of a school different from those we have so far discussed, do not find this starting point problematic. For example, the French philosopher Maurice Merleau-Ponty did not find it a barrier to understanding other minds or the world to begin with consciousness. Rather, consciousness is the indispensable key. But Merleau-Ponty radically "reunderstood" the idea of consciousness.

How is the body essential to communication?

Awareness is mediated or takes place through a body. So it makes no sense to talk of consciousness apart from body, to talk of mind-body dualisms. Merleau-Ponty goes so far as to say we are our bodies. Let's look at a distinction he makes that will clarify his idea of body and help us understand how he conceives of our relations to others.

He distinguishes between "my body for me" and "my body for others."

My body for others is the one that biologists, chemists, and other scientists can deal with objectively. It is not what *I* experience. We don't feel like a combination of chemicals and processes. We don't experience ourselves as bare Cartesian consciousnesses with extended bodies. Our body is the medium through which we both perceive the world and are located in that world. I do not simply see colors and shapes or utter meaningless sounds. I see the red rug against the background of the beige wall; I hear the conversation between two people and it makes sense to me; I discuss the ballet, my studies, or the weather with other individuals. All these activities involve a social context. This means that our body "as lived" is neither an external object that is described scientifically nor purely a subject that is felt apart from its involvement with a world. Instead, it is a "style" of existing, participating in both the external and the internal but not equal to either one.

Our bodies also reveal our separateness from others. Their very materiality points out individuality. They remind us we can never experience another in quite the same way we can experience ourselves. The other person's grief is his or hers; my grief is mine. But body also reveals our coexistence and is the means by which we communicate. I know the other as a consciousness in the world, as another "style" of existing. I experience the other person as grieving, enjoying, or whatever. And I know I can have a dialogue with another. Body in all its modes of perception reveals our interrelatedness with other human beings in society and history. This whole complex of the lived body, Merleau-Ponty claims, is what constitutes the human condition, our life as people.

We are also in the world. The relationship between self and world is primary, and life is a process of articulating and refining that relationship. By growing and maturing we learn a multitude of things that make a difference in how we live and relate to others. As children we learn to walk and talk. We may later learn to use tools such as computers and telescopes. We thus learn to change the world and are in the process changed by it as we learn.

Most of us would not think in terms of body for me, body for others, and world, with such philosophical sophistication. But what it means to be a person living with others in the everyday world *is* something we reflect on. It's hard to avoid being aware of the world and of other people. We constantly find ourselves either in conflict or agreement with others. Almost always the question of freedom in some sense is involved. Think of the last time you walked into an elevator with some friends and saw a "no smoking" sign on the wall. You were dying for a cigarette. Many of the passengers were nonsmokers, and you knew that smoking would annoy them, even bring physical discomfort. Were you free to light up in the elevator?

Some would argue that your need for a smoke is biologically and chemically determined, that you have become addicted to the nicotine, and you just can't stop smoking. Others would push the problem further by insisting that you did not even really have a choice to begin smoking or not. Everyone in your family smoked, and this circumstance, combined with social pressures when you were a teenager, led you to develop the habit before you were even aware you had it. You can think of a hundred factors in your past, all influencing you to smoke. These views amount to saying that you were not really free to choose to have a smoke; you just *had* to.

The opposite view would maintain that things do influence us, but that we can also influence and act on things. In the philosopher Jean-Paul Sartre's view, nothing is responsible for what "I" do or what "I" am but myself. He says we are "condemned to be free." We are responsible for our actions and what our actions make us into. If my actions are determined only by outside influences, as the behaviorists believe, I am not my own lived body but a body for others, an object and not a person.

From an individual point of view the responsibility to smoke or not to smoke is thus mine. Perhaps I was influenced to become a smoker, but I am totally free to continue or stop. It is so much easier to view ourselves as objects, Sartre says, determined by factors beyond our control. If we do not see ourselves as responsible for our actions we need not feel the anxiety that decisions entail.

At a social level, are you free to light up in the elevator and inflict your habit on the nonsmokers? It is true that you could smoke in spite of the prohibition. Prohibitions curtail freedom in some sense. But why? Because the exercise of your freedom may offend or injure another. Sartre believes there is necessarily antagonism between people, each of whom is unique and thwarted by others with whom he must somehow get along.

Sartre and other existentialists are saying that society's norms are relative. We have to make our own decisions. But Sartre also says we must choose with the good of everyone in mind. It is difficult to understand how one can decide for one's own good and everyone else's at the same time. Many thinkers have criticized Sartre for stressing that the individual is absolutely free while arguing that the choice must take others into consideration.

Are we responsible only to ourselves for our own actions? Do we have any "social" responsibility? If human beings need society in order to live, must they make compromises with their own immediate desires to guarantee their own survival and benefit in the long run? These questions imply that considering what is human must take into account both individual and social dimensions. What is most essential to people can be understood many ways. We can, as Sartre does most of the time, maintain that the self is primary. Or we can argue that the society in which the self exists must take precedence for the individual to survive, in fact, for the individual to have any sense of "self" at all. A few modern thinkers, among them Max Scheler and Alfred Schütz, emphasize that the social element is integral to our understanding of human nature.

Max Scheler argued that close examination of our everyday experiences provides the necessary clue to the resolution of the problem of other minds. We should not depend on reasoning from analogies. Instead, detailed description of what occurs in our conscious awareness of others reveals that we *do* know others in an immediate and direct way. Scheler is willing to admit that some aspects of other people are not accessible to us, but he maintains that we can directly experience another's pain, for example, in his or her crying or moaning.

Why do Scheler and Schütz think philosophers must begin with the idea of "we"?

But what is it that we directly experience, what is it that is shared between two selves? Scheler is forceful in his rejection of the argument by analogy for the existence of other minds because he's convinced that it's a pseudo problem, although for reasons different from those Ryle suggested. The argument from analogy, Scheler claims, assumes that what we know first is only our own self, a completely wrong perception of our actual experience. Self-knowledge is not prior to knowledge of others; rather, others are basic to our immediate experience in the world. This means that we have access to other minds directly. And we know our own "self" by separating and distinguishing it from all that is around us. Self is inferred from others and not others from knowledge of self. A child is not born with a sense of self or even with what an adult would call a self. Scheler agrees thus far with Sartre: The self must be created. However, Scheler would say individuality is radically dependent on the community in which it is originally involved. The child learns to interact with its family and their circle. It learns to smile, walk, talk, eat, play. These are ways it not only communicates but also learns to become independent and detached from others while still related. Gradually the child becomes autonomous, but what it learned is dependent on the social environment. Self emerges from relationships and is defined in terms of them. Once the child learns to observe and reflect on the behavior of others, he or she has basically already learned through interaction, direct experience, what he or she is observing. For instance, a child learns from an original closeness to others what pain, joy, sympathy, and feeling in general are.

Human beings for Scheler are both "private" and "shared"; they can be explained in terms of immediate experience—"intuitive" discovery—as we've just discussed. But we can also discuss people "scientifically" as chemicals and processes. Scheler's concern was to use both approaches simultaneously by investigating the interaction between the material and "spiritual" elements. The "link" in this interaction is investigated in his study *The Nature of Sympathy,* in which he analyzes human feeling. Scheler says feeling provides access to the larger universe of all living things. The person is not a thing in isolation but a "unity of activity." Feelings, rather than isolating us, indicate our interrelatedness, our "points of contact" with other beings and things. And to feel love is not only to recognize or realize our connectedness but also to place a value on the object in question. Without feeling, values would not be accessible to us, and without love we could never understand them.

Scheler's view of value is similar to Plato's and Augustine's. Scheler, who is a religious as well as a philosophical thinker, says there is a hierarchy of values in the order of creation and in our world of experience. Some things are intrinsically worth more than others to us as human beings. He identifies three basic levels of value. We are drawn to the higher levels, each of which corresponds to a specific kind of knowledge. First, at the lowest level, is scientific knowledge, which is cultivated in order to control the social order and nature. The second is metaphysical knowledge, which deals with the basis of scientific knowledge, the principles on which it is founded. Metaphysical knowledge reflects the human being as speculative, as a knower in the classic sense. The third is what Scheler calls "religious" knowledge. It is the highest level and is concerned with salvation and knowledge of "absolute being."

Scheler's investigation of being human was concerned with all living things, then with more detailed study of the social, cultural, and historical part of our experience, and finally with his pervasive interest in questions of value and knowledge. Alfred Schütz was most concerned with the second of these areas, social relations, as the basis for his understanding of human beings. He shares Scheler's rejection of analogy and inference as a way to know others as well as his attention to shared experience as a viable alternative. Schütz, however, explores in more detail what a "we-relationship" implies.

Considering his interests in both philosophy and sociology, the emphasis Schütz places on social relationships is understandable. He was most interested in "intersubjectivity," the interaction of persons with one another. Both Schütz and Scheler used the "phenomenological" method of Edmund Husserl. All were convinced that philosophy must be grounded in the description of concrete experience. Such description reveals the essential structure of whatever appears to us and is the content of our consciousness. Most of Schütz's attention was directed to the social situation in which our immediate experience of others takes place: a "communicative common environment" where people share something. A student of Schütz's thought, Helmut Wagner, explains the insight.

Of course, the situation is elliptical: it has two subjective foci. Each of the persons in it lives through his own experience of the situation, of which the other is a part. But he not only experiences himself in the situation, he experiences the experiencing of the situation by the other. This is the experience of the "We."

It is mutual and shared understanding, then, which Schütz views as the important element in such experience. We don't look on the other person as some projection of *our* experience, but are aware of that person as a being in his or her own right. This is different from merely empathizing, which implies that we use our experience to judge another's. Schütz is concentrating on what is common to the experience we and the other share. Thus, Schütz is interested not so much in the experience as in what the experience is *of*, its content. We are involved and in the midst of what we experience, our "life-world."

Could we choose not to be involved or perhaps to be less involved with others and with the world around us? Aren't there different levels of communication? Schütz recognizes that we often discover that we're not

Viewpoint

Yet the world of my daily life is by no means my private world but is from the outset an intersubjective one, shared with my fellow-men, experienced and interpreted by Others; in brief, it is a world common to all of us. The unique biographical situation in which I find myself within the world at any moment of my existence is only to a very small extent of my own making. I find myself always within an historically given world which, as a world of nature as well as a sociocultural world, had existed before my birth and which will continue to exist after my death. This means that this world is not only mine but also my fellow-men's environment; moreover, these fellow-men are elements of my own situation, as I am of theirs. Acting upon the Others and acted upon by them, I know of this mutual relationship, and this knowledge also implies that they, the Others, experience the common world in a way substantially similar to mine. They, too, find themselves in a unique biographical situation within a world which is, like mine, structured in terms of actual and potential reach, grouped around their actual Here and Now at the center in the same dimensions and directions of space and time, an historically given world of nature, society, and culture.

ALFRED SCHÜTZ, "Symbol, Reality, and Society"

actively participating in a given situation. Rather than being aware of a shared "we-relationship," we're outside it and separate from the direct experience. We "observe." But in this condition as observer we're removed from the immediate insight possible only to those *in* the shared experience. This means as observers we have to make inferences or draw conclusions or project what we might feel *if* we were involved in order to come to an understanding of others. It is *as if* there were a problem of other minds. Social relationships in Schütz's view are most completely described in terms of directly experienced situations where there's shared involvement. But he recognized that in today's world most of us tend to "back off" from others, relate to them "objectively." For Schütz this means we are less experientially involved. Because of it we tend to view other people as distant and remote.

Do we relate to others primarily through conflict?

The profound difference that the adoption of either of these two attitudes can make in our relationship to others and our view of what it means to be a person can be seen clearly in the difference between the theories proposed by Jean-Paul Sartre and Martin Buber. Sartre argues for the uniqueness and priority of the self such that conflict and distance are fundamental characteristics of our dealing with others and knowing ourselves. Buber proposes that respect, which results in meeting another rather than separating oneself from the other, is the mode of relating that reveals our basic humanity and self-worth.

Emphasis on the individual rather than on "human nature" is characteristic of Sartre's philosophical position. Traditionally, he says, we've understood human beings as created, somewhat like a pair of scissors or some other manufactured article. Someone had an idea of their function and made them in accord with this concept. The case is just the reverse Sartre claims. There is no "God-Creator" of human beings, no "supernal artisan." Consequently, there's no idea of "human nature" according to which we're defined. We exist first of all and define ourselves as human selves afterward. There is no one or nothing to tell us who or what to be, only a human *condition,* a situation, in which we make ourselves.

Our human existence is in two modes: what Sartre calls "being-in-itself," which is existing in the way a stone, for example, might be said to "be"; and "being-for-itself," which refers to existence as a conscious subject. In the second case, the individual confronts a future and is responsible for what he or she is and is to become. There is nothing "behind" what we are, literally nothing, as the title of Sartre's major work, *Being and Nothingness,* indicates. The characteristic distinguishing being-in-itself (being) from being-for-itself (consciousness) is just the directedness toward what is perceived, reflected, remembered, and felt. Our consciousness isn't of a "self" that was determined previously. "Self" is really only our conscious acts reflected back to us. Sartre's example of what happens with a mirror helps to clarify this point. When we see ourselves in a mirror, what's there is a reflection, not anything "behind" the mirror. So, too, there's no essence or substance in Descartes' sense behind our existence.

But this consciousness, being-for-itself, depends on what Sartre calls "nihilations," or negations. We're aware of things in terms of what they are not. This book is not the chair you're sitting in or the desk you're sitting at. We know things only by separating them from all the things they are *not*. We sense, however, that self-knowledge is somehow different from knowing things. This is due, Sartre claims, to the impossibility of human beings' becoming reduced to things, although we often try to do just that. Consciousness is always changing, remaking itself. It "is not what it is." In contrast, things are what they are until they are destroyed. Since being-for-itself is continually making itself into something else, it's easy to mistake our fantasies or false identities as facts. We're prone to self-deception, or what Sartre calls "bad faith."

It is because the self is continually remade, dependent for its definition on nothingness, and so easily misled by bad faith that our relations with others are conflictual. For Sartre, "hell is other people" because we make the mistake first of living in bad faith; that is, we play roles or are unaware of our self-deceptions. Second, we ask of human relationships what they can't provide, our own self-definition. We're inauthentic, and this dooms our relations with others. We're like the woman in Sartre's example of bad faith. She agrees to go out with a certain gentleman, knowing what his intentions are. She doesn't want to make a decision, even though she knows she'll eventually have to do so. His advances are interpreted as respectful and acceptable behavior because she hides behind her fantasy to avoid having to take a position and decide on her own course of action. The entire situation is simply intolerable.

More recently Sartre has offered another, significantly different, description of human relationships. In his *Critique de la raison dialectique* [Critique of dialectical reason], he distinguishes between purposeful human action (*praxis*) and the world of worked-over matter in which we live and act (the *pratico-inerte*). Affirming that through his action "man produces his life in the midst of other men," Sartre attempts in this difficult work to elaborate the social theory that will allow human beings to act in concert to overcome the violent conflicts that arise from economic scarcity, and so, to liberate themselves, if not from having to work, at least from oppressing and exploiting one another. Scholars disagree whether this later position contradicts his earlier work. It is interesting to note, however, that Sartre does envision the possibility of cooperative efforts rather than conflictual or confrontational relations among persons.

Buber begins his work *I and Thou* by pointing, like Sartre, to two basic

Can we relate to others through respect?

modes of being, but he argues that the distinction between persons and things so important to Sartre doesn't reflect our immediate experience. We can take a twofold *attitude* toward things and people in the world, and this attitude "is twofold in accordance with the two basic words [we] can speak. The basic words are not single words but word pairs. One basic word is the word pair I-You. The other basic word is the word pair I-It."

In Buber's view we can have an I-Thou or an I-It attitude toward either persons or things. Sartre's description of detachment from other people and things falls under Buber's category of an I-It relation. There is a passion for control, manipulation, and distance. It makes no difference whether this attitude is directed toward persons or objects. What is important is the kind of relationship such an attitude implies, use of the other rather than respect for the other. Buber would agree to the importance of an I-it or controlling attitude in some circumstances. It does provide a reliable and public basis for scientific knowledge. His disagreement is with those who live only at the I-it level. Suppose, in our manufacturing of consumer goods, we totally neglected nature conservation? Or suppose we treated all other persons as though they were put here only for our own convenience?

The I-Thou attitude is important for human existence because it reflects participation in living rather than the observation of life. Unlike the static contrast of things and persons, the pair I-Thou has a dynamic quality. It's spontaneous, and we can't manipulate it. We can only accept the opportunity for such a relationship when it presents itself to us. To speak objectively of "people" and "things" implies that we adopt the attitude of observers. But we can let go of our desire to control and to observe both things and people from a distance; we can approach a tree, our pet horse, our parents, our lover in respect and appreciation. Buber argues that the quality of any relationship we may hope to achieve depends on our adopting an attitude of openness and respect for the other.

Where Sartre denies the existence of a Creator and thus argues for our self-creation, Buber presents a case for the existence of God as present to some degree in all I-Thou encounters. Only God never refuses to enter into an I-Thou relationship with another. The risk involved in letting go of our controlling attitude is what accounts for people's shrinking from the uncertainty of I-Thou relationships. Buber even argues that the threatening character of the experience is what explains why people deny that God, the eternal you, exists.

Apart from the religious aspects of Buber's position, it can be applied to experience in a general way. Everything that we experience is potentially in relation to us. If not, we wouldn't be aware of any person or any object that appeared to us. It wouldn't "be" for us unless we responded to it. How many times in class have you *not* been aware of the warmth of sunlight on your hand as you wrote, or the texture of the wood in your desk, or the lost expression on your fellow student's face? Unless we interact with these, attend to them, they are nonexistent for us as far as our lived experience is concerned. Rain, sun, wind, and trees are the same *things* for us as for an aborigine. Yet we don't experience them in the same manner. Why? If we were to adopt a position like Buber's the response would be because they are "its" for us. We've replaced receptivity with manipulation and distance. We've lost the attitude of respect.

Deciding between the positions of Sartre and Buber is not simply a matter of preference. Any evaluation of human behavior and attitudes must return to the question of the relationship between mind and body that we have discussed in this chapter. It seems that being human is something that we are constantly involved in, and part of that involvement includes our attempt to understand just what such a project entails. Understanding what it means to be a person poses one of philosophy's most basic challenges.

Summary

The Problem of the Self: The philosophical question "Who am I?" arises in everyday life. It involves our self-image, our social situation, our decisions, and the meaning of our lives. To respond to the question we must consider not only how we might describe our own self but also how we can know other selves.

Descartes and His Critics: Descartes' skeptical method led him to conclude that he was a thinking substance, that the external world provides the basis for our perceptions, and that mind and body are two separate but related entities. David Hume, who disagreed with Descartes' resolution of the question of the self, argued that there is no substantial "self." Emphasizing sense experience, Hume concluded that the "self" is only a bundle of perceptions. Gilbert Ryle also criticizes Descartes' views, but he objects to them on the basis that Descartes made a logical rather than a perceptual mistake.

Other Options besides Descartes' Position: The contemporary "behaviorist" school argues that a person can best be understood in terms of his or her observable behavior. Arthur Schopenhauer proposed that individually and socially we are our own desires, the product of will. Friedrich Nietzsche presented a case for the "superman" as the ideal for the human "will to power." William James introduced the view that we should define consciousness as a relation between mind and objects. We can only know what we experience; our knowledge of "self" is acquired through our experience of ourselves in relation to other things and other persons.

The Problem of Other Selves: Contemporary philosophers have debated Descartes' attempt to explain our knowledge of others by drawing an analogy between what we experience and what we observe about other people. Wittgenstein held that it's impossible to understand others (and indeed one's own experience) if we begin, as Descartes did, with the isolated individual. A. J. Ayer argues that we need not have an idea of "person" in order to attribute consciousness to persons, whereas P. F. Strawson maintains that the idea of consciousness presupposes the idea of persons.

Our Relations to Others: Maurice Merleau-Ponty has expressed the view that our awareness is mediated through our body and that a mind-body dualism is senseless for that reason. Our lived body is, in fact, what constitutes our life as persons. Jean-Paul Sartre held in his early work that our relationship to others is necessarily conflictual. Max Scheler stressed awareness rather than analogical reasoning as the way to know others while Alfred Schütz explored "intersubjectivity" and the nature of "we-relationships." Martin Buber's description of the I-Thou relationship emphasizes an attitude of openness and respect toward others.

Suggestions for Further Reading

Mortimer Adler's *The Difference of Man and the Difference It Makes* (New York: Holt, 1967) surveys a wide range of disciplines dealing with the question of human beings, including the biological and social sciences, and organizes the issues in terms of the philosophical questions involved.

Another interdisciplinary approach to the subject of human nature is Leslie Stevenson's *Seven Theories of Human Nature* (New York: Oxford University Press, 1974). Each of the seven views, Plato, Christianity, Marx, Freud, Sartre, Skinner, and Lorenz, is presented in light of the theory of the universe that provides the background for it. Views of the human condition implied by each position are also discussed.

An interesting summary of various arguments in the analytic tradition can be found in the collection of essays edited by Harold Morick, *Wittgenstein and the Problem of Other Minds* (New York: McGraw-Hill, 1967). This collection presents explanations of Wittgenstein's position and criticisms of his views. Morick also edited *Introduction to the Philosophy of Mind* (Glenview, Il: Scott, Foresman, 1970). The essays in this volume include discussions by philosophers from Descartes to Strawson on the questions of "self" and self-knowledge.

For a general introduction to the history of the mind-body problem in philosophy from classical thought through the beginning of the twentieth century with William James, see Joan W. Reeves, *Body and Mind in Western Thought* (Baltimore: Penguin, 1958).

Inquiry

Abortion: Life and Liberty

In 1973 the United States Supreme Court made a crucial but controversial decision on abortion. The decision was crucial because by and large it resolved the legal questions surrounding abortion; it remains controversial because it did not resolve the moral questions.

Essentially, the Court ruled that during the first trimester of pregnancy the decision to abort is a medical decision, one to be made by the attending physician in consultation with his or her patient on the basis of an assessment of the threat an uninterrupted pregnancy would pose to the patient's well-being. If the doctor decides that the patient's pregnancy should be terminated, that decision "may be effectuated," the Court held, "by an abortion free of interference by the State." In the second trimester, however, the Court ruled that the state's "important and legitimate interest in preserving and protecting the health of the pregnant woman" is "compelling." At that point, the state may intervene to regulate abortion procedures "to the extent that the regulation reasonably relates to the preservation and protection of maternal health." Finally, the Court ruled that the state has "*another* important and legitimate interest in protecting the potentiality of human life." This interest is "compelling" after "viability," when the fetus "presumably has the capability of meaningful life outside the mother's womb." At that point, the state may regulate and even prohibit abortion except when it is necessary to preserve the mother's life or health. Citing medical authority, the Court noted that viability is usually placed at about twenty-eight weeks, but may occur as early as twenty-four weeks.

The debate over the morality of abortion usually centers on a philosophical question the Supreme Court did not attempt to resolve as such: the question of the fetus' status as a human being. From a moral point of view, it is generally, although not universally, accepted that if the fetus is a human being, or a person, then abortion is homicide. But is the fetus a human being? Is the fetus a person?

The biological facts of fetal development are not in dispute, but the interpretation of them is. Those who *oppose* legalized abortion and question the Supreme Court's decision usually argue that the fetus is at least potentially a human being, capable of self-awareness, rational thought, and love. Moreover, they remark, from the moment of conception its genetic code ensures its individuality. In addition, they cite the well-known facts that the fetus' brain activity may be detected at ten weeks and its heart activity, at twelve. By that time, they point out, the fetus already has a face, arms and legs, and fingers and toes. It is a human being, they maintain, and because it is a human being it has

a right to life. Those who *support* legalized abortion frequently respond that although the fetus may be "human" in a limited, biomedical sense of the term, it is not a human being or a person in any ordinary sense. For instance, it is not aware of itself as a person among other persons, and it is incapable of rational thought. In particular, they hold, the fetus, at least in the early stages of its development, is not a person in any generally accepted moral sense. It is not a subject of rights, so it does not have a clear and unconditional right to life.

Disagreement about the mother's rights and responsibilities also marks the abortion controversy. Proabortionists often argue that the decision to abort is a matter of individual conscience and choice and that the state cannot legitimately intervene to outlaw abortion because such intervention would violate the pregnant woman's right of privacy. They emphasize the detriment the state would cause the woman by restoring or enacting paternalistic antiabortion statutes denying her the right to choose. They point out that childbirth may deprive a woman of the life style she prefers and force her to accept a radically different future against her will. Among other things, it might mean that she would have to suffer physical discomfort, or psychological damage, or both. She might have to shoulder the financial burden of giving birth to the child and caring for it; she might have to abandon her educational and career plans. She might have to bear the stigma of unwed motherhood. In such cases, proabortionists argue, the woman should be permitted to reach her own decision to terminate or not to terminate her pregnancy. After all, it is her body and her future. Antiabortionists respond that the unborn child's right to life is more fundamental and more compelling than the mother's right of privacy. The mother has a responsibility to nurture the potential life developing within her, and the inconvenience pregnancy and childbirth might cause her does not justify aborting that life.

In reaching its decision, the Supreme Court weighed such arguments. It concluded that the right of personal privacy, as defined and guaranteed by the Ninth and the Fourteenth Amendments to the Constitution, includes the woman's right to terminate her pregnancy. However, the Court ruled, "this right is not unqualified and must be considered against important State interests" in the regulation of abortion, as outlined above.

Morally, is abortion acceptable? Legally, should it be permitted? Despite the Supreme Court decision, there is no consensus in American society. Indeed, today few issues are as divisive and emotionally charged. Reasonable people vehemently disagree with one another, not only about the fetus' humanity, but also about the relative merits of its claim to life and its mother's claim to freedom. What do you think? In defining your position, specifically consider these questions:

Is the fetus a human being? If not, why not? If so, is it a human being from the moment of conception or does it become human in the course of its development? In formulating and defending your answer, try to explain as clearly as possible what you mean by the word "human" in this context.

In delivering the Supreme Court's 1973 decision, Justice Blackmun said, "We need not resolve the difficult question of when [human] life begins. When those trained in the respective disciplines of medicine, philosophy, and theology are unable to arrive at any consensus, the judiciary, at this point in the development of man's knowledge, is not in a position to speculate as to the answer." However, the Court's ruling that the state's interest in protecting the fetus' life becomes compelling after the fetus achieves viability might be taken as an ad hoc answer to that question. In your opinion, what should be the law's role in determining whether or not the fetus is a human being, or when human life begins?

Some critics of the Supreme Court decision

have argued that "viability" is not a proper criterion for human life. Although it *apparently* reflects the state of fetal development, it *actually* reflects nothing more than the state of medical science. In addition, they point out, doctors disagree about when the fetus is viable, and lawyers wonder just what "viability" means. Those who press these arguments generally maintain that the fetus should be considered a human being, entitled to the law's protection, from the moment of conception. In your opinion, is the Court justified in identifying viability as the point at which the fetus' rights become compelling?

Those who support legalized abortion frequently argue that the unenforceability of anti-abortion statutes renders them socially harmful. Criminal abortions are notoriously dangerous because "abortion mills," which are not regulated by governmental agencies, need not and all too often do not conform to the professional standards of safe medical practice. Thus, anti-abortion statutes victimize the poor, who cannot afford to travel to another state or another country for a properly supervised legal abortion under medically safe conditions. In your opinion, is this a strong or a weak argument for legalizing abortion?

Finally, many hold that although abortion should not be outlawed in all cases, neither should it be permitted in every case. In your opinion, if abortion is ever a morally acceptable alternative to continued pregnancy and childbirth, *when* or *under what circumstances* is it justified? Is abortion acceptable, for instance, when the pregnancy or the prospect of childbirth poses a threat to the mother's physical health? When it poses a threat to her psychological well-being? When it imposes a financial strain on the family? When the mother is unwed? In the case of rape? In the case of fetal defects? In a case where it would interrupt the mother's education or force her to give up her career? And how would you decide?

Inquiry

Lord of the Flies:
The Terrors of
Dehumanization

The sky was ominous and dark; lightning ripped the blackness with terrifying force. Dance and chant held back the horror as the boys surrounded the thing crouched in the middle of the circle. The frenzied beat of their cries, "Kill the beast! Cut his throat! Spill his blood!" was magnified by the pounding of their sticks, the tearing of flesh, and the smell of blood on the sand. As the rain burst on the island, the dead boy lay on the beach, and the dead parachutist he'd discovered blew out to sea. What began as an idyllic tale of British schoolboys on a tropical island becomes a story about the dark side of human nature.

With the rest of the world engaged in atomic war, the boys found themselves marooned after a plane crash. Awaiting rescue, they attempt to set up a civilized society, and leaders emerge from the group to organize and direct their activities. The intellectual and rational Piggy is mocked and ignored. Ralph, orderly and democratic, is overwhelmed by Jack Merridew's passion for dictatorial rule and violence. Simon is an introspective epileptic whose differences from the other boys force him to confront himself and his limitations. It is Simon who discovers that the Beast, so feared by the boys, is not supernatural at all. The Beast is human—a dead man. Before he can share this knowledge with the other boys he is sacrificed. The event is similar to the way the boys had killed a pig during the hunt and left its head on a spike as a gift for the Beast.

Simon's death also signifies the demise of the group's social manners, morals, and conscience. The loss of control to frenzied passion and of reason to the urge to kill results in dehumanization. Any attempt to become an individual simply by rebelling against the rules of society is doomed because the health of the social order depends on the recognition and acceptance of human frailty. Unless each person takes responsibility for this, neither the individual nor society can be human.

In his first and best-known novel, *Lord of the Flies,* William Golding is concerned with fundamental human characteristics that he feels are directly related to society. Philosophers (and novelists) have often argued about what these characteristics are and whether or not they have a connection with social structure. This debate is sometimes referred to as the "nature vs. nurture" controversy. One side holds that nature is responsible for the kind of being we become; we are whatever we are because of our genetic makeup, or the biological and physical laws governing our existence, or all three. The other position presents "nurture," or our society and surroundings, as primarily responsible for how we develop as adults. Our environment and

culture are responsible for who we are. Golding's novel presents us with human beings who "revert" to savage existence once they are beyond the controls of "civilization." He asks us to consider why this happened to the boys in the story and what might be done, if anything, to alter the outcome. In the light of Golding's story, consider the following questions about human nature, society, and their relationship.

"Civilized man" has frequently used the terms "savage" and "primitive" to refer to people whose life style does not measure up to certain standards. What is a "savage"? Does the term refer to a predatory being lacking reason and living in some animal state? Does it refer to human nature free from society's restraints to express itself naturally? Or does it reflect a value judgment based on a particular view of what is good and desirable rather than a description of what is the the case?

Many animals are social, organized and united by common interests or needs. Is human society different and if so how? Are civilization and society the same thing? Is civilization something that brings out human potential, or does it restrict it? What standards would you use to answer these questions?

How much do you think being "human" depends on biological, genetic, and evolutionary factors as opposed to social ones? Would you argue for one's being more important for our self-definition than another? If so, why? Does the phrase "human nature" refer primarily to anatomical and physiological attributes or to psychological and moral ones? If you consider both to be related, explain how.

Do you think that using reason in attempting to understand ourselves has any benefit? Would understanding have a bearing on the potential for human change? *Can* human beings change? If so, in what ways and how much? Do you agree with Golding that "innocence" must end if we are to realize our human potential? What can Golding mean by innocence, and how can we determine what human potential is?

Are the defects in the social order traceable, as Golding has said, to the defects in human nature? Must the individual be held responsible for moral choice even if human nature is defective and imperfect? If so, and if the individual is part of the social order, can the individual ever overcome the limitations of an imperfect social order as well?

Do you think that language, particularly names, has a role in establishing self and social identity? How are names used? In what ways can they indicate the kind of relationship existing between individuals? A person's sense of individuality?

Philosophy begins in wonder. And, at the end, when philosophic thought has done its best, the wonder remains. There have been added, however, some grasp of the immensity of things, some purification of emotion by understanding.

ALFRED NORTH WHITEHEAD

. . . the business of science involves more than the mere assembly of facts: it demands also intellectual architecture and construction. Before the actual building comes the collection of materials; before that, the detailed work at the drawing-board; before that, the conception of a design; and, before that even, there comes the bare recognition of possibilities.

STEPHEN TOULMIN

Chapter 2

INHABITING A UNIVERSE:
Science and Significance

Chapter Survey

Wonder: The Source and Principle of Inquiry

What kind of attitude is wonder?
How does wonder lead to myth, philosophy, and science?
What are scientific concepts about?
How does myth symbolize the unknown?

Cosmological Conviction

What do myth, philosophy, and science have in common?
What do the Babylonian and Hebrew myths tell us about human beings and the world?

The Development of the Scientific Attitude

Why did science develop in Greece?
How did the pre-Socratic philosophers of nature contribute to the development of science?
What was Aristotle's conception of science?
How does Galileo's explanation of the world differ from Aristotle's?

The Nature of Scientific Explanation

What is a fact?
What is a scientific law?
How does the idea of cause function in scientific explanations?

Edmund Husserl
1859–1938

At the end of a long and immensely productive career, Edmund Husserl had lived through World War I, and, as an Austrian of Jewish ancestry and a professor of philosophy, he had been exposed to the racial hatred and the irrationality that would lead to World War II. The real significance of his life, however, doesn't lie in these external facts. "Although he lived through dramatic times," Maurice Natanson writes, "the drama of his career was inward; it consisted in the discovery of a new terrain of consciousness and of an extraordinary method for the disclosure of its scope and structure."

What is consciousness? Husserl saw that to be conscious is always to be conscious of something. Consciousness is always actively oriented toward its object. The very essence of consciousness, he maintained, is its "intentionality," its directedness. "Being genuinely alive," he wrote, "is always having one's attention turned to this or that, turned to something as an end or a means, as relevant or irrelevant, interesting or indifferent, private or public, to something that is in daily demand or to something that is startlingly new." That simple insight is the key to Husserl's philosophical achievement.

In "Philosophy as Rigorous Science," Husserl declared that "the highest interests of human culture demand the development of a rigorously

scientific philosophy; consequently, if a philosophical revolution in our times is to be justified, it must without fail be animated by the purpose of laying a new foundation for philosophy in the sense of strict science." His lifelong struggle was to develop a radically "presupposi-

tionless" philosophy—a philosophy that would take absolutely nothing for granted—which he called "phenomenology." The method he defined (and continually refined) to accomplish this consists, essentially, in a certain suspension of belief in the world as its practitioner moves from the natural to the phenomenological attitude.

From the natural standpoint, the familiar world in which we live with others is simply there before us. We don't ordinarily doubt its reality. We

might occasionally be surprised to find something different from what we'd expected, but in general we have a common sense trust in the world we experience together. Thus, Husserl wrote, "This 'fact-world' . . . I find to be out there, and also take it just as it gives itself to me as something that exists out there." *This is the natural attitude; its central claim is that what we perceive really exists and that it really is what it appears to be.*

When we adopt the phenomenological attitude, by contrast, we suspend this naïve acceptance of external reality: "We put out of action the general thesis which belongs to the essence of the natural standpoint, *we place in brackets whatever it includes respecting the nature of Being."* This is not by any means to say that Husserl denied the world's reality; rather, in describing the objects of intentional consciousness, he barred himself from making judgments and assumptions about their existence.

In this way, Husserl hoped to penetrate to the origins of our experience: He hoped to describe "pre-predicative" experience, things as they immediately present themselves to us before we make judgments about them. The word "radical" means "relating to roots," and in a sense Husserl's radical idea of phenomenology as a presuppositionless philosophy entails a search for beginnings, a quest for the roots of our conscious life.

INHABITING A UNIVERSE

Wonder: The Source and Principle of Inquiry

He had been in the crow's nest for hours keeping watch for whales. The sea was rolling rhythmically far beneath his feet. It was as if he were at the top of the world, with all life swimming below him. The winds blew, and the currents flowed, and the waves rose and fell. His business was to keep a sharp eye, to survey the vast expanse of ocean for the monsters of the sea so that their riches might enrich the lives of men. After all, a whaling ship can't kill whales until the lookout sees them!

But Ishmael, perched so high above the ship's deck, "kept but sorry guard." He was taken in by the immensity of nature around him. How, then, could *he* possibly take *it* in? The young lookout found himself lulled by the harmony of his thoughts with the movement of the waves. He drifted, losing his identity to the bottomless ocean. Time and space were everywhere and nowhere. His life was not his, but only borrowed from the world around him; it was the sea's.

Be careful not to move your foot, young man. Don't allow your hand to lose its hold. You are but an inch away from falling to your death. Your screams will be smothered in the vast expanse around you. Know that involvement and detachment are merely different postures we assume toward the universe we inhabit.

Herman Melville's *Moby Dick* is an instructive example of the tension that can exist between a philosophic and a scientific attitude toward nature. It tells the story of young Ishmael and his adventures aboard a New England whaling ship in the nineteenth century. We come to see quickly, however, that Ishmael's experiences reflect a complex involvement with nature. He has a mythic, almost mystical, understanding of the sea. But he is also aware of the technological elements of the whaling industry, and from this perspective he is an exact observer of the sea and its marine life.

This brief episode from *Moby Dick* introduces our main topics for this chapter. We'll see how wonder about the things that surround us—oceans, marine life, celestial bodies, a blade of grass—may lead us to ask questions about the origins and purposes of the universe. These questions yield different types of answers depending on whether they are asked from a philosophic or a scientific point of view. We'll compare these points of view and explore their connection to mythology. Later in the chapter we will discuss some key concepts used in science as well as in philosophy: fact, law, and cause. .

What kind of attitude is wonder?

To begin disentangling the points of view we've called scientific and philosophic, let's look at the attitude behind the emergence of both science and philosophy: the attitude of wonder.

Wondering about origins, about where things come from and how they come to be, often inspires people's imaginations. Both philosophy and science are rooted in this attitude, this awareness that leads us to see that there is so much we do not know. Both philosophy and science are concerned with discovery, with coming to terms with the unknown. And *what* it is that is unknown is not only ourselves. It is everything around us: the entire universe of which we find ourselves a part.

In this state of wonder our attention is directed and arrested by things; we cease to be self-centered and inner-directed once we are caught up, like Ishmael, in what is all around us. Wonder is the attitude of the child fascinated by the blade of grass moving in the wind or of the astronaut awed by seeing the earth shining against the black immensity of space or of the person noticing how an oak has developed from an acorn. This amazement that what is, is leads to the questions "Why?" and "How?"

How does wonder lead to myth, philosophy, and science?

Once we become aware of our amazement by asking why or how, we have the beginning of both science and philosophy. We begin to scrutinize our involvement with things. We realize that things are governed by their own laws, independent of us, and we relate ourselves to things through our inquiring about them. Our questions and inquiry become the critical check on our reveries. They help us develop rules about the way we are to deal with the unknown and how we are to think about it.

Ishmael was fascinated by the sea and by the details of whaling. But whoever keeps watch on the masthead is expected to keep his wits about him. He must make all his scientific knowledge help him spot whales. It is necessary to learn, both from continued observation and from "lore," what to expect from the unknown, the whales, and when to expect it. The person on watch and the crew also need to be able to communicate with each other; thus they need rules about whale watching and whales in general that will enable them to do their jobs. They must be able to predict.

Science too begins with information derived from disciplined observation. This means that scientific information and the rules derived from it are necessarily public; they presuppose the pooled results of observation and experimentation. Those results are the information that has proved reliable and has thus become the accepted basis for prediction. Science not only seeks to know but also to manipulate its object in order to learn more about it, to learn the facts about it. Science has both a theoretical and a practical side. By contrast, a philosopher concerned with how we know may also be concerned with facts, but will not usually be interested in manipulation aimed at practical results.

Because we are complex, our responses to life situations are complex. Ishmael developed much more than a detached scientific attitude. He said he "kept but sorry watch"; that is, he also remained intensely involved in his experience. Focusing on this alone and asking "Why?" yields a different kind of answer or account of the time spent on the masthead.

The immensity of the sea and the sailor's aloneness with it in a vulnerable situation led him to give priority at that moment to "the problem of the universe revolving" inside him. The sailor is maintaining a vigil, but it is a vigil on the meaning of his life. He could be led to reflect on his own finitude, why he is alive and how he can make the most of the time he has left. He may also be led to think about the rightness and wrongness of his and others' actions. And perhaps he may consider his relations to other people. These issues are often the concerns of philosophers. They are not directly related to the business of science. But the issues dealt with by both disciplines, whether they are the same or different, arise from the same source.

Viewpoint

The invariable mark of wisdom is to see the miraculous in the common. What is a day? What is a year? What is summer? What is woman? What is a child? What is sleep? To our blindness, these things seem unaffecting. We make fables to hide the baldness of the fact and conform it, as we say, to the higher law of the mind. But when the fact is seen under the light of an idea, the gaudy fable fades and shrivels. We behold the real higher law. To the wise, therefore, a fact is true poetry, and the most beautiful of fables. These wonders are brought to your own door. You also are a man. Man and woman and their social life, poverty, labor, sleep, fear, fortune, are known to you. Learn that none of these things is superficial.

RALPH WALDO EMERSON, "Nature"

Philosophers are concerned with many issues, including the human situation, the ultimate constituents and structure of the universe, ethical problems, and determining what and how we can know. As you can see, sometimes philosophy and science overlap. Above all else, both are concerned with knowing; and historically they have always been closely related. Scientists like Newton, Einstein, Heisenberg, and Eiseley have a strong philosophic side; and philosophers like Kant, Whitehead, Russell, Bergson, and Wittgenstein have a strong scientific side.

In ancient Greece there was no real distinction between philosophy and science. Pre-Socratic thinkers, whom we might call philosophers of nature, tried to determine what the universe was made of and how the changes in it occurred. They assumed we could have fairly accurate knowledge of external things. Modern philosophers are skeptical about this assumption. They tend to focus more on the way we think about the external world than on the world itself.

What are scientific concepts about?

What exactly are scientific concepts about? Do they describe the external world as it is, or are they mental constructs that help us interpret what we see? Are they somehow both these things?

For example, the Ptolemaic conception of the universe with the earth at the center was superseded by the Copernican conception, which has the sun at the center. Did reality change, or did our picture change? Both the geocentric and the heliocentric views are now curiosities, relics. And this is true even though both were based on careful observation. Perhaps scientific views tell us more about how people think than about the structure of the universe.

The stars and the sun do appear to revolve around us, around the earth. And as long as our reference point is the earth, then there is something correct about the Ptolemaic picture. However, it did not account very well for facts like the retrogradation of planets. From the earth, planets appear to stop, go backward, and then go forward again in their orbits. Copernicus changed the reference point to the vicinity of the sun and accounted for such facts. Retrogradation is only "apparent" motion. But the Copernican revolution, as it is sometimes called, also led people to distrust their senses. Reality became, by definition, something other than what is naïvely perceived.

The history of science with its ever new theories suggests that the structure of the universe is not entirely known and perhaps can never be known. Theories and models of it are the human way of responding to this fact. Scientific explanation attempts to extend the range of knowing by constructing theories on the basis of what we can observe or calculate. And by continually reinterpreting what is available to us, we can change our theorizing about the unknown. Thus theories may reveal more about how we think than about what is "out there." In any case, they do reflect the intimate and mysterious association between human beings and their environment.

Wonder, as we've seen, leads us to both philosophic and scientific explanation. It leads us to want to create order and bring significance to our experience. But, returning to Ishmael for a moment, we can see that wonder involves yet another kind of human attempt at symbolizing the unknown.

How does myth symbolize the unknown?

Ishmael is a sailor, but he is also telling the story of Captain Ahab's search for the great white whale, Moby Dick. Moby Dick symbolizes evil in the story, and Ahab is obsessed with its destruction. One of Ishmael's functions as narrator is to record the immensity of the human moral dilemma, the incomprehensible fact that evil is part of the human condition. And the story of Ahab's destruction also indicates that a person might be destroyed in the process of trying to rid the world, or himself, of evil. At this level, Ishmael's personality and personal experience fade into the background, and the story is a myth.

The theme of evil and human attempts to deal with it are always found in myth, along with accounts of the origin and structure of the world. Myth is yet another way of picturing the world, structuring our experience. The issues dealt with in myth may also be dealt with by philosophy or science, or both. But the dramatization in mythic or story form of these perennial themes arises from a more personal, subjective point of view. Myth reflects a systematic and organized way of dealing with the world, but we do not try to verify it through experimentation. In myth, the earth and human beings are always the center of accounts of the universe; there never was a Copernican revolution in myth. As we shall see in the next section, myth is a fundamentally different kind of account than science and philosophy, one from which we learn different things about human beings and their "lived world." But myth is also an important precursor to philosophy and science.

Cosmological Conviction

Archaeologists' discoveries in the Near East have immensely increased our knowledge of the roots of Western culture. For example, despite profound differences between ancient Mesopotamian, Greek, and Hebraic societies, all arose from the same cultural matrix. This issue of the pre-Christian roots of the Western heritage concerns Cornelius Loew in his study *Myth, Sacred History, and Philosophy.*

Early cultures shared what Loew calls "a cosmological conviction"; that is, they shared a "persuasion" that the "meaning of life is rooted in an encompassing cosmic order in which man, society, and the gods all

What do myth, philosophy, and science have in common?

participate." "Cosmos" is from the Greek word *kosmos,* which is usually understood to mean "order." A "cosmos" is "a universe conceived of as an orderly arrangement." Our sense of cosmos, or world, or our orientation toward life is formed in the light of something or someone "experienced as an exterior force."

To explain the idea of something experienced as an exterior force, Loew traces the development of cosmological convictions from about 4000 B.C., beginning in Mesopotamia. He finds that the outside power has variously been understood as "gods, the highest good, the truth, the Holy Spirit, the law of nature, the nation." In each case, it is understood to exercise ultimate authority over the people and their world because for them it represents an ultimate value.

All these ancient societies expressed their convictions—their answers to questions about the order of the world and their place in it—in the form of myth. The form was modified by the Hebrews to become a sacred history. The Hebrews were acutely aware of their relationship to their deity. They saw many events of their history as having cosmic significance. Moses' receiving the Ten Commandments from God is part of their sacred history, for example.

When Greek civilization emerged, myth continued to be important. But an entirely new phenomenon—philosophy—appeared to express the people's basic persuasion about the cosmos. Early Greek philosophy was intimately connected with both the mythic attitude and natural science. And, as we shall see, Greek philosophy analyzed myth and religion critically.

Philosophic, mythico-religious, and scientific orientations toward the world reflect a common concern. Philosophy and science also sought answers to questions about the order and structure of the world. In their search for truth and in their need to develop a picture of what reality is like, philosophy and science resemble myth. But how did a sense of cosmic order emerge in the first place?

The ancients closely observed seasonal changes and the movements of heavenly bodies. They concluded there were connections between the events in the natural world and the structure of the social order. Just as heavenly bodies and processes in nature followed laws, so too should society. In Babylonian myth the god Marduk was responsible for the order of nature, just as the king was responsible for the laws that should be followed in society. For example, the Code of Hammurabi, the first fairly complete legal code we have, expresses a new idea: Punishments shall fit crimes. In both nature and society there should be a balance, a justice. This attitude expresses a belief in the rationality of the universe, and it implies that human experience and the world can be understood because they are analogous.

This sense of connection between nature and society is basic to the cosmological conviction. Loew has investigated the Mesopotamian search for both order and meaning in the world, and his studies have led him to five conclusions about Mesopotamian culture:

1. Every aspect of reality is permeated by a cosmic order.
2. The divine society of the gods constitutes the cosmic order.
3. Society is to be understood through the study of changes in the heavenly bodies.
4. The divine society of the gods is the macrocosm (large picture) of which human society is the microcosm. Their organization and governance should correspond.
5. The function of keeping human and divine orders in harmony belongs to the priests and kings.

With a few substitutions, the basic premise of an ordered universe and the necessity for people to be in harmony with it holds even for our modern technological society. Today we would argue that there is in some sense an order or pattern to the world. We come to understand this order through observation. Universal scientific laws reflect this order. And from a scientific point of view the abstract principle of organization is substituted for the personal external force. The pattern of the physical as well as the social world is understood in terms of its conformity to scientific laws (through the natural and social sciences). But perhaps the priestly and kingly function of keeping harmonious order has been assumed less by priests than by politicians, doctors, and lawyers.

Let's begin exploring how cosmological convictions developed in the West from myth to philosophy and science by examining two Babylonian myths. The first is a creation story, the Enuma Elish, which was first written down around 2000 B.C. It begins with a description of the primordial situation, the situation before the creation of the world.

What do the Babylonian and Hebrew myths tell us about human beings and the world?

When a sky above had not [yet even] been mentioned
[And] the name of firm ground below had not [yet even] been thought of;
[When] only primeval Apsu, their begetter,
And Mummu and Tiamat—she who gave birth to them all—
Were mingling their waters in one;
When no bog had formed [and] no island could be found;
When no god whosoever had appeared,
Had been named by name, had been determined as to [his] lot,
Then were gods formed within them.

It is not uncommon for primitive peoples to connect the origin of the universe with water, an element they see as "causing" growth. Mummu-Tiamat and Apsu are fertile waters, symbolizing the source of life, as rivers were observed to mingle with the sea. Water teemed with life; rain was seen as the semen of the earth.

The primordial situation is also chaotic, "undetermined"; it is not yet a cosmos. Marduk goes on to create order by forming the universe as we experience and depend on it. Land is formed to go under our feet. The sky and stars are formed to go over our heads. Lastly, when the stage is set, Marduk creates human beings, who are to serve the gods through their religious duties. Their task is to reflect and maintain the divine order established at creation. The myth celebrates the victory over chaos by recognizing a pattern in the world and meaning in experience.

A later Babylonian myth, the epic of Gilgamesh (also first recorded about 2000 B.C.), does not concern itself with the ordering of the universe, but tells of the rebellion against the earlier conviction that human beings were put on earth to serve the gods. Gilgamesh, like the Biblical genesis, reflects the considerable tension that develops between the human and the divine orders. It also records attempts by the ancients to remedy the problem.

Gilgamesh is the energetic and arrogant king of the city of Uruk. The goddess Aruru creates a companion for him, Enkidu, to redirect his oppressive behavior. Enkidu is a primitive being—much like Adam before the Fall—but one who is "civilized" or humanized by a prostitute. After a challenge fight, Gilgamesh and Enkidu become fast friends and go on many dangerous adventures together. Gilgamesh tells him that it is important to leave a heroic legend of brave acts behind, in fact, that this is what counts.

The gods decide it was unfair that Enkidu helped Gilgamesh kill the Bull of Heaven. When Enkidu's insult of the goddess Ishtar follows, the gods

Viewpoint

Philosophy, in one of its functions, is the critic of cosmologies. It is its function to harmonise, refashion, and justify divergent intuitions as to the nature of things. It has to insist on the scrutiny of the ultimate ideas, and on the retention of the whole of the evidence in shaping our cosmological scheme. Its business is to render explicit, and—so far as may be—efficient, a process which otherwise is unconsciously performed without rational tests.

ALFRED NORTH WHITEHEAD, Science and the Modern World

decide that he must die. Heartbreaking sorrow fills Gilgamesh. He begins to fear his own death and to lose confidence in the heroic ideal. He goes on a dangerous journey in search of the legendary plant that will ensure eternal youth. With tremendous effort Gilgamesh retrieves the plant, but a snake steals it. An anguished Gilgamesh returns to Uruk, humbled and recognizing death's inevitability.

Perhaps the appeal to modern readers of the Gilgamesh story is in its tone of resistance to the previously accepted conviction that human beings are to work and manage the earth in the service of the gods. Humanity returns to the earth at death. Yet, because they know that death must come, the heroes of ancient legend—who were often at least partially divine in origin—can think about overcoming it. Can humanity, instead of the gods, rule the natural order?

The Biblical genesis is concerned with the perennial themes of the origins of the universe, earth, humanity, and evil. Much of the material was taken by the Hebrew writers from earlier Mesopotamian accounts, but it was altered to express their belief in one God, Yahweh. The Hebraic account, like the Babylonian, also tells how God causes creation to take place. Here too God is represented as having human qualities, a voice, for instance, and wrath.

In Genesis, the first book of the Bible, the primordial condition is again chaotic, "without form." And water once more indicates the potential for life. As in the Babylonian myth, God proceeds to bring order out of chaos. He sets the stage for the culmination of creation: human beings.

Biblical writers didn't know any more than we do how the universe was formed. The six days of creation are not intended to be geological eras. Biblical writers did not set out to prove a scientific theory about how the universe came to be, but they did try to express their particular cosmological conviction. Creation is the beginning of their sacred history; it thus confers meaning by delineating their special relation to a deity.

Like all primitive and ancient peoples, the Hebrews' universe was human-centered. The earth is the center of the universe, and man is the most important part of Creation. And, as in the early Babylonian creation story, there is a harmonious relationship between God and His creatures. In Eden, all needs were provided for. The image of the tree of life, often found in Babylonian stories too, is present in the Genesis account. Some scholars argue that it could be interpreted as providing access to immortality. Another tree, the tree of the "knowledge of good and evil," signifies the possibility to choose for oneself what's good and bad, right and wrong. Such a choice implies moral autonomy, a human independence to make decisions about right and wrong. In the Biblical genesis this right belongs to God alone. To try to usurp it, as Adam and Eve did when in the story they ate the fruit of the tree, meant that humanity tried to assert its individuality and independence in opposition to the divine plan for the cosmic order. Thus the desire to "become as gods," which is at the heart of the story, led to death, suffering, and evil in the world. Moreover, having lost their proper relationship to God, Adam and Eve also found themselves out of harmony with the other creatures. Upsetting the harmony of the world is clearly their responsibility, and they must accept the consequences.

Both the Babylonian myths and the Hebraic sacred history are serious attempts to find order and meaning in the universe and a pattern in human experience. Myths contain a glimmer of the scientific attitude. Mythic cosmogonies (creation stories) have their own ideas of law, cause, and observation. But the ancients did not investigate natural law apart from God, its animating force. Nor were causes systematically examined. Events had supernatural causes as often as not. The ancients did realize that events needed explanation in terms of causality, but observation did not become useful scientifically until it was disciplined by experimentation and aimed at finding natural causes.

Myth describes moral dilemmas and human anguish in a way that philosophy and science cannot, however. Although scientific views may have ethical consequences, science simply is not concerned with describing the moral realm. Science does not replace myth; it has a different function.

The Development of the Scientific Attitude

Let's move from the Babylonian and Biblical accounts of the universe and the human condition to those found in early Greek culture in the eighth and sixth centuries B.C. Erich Auerbach opens his classic study *Mimesis* with an essay in which he compares the Homeric Greek and the Biblical approaches. The Hebrews, in presenting their sacred history, told simple stories, sparsely described. But the Homeric epics concentrate on the detail of particular things, events, and persons.

An examination of the eighth century epic the *Odyssey* will illustrate this difference. This is the story of Odysseus' attempt to return home after fighting for ten years in the Trojan War. Because of his superior cunning and the help of the gods, Odysseus is reunited with his kingdom and family. But it takes him twenty years. The *Odyssey* tells of his voyages and trials in great detail. Such things as food at banquets, the women's wash days, athletic contests, customs of all the people Odysseus meets, the landscape, and the sea are richly and eloquently described.

By contrast, Biblical stories are shrouded in mystery. No one knows what Adam and Eve looked like, what they wore after the Fall, or what they ate.

Biblical figures become full individuals only by being seen as part of the Hebraic sacred history. This is not to say that one culture is superior to another; it is simply to point out how different the world can seem to people whose cosmological convictions differ.

What does this example of the Greek penchant for minute description tell us about the Greeks or about the development of the scientific attitude? Most experts agree that Western philosophy began with the Greeks and that even if mathematics and natural science didn't begin in Greece, the Greeks gave them a big push in the modern direction.

To consider these issues we'll have to examine the Greek notion of the deity. The Greeks didn't have just one god; they had a whole pantheon of very human deities. Gods differed from humans only in strength and immortality. Otherwise they had the same squabbles, loves, jealousies, and petty concerns. The Greeks saw gods everywhere—behind each storm at sea, each turn of fate, each accident, each bit of regular or irregular behavior, each strong feeling. Everything needed an explanation; there was a cause to every event. But their detailed, precise explanations of causality usually referred back to the pantheon of gods. Even Odysseus' cunning—an important attribute because of the later Greek emphasis on human reason— is augmented by the gods. The Greek way is a complicated way to see reality. It is rich in detail and beauty, but some thinkers came to see it as inadequate.

Why did science develop in Greece?

Viewpoint

We are in the world, as bodies among bodies, not only as observers but as active experimenters. We could not ever be observers unless we were sometimes active experimenters, and we could not ever be experimenters unless we were sometimes observers. To observe is to learn what obstructions there are in the environment: and to experiment is to act with a view to perceiving what happens when we act in a certain way. It is a commonplace that scientific knowledge generally comes, not from passive observation of the course of nature, but from observation of the results of deliberate interference. In this respect scientific exploration of the world is continuous with a child's exploration. A child may be watched fixing its relation to other things, and determining their nature, by experiment, that is, by observing the results of its calculated interferences.

STUART HAMPSHIRE, Thought and Action

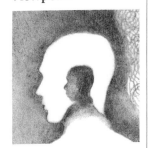

How did the pre-Socratic philosophers of nature contribute to the development of science?

The appeal of Greek religion was more to imagination than to reason, and most Greeks took Olympian religion seriously. But others raised doubts about it. For these individuals, the function of religious myth and deities to interpret nature and its processes and to make human beings feel at home in the world began to be taken over by human reason itself.

In the sixth century B.C. we have the first indication that it is possible to assume a different attitude toward the world than the mythico-religious. From his wonderings about nature, Thales, the Greek philosopher of nature, tried to find an explanation for why things are as they are. He sought his explanation in terms of natural causes because he thought the facts required it. He and some of his successors (as observant as the legendary Odysseus but in their own way) asked an entirely new question about the universe. They asked what raw material it was made of. Thales chose water as the source and principle of all things.

Thales' choice of water as the primal element is interesting not only for its possible mythological connections but also for what it may reveal about the development of observation. Water is not only teeming with life (oceans, lakes, and rivers) but also can easily be observed to change states. One doesn't need a lot of complicated scientific equipment to see water become a solid or a gas. Water seems like the universal solvent.

Thales' pupil Anaximander also said there was a primal stuff, but he called it the "unlimited." He thought it must be without, or prior to, properties. Another philosopher, Anaximenes, after observing the facts about the formation of clouds from condensation of moisture in the air, determined that air must be the source of all things. That air or water should be a first principle seems patently false to the modern mind. But what originated with the Greeks were explanations based on observation without superstition. Many of the Greek philosophers of nature (commonly called pre-Socratics) also believed in gods. But they didn't let the gods interfere with their new type of explanation.

Early philosophers did not sharply distinguish the scientific from the philosophic or the mythic. These were later distinctions, and we see the birth of a new world view only by hindsight. The important thing about these innovations is not their scientific correctness, but the assumption that the universe is natural and that its principles can be grasped by human reason. All the new philosophers of nature were looking for the reality behind the appearances, the one behind the many, the natural cause behind the effect. And instead of seeing gods, they saw a natural principle to explain what they took to be the facts.

Thales is also important because he predicted an eclipse, thereby furthering the development of astronomy. And in generalizing the land-measuring techniques of the Egyptians he furthered the science of geometry.

We can see in all this that the Greek concern for giving explanations of the visible realm, their concern for detail, indicated an extraordinary sensitivity to what makes up ordinary experience. Scientific and philosophic attitudes had found rich soil for development.

Later philosophers scoffed at the anthropomorphic gods as explanations for natural phenomena. But science and philosophy never completely replaced religion and myth. They became important alternatives. Through science and philosophy confidence in the human ability to know was increased. And in Greece, unlike in Babylonia and Judea, people became more like gods—in a sense.

In thinking about conduct, the Greeks learned to observe their own actions and the actions of others. On the basis of their observations, they developed notions of right and wrong. Theoretically, they could then control their lives in more ways. On the scientific side, Greek observation led to a rapid development not only in the areas we've already mentioned but in medicine as well. Diseases were seen to have natural causes. Symptoms were not necessarily god-sent; instead, they were clues to the underlying illness. By our standards Greek medicine was primitive, but not much progress was made for over 1,500 years after the Greek achievement. Not until the Renaissance alchemist Paracelsus discovered that substances normally poisonous to the human body could be beneficial if given in small amounts did medicine really begin to make progress.

So the Greeks made progress through disciplined observation, trying to figure out not only what things were made of but also how they changed. A famous pre-Socratic of the fifth century B.C., Parmenides, decided that knowledge was impossible on the basis of sense perception. He favored a method of reasoning that was purely "a priori," that is, "independent of observation." He began with an intuitive, self-evident principle and deduced what he took to be a correct picture of reality from that principle without ever once having recourse to his senses. He concluded that his predecessors were inconsistent when they spoke at the same time of existent "stuff" and empty space. According to Parmenides, there *is* only what there *is*, and one should never speak of what isn't as if it were.

It was over the question of change that Parmenides disagreed with earlier thinkers. Earlier philosophers of nature tried to account for change, to find its laws. But Parmenides said change, or motion, was illusory. His argument went like this:

It is. (That is, it is self-evident that there is something.)
If "It is," then it is not the case that "It is not." (That is, there is no "nothing.")
It is eternal. (For if It was created or could be destroyed, then It would

be nothing. But we have already established that there can be no "nothing.")

It is equally real in all directions.

Therefore, It is spherical. (That is, the sphere is the only figure which is "self-contained.")

There are no "holes" in It. (If there were, those places would be nothing, but there is no "nothing.")

Therefore, there is no motion. (Motion would require It to move to where It is not, but there is nowhere that It is not, since It is.)

Parmenides was arguing that change means something comes into being that wasn't before. But it's impossible to claim that anything can come either out of being (what is) or out of nonbeing (what isn't). In the first case, if something comes into being from being, "It" already is. In the second, for something to come into being from "nonbeing" implies that nonbeing is "something," and that's plainly a contradiction. Both positions are therefore absurd. The only course open, in Parmenides' view, is to assume there is no

Viewpoint

An analysis of the specific experimentally verified theories of modern physics with respect to what they say about the object of human knowledge and its relation to the human knower exhibits a very rich and complex ontological and epistemological philosophy which is an essential part of the scientific theory and method itself. Hence, physics is neither epistemologically nor ontologically neutral. Deny any one of the epistemological assumptions of the physicist's theory and there is no scientific method for testing whether what the theory says about the physical object is true, in the sense of being empirically confirmed. Deny any one of the ontological assumptions and there is not enough content in the axiomatically constructed mathematical postulates of the physicist's theory to permit the deduction of the experimental facts which it is introduced to predict, co-ordinate consistently and explain. Hence, to the extent that experimental physicists assure us that their theory of contemporary physics is indirectly and experimentally verified, they ipso facto *assure us that its rich and complex ontological and epistemological philosophy is verified also.*

WERNER HEISENBERG, Physics and Philosophy: The Revolution
in Modern Science

change and that all reality is motionless and eternal. To think otherwise is to confuse appearances with reality.

If we begin by assuming that sense perception leads only to illusions, then we refuse to accept it as evidence. Parmenides, who may have thrown the baby out with the bathwater, arrived at some startling conclusions. However, even if we decide sense perception *can* lead to knowledge, Parmenides makes us ask about our naïve dependence on it. How distorted are the views based on it? And would science be possible if Parmenides' arguments were widely accepted?

It was clear to later thinkers, especially to the Greek philosopher Aristotle, that knowledge must begin with sense experience. The senses are our only avenue to what is "out there." Science, Aristotle held, tries to account for change and differentiation in the world, and our only clue to the *why* of change is our sense experience. Parmenides supplied the ideal for scientists and philosophers. He thought that knowledge should be characterized by absolute certainty about reality, but his description of the real made it impossible to develop a method by which they could know it. Many contemporary thinkers disagree with Parmenides' ideal. They say that we can have only approximate or partial knowledge of reality. And skeptics, both ancient and modern, think we can't know reality at all.

What was Aristotle's conception of science?

Aristotle did something entirely new, something essential to the development of science and philosophy. He systematically criticized the opinions of his predecessors, and he consciously placed his own philosophy in a tradition. He saw his ideas as answers to problems that had been generated but not adequately dealt with by earlier thought.

We'll look briefly at Aristotle's idea of science, since we can trace our modern idea of science to it. The Greek word usually translated as "science" is *episteme*. It means "knowledge." Aristotle said that each branch of knowledge, each science, asks questions about a specific subject matter. And each science also has its own rules. For instance, he thought the subject matter of physics is change or motion; so the physicist asks what it is to be a moving thing. The subject matter of biology is life. What is it to be a living thing? Ethics and politics are sciences too, but they are practical sciences. They are concerned with effecting change in the human realm. They ask what it is to be a good human being and to have a good state. The subject matter dictates how we should approach it. For example, to develop a political philosophy we need to observe different states or governments and investigate their principles of organization. After comparing many we will be in a position to determine which one will foster the best life for human beings.

Aristotle's explanations did involve reference to the supernatural. It is true that he focused on what sense experience could tell him. He guided his observation by trying to identify the natural reasons—he called them causes—of a thing's existence. For instance, he tried to determine the material out of which a thing is made, the end for which it was made, and its distinguishing characteristics. But Aristotle thought there was nothing we can observe that could account for the variety, the change, or the wonder of it all. There must be a deity, an ultimate principle of explanation, a "final cause" of the world. Aristotle called this deity the "unmoved mover." Although the unmoved mover is not a personal god, it is an answer to the question "Why?"

Philosophy, for Aristotle, is done for its own sake. Human beings by nature desire to know and enjoy speculating. Out of wonder they enjoy asking questions and looking for answers. And while engaged in this activity, Aristotle held, human beings were most "godlike"—most themselves.

How does Galileo's explanation of the world differ from Aristotle's?

Aristotle was the authority in science and philosophy for centuries. Not until the Renaissance did scientists seriously question explanations based on concepts such as the "unmoved mover." How, after all, can observation yield evidence about a deity? The Renaissance scientist and mathematician Galileo (1564–1642) said that observation leads to knowledge of nature. And we do not have to postulate a deity to explain nature. Galileo said scientists must restrict themselves to describing "primary qualities." Matter, of which nature is made, can be described only in terms of the properties it has independent of an observer: size, shape, number, mass, and velocity, or rate of motion. Nature is still thought to be rational and orderly, but it is conceived entirely in mathematical terms. Scientific truth is a matter of becoming aware of nature's mathematical structure. By restricting ourselves to primary qualities we will have a more limited view, but it will be more accurate.

If science can yield the same kind of certainty that mathematics can, it must be on the right track, Galileo said. This again is an example of how assumptions or starting points influence what we find. Only those aspects of the world that can be "mathematicized" will be sought. This concept of science has been enormously influential, resulting in many advances. Galileo's work led to the new idea of scientific explanation, and the success of this mode of explanation led to a new concept of nature. So we see how explanations influence how we see reality.

But Galileo thought we must also be critical of sense perception. Science should not deal with color, sound, or odor. These "secondary qualities" are not properties of objects; they are in the subject and lead only to a distortion of our representation of nature. Sense perception may be our only avenue to truth, but we must be critical of interpretations based on it. This is the legacy of the Copernican revolution. The universe just isn't the way it looks.

Galileo said we should not look for "final causes" for motion and change, such as the "unmoved mover." Science should simply describe how motion occurs, not why it occurs. Modern scientists, for the most part, agree that science is concerned with "How?" rather than "Why?"

We have been concerned so far with explaining how myth, philosophy, and science can be different expressions of the human urge to know. And we've tried to show how the scientific attitude could have emerged. In the next section, we'll look at what a few contemporary philosophers of science have to say about some of the key concepts used by scientists.

The Nature of Scientific Explanation

Most people would agree that science deals with objective facts about the world. It is also generally assumed that science does this in a rigorous and systematic way, so that through observation and experimentation it is able to discover general laws. From these laws verifiable predictions can be derived. Several of the terms here, however, have to be examined quite carefully. It is easy to take for granted words like "fact," "observation," "experimentation," "law," and "verification." They seem so straightfor-

Viewpoint

If the seeming feuds between science and theology or between fundamental physics and common knowledge are to be dissolved at all, their dissolution can come not from making the polite compromise that both parties are really artists of a sort working from different points of view and with different sketching materials, but only from drawing uncompromising contrasts between their businesses. To satisfy the tobacconist and the tennis-coach that there need be no professional antagonisms between them, it is not necessary or expedient to pretend that they are really fellow-workers in some joint but unobviously missionary enterprise. It is better policy to remind them how different and independent their trades actually are. Indeed, this smothering effect of using notions like depicting, describing, explaining, and others to cover highly disparate things reinforces other tendencies to assimilate the dissimilar and unsuspiciously to impute just those parities of reasoning, the unreality of which engenders dilemmas.

GILBERT RYLE, Dilemmas

ward. Yet when we look at them critically we find many philosophical difficulties just beneath the surface. To illustrate, we'll consider three basic ideas we've been dealing with in this chapter, ideas that are immensely important for both science and the philosophy of science: the ideas of fact, law, and cause.

What is a fact? This question has generated a tremendous amount of discussion among philosophers of science. Contemporary philosophers think we have been mistaken in assuming that facts must be a kind of *things.* It is easy to find tables and chairs and rocks "out there," but are these things facts? We can state facts *about* tables and chairs and rocks, such as their size, weight, and shape, but the rock or table or chair is not itself a fact. If facts, then, are not "things" in any substantial sense, what are they?

One contemporary view, which many philosophers today find satisfying, is that "facts are what true statements state." N. R. Hanson believes that it would be completely wrongheaded to ask whether facts are material or mental things. What we can meaningfully ask about material objects and mental phenomena are not the same kinds of questions we can ask about facts. It is a fact that $2 + 2 = 4$ and that water evaporates during warm weather. Asking a question about either of those facts is not the same as asking a question about what 2 is or what water is.

If we accept that facts are what true statements state, then it should obviously follow that there can be many different kinds of facts about any one situation. For example, when we look at Velazquez's painting *The Maids of Honor,* a number of true statements can be asserted about it, thus, many different kinds of "facts." For instance:

1. This work is oil paint on canvas.
2. The oil paint used by Velazquez has the following chemical composition . . .
3. *The Maids of Honor* hangs in the Prado Museum in Madrid.
4. *The Maids of Honor* was painted in 1656.
5. The king and queen are reflected in the mirror in the background.
6. The painting contains a self-portrait of Velazquez.
7. Velazquez worked these figures around an X-like design, just as he did in most of his larger works.
8. The method of painting the princess' hair distinguishes this as the baroque style, not the earlier Renaissance style.

Perhaps very few of the foregoing sentences are of scientific interest. This is important to realize because it suggests that although science is interested in "the facts," it is not interested in *all* the facts. Some facts are scientifically indifferent. In some areas, such as myth, a scientific attitude may even be misguided.

If science is not interested in all the facts, can we ever claim that the facts in which science *is* interested are all that's important or even necessary? To claim this would be a form of "reductionism." It would be reducing a number of options or statements to one alone and arguing that this one is the most basic. If we were to adopt a reductionist attitude about the Velazquez painting, we would be very hard pressed to deduce statements (3) through (8) from statements (1) and (2). Reductionist models are out of place in some contexts and inappropriate for some purposes.

Facts, in Hanson's terms, are "theory-laden," or context-bound. The facts you deal with will be dictated by your interests. If you are a furniture mover or an art thief, the things about Velazquez's work that emerge as facts will probably be different from those that concern the art critic. If you are a psychoanalyst, the facts you discover about a work of art will probably not be identical to those the historian discovers. To take another example, the "fact" that "this Gothic tower was paid for by donations from the local peasants and is an expression of their piety" is very different from the "fact" that "this Gothic tower is symbolic of male genitalia." Both assertions can be true about the same tower.

Anthropologists have reported that members of certain African tribes fail to recognize snapshots of themselves as human likenesses. This indicates that seeing those black, white, and grey color patches *as if* they were three-dimensional, living beings is a learned activity and is in no way "innate." A statement like "This is the chief and his daughter" expresses a "fact" only within the context of a "game" with whose special rules we're acquainted. Similarly, returning to the Velazquez painting, "The king and queen are reflected in the mirror in the background" becomes a true statement only within a certain aesthetic context. To learn to see those color patches as the king and queen requires that we assume a particular intellectual and emotional stance. This, in turn, requires that we disregard certain facts, like the fact that the painting is "really" two-dimensional or the fact that the paint reflects the daylight passing through a museum window.

What we've discovered to be true of *The Maids of Honor* is true of the world: What is considered to be a fact depends on the context, and context is often defined by our interests and theories. You'll remember that for Galileo only statements based on calculation of mass and velocity revealed "facts" about nature. Aristotle, on the other hand, thought it was a fact that all things have a final cause. And it was a fact for Ptolemy that the sun revolves around the earth. Suppose you saw a half-eaten sandwich on the table. Could this fact be a "clue"? Could it be "evidence"? Yes, but only if you were trying to solve a problem where that information would be pertinent. Independent of such a problem, there would be no clue at all.

The contemporary Austrian philosopher Ludwig Wittgenstein has suggested that "seeing" is always "seeing as . . ." To see anything at all is to see it in a particular context. In *Philosophical Investigations,* Wittgenstein reproduced a line drawing from a psychology book. It was a "duck-rabbit," a sketch that could be seen either as a duck or as a rabbit, but not as both at once. What would it mean to ask "Yes, but what is it *really?*" Is it really a cartoon of a duck? Or is it a sketch of a rabbit? It depends on whether you *see* it *as* a duck or *as* a rabbit. If you say it is really an irregular line, you're doing the same thing as the person who says of Velazquez's painting that it's really blotches of colored oil on a canvas. Both blotches of oil on canvas and irregular lines are such only in a given context.

Thinking about contexts forces us to consider the other terms we mentioned in our characterization of science. We said that through *observation* and *experimentation* science is able to formulate general laws from which verifiable predictions can be derived. This characterization is certainly valid. But for contemporary philosophers it is a naïve philosophy of science since it suggests that scientists simply begin by observing. If you were told just to "start observing" and to come up with some general laws, you'd want to know what you were supposed to observe! But if I ask you to observe what happens when the hot valley air meets the cold ocean air, I have already set up a context, a theoretical framework, for your observations. What was the case with "facts," then, is also the case with "observation." A "scientific observation" is also a "theory-laden activity." The implication is that there are no "raw observations," just as there are no "raw data."

For a long time, philosophers of science associated with the school known as "logical positivism" tried to show that all statements in science revert to "raw data." These data were usually conceived as being pure, neutral sense data such as color patches, sounds, odors, and sensations, and statements about objects and experiences had to be reducible to these basic elements. Furthermore, statements we construct must be made by combining these qualities as though they were building blocks.

Sounds, colors, odors, and sensations are always of something; they are always bound up with our perception of things. No one ever hears a pure sound. We hear the sound of a train, a piano, a dog barking, and so on. These perceptions also always have a context. We hear a train while walking, conversing, or trying to fall asleep. Sense data do not describe how we perceive. The positivists' attempt to break perception down into simple building blocks reflects their desire to achieve the objectivity of mechanical science. Physics made great advances by reducing nature to particles that could be dealt with mathematically, or objectively. Positivists tried to imitate this success in the realm of perception; they tried to make what is essentially a very subjective process as objective as science was. Eventually the positivistic program of reducing everything to sense data was abandoned. At this point Wittgenstein's alternative of "seeing" as "seeing as . . ." became very attractive.

What we've said here about "facts" and "observations" is even more true of "experiments." An activity becomes a scientific experiment only in a theory-laden context. Dropping metal balls from the Leaning Tower of Pisa may be a scientific experiment in one context and perversity in another!

As an experiment, dropping metal balls from the Leaning Tower of Pisa may illustrate some fact about how all objects fall. All objects fall, the scientist might assert, at a rate of 32 feet per second squared. What kind of statement is this? Since it purports to state something that occurs every time a body falls, it evidently states a necessary feature of the world and so has the status of a law in science. The topic of laws is at once more exciting and more complicated than the others we have discussed; it's at the very heart of the philosophy of science.

What is a scientific law?

For modern philosophers of science, one of the main problems is trying to establish the logical status of propositions or statements that express scientific laws. Since David Hume's time (the eighteenth century) it has generally been held that there are basically two kinds of meaningful assertions: analytic propositions and synthetic propositions. These important terms were later used by Immanuel Kant. Analytic propositions are "statements whose negation leads to a self-contradiction." In other words, they're statements we can't deny without falling into contradictions. According to this definition, the following are "analytic":

1. All bachelors are unmarried males.
2. Every one-eyed white ant with a wooden leg is either parasitical or not parasitical.

Negate the first statement (Some bachelor is not an unmarried male). You are now actually asserting the self-contradictory proposition that some bachelor is not a bachelor because bachelors *just are* unmarried males. The second example may not, at first glance, seem to be like the first, until you notice that its negation leads to the contradictory assertion that "some ant is both parasitic and not parasitic."

Notice a few other characteristics of analytic statements. Given the rules of the language in which they are assertions, they are somehow "necessary." They couldn't be false without our language being very different from what it is. Also, they are a priori, that is, their truth is established independently of observation. If you wonder about the truth of any analytic proposition you'll have a terrible time doing empirical research! Can you imagine a sociological questionnaire or a census form asking:

1. Are you a bachelor?
2. If so, are you also a male?
3. And are you unmarried?

Because they are a priori, analytic propositions are apparent "tautologies." A tautology is a self-contained redundant or repetitious statement. As such, analytic propositions are not "about the world." When you have learned that A = A, or that bachelors are unmarried males, it is not obvious that you have learned about anything "out there" (or, for that matter, "in here"). But you have become acquainted with certain conventions and rules governing the use of the language.

"Synthetic" propositions are the opposite of analytic ones in every respect. Their negation does not lead to a self-contradiction. They are not "necessary" but "contingent." Their truth must be established a posteriori; it is dependent upon observation. They are not "empty" or circular statements but refer to things outside themselves. They are "about the world." For instance:

1. There are some cherry trees in Golden Gate Park.
2. Brutus killed Caesar.

In each case, the negation of these statements is logically consistent. To say "There are no cherry trees in Golden Gate Park" is false, but it is not self-contradictory. Both these propositions are true, but they might have been

Viewpoint

It is obvious that truth in general depends on both language and extralinguistic fact. The statement "Brutus killed Caesar" would be false if the world had been different in certain ways, but it would also be false if the word "killed" happened rather to have the sense of "begat." Thus one is tempted to suppose in general that the truth of a statement is somehow analyzable into a linguistic component and a factual component. Given this supposition, it next seems reasonable that in some statements the factual component should be null; and these are the analytic statements. But, for all its a priori reasonableness, a boundary between analytic and synthetic statements simply has not been drawn. That there is such a distinction to be drawn at all is an unempirical dogma of empiricists, a metaphysical article of faith.

WILLARD VAN ORMAN QUINE, "Two Dogmas of Empiricism"

false under different conditions. That's what contingent means. They are both a posteriori because to establish their truth requires some form of empirical investigation.

There have been some efforts in the history of philosophy, like Immanuel Kant's, to show that there may be other forms of meaningful statements besides analytic and synthetic ones. More recently, the American philosopher Willard Van Orman Quine has argued that the traditional distinction between analytic statements, whose truth is a matter of definition, or language, and synthetic statements, whose truth is a matter of fact, or experience, is misleading and simplistic. While acknowledging that science taken as a whole has a "double dependence" on language and experience, he suggests that "it is nonsense, and the root of much nonsense, to speak of a linguistic component and a factual component in the truth of any individual statement."

Still, for the great majority of philosophers since Hume's time, the two categories—analytic propositions and synthetic propositions—have exhausted the possibilities. Moreover, distinguishing between them, however informally, has proved valuable. Let's assume, then, that propositions are either analytic or synthetic. To ask what sort of statement "laws of science" are is to ask whether they are analytic or synthetic.

It should come as no surprise that rationalistic philosophers (those who argue, as Parmenides did, that thought and reason are primary) view scientific laws as analytic propositions. Empirically oriented philosophers (those who argue that sense experience is most important) have generally viewed scientific laws as synthetic propositions. It makes considerable difference which of these positions you adopt.

For example, take the laws of Newtonian physics you learned in your introductory physics class. Newton's second law, $F = ma$, or his law of gravitation, $F = Gm_1m_2/d^2$ might serve here. The first means "force equals mass times acceleration"; the second, "every particle of matter in the universe attracts every other particle with a force directly proportional to the product of the masses of the particles and inversely proportional to the square of the distance between them."

If you are of rationalist orientation, you will believe these laws have no exceptions. You might even claim that they *could* have no exceptions. They would be like definitions because they define the rules by which the game is played. For anything to be considered an event in physical reality, the phenomenon would necessarily have to take place according to these laws.

This interpretation has definite strengths. It accounts for the feeling that metal balls don't just *happen* to fall at a constant rate of 32 feet per second squared. Accepting this law means we hold that this is the way things have always been and always will be. The rationalist interpretation also has weaknesses, however. First, analytic propositions are such that if you put them in the negative they contradict themselves. How could we explain the fact that we can understand what denying the law of gravitation means? It is easy enough to imagine a world in which objects rise and fall at random and occasionally just hover. Furthermore, we said analytic statements are tautologies and as such "empty" and not "about the world." Yet these laws certainly seem to say something "about the world." Finally, they seem to be discoverable only through observation. If this is the case, they are a posteriori.

Empiricists, on the other hand, interpret the laws of science as empirical generalizations. If in all known cases hot air has been observed to rise above cold air, we may generalize and say hot air rises above cold air. Still, we will watch cautiously for counterexamples, and we are prepared to modify the "law." As an empiricist, you might view the laws of science simply as ways of organizing experiential data that facilitate predictions.

The clear strength of the empiricist position is that it allows scientific laws to be a posteriori and about the world. It can also accommodate new data since its theoretical structure is not rigid. Where the rationalist posture was strongest, though, the empiricist view is weakest. The rationalists know it doesn't just happen that weights fall at a constantly accelerating rate. It is this apparent necessity that empiricists cannot explain. From their point of view fishing weights have always sunk in water while the cork floats on the surface as if by a series of coincidences. Still, just because the sun has risen every morning throughout recorded history doesn't mean that it will rise of necessity tomorrow. Ultimately it is not logic but conviction that tells us something "necessary" about the world.

As Quine suggested, the actual business of doing science seems to involve both language and experience and both the rational and the empirical approaches. Observation, as we've seen, is not pure; it is conditioned by interests and theories, that is, by the assumptions we hold about the world. Theories are modified or confirmed by further observation and experimentation, that is, by further empirical research. But the rules by which this observation takes place involve convictions we must call "rationalist." For example, observation does not supply the concept of causality. All we observe, as Hume pointed out, is that one event follows another; we do not observe that one event *must* follow another. The mind supplies the necessity. This is not to say that events do not have causes; it's just that we can't see them and so do not know anything about them with certainty. We operate "as if" the sun will rise tomorrow morning.

How does the idea of cause function in scientific explanations?

Thus we are brought to another important concept in science and philosophy: causality. A traditional definition of causality is related to the notion of "laws." This definition seems to have governed much philosophical and scientific thought at least through the nineteenth century. It continues to be influential in some circles today.

According to this view, to say that x causes y is to say that whenever event x takes place, event y follows of necessity. Newton's physics seems to presuppose this definition. Here's a description of Newton's mechanized, mathematicized world offered by the contemporary physicist and philosopher Werner Heisenberg in *Physics and Philosophy*. You'll notice that Newton's world is almost identical to Galileo's:

The world consisted of things in space and time, the things consist of matter, and matter can produce and can be acted upon by forces. The events follow from the interplay between matter and forces; every event is the result and the cause of other events.

It's easy to understand causality in these terms. We can all come up with illustrations: The image of billiard balls knocking other billiard balls about immediately comes to mind. But using such a model makes it difficult to see how a physical event could cause a mental event or vice versa. We know how a billiard ball strikes another billiard ball and passes on its momentum, but where does a physical event "strike" a mental one?

It is important that we analyze the definition of cause before accepting it. The first critical comment we can make is this: Although the proposed definition of causality does seem to apply to the world of billiard balls, pulleys, and falling apples, developments in twentieth century physics cast doubt on its absoluteness and universal applicability. The implications of Heisenberg's "uncertainty principle" are that on the subatomic level this model simply does not apply. Only a statistical interpretation of subatomic particles is possible. Heisenberg concluded that there really is *no* causal sequence at this level, that the data are such that only statistical probabilities can be stated.

Influenced by Heisenberg's work, scientists like Sir Arthur Eddington have urged that what is true of the subatomic world is true of the larger world as well. This means that the causal model we've been discussing has no application at all! Others, like Einstein, argued that Heisenberg had, in a sense, misunderstood his own principle. The causal model does apply to the subatomic world, but there are practical difficulties in demonstrating it. Obviously, we will not be able to decide here which position is "correct." What we can say, however, is that Heisenberg and Eddington have shown it is possible to reject the simple causal model without rejecting science itself.

We have already noted how "facts," "observations," and "experiments" are "theory-laden." We may further suggest that what is to count as a "cause" will depend very much on the context. The interests of the investigator, and the theoretical structure within which he or she is operating, will be important. Again, N. R. Hanson, in *Observation and Explanation,* asks us to consider the following possibilities when attempting to establish the cause of an airplane accident in which the pilot is killed:

1. *The engine stopped, at night, over the Rockies.*
2. *Insufficient care had been given, during the last 100-hour inspection, to the fuel strainers, which* post mortem *examination proved to be clogged.*
3. *The pilot had probably not acquainted himself with meteorological conditions en route; at least the FAA Flight Service has no record of his having done so.*
4. *The weather data broadcast during the fatal flight was not current for the locale of the disaster.*

Viewpoint

Science certainly cannot be charged with responsibility for having brought forth this depersonalized, this devalued, this demoralized common world of ours. Yet insofar as the scientist has not been a philosopher who has been aware of the limits of his objectifying work, of the need of its complementation by the work of others devoted to truth of another sort than his truth, insofar as he has been unaware of the moral element in his own activity, he bears some share in our common failure.

The human problem of our time cannot be stated by the use of such phrases as "science in conflict with morality." Our situation is not one of conflict between great forces. It is better described as a situation of emptiness. Life for man has become empty because it is without great purposes and great hopes and great commitments, without a sense of participation in a great conflict of good and evil. We shall not emerge out of this situation by passing judgments on one another in our various communities and callings, nor by trying to find out which one of us— scientific community, or economic, or religious or political—has led the rest of us astray. But we are challenged in all these spheres to become something more than we have been, not scientists only, or logicians only, nor theologians only, but philosophers, lovers and seekers of that inclusive wisdom which is an affair of whole selves in a whole world.

H. RICHARD NIEBUHR, "Science in Conflict with Morality?"

All these propositions (and more) could be true simultaneously. What will count as the "cause" of the crash will depend on the interests of the investigator. The aircraft designer, the mechanic, the psychologist, and the FAA flight examiner will each concentrate on very different elements of the story. No *one* thing emerges as *the* cause. This analysis shows the "theory-laden" nature of the notion of causality. According to our earlier definition, saying that x causes y is saying that given event x, event y follows of necessity. It now appears that this model is simply not rich enough to provide answers to all the questions we may ask about the world that surrounds us.

Scientific explanation is made possible through the concepts we've been discussing. We've seen that theoretical contexts and historical periods influence their meaning. What counts as explanation seems to depend on a cosmological conviction or a world view. Aristotle thought his world was completely knowable, so he felt confident describin events in terms of final causes. Galileo, however, believed that the knowable world was restricted to "primary qualities," that is, that we could explain *how* there is motion or change, but not *why*. And modern physics, when it describes subatomic particles, has trouble with the very notion that a cause must precede an event! The Aristotelian, the Galilean, and the contemporary views of science and reality all hold that the universe we inhabit is a cosmos. They all posit an order to nature that we can understand and explain, if only in terms of statistical probabilities.

The myths we discussed earlier in this chapter raised ethical questions, and so, of course, does science. Mythology presents convictions about how the world is organized, and these convictions imply how people ought to behave to maintain the world order. For instance, in the Biblical genesis Adam and Eve are required to tend the garden. Is this still in some sense a viable idea today? Does our knowledge of the environment—a product of scientific investigation—imply a way in which we *ought* to act toward nature? Does scientific knowledge dictate attitudes of detachment and manipulation? If wonder gives rise to science, does science necessarily destroy wonder? Is it possible to experience a certain involvement in nature without abandoning science? Should scientists be held accountable for the ecological, social, and political consequences of their advances? How can we attempt to resolve the value problems scientific advances pose? Science, like myth, raises philosophical questions not only about explanatory theories and models but also about their human and social implications.

Philosophy's role is to make explicit what myth and science assume and imply about the world and about our lives together in it. Philosophy's role is, first, to question what they take for granted and, second, to assess their theoretical and their practical consequences. Perhaps this is what Whitehead meant in writing that "Philosophy, in one of its functions, is the critic of cosmologies." If this is so, then from both the individual and the societal points of view philosophical reflection and analysis are not luxuries. Indeed, they are necessities.

Summary

Wonder: The Source and Principle of Inquiry: Wonder at being—amazement that what is, is—leads to the questions "Why?" and "How?" Both philosophy and science begin with this sense of wonder. Although mythical accounts differ fundamentally from philosophical and scientific explanations, myth does reflect a systematic and organized way of dealing with the world.

Cosmological Conviction: Cornelius Loew explains that a "cosmological conviction" is a "persuasion" that "the meaning of life is rooted in an encompassing cosmic order in which man, society, and the gods all participate." Babylonian myths and Hebraic sacred history express cosmological convictions.

The Development of the Scientific Attitude: Greek religion appealed more to imagination that to reason; inquiring about the ultimate "stuff" of the universe, pre-Socratic philosophers of nature adopted a more critical attitude. Parmenides argued that knowledge cannot be based on sense perception; Aristotle held, however, that science should account for change and the only clue to the reasons for change is sense experience. During the Renaissance, Galileo maintained that scientists should limit themselves to describing "primary qualities," such as mass and velocity.

The Nature of Scientific Explanation: The assumptions and interests of the investigator will direct his or her attention to certain things as facts and causes, which may be called theory-laden, or context-bound. Although the status of its laws is disputed, science has a "double dependence" on language and fact; scientific activity involves both reason and experience.

Suggestions for Further Reading

In *The Greek Experience* (New York: Mentor Books, 1957), C. K. Bowra communicates the spirit of classical Greek civilization and discusses the early relations between philosophy and science.

Arthur Koestler's *The Sleep Walkers* (New York: Macmillan, 1959) is an enjoyable history of the pre-Socratic cosmologists.

In *Physics and Philosophy: The Revolution in Modern Science* (New York: Harper & Row, Harper Torchbooks, 1962), Werner Heisenberg explains the overthrow of traditional physics and examines philosophically interesting aspects of recent scientific thought.

A philosopher and historian of science, Thomas S. Kuhn offers a theory to account for revolutions in scientific thought in *The Structure of Scientific Revolutions* (Chicago: The University of Chicago Press, 1962).

Stephen Toulmin addresses the related problems of defining scientific activity and establishing criteria for scientific merit in *Foresight and Understanding: An Enquiry into the Aims of Science* (New York: Harper & Row, Harper Torchbooks, 1963).

A stimulating introduction, N. R. Hanson's *Observation and Explanation: A Guide to Philosophy of Science* (London: Allen, 1972) is especially valuable for its clarity.

Inquiry

Science and Society: The Possibility of Social Science

In a very general sense we use the term "science" to refer to a body of knowledge—as in the "science" of auto mechanics or piano tuning. But more particularly, the term refers to the method of study rather than to the content of the study. The "scientific method" is really a combination of methods. It is, however, based on the philosophical position that argues knowledge is obtained through direct observation. The result is a set of hypotheses about the natural world closely related to observations of that world. For these hypotheses to count as "scientific," it is usually held that they must accomplish the following:

1. They must give us new knowledge, knowledge not already implicit in prescientific observation;
2. They must explain—they must relate what we don't understand to what we do understand in such a way that we can derive the former from the latter; and
3. They must allow us to make verifiable predictions about the world.

The first two characteristics relate to understanding as a goal of the scientific process. The third, prediction, depends on this understanding. Another aspect of scientific method, control, or the use of understanding and prediction to direct events or objects in a specific manner, will be considered in the next Inquiry, which raises ethical questions in addition to epistemological or knowledge-related ones.

It is easy to see how understanding and prediction apply to the physical and biological sciences. For example, we observe objects in motion and arrive at an understanding of the laws of motion. We can then predict the movement of objects around us. We can even construct objects that move in a direction, at a speed, and in a manner we've designed. But it is difficult to comprehend how observation leads to understanding and prediction when we are concerned with such nonmaterial entities as human nature, democracy, or culture. These things are not observable in the same way that plants or stars or rocks are. If we consider science as a method rather than a body of knowledge, can there be *social sciences?*

Answers run from an emphatic, unqualified yes to an equally emphatic unqualified no—with many in between. We get affirmative responses from such social theorists as Émile Durkheim, Sigmund Freud, and B. F. Skinner. For all their differences, these men did not doubt that the same causal model that worked in Newtonian physics could also be applied to explain human behavior. At the other extreme, we get negative answers from certain religious thinkers who deny that a human being is fully part of the natural world and that human beings can be completely understood in naturalistic terms. Yet another point of view is represented by some existentialists who claim, following Jean-Paul Sartre, that there is no such thing as "human nature." Political activists espouse another position: that "social scientists" should not even be trying to observe and theorize objectively. Instead, they should be committed to effecting social change. Marx even argued, "The philosophers have only *interpreted* the world in various ways; the point, however, is to *change* it."

Somewhere between these extremes is a group of philosophers and social scientists who hold that there *can* be a scientific study of human beings. However, the subject matter of this study, the human being, is so unique that social science must generate its *own* criteria and methods. The criteria and the methodology of the physical sciences cannot fruitfully be applied to the study of human beings.

The "hard-minded" philosophers of social science say that for anything to count as scientific activity, it must be based on the models provided by the most successful sciences, especially physics. These philosophers often emphasize measurement, predictability, laws, and some form of the causal model. Does the difference in the subject matter of the social sciences as opposed to the physical and biological sciences make the application of scientific method impossible, or does the difference make it even more necessary if we are to acquire understanding of human beings and their relationships?

Measurement is considered an important aspect of scientific method. It is, however, harder to apply such a criterion to phenomena like social attitudes than to distances in space. If measurement in the social sciences is difficult to quantify (to assign a numerical number to), in what sense is measurement in physical and biological science the same as measurement in social science? If techniques like sampling and statistical survey are used, how might we check that the variables are constant? What and how do the social sciences "measure"?

Many people think of experimentation and science as interchangeable concepts. But experimentation depends on the ability to control the various elements and conditions related to the experiment. It is possible to control variables in a chemistry laboratory when conducting an experiment to determine the effect of a liquid on a particular metal. If we were to try to determine the effect of a certain form of government on family structure, would it be possible to control people and their organizations and all the variables that might affect the outcome of our investigation? Would failure to control the variables seriously affect the "scientific" nature of our inquiry? What alternatives or corrective techniques might be available to the social scientist to correct for such failures? Are they reliable?

The social scientist, unlike the physical or biological scientist, is part of the very thing that he or she is investigating. When studying a particular social class or family structure, for example, the social scientist does not cease to be a member of a social class or a family. Does this make it impossible for the social scientist to be unbiased in the investigation, to conduct "value-free" research? Is objectivity possible in *any* application of scientific method, particularly in the application of scientific method by the social sciences?

A difficulty frequently encountered by social scientists is the tension between the positive and the normative aspects of their investigations. They describe and attempt to understand a phenomenon such as poverty. Sometimes they make predictions about what they've investigated, for example, the effect of poverty on the number of crimes that can be expected in a community with subsistence-level incomes. But is it also their role to consider not only what is, but what ought to be? Is the social scientist, as scientist, required to suggest possible solutions to social problems? Are such plans dependent on nonscientific factors? If so, how much, and what might these factors be?

If social science must develop its own criteria, based on, but not identical with, the method of the physical and biological sciences, what elements would remain the same in both? What ones would change or be modified? In what sense could they all be considered "scientific?"

Inquiry

The Moral Responsibility of the Scientist

There can be little doubt that the world in which we live has been changed and will probably continue to change as a result of scientific discoveries. Research in pure science has led to applications affecting our daily lives—electricity, automobiles, and telephones. But frequently a social situation (take international relations, for example) precipitates scientific research for the purpose of altering the present situation. The results might be the development of atomic weapons, alternative energy sources, or more efficient means of communication. If we can establish that there is a relationship between science and society, can we also establish whether or not the scientist is, can, or should be divorced from the application of his or her discovery?

Some defenders of the scientific establishment have pointed out that "science" does not make the decision to explode bombs, apply DDT, or build nuclear power plants; rather, such decisions are made by politicians. They argue that science itself is politically and morally neutral. The use of science by nonscientists is what has to be controlled. This idea, which has some plausibility, has recently been examined by the philosopher Herbert Marcuse.

Marcuse claims that the very neutrality of science is itself a form of ideology. Inherent in the goals and methods of science, he argues, is the domination of nature, and science makes no

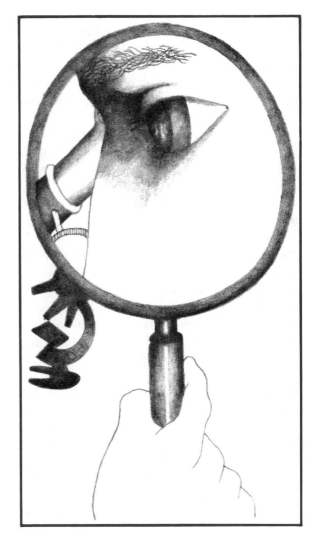

distinction between human beings and nature. Hence, the unspoken goal of the domination of human beings is inherent even in "pure" science. Science fills any vacuum. According to this line of reasoning, the German physicians who performed experimental operations without anesthesia on prisoners in concentration camps were not aberrations. They were in the mainstream of science. From his Marxian position, Marcuse thinks we must recognize that science is implicitly political and confront it with explicitly political demands that require it to serve humanistic goals.

The issue Marcuse raises is critical not only for the biological and physical sciences but for the social sciences as well. In a well-publicized debate with the humanistic psychologist Carl Rogers, B. F. Skinner argued that the human being is totally and irrationally controlled by such things as moral and religious upbringing, ethical and legal sanctions, TV commercials, and social prejudices. Since he held that it was human destiny to be controlled, Skinner argued that we should submit to rational, scientific control. Rogers replied that moral and political goals could not be derived from science, hence, that Skinner's proposal was inconsistent. Like Marcuse, Rogers questions the very notion of a value-free social science.

Forms of psychological control have become continually more sophisticated, subtle, and—to many—downright frightening. Neurological experimentation on the brains of animals has resulted in the discovery of certain control centers, including a "pleasure center." An electrode implanted in the pleasure center by a relatively simple operation can literally make *any* activity pleasurable. The political implications of this fact are staggering. Just in case this argument sounds "academic," recall that it comes at a time when newspapers are reporting cases of frontal lobotomies performed on "troublemakers" in prisons in order to pacify them. Other reports describe experiments on people suffering from syphilis. They were given fake medicine, and their degeneration was studied over a period of many years in order to discover the effects of untreated venereal disease. Is the question "How different is this from the activities of the Nazi physicians?" simply rhetorical?

These arguments and examples force us to consider some fundamental questions about the nature, direction, and consequences of scientific research. Let us consider the individual scientist first. Should the chemist who discovers a new drug be held responsible for its application? If you argue that the chemist *is* responsible not only for publishing data regarding the discovery and properties of the drug but also for its effects on human beings and the environment, does this responsibility extend to making sure the drug is used only by those who would not be harmed by it?

Suppose that you think such a responsibility is entirely too much to place on the scientist alone. You suggest that questions of the application of scientific discoveries should be left to other segments of society. Can other members of society make an intelligent and informed decision without the scientist's input, particularly if the scientist is the "expert" and the one most qualified to ascertain the consequences of his or her investigations?

Sometimes the scientist does express concern over the application of scientific information. For example, increased sensitivity to ecological issues precipitated a heated debate in the scientific community over the conditions for construction of nuclear power plants to serve energy needs. When voters in California were asked to decide the issue, they found "experts" on both sides of the question. Did scientists who didn't share their expertise with the public abrogate their responsibility? Did the voter have a responsibility to become as informed as the scientist? If consequences are only probable, and not certain, how far does our moral responsibility extend? Is the scientist responsible for the consequences of

his or her discovery only after they are known?

Science affects both our environment and ourselves. New knowledge in the field of genetics, for example, raises a particularly difficult question of responsibility. In the early 1960s a technique called cloning, making exact copies of an individual organism, a genetic duplicate, was developed. Most scientists are convinced that the technique can be eventually applied to animals and humans. We could reproduce an unlimited number of individuals with the appearance and capacities of an Einstein or a Hitler. If this is possible, should it be done? Who decides and on what basis? Must the geneticists who worked on the technique be responsible for educating governments to its potential use and abuse? Are they in any sense responsible for the decisions that such government officials might make about the matter?

If science and society are so intertwined, who should assume the responsibility for the direction of scientific research? Why? What problems can be anticipated?

Do you agree with Marcuse that science is implicitly political? If so, who should make decisions about its control? If not, does your answer change?

Words and deeds are quite indifferent modes of the divine energy. Words are also actions, and actions are a kind of words.

RALPH WALDO EMERSON

Some gross and confused conceptions men indeed ordinarily have, to which they apply the common words of their language; and such a loose use of their words serves them well enough in their ordinary discourses or affairs. But this is not sufficient for philosophical inquiries.

JOHN LOCKE

Chapter 3

COMMUNICATION
From Rituals to Reasoning

Chapter Survey

What Is Communication?
What makes up "communication"?
How do animals communicate?

Nonlinguistic Communication
What and how do the arts communicate?
What forms of communication do religions use?
What and how do rituals communicate?

The Uses of Language
What is the symbolic nature of language?
What functions does language serve?

The Performative Use of Language
What are "performatives"?
How can words accomplish actions?

Evaluating Arguments
What is logic?
What is an argument?

Validity
What is a valid argument?
How can you set about clarifying arguments?

Attacking Arguments
How do arguments go wrong?
What methods are available for attacking arguments?

The Form of Arguments
How can arguments formally resemble one another?
What is the value of identifying an argument's form?

Counterexamples
What is a "counterexample" to an argument?
How does argumentation proceed?

Ludwig Wittgenstein
1889–1951

"The difficulty in philosophy is to say no more than we know."

Ludwig Wittgenstein undoubtedly did more than anyone else to shape recent philosophical thought in English-speaking countries. After his death, Gilbert Ryle attested, "Philosophers who never met him—and few of us did meet him—can be heard talking philosophy in his tones of voice; and students who can barely spell his name now wrinkle up their noses at things which had a bad smell for him." His extraordinary influence is not altogether surprising, however; Wittgenstein was an extraordinary person. Trained as an aeronautical engineer, he was also a mathematician, a musician, a sculptor, an architect, a devotee of cowboy films, a fine writer, and, above all, a brilliant, passionate thinker.

Written under difficult circumstances during his service in World War I, Wittgenstein's first important work was Tractatus Logico-Philosophicus. He explained in its preface that "the whole sense of the book might be summed up in the following words: what can be said at all can be said clearly, and what we cannot talk about we must pass over in silence." The work's central thesis is that meaningful propositions depict reality. "A proposition is a picture of reality," Wittgenstein argued. "A proposition is a model of reality as we imagine it." According to this picture theory of meaning, as it came to be called, the propositions of ordinary language correspond, if they have any meaning, to possible states of affairs in the world. If the facts they picture are indeed facts, they're true; if not, they're

false. A proposition "can be true or false only in virtue of being a picture of reality."

Since the Tractatus presented, in its author's words, "the final solution of the problems," Wittgenstein gave up philosophy to become, in turn, a schoolmaster, a monastery gardener, and an

architect. Some years later, however, in a period of renewed philosophical activity, he came to recognize that we use language not just to form declarative sentences about matters of fact, but in many different ways. "Think of the tools in a tool box: there is a hammer, pliers, a saw, a screwdriver, a rule, a glue-pot, glue, nails and screws.—The functions of words are as diverse as the functions of these objects." The meaning of a word, he now argued, is neither the object to which that word might refer nor the thought, the "mental content," it might express; rather, its meaning is its practical use in a given situation. Indeed,

"thinking," he wrote, "is essentially the activity of operating with signs," that is, generally, using language.

Wittgenstein also compared the different ways we use language to games. In his later work, he occasionally sketched simple scenarios, which he called "language-games," to illustrate a point. The notion of language-games has more than methodological significance; Wittgenstein wrote that "the term 'language-game' is meant to bring into prominence the fact that the speaking of language is part of an activity, or of a form of life."

Generally, however, Wittgenstein's conception of philosophy as an activity whose goal was to clarify thought by examining language didn't change. Linguistic analysis, the philosophical movement his work inspired, has as its primary objective the descriptive investigation of language uses and the logical analysis of ideas. In The Blue and Brown Books, Wittgenstein said, "Philosophy, as we use the word, is a fight against the fascination which forms of expression exert upon us." In Philosophical Investigations, he further explained that "philosophical problems arise when language goes on holiday," when we think we're saying something meaningful, but we aren't. "The confusions which occupy us arise when language is like an engine idling, not when it is doing work." This understanding of philosophy as a descriptive, analytic activity focusing on language is Wittgenstein's major contribution to contemporary Western thought.

Chapter 3

COMMUNICATION

What Is Communication?

What do you first think of when you hear the word "communication"? Your immediate response might include such activities as speaking, hearing, writing, and reading and such media as radio, television, books, and newspapers. But are these the only means of communication? Although philosophers have often concentrated on means that, like these, depend heavily on language, there are in fact many other ways in which communication takes place.

The origin of the term "communication" is the Latin *communis,* meaning "common." Thus the verb "to communicate" literally means "to make common." We take for granted someone else's understanding or deciphering of the "code" represented by our talking or laughing. A need or desire may be communicated and a response elicited quite automatically. If a person cries, that person is probably upset; if a child throws a tantrum, that child has probably been denied something; and if someone rushes toward you and gives you a hug, that person is probably pleased to see you. The arched eyebrow, the blush, the shift in bodily position, the "look that can kill," all "speak" to us. We usually know what these things mean without thinking about them.

"Body language" and "nonverbal communication"—subjects of best-sellers today—are means of our human interconnectedness, just as words are. They are the ways we reach out to one another. Our inner responses to these means indicate the complicated network of relationships that make up our shared human world.

By looking at other cultures, we can see that communication depends on a shared world or shared experience. For example, it is not a custom in China to wave one's arm as a greeting. (Let's put aside difficulties in communication created by differences in language.) The Chinese unfamiliar with the Western custom would not understand the gesture. The

What makes up "communication"?

intended greeting would not be communicated; indeed, the gesture might be misinterpreted as a threat. And even if some Chinese did understand, waving still would not be a terribly meaningful greeting. For communication to take place, something must get through to us, and we must hold it in common.

We communicate the intangible. No one touches, hears, or sees a thought or feeling. The tangible—what can be touched, heard, or seen—can't be communicated in the normal sense of the word. I can give you my book, but I can't communicate it as a physical object with its cover and pages. I can own it, or you can own it, or we can each own a half, or we can alternate ownership. The ideas in the book, though, can be communicated, for when I impart them to you I don't cease to possess them too. When communication of an idea has occurred, we have the idea in common. A meaningful connection has been established.

How do animals communicate?

Language is important for human communication, but it is, as we've seen, not necessary for communication. Animals communicate without the use of language in many ways. For instance, one animal can communicate its fear to another and so warn it of approaching danger by crying out; it can

Viewpoint

If we hope to understand human language and the psychological capacities on which it rests, we must first ask what it is, not how or for what purposes it is used. When we ask what human language is, we find no striking similarity to animal communication systems. There is nothing useful to be said about behavior or thought at the level of abstraction at which animal and human communication fall together. The examples of animal communication that have been examined to date do share many of the properties of human gestural systems, and it might be reasonable to explore the possibility of direct connection in this case. But human language, it appears, is based on entirely different principles. This, I think, is an important point, often overlooked by those who approach human language as a natural, biological phenomenon; in particular, it seems rather pointless, for these reasons, to speculate about the evolution of human language from simpler systems—perhaps as absurd as it would be to speculate about the "evolution" of atoms from clouds of elementary particles.

NOAM CHOMSKY, Language and Mind

express pain by screaming or whimpering; it can show affection by tender touches or soft sounds.

There is a great deal of debate over the extent to which animals can communicate ideas or even *have* ideas. Many philosophers, such as Aristotle and Descartes, have thought that the possession of language and reason sets human beings apart from other species.

A major difficulty in discussing nonhuman communication is to decide just what counts as having an idea or being able to understand a language. A well-trained dog can respond to certain commands just as accurately as an intelligent human being, but no dog is able to read books on advanced mathematics—or even elementary mathematics! So, can dogs understand a language? Can they think? Whatever answer we give to these questions, there is no doubt that animals communicate information and feelings; and it is clear that, being animals too, we share some of their means of communication.

However, human beings are the animals we know best, and they seem to have by far the most sophisticated and complex techniques for communicating. Human beings have language, in fact many languages, and they are usually complicated and effective tools for communicating all sorts of things. Accordingly, in this chapter we'll focus on the various ways in which we use language to express ourselves and to communicate with other persons. We'll also evaluate one of the tools philosophers use to communicate; that is, we'll discuss the logical evaluation of arguments. It would be a little too simple, though, to imagine that language is the only communication tool we have that other animals don't have. For the moment, let us look at some of the nonlinguistic, or at least partially nonlinguistic, ways in which humans but not the other animals communicate. Specifically, let us look at art and ritual as partially nonlinguistic means of human communication. Both give us a sense of shared experience and a life in common.

Nonlinguistic Communication

First, let us consider how the arts communicate, how they articulate our shared experience. Clearly, some of the arts—such as poetry, novels, songs with lyrics, plays, and films—use language in various ways. But notice that even in this list means other than language play a prominent role. It is admittedly hard to think of a poem or a novel that doesn't utilize language. But songs, even when they have lyrics, also have music, which may stand on its own; and films, in the early days, were almost completely without language. And then there are the arts that may not use language at all: sculpture, symphonic music, painting, pantomime, architecture, and dance.

What and how do the arts communicate?

We know that art communicates, but sometimes it's hard to put into words exactly *what* is communicated by a symphony, say, or a painting. But this may just show that art is another *kind* of communication, one that is not easily (if at all) translated into the linguistic kind.

There is romantic music and music that inspires patriotic pride. Some philosophers have argued that even though music may not often communicate explicit ideas, it does convey emotions and feelings. There is funeral music and 'dance music; there are many kinds of religious music. Even without words, a musical composition may *express* what the composer feels or what the composer knows about human feeling. When the music elicits our response, communication has occurred.

What holds for music holds for the other arts as well. A painting of the Crucifixion communicates something different to us than does a painting of a group of peasants celebrating a festival. The classic lines of the Parthenon in Athens evoke in us a different emotional response than do the glass-covered heights of a modern skyscraper.

Many philosophers have debated the nature and function of art; it would be incorrect to suggest that they have reached a consensus on these problems. Any simple characterization of art runs the risk of failing to do justice to the variety within the arts; it may also miss the complexity of the art objects themselves and of our responses to them. This complexity suggests the richness of our shared experience and the limitless possibilities of communication it affords. Leo Tolstoy may or may not have been justified in describing art as "a means of union among men joining them together in the same feelings"; however, it is clear that the nonverbal arts, no less than language, are forms of human communication.

What forms of communication do religions use?

Second, the religions of the world furnish many examples of communication among people. In fact, if we think of each religion as a community of persons, we can readily see why this should be so. "Community" comes from the same Latin word as "communicate": It means a group having certain things in common. Thus, a community requires communication, and communication always establishes a community, if only of two persons. The existence of a religious community, even one that is worldwide, involves reinforcement through the continual communication among its members of those things that bind them together into one group.

Religions use language in praying, in preaching, in rituals, in hymns of praise, and in their sacred writings. Religions also use art. (The American philosopher George Santayana was so impressed with the aesthetic dimension of religion that he was attracted to Catholicism *as* art, admiring its beauty while disbelieving its dogmas.) Magnificent cathedrals, sublime paintings, and glorious hymns are art objects in their own right. But they may also be used to communicate feelings, thoughts, and even theological insights and doctrines among the believers. A hymn, for instance, may serve to stir emotions (even among nonbelievers), but its words will also communicate certain ideas, perhaps concerning the nature of God or the believer's personal relationship with the divinity.

But there is another way, besides language and art, in which religions communicate. They communicate through ritual or ceremony. Can we think of a religious ceremony itself, apart from the words spoken or the music played, as an act of communication? It surely fits our working definition of communicative acts: A ceremony does establish meaningful connections among the participants. A ceremony elicits an emotional response or transfers an idea; it makes the participants feel part of a larger whole. And all religions have rituals. To cite some familiar examples: In Judaism, there is Passover and the Bar Mitzvah ceremony; and in Christianity, there is Baptism and Communion.

You might think that these activities are too dependent on the words that accompany them or that provide the background theology to be taken as really separate forms of communication. It is certainly true that language is frequently a major part of religious rituals and that there are verbal explanations and even justifications for the various rituals. But there is reason to believe that in fact the ritual activities themselves are more important in providing a sense of community than the words or explanations that go along with them.

What and how do rituals communicate?

Viewpoint

When the public ceremonial of the State has been reduced to the barest simplicity, private clubs and associations at once commence to reconstitute symbolic actions. It seems as though mankind must always be masquerading. This imperative impulse suggests that the notion of an idle masquerade is the wrong way of thought about the symbolic elements in life. The function of these elements is to be definite, manageable, reproducible, and also to be charged with their own emotional efficacity: symbolic transference invests their correlative meanings with some or all of these attributes of the symbols, and thereby lifts the meanings into an intensity of definite effectiveness—as elements in knowledge, emotion, and purpose—an effectiveness which the meanings may, or may not, deserve on their own account. The object of symbolism is the enhancement of the importance of what is symbolized.

ALFRED NORTH WHITEHEAD, Symbolism: Its Meaning and Effect

For example, in Judaism the keeping of the Sabbath is a venerable tradition that involves a number of prohibitions against different forms of work on the seventh day. In the Old Testament the commandment to keep the Sabbath holy is given twice: in Exodus 20:8–11 and in Deuteronomy 5:12–15. In the first passage, the Israelites are told to keep the Sabbath because God rested from his Creation on the seventh day. In the second passage, however, they are told to keep the Sabbath because God delivered them from Egypt, where they had been enslaved.

Is one of these verbal explanations for the ritual of keeping the Sabbath simply wrong? In *The Forgotten Language*, Erich Fromm attempts to reconcile them by invoking the Biblical concept of work and rest. "The Sabbath," he suggests, "symbolizes a state of complete harmony between man and nature and between man and man." This is so because work is man's interference, whether destructive or constructive, with the physical world, while rest is a state of peace between man and nature. Furthermore, the Sabbath extends the idea of peace from the natural to the social realm. Having suggested this view of work and rest, Fromm goes on to argue that the God of the Old Testament

> *must "rest" not because he is tired but because he is free and fully God only when he has ceased to work. So is man fully man only when he does not work, when he is at peace with nature and his fellow men; that is why the Sabbath commandment is at one time motivated by God's rest and at the other by the liberation from Egypt. Both mean the same and interpret each other: rest is freedom.*

However, there is another possible explanation for the two conflicting statements. It's simply that the ritual was in fact well established independently of either explanation. Only later did people attempt to provide a reason for it, and at different times they offered different reasons.

Whatever the historical sequence of events, the passages do show that one and the same ceremony or activity can be explained in quite different ways. This indicates that the ritual has a stability and an importance in the community quite apart from any particular theological justification for it.

One of W. H. Auden's last poems, "Archaeology," contains some lines that express this importance of rituals:

> *I'd swear*
> *that men have always lounged in myths*
> *as Tall Stories,*
>
> *that their real earnest*

Only in rites
can we renounce our oddities
and be truly entired.

Do the rituals apart from the words, however, really serve as means of communication? And if so, what is communicated? As with art, we are faced here with the difficulty of "translating" one form of communication (ritual) into another form (language). Some elements of the communication may be outlined, however. Rituals bind individuals together into one community through the regular performance of certain ceremonies. The feeling, if not the intellectual belief, that there is a world order, that the world and existence are meaningful, may be shared through the ritual. Through it the participants identify with something larger than themselves. They identify with the community's values, beliefs, and feelings, and then with the universe, God's creation. Ritual, in uniting the participants, thus points to the cosmic dimension of religion.

In our example of the Sabbath, for instance, the believers see the seventh day as really holy. It coincides for them with a wider structure of time. That is, by seeing their activity, rest on the seventh day, in relation to a divine model, God's rest from creation, they have sanctified and made meaningful a portion of their time. By seeing their rest on the Sabbath as an acknowledgment and commemoration of God's intervention to free them from bondage, they have similarly sanctified a part of their time. They have, so to speak, put it into perspective.

Of course, in practice the activities of rituals are usually bound up with certain words, and, at least among the more philosophically minded, with theories and explanations and justifications. But the language used in rituals is often transformed from its ordinary use. There are special phrases and even special styles of speech. One example is the English use of "Thou" for addressing God. This solemn language serves, along with the special actions that may be performed at holy times and in sacred places, to distinguish the ritual from everyday existence and thus to endow it with unique significance.

We shouldn't think that all rituals are parts of religions, however. Is Christmas shopping, a major ritual for most of us, really a part of Christianity? What about the exchange of Christmas cards? And what about the clearly secular rituals? Mircea Eliade, a prominent historian of religion, has aptly said, "the modern man who feels and claims that he is nonreligious still retains a large stock of camouflaged myths and degenerated rituals." Eliade goes on to mention the marriage ceremony (even when separated from any religious aspect), housewarming parties, and, of course, one of the most important rituals in modern America, the celebration of New Year's Eve. Here is an activity that for many is as highly structured and predictable as a religious service; yet, there is probably no "explanation" or "justification" behind it. It may symbolize ending a cycle of time and beginning afresh with a clean slate. By participating in these ceremonies (birthday parties might be another example) we find meaning within the flow of time.

A final example of nonlinguistic communication may be taken from what the sociologist Robert Bellah has called our American "civil religion." This "religion" is related to Judaism and Christianity in its appeal to God and His providence but is not to be identified with either of them. It has its own sacred writings (the Declaration of Independence, the Constitution), its own heroes or saints (Washington, Lincoln), and its own, partly nonlinguistic rituals: the president's annual State of the Union message, the dignified proceedings of the Supreme Court, the fanfare of party conventions, the slow processes of the Congress, the ceremonies accompanying the funeral of a president. Through such rituals, the people of a nation are bound together into a community, and feelings of national pride and solidarity are communicated.

It appears, then, that human communication takes place in a variety of ways without the use of language or at least without language as the only means involved. However, it is probably language that first comes to mind when you think about communication. That's not surprising: Language is a powerful and versatile instrument for communication among human beings.

From a philosophical point of view, there are excellent reasons to examine the ways we use language in our everyday lives. Following Ludwig Wittgenstein, linguistic analysts have shown that if we pay close attention to our ordinary language we may learn a great deal about our conceptual framework, which is the basis of communication. J. L. Austin, one of the most influential "ordinary language" philosophers, offered three reasons to justify the linguistic analysts' concern with language:

First, words are our tools, and, as a minimum, we should use clean tools: we should know what we mean and what we do not, and we must forearm ourselves against the traps that language sets us. Secondly, words are not (except in their own little corner) facts or things: we need therefore to prise them off the world, to hold them apart from and against it, so that we can realise their inadequacies and arbitrarinesses, and can re-look at the world without blinkers. Thirdly, and more hopefully, our common stock of words embodies all the distinctions men have

It's clear, then, that we stand to gain from the analytic study of everyday language. But how do we use language? And for what purposes? Let's consider some of the obvious ways we commonly put our language to work.

The Uses of Language

Clearly, language can be used to communicate many of the same things that are often communicated by other means. For instance, we can communicate our fear not only by screaming or trembling but also by uttering certain words such as "I'm scared!" Similarly, we can communicate our pain by holding our heads and moaning or by saying "My head aches."

However, language has many other uses that are dependent on what is sometimes called its "abstract" nature. Through language we can not only express our present fear but also tell someone about having been afraid ten years ago. It would be hard to do this merely by trembling! This capacity of language to abstract from the immediate environment enables a person to hand down traditions, to relate ancient events, and to speculate about the distant future. It enables people to communicate about things they have never directly experienced.

What is the symbolic nature of language?

This power of abstraction seems to be connected with the symbolic nature of language. Utilization of symbols can, in part, replace our immediate responses to our surroundings. To see how this can work, let's look a little more closely at our example of being afraid. What exactly is it that is communicated when person A tells person B that A is scared?

It may be that the fear itself is communicated; that is, B may come to be scared also and even scared of the same thing that A is. But the fear itself may not be communicated. B may be completely out of danger and know it and thus feel no fear at all. B may not even worry about A, but just note A's difficulty. So in this case is anything being communicated, that is, being shared between A and B?

If we overheard A's words, we might later report, "A told B that A was scared." What seems to be communicated when A delivers his message is the symbolic assertion "that A is scared." A, of course, feels the fright directly, but we may assume that he also understands that these words, "A is scared," describe his own situation. B, on the other hand, may just understand the words and not feel the fright.

Once we are able to manipulate such symbols and to communicate by means of them apart from having certain feelings or physical responses, we can proceed to more varied uses. We can think about our having been afraid in the past and even laugh about it now. We can observe someone else's being afraid and have a whole range of responses other than becoming afraid ourselves.

Indeed, language can perform a number of different functions within human life and within the different kinds of communities to which people belong. In *Philosophical Investigations,* Wittgenstein has given a sample of the variety of functions of which language is capable:

> *Giving orders, and obeying them—*
> *Describing the appearance of an object, or giving its measurements—*
> *Constructing an object from a description (a drawing)—*
> *Reporting an event—*
> *Speculating about an event—*
> *Forming and testing a hypothesis—*
> *Presenting the results of an experiment in tables and diagrams—*
> *Making up a story; and reading it—*
> *Play-acting—*
> *Singing catches—*
> *Guessing riddles—*
> *Making a joke; telling it—*
> *Solving a problem in practical arithmetic—*
> *Translating from one language into another—*
> *Asking, thanking, cursing, greeting, praying.*

In fact, Wittgenstein talks not so much about language as about language-games. He emphasizes the place of language within a wider context of practice, a form of life. That this context is crucial may be seen from the different functions the same words may have. Consider, for example, the sentence "Joe shot Bob." The function of this sentence and our reaction to it can vary considerably depending on whether it is spoken as:

1. An accusation by an eyewitness to the crime
2. A narration by a historian
3. A line in a play
4. A sentence in English to be translated into German

Philosophers have sometimes spoken as though the primary, or even the sole, function of language is its use in making statements of fact, sentences intended to describe an object or report a situation. Such statements occur regularly in scientific writing and in everyday conversation, and they can be evaluated as true or false depending on whether or not the description matches the facts. For instance, that water freezes at 0°C (or 32°F) and boils at 100°C (or 212°F) is a statement of fact. It describes the "behavior" of water; more accurately, it describes the physical state of water under different conditions. Its truth in a given case can be demonstrated by a simple experiment, and its probable truth in all cases can be established, more or less satisfactorily, by a large number of observations. To take another example, that the book is to the left of the desk lamp may be a statement of fact. It would be easy enough to determine whether it's true or false. This use of language to describe objects and report situations is common. But Wittgenstein's point was that language has a wide variety of uses in addition to describing and reporting.

One important type of sentence that doesn't fit into the category of descriptions is the imperative (Wittgenstein's "giving orders"). "Shut the door" doesn't describe the door, and it isn't true or false. But the sentence can be judged to be reasonable or unreasonable; we can ask "Why?" and expect some reason to be given. Other sentences, such as "There's a draft," or "We'll be overheard," might serve as justifications for the command. And the person being addressed can object to the reasonableness of the command as well as to the authority of the person giving the command.

We might also mention a use of language that is quite complex, namely, its use in poetic and metaphorical contexts. A verse of a poem may describe, but it also may evoke feelings or ideas by means of the association of sounds

Viewpoint

244. How do words refer to sensations?—There doesn't seem to be any problem here; don't we talk about sensations every day, and give them names? But how is the connexion between the name and the thing named set up? This question is the same as: how does a human being learn the meaning of the names of sensations?—of the word "pain" for example. Here is one possibility: words are connected with the primitive, the natural, expressions of the sensation and are used in their place. A child has hurt himself and he cries; and then adults talk to him and teach him exclamations and, later, sentences. They teach the child new pain-behaviour.

"So you are saying that the word 'pain' really means crying?"—On the contrary: the verbal expression of pain replaces crying and does not describe it.

LUDWIG WITTGENSTEIN, Philosophical Investigations

or by the use of analogies. To cite a trivial example, we may speak, for instance, of comparing someone to a summer's day, which is not meant literally as a description of fact because a person and a day are quite different things.

J. L. Austin claimed that "many traditional philosophical perplexities have arisen through a mistake—the mistake of taking as straightforward statements of fact utterances which are *either* . . . nonsensical *or else* intended as something quite different." It is this last error which Austin hoped to correct by analyzing utterances that are not statements of fact, but that are certainly not nonsensical, since they play a well-defined role in language. We have already seen one such example with imperatives. Now let's look at some more.

The Performative Use of Language

What are "performatives"? Austin begins by talking about what he calls "performative" sentences or utterances. These he defines initially as utterances that do not describe or report anything and that thus are not true or false. However, they are an activity or at least part of an activity. Examples are abundant: "I promise to be there," "I thank you for the present," "Strike three!" (said by the home-plate umpire). Performative utterances are often expressed by a first-person singular verb, as in our first two examples, and sometimes by a first-person plural verb, as in "We give thanks to Thee, Lord God Almighty" (Revelation 11:17).

That such sentences differ from "ordinary" descriptions may be seen by comparing them to actions that do not involve language at all. A promise can be made by a nod of the head at a certain moment just as well as with a sentence. Thanks can be rendered by a smile. And the umpire can simply make a certain gesture, usually with his closed fist, and not say anything at all. The utterance "strike three" is just a linguistic way of performing an action that can be done just as well without any verbal language. In contrast, try to imagine how scientific laws, for instance, could ever be formulated and communicated without a language, indeed, a rather sophisticated language!

An important feature of performative sentences is that they are typically tied up with various aspects of human life, with a particular community, and even with rituals. The umpire's "strike three," for instance, makes sense only within the structure of the rules of baseball. It also is tied up with the umpire's having a certain authoritative position within that structure; a spectator's yelling "strike three" doesn't accomplish at all the same thing as the home-plate umpire's yelling it. And someone else's later saying "The umpire called him out" is just an ordinary description.

Austin and others have given detailed classifications of such performative uses of language. A few examples may be of interest here. Certain sentences *commit* the speaker to certain actions in the future, for instance, "I promise to be there." Likewise, sentences involving "I plan," "I guarantee," or "I vow" typically establish such commitments. Austin called such utterances "commissives."

A second class of performative sentences involves attitudes and social behavior. Examples are "I thank you," "I apologize," "I criticize," and "I praise," or "we praise." Such performatives are related to standard ways of communicating certain feelings or attitudes, and Austin called them "behabitives."

How can words accomplish actions?

A third class includes such expressions as "I affirm," "I deny," "I mention," and "I argue." Austin called these "expositives," since they "make plain how our utterances fit into the course of an argument or conversation, how we are using words." Generally, he said, such performatives "have reference to the communicational situation."

The function of expositives can be served by other means. Often we don't say "I affirm"; we just affirm, perhaps with a certain tone or intensity. Information on how words are to be taken has been called "metamessages," that is, messages telling us how sentences are to be understood. For example, "That is a good car" might be said in a firm voice as a declaration, or it might be said in a questioning tone, or it might even be said with a slight stress on "good" as a note of sarcasm. Through such metamessages, whether they're made explicit by expositives or not, we understand the force of a particular communication. We understand whether the speaker is affirming or denying, reporting or questioning, conjecturing or swearing, or perhaps just kidding.

Now, as Austin himself emphasized, in practice the various forces and uses of language can't be sharply separated. If I praise someone for doing something, I am expressing an attitude toward that person and also committing myself in certain ways (maybe to encourage similar behavior in the future and not to punish such action). I'm also implying that I have certain beliefs about factual matters, for instance, that the person I'm praising really did a particular deed or that he or she did it for a particular reason.

We have seen that descriptions are judged to be true or false, and imperatives, reasonable or unreasonable. Commissives (a promise, for instance) may be sincere or insincere, as may behabitives (thanks, for example, or an apology). There may be no exact answer to the question "What does that mean?" in every situation. But we must make some attempt to distinguish the various uses of language if we are to evaluate sentences in ways appropriate to them and if we are to understand correctly their role in communication.

In the next section we'll consider the groups of linguistic symbols known as arguments. To a great extent, although not exclusively, the branch of philosophy known as logic is concerned with the analysis of arguments. Focusing on the analysis of arguments will throw some light on the relevance of logic to other areas of philosophy. And it will also be relevant to every form of human communication that demands precision and clarity. This includes disciplines such as physics, astronomy, anthropology, history, literary· criticism, art history, journalism, and law. It also includes term papers, exams, lectures, and textbooks. The backbone of these forms of communication is logical argumentation.

Evaluating Arguments

What is logic?

Arguing is not an activity peculiar to logicians, philosophers, teachers, or any other special group. In all academic areas as well as in everyday life, people present arguments, reasons and evidence, to persuade other people to believe certain things. What is peculiar to logic as a branch of philosophy is the attempt to look at arguments more carefully than is usually the case and to formulate the criteria for good or bad arguments in a systematic way.

Most of us probably have a rough, intuitive idea of what a good argument is and what a bad argument is. Scientists—even those with no professional or formal training in philosophy—take great care when setting up an experiment to test a hypothesis to discover just what is needed to provide good evidence (that is, to supply a good argument) for or against the hypothesis. Historians rely on more or less implicit criteria for evaluating arguments when they sift evidence and balance contradictory reports for the purpose of establishing what really happened or what motivated a certain historical figure. Lawyers, judges, and juries must make similar judgments. And as citizens, consumers, and private individuals, all of us are called on, at least sometimes, to evaluate arguments when we listen to political speeches, editorials, commercials, and sermons. Logic tries to make explicit and systematic that which is usually only implicit in our evaluation of arguments.

What is an argument?

For our purposes here, we'll consider arguments to have at least one premise and a conclusion. The conclusion is what the argument is designed to establish or to convince us of; the premises present the evidence supporting the conclusion. The following, for instance, is a deductive argument (one in which the conclusion follows necessarily from the premises):

All people are mortal.
Socrates is a person.
Therefore, Socrates is mortal.

Here the premises, two in number, are "All people are mortal" and "Socrates is a person." The conclusion is "Socrates is mortal." That the latter statement is supposed to follow from the premises is indicated here by the word "therefore." "Thus" and "consequently" may also be used.

By contrast, inductive arguments are designed to show only that the premises make the conclusion more or less probable. Consider, for example, this one:

Sean is an Irish Catholic.
80 percent of Irish Catholics are Democrats.
Probably, then, Sean is a Democrat.

It should be clear that here the premises do not warrant our concluding that Sean certainly is a Democrat. Sean might very well be one of the 20 percent of Irish Catholics who are not. But they provide some evidence for the claim, good enough to bet on, we might say. We can conclude that Sean probably is a Democrat.

Actually, one of the first places where considerations of probability figured was in games of chance. In poker, a flush is a hand with all five cards in the same suit. If a poker player has four hearts and draws one card, what are the chances of his or her getting a flush? One can formulate this practical problem in terms of an argument as follows:

I have four hearts.
I draw one card.
Thus, I draw another heart.

The question is, what degree of confidence should I place in the conclusion, that is, what degree of support do the premises give for the conclusion? There are 13 hearts in the deck of 52 cards. Since the player already has 4 hearts, there is a chance of 9 in 48 of his or her drawing another heart, so that the conclusion is 9/48 probable. The player may or may not consider this good enough to bet on.

Science is another area where probability considerations arise. The actual framing and testing of scientific hypotheses and laws is a complex process. It seems to depend in part on historical and perhaps even psychological factors. One type of argument that occurs is the following: A scientist observes that an event of type A is always followed by an event of type B. (A simple example of this might be that one's reducing the temperature of water below $0°C$ is always followed by the water's freezing, or that one's letting go of a rock is always followed by the rock's falling.) If the scientist observes enough cases of this kind of connection, he or she may formulate a general principle of the form "Every A is followed by a B" and argue that his or her evidence supports this claim.

Clearly, how much support the evidence gives the conclusion depends on how many cases the scientist has observed. But no matter how many individual cases there may have been, the possibility always remains that the next case observed will prove the general principle false, so that such a generalization is supported only up to a certain degree of probability.

There are other sorts of arguments, however, where the claim is that the premises provide absolutely sufficient evidence for the conclusion. Such arguments are the rule in mathematics, but they also occur in everyday life. Some arguments merit this claim; some do not. This is not surprising, since we ordinarily distinguish good reasoning from bad reasoning and convincing evidence from irrelevant considerations. But, in a given case, how can we decide whether a particular argument is a good one or bad one?

Viewpoint

Criticisms of the use of "he," "man," etc. as gender-neutral terms may claim that this use is (1) an effect of the lower status of women, or (2) a cause of unfairness. I argue for the less obvious second claim, showing first that taking a description to apply to males makes it difficult to apply it to females.

The argument that a word cannot have both a neutral and a specific use is rejected on comparison with unmarked adjectives. The argument against gender-neutral uses because of potential ambiguity is also rejected.

However, some neutrally intended, unambiguous uses of "he" and "man" do fail to be gender-neutral. Consider the first line of the famous syllogism: All men are mortal. This is usually intended to be about the whole human species. But the second line usually reads: Socrates is a man. And the occurrence of "man" in this sentence is not a neutral use. Replacing "Socrates" with the name of a female human changes the truth value of the sentence (or the meaning of "man"). Thus the customary inference is invalid if the occurrence of "men" is intended to be gender-neutral. Instead of a paradigm of valid inference, it is an equivocation.

I conclude that such uses of "man" etc. where a gender-neutral term belongs are instances of a common practice in which the name of a high-status member or subset is used as a generic name for the whole class to the disadvantage of the remaining members of the class.

JANICE MOULTON, abstract of "The Myth of the Neutral 'Man' "

Validity

The study of probability considerations in arguments is treated in what is called inductive logic; the study of questions of validity and invalidity is treated in deductive logic, our concern here. Those terms, "validity" and "invalidity," are important. In dealing with questions of conclusive evidence, the evaluative term used to describe a good argument is "valid." Bad arguments are those whose evidence is not conclusive; they are called "invalid." Put another way: A "valid" argument is one in which the premises provide conclusive evidence for the truth of the conclusion; an "invalid" argument is one that is not valid.

What is a valid argument?

For our purposes in deductive logic, an argument whose premises establish its conclusion with only a certain degree of probability is simply invalid. The formal study of deductive logic deals extensively with validity and invalidity, and it attempts to formulate procedures for distinguishing valid arguments (good ones) from invalid arguments (bad ones). Let us look first at a real argument, not one made up for the sake of an example, and analyze it in terms of its premises and conclusion.

In October 1971, the Episcopal bishop of California, the Right Reverend C. Kilmer Myers, became the center of a controversy by claiming that women should not be allowed to be Episcopal priests. Such controversies have, of course, continued up to the present in a number of religious groups. The following is an excerpt from an article in the *San Francisco Chronicle* of October 23, 1971:

> *The bishop's argument for refusing women priestly orders will be advanced today or tomorrow during floor debate on the issue.*
>
> *In a statement prepared for delivery to the 700 delegates gathered in Grace Cathedral he said the Episcopalian priesthood is "a masculine conception."*
>
> *"Christ is the source of priesthood," the prelate declared. "The sexuality of Christ is no accident nor is His masculinity incidental. This is the divine choice. Jesus continued that choice in His selection of men to be His apostles."*

This is claimed by the reporter to be an argument. What are the premises and conclusion? It is clear that Bishop Myers has not been kind enough to us logicians to formulate his argument in terms of premises followed by a "thus" or a "therefore" and his conclusion. But this is typical of the way people argue in real communication situations: Premises and conclusions are frequently mixed together with rhetoric, jokes, appeals to prejudice and emotion, and the like. We have to dig a little, and sometimes even alter the arguer's original words, in order to extract an explicit argument.

How can you set about clarifying arguments?

The conclusion of Bishop Myers's argument seems to be something like women should not be Episcopal priests, even though he may not spell that out explicitly. Unpopular conclusions are sometimes easier to present if they're not put too plainly. His premises appear to include some historical claims (Jesus was a man; all his apostles were men) and a theological claim (Christ is the source of priesthood).

But there also seems to be something else that is only hinted at by the statement that Christ's masculinity is not accidental. This hidden premise seems to be that priests must share whatever properties or characteristics Christ had. This is not spelled out, but it does appear to be the assumption on which the argument depends. The fact that Jesus chose only men to be apostles is appealed to as an indication that this hidden claim is correct.

Thus, if we were to try to make explicit exactly what claim Bishop Myers was making, we might get the following:

> *Christ was a man. Since Christ is the source of the Episcopal priesthood, whatever characteristics he had should be shared by Episcopal priests. (This is confirmed by the fact that Christ chose only men for his apostles.) Therefore, men only (and not women) should be Episcopal priests.*

Actually, we have here a rather complicated situation, since the second premise is itself supported by additional considerations. That is, the second premise (of *this* argument) is itself the conclusion of another argument designed to support it. We might thus give a final analysis, making explicit the additional hidden premise that no women are men (a biological fact), as follows:

1 *(a)* Christ was a man.
(Christ is the source of the Episcopal priesthood; thus)

   (b) Whatever characteristics Christ had should be shared by Episcopal priests.
(This is confirmed by the fact that Christ chose only men as his apostles.)

   (c) No women are men.

Therefore, no women should be Episcopal priests.

This makes a reasonably plausible argument—we will examine it more closely later on—and seems to capture the essential points of Bishop Myers's argument. From now on we will refer to our reconstruction as argument 1 and speak of a possible defender of it as "the arguer."

Additional considerations are involved at this stage, but we have kept them to the side for the sake of simplification. Our short newspaper clipping has already gotten rather complex! One consideration is that sometimes, of course, we can just ask the arguer to clarify what exactly he or she means as the premises and conclusion. Similarly, if there is any terminology that is unclear, any word that we don't know or that is ambiguous, we can just ask. Arguments in actual conversation are often full of such questions and answers. All this is not so much evaluating the argument as it is just getting clear what the argument is in the first place.

When an argument is presented in print or in lecture, it is not so easy to clarify such points if the speaker has not been completely explicit from the beginning. And such clarity is not the rule. In our example, there is the additional complication that we have a reporter's presentation of someone else's argument; it is always possible that such reports may be incomplete, misleading, or even quite inaccurate. To become clearer about the arguer's intentions, one could try to check other writings by the same author. Or, as in our case, we could check the numerous later debates on this same issue to see if the premises involved are clarified. Usually, our common background and grasp of a common language convince us that we understand the speaker or writer. But we have seen that even this common language is complex and many-layered. The basic principle is to try to be as clear as possible when presenting arguments and always to seek clarity when trying to understand others' arguments.

One final point in this section: How do we know that Bishop Myers's argument is meant to be a deductive argument rather than an inductive one? Perhaps the only certain way would be to ask him. But there are clues. First, there are none of the terms that typically accompany inductive arguments: "probably," "likely," "good bet," and the like. Also, none of the premises, either in the original statement or in our reconstruction, involved statistics or percentages. In fact, one of Bishop Myers's statements explicitly denies any kind of probability: Jesus' masculinity is no accident; it is the result of the divine choice. This suggests that the connections among the statements are seen as necessary rather than merely probabilistic.

Attacking Arguments

We earlier defined a valid argument as one in which the premises provide conclusive evidence for the truth of the conclusion. We can also say that a valid argument is one in which *if* the premises are true, *then* the conclusion must be true. Reflection on this second definition will lead us to recognize two methods of attacking an argument.

How do arguments go wrong?

As we've already seen, in practice the purpose of presenting an argument is typically to convince someone—the listener, the reader, or even the arguer—of the truth of the conclusion. There are two sorts of things that can go wrong with an argument from the point of view of its effectiveness in convincing someone to believe the conclusion. One is that one or more of the premises may be false; that is, we may be reasoning from incorrect information, mistaken political beliefs, and so on. The other sort of thing that can go wrong is that we reason incorrectly; that is, the argument may be invalid. And, of course, it may be that both things go wrong at once: We may reason incorrectly from false premises.

Let's call a valid argument with all true premises a *sound* argument. If we admit that an argument is sound, then we should accept the conclusion. If we wish to attack an argument by denying that it convinces us of the truth of the conclusion, we can take two approaches. We can attack the truth of the premises either by showing that one or more are false or, more easily, just by raising serious doubts about their truth. And we can attack the method of argument or reasoning itself by claiming that the argument is invalid. If we want to devastate an argument, we might try both lines of attack. In his *Physics*, Aristotle criticized the arguments of some of his predecessors in these terms: "Their premises are false and their conclusions do not follow."

What methods are available for attacking arguments?

In connection with the first line of attack, the premises of an argument may well involve scientific facts, historical facts, claims about what is right or wrong, or even theological claims. Logic alone will not help us to answer

---

Viewpoint

"I don't know what you mean by 'glory,'" Alice said.

Humpty Dumpty smiled contemptuously. "Of course you don't—till I tell you. I meant 'there's a nice knock-down argument for you!'"

"But 'glory' doesn't mean 'a nice knock-down argument,'" Alice objected.

"When I use a word," Humpty Dumpty said, in rather a scornful tone, "it means just what I choose it to mean—neither more nor less."

"The question is," said Alice, "whether you can make words mean so many different things."

"The question is," said Humpty Dumpty, "which is to be master—that's all."

LEWIS CARROLL, Through the Looking Glass

the factual question whether or not certain scientific premises are true. Thus, if we wish to attack an argument involving premises concerning physics, say, using our first method, we have to know something about physics already, or do some research, or ask an expert. Logic will tell us our method and may sharpen our critical abilities, but it can't tell us scientific facts.

The peculiar province of logic is concerned with attacks of the second kind: showing arguments to be invalid. Indeed, basic courses in logic have as at least one of their main goals helping people to see when arguments are valid or invalid. To examine this method, however, we need to introduce some additional considerations concerning the form of arguments.

The Form of Arguments

Certain arguments are alike in certain ways. Consider arguments 2 and 3:

2   Ford is President and Rockefeller is Vice-President.
          Therefore, Ford is President.

3   Humphrey is President and Muskie is Vice-President.
          Therefore, Humphrey is President.

Arguments 2 and 3 clearly have some similarities. Both have only one premise (in contrast to our earlier argument). This one premise is in each argument a conjunction, or joining together, of two simpler sentences linked by the word "and." Moreover, in each the conclusion is identical with the first conjunct (the left-hand "sentence" before the "and") of the premise.

How can arguments formally resemble one another?

Both 2 and 3 are *valid* arguments. Remember that, in considering questions of validity and invalidity, we are not concerned with whether the premise and conclusion happen to be true or false; we are concerned only with whether the premises give conclusive evidence for the truth of the conclusion. In argument 2 it happens (as a matter of historical fact) that the premise and the conclusion are both true (as of June 1976). But that fact doesn't make the argument valid. What *does* make argument 2 valid is the fact that *if* the premise is true, then the conclusion must be true also. And this is so.

In argument 3 it happens (again, as a matter of historical fact) that the premise and the conclusion are both false. But this tells us nothing about the argument's validity. What makes 3 valid is the fact that if the premise were true, then the conclusion would have to be true too. That is, if it were the case that Humphrey were president and Muskie vice-president, then it would have to be true that Humphrey were president. That this is a valid argument is a matter of logic; that the premise and the conclusion are false is a matter of political history.

By now you may have noticed a more general principle: *Any* argument whatsoever that is similar to argument 2 (or to 3) in the ways mentioned three paragraphs back will be valid too. That is, any argument whose sole premise is a conjunction of two sentences and whose conclusion is the first conjunct will be valid. We can express this general principle by saying that any argument of the *form*

> P and Q
> Therefore, P

will be valid.

Another way of saying this is: If you replace the two Ps by a sentence and replace the Q by a sentence, then you will have a valid argument. The justification for this claim is that if the conjunction of two sentences is true, then the first conjunct must be true too.

What is the value of identifying an argument's form?

The point of shifting to the *form* of arguments 2 and 3 is that we can study at one time the validity of many arguments. Instead, in other words, of dealing with 2, and then dealing with 3, and so on, we can just convince ourselves that any argument of a certain form is valid and then deal with 2, 3, and others like them as particular cases of that general principle.

The following are all forms of valid arguments. One problem for the second Inquiry following this chapter is to see if you can find a justification for the validity of arguments of a given form and construct particular arguments having that form. [We just did *(a)*.]

(a) P and Q. Therefore, P.

(b) P and Q. Therefore, Q.

(c) If P, then Q. P. Therefore, Q.

(d) P or Q. It is not the case that P. Therefore, Q.

(e) P. Therefore, P and P.

We've sketched a method of showing when an argument is valid. Namely, first we justify a general form of argument (usually by considerations of the meaning of certain English words), and then we show that a particular argument has that form. Let us now turn to the problem of showing that an argument is invalid.

Counterexamples

The form of an argument determines its validity or invalidity. But its content—the particular sentences involved—determines the truth or falsity of its premises and conclusion. A claim that an argument is valid is essentially a claim that a certain form represents correct reasoning. Thus, to undercut this claim, all we need to do is to find an invalid argument that has the same form. But how can we tell that an argument is invalid?

Well, there is one clear-cut case in which an argument *must* be invalid: when the premises are all true but the conclusion is false. So to claim that an argument is invalid, we can try to find another argument of the same form whose premises are all true but whose conclusion is false. It will be sufficient for purposes of communication if the people we are arguing with agree that the premises are true and the conclusion is false, so we may tailor our example to our common background.

This procedure sounds complicated, but it corresponds to something that is done frequently in ordinary arguing. When we wish to attack an argument, we may say something like "Why, that's like saying . . ." and then proceed to give an unacceptable statement or argument that is enough like the original one to cause the arguer a difficulty. For instance, government officials have sometimes defended our selling arms abroad, often to both sides of a potential conflict, by arguing "Well, if we don't sell arms to them, they'll just buy them somewhere else, so we might as well make a profit on the sales." A critic of such sales might respond, "Why, that's like saying that since criminals are obviously going to get weapons from somewhere, the government might as well supply them and make the profit."

What is a "counterexample" to an argument?

This procedure is sometimes called giving a counterexample to the claim that arguments of a certain form are valid. Let us illustrate it with argument 4:

4   Ford is President.
         Thus, Ford is President and Rockefeller is Vice-President.

Is this argument valid? Clearly the premise and the conclusion are true (as of June 1976), but does the premise give conclusive evidence for the truth of the conclusion? Intuitively we might have our doubts, since part of the conclusion isn't even mentioned in the premise. That the premise doesn't give such conclusive evidence may be shown by presenting this counterexample:

5   Snow is white.
         Thus, snow is white and the earth is flat.

Both arguments 4 and 5 have the same logical form

P
Thus, P and Q.

However, the premise of 5 is true, while its conclusion is false (since the earth isn't flat). Thus 5 is invalid. But now, since arguments 4 and 5 have the same logical form, 4 must be invalid too. So we have shown that 4 is invalid, even though it has a true premise and a true conclusion, by giving 5 as a counterexample.

A further problem for the Inquiry is to try to show that the following five arguments are invalid by isolating their forms and then presenting a counterexample. [We just did *(a)*.]

(a)   Ford is President.
Thus, Ford is President and Rockefeller is Vice-President.

(b)   Nixon is President or Ford is President.
Therefore, Ford is President.

(c)   If Nixon resigned, then Ford is President.
Ford is President.
Thus, Nixon resigned.

(d)   Snow is white.
Therefore, God exists.

(e)   The earth is round or iron is heavier than water.
Thus, the earth is round and iron is heavier than water.

Actually, one final complication must be mentioned: There is no sure way to tell if we have in fact isolated *the* form of an argument. It is possible that we might overlook the formal connection between the premises and the conclusion on which the arguer was relying. If this happens, the arguer can just point out our oversight to us. We can then either agree that the argument is valid or try to construct a better counterexample. An illustration of how this problem might arise is furnished by argument 6:

6   Ford is President.
Thus, Ford is President and Ford is President.

Now, we *might* analyze this as being of the form

P
Thus, P and Q

and conclude that it was invalid, as we did with arguments 4 and 5. But this would be a mistake since 6 also falls under the general form

> P
> Thus, P and P.

And, as we saw in example *(e)*, any argument having this form is valid. Our mistake lay in thinking that we had completely analyzed the form of argument 6 when we hadn't. We did not notice that the conclusion of the argument is a conjunction of one sentence with *itself* rather than with another unrelated sentence. This sort of problem is part of clarifying the argument (in this case, clarifying the logical form) rather than simply being part of evaluating the argument.

It is possible to use the counterexample method to attack an argument even when we aren't sure whether we want to question the truth of the premises or the validity of the argument. We simply try to construct an argument that parallels as closely as possible the original argument, but which has a conclusion that is clearly false or at least is unacceptable to the arguer. The arguer may then respond by accepting our attack and giving up his argument. Or he may respond by claiming that our counterexample overlooked something present in the original argument. In other words, he may say that in fact the two arguments are not similar at a crucial point. The attack and defense can then continue back and forth.

How does argumentation proceed?

Let us illustrate the method in some detail by attacking our first argument, the one designed to show that women should not be Episcopal priests. Recalling what the argument is, consider argument 7 which is similar in form and content:

7 *(a)* Christ was a Jew.
(Christ is the source of the Episcopal priesthood); thus

(b) Whatever characteristics Christ had should be shared by Episcopal priests.
(This is confirmed by the fact that Christ chose only Jews as his apostles.)

(c) No non-Jews are Jews.
Therefore, no non-Jews should be Episcopal priests.

This argument is exactly the same as argument 1, except that Jews and non-Jews are used instead of men and women.

Let us suppose that the arguer for 1 would not accept the conclusion of 7. Accepting it would, of course, drastically curtail the number of Episcopal priests. But premises *(a)* and *(c)* seem obvious enough, and they're of the same form as the corresponding premises of argument 1. And premise *(b)* is identical with premise *(b)* of argument 1. Thus the defender of 1 would either have to admit that his original argument was not sound, in which case our attack was successful. Or he would have to show some relevant difference between arguments 1 and 7 such that 7 is not an adequate counterexample to 1.

We could put this point rather informally by saying that argument 1 against women priests works just as well against non-Jewish priests, since Christ was a Jew as well as a man, and all his apostles were Jews as well as men. Indeed, it is clear from the idea of the election or "chosenness" of Israel that theologically speaking Christ's Jewishness was not an accident but a crucial feature of God's plan for salvation. And, of course, there are many other characteristics that Christ and all his apostles shared but that the arguer probably would not want to require of Episcopal priests, such as their being speakers of Aramaic, alive in the first century A.D., and living in Judea.

It would be unfair to the arguer and misleadingly simple to state that the above considerations demolish argument 1 once and for all. Of course, the arguer might be persuaded by our remarks and give up the objection to women priests. But various avenues are open to him. First, he might claim that our reconstructed argument 1 simply does not do justice to his argument or even that he was misquoted in the newspaper. And he might then go ahead to present us with an explicit argument that is not subject to the difficulties mentioned. He might also say that our reconstruction is basically correct, except that it fails to make clear what is a relevant difference between Christ's Jewishness, which is a characteristic Episcopal priests need not share, and his manhood, which is a characteristic they must share. The arguer might then present us with additional premises that try to spell out what the difference is and justify it in some way. He might also just want to revise some of the premises, for instance, the second one, so as to overcome the objections.

We might then be persuaded by the revised version or we might proceed to attack it again. This process can continue until agreement is reached or until we become too tired, disgusted, or angry to try to communicate further. Our particular example of women priests is the subject of ongoing discussion, and it would be presumptuous of us to try to deal with all the possibilities for argument here. But such analysis and explicit treatment of arguments are necessary for an eventual reasoned agreement.

We've now seen how an analysis of an argument might proceed. Argument is one way in which we attempt to arrive at mutual understanding and to persuade one another, and these attempts are central to human communication. For instance, careful attention to argumentation may help us deal with prejudices and impulsive or violent actions. In our example concerning the Episcopal priesthood we've seen how questionable opinions about women and minorities might be tested. Often a suicide can be reasoned with, argued out of his or her intention. Careful reasoning, whether alone or in dialogue, may lead us to make wiser decisions about a lot of things. Analysis and evaluation of arguments, including ones we meet in everyday life, are important features of communicating through the means of language.

Summary

What Is Communication? Communication is the sharing of thoughts and feelings. All animals, human and nonhuman, can communicate by a variety of means without the use of language, but human beings have many methods of communication peculiar to them.

Nonlinguistic Communication: The arts may serve as means of communication; music, for example, in communicating may evoke feelings, as may paintings and architecture. Religious communities, whose members have ideas and feelings in common, use many means of communication, including language, art, music, rituals, and ceremonies. Rituals are also important in nonreligious contexts.

The Uses of Language: Language commonly serves to describe or report matters of fact, but it has many other uses besides this one of making true or false statements. Imperatives, for example, are neither true nor false, but they make sense, and may be judged to be reasonable or unreasonable.

The Performative Use of Language: Austin has called attention to performatives, linguistic utterances that are primarily acts rather than descriptions or statements of fact.

Evaluating Arguments: Logic is largely, though not exclusively, concerned with evaluating arguments. An argument has a conclusion and at least one premise that provides evidence that the conclusion is probably or certainly true.

Validity: A valid argument is one in which the premises provide conclusive evidence for the conclusion. In the actual evaluation of arguments, the first task, not always an easy one, is to discover what the premises and the conclusion are.

Attacking Arguments: An argument may have false premises or it may be invalid; thus, you may attack an argument's premises, or its logic, or both.

The Form of Arguments: Different arguments may have the same logical form. An argument's form determines its validity or invalidity.

Counterexamples: To show that an argument is invalid, you may try to construct another argument of the same form that has true premises but a false conclusion, so it must be invalid.

Suggestions for Further Reading

A good introduction to the subject of language, William P. Alston's *Philosophy of Language* (Englewood Cliffs, NJ: Prentice-Hall, 1964) is in the Foundations of Philosophy series.

A number of historical studies focus on the development of analytic philosophy in this century. J. O. Urmson's *Philosophical Analysis: Its Development between the Two World Wars* (New York: Oxford University Press, 1956) is a noteworthy history of logical atomism and logical positivism. G. J. Warnock's *English Philosophy Since 1900* (New York: Oxford University Press, 1966) is an excellent brief survey of the work of such contemporary philosophers as G. E. Moore, Bertrand Russell, Ludwig Wittgenstein, and Gilbert Ryle.

David Pears's *Ludwig Wittgenstein* (New York: Viking, 1970) is a popular introduction to Wittgenstein's thought in both his early and his later periods. It is in the Modern Masters series.

In *The Language of Morals* (New York: Oxford University Press, 1964), R. M. Hare argues that "in a world in which the problems of conduct become every day more complex and tormenting, there is a great need for an understanding of the language in which these problems are posed and answered. For confusion about our moral language leads, not merely to theoretical muddles, but to needless practical perplexities." In *Word Politics: Essays on Language and Politics* (Palo Alto, CA: Freel, 1972), editor Max J. Skidmore has compiled an unusually fine anthology of short articles on recent abuses of language.

Among the many well-written first books in logic, the most readable and useful is Ronald Munson's *The Way of Words: An Informal Logic* (Boston: Houghton Mifflin, 1976). Munson entertains as he instructs; we highly recommend his work.

Finally, in *The Underlying Reality of Language and Its Philosophical Import* (New York: Harper & Row, 1971), Jerrold J. Katz discusses the philosophical significance of recent developments in linguistics.

Inquiry

"Let the People Sing His Praises!" Analyzing Religious Language

"Evidently," a theologian recently asserted, "talking about God occurs in a context of its own, different from the language in which tables and chairs are described or the weather is forecasted." But what is the context peculiar to religious language? How does religious language differ from ordinary and scientific language? What can the philosophical analysis of religious language reveal?

Although it's apparently simple, religious language is actually quite complex. To cite a familiar source, the Bible contains many sentences that seem to be straightforward, matter-of-fact descriptions: for instance, that David was the son of Jesse or that Joshua conquered Jericho. But it also contains imperatives like "Thou shalt not kill" or "Let us praise the Lord!" And then there are other sentences that appear to be descriptive but that don't describe ordinary facts about the world: for instance, "God created the heavens and the earth" or "The Word became flesh."

Consider a sentence like "God exists." Some people (including some philosophers) take this to be a factual statement about the existence of someone or something (although not a material object). They consider it the same as saying "The Eiffel Tower exists" or "Passenger pigeons don't exist any more." Taking it in this way leads inevitably to questions of evidence. As a

practical matter, I know that the Eiffel Tower exists because I have seen it, or seen pictures of it, or read about it, or know people who have seen it. Similarly, I know from historical reports that passenger pigeons did exist in great numbers earlier in this century, but that people then killed so many of them that they are now extinct. But what sort of evidence is appropriate for a claim about God's existence?

An influential group of twentieth century philosophers known as logical positivists claim that there is no way we can prove by observation the truth or falsity of the sentence "God exists." Therefore, they claim, such a sentence is neither true nor false but meaningless. Sentences like "God exists" are meta-physical; that is, in attempting to say something about the ultimate structure and purpose of reality, those who formulate them go beyond the world of everyday experience and, indeed, beyond the physical order, to some spiritual realm. The logical positivists object that sentences going beyond our everyday experience are likely to be nonsensical. They may seem to convey some factual information about the world, but they don't actually describe events or report facts.

The logical positivists reached this conclusion by applying to metaphysical statements the criterion of meaning known as the verification principle. Noting that the precise formulation of this principle is a complicated matter, A. J. Ayer has explained that

> roughly stated, it lays it down that the meaning of a statement is determined by the way in which it can be verified, where its being verified consists in its being tested by empirical observation. Consequently, statements like those of metaphysics to the truth or falsehood of which no empirical observation could possibly be relevant, are ruled out as factually meaningless.

Some people, of course, have tried to prove that God exists through various sorts of argument; thus they claim that there is indeed evidence relevant to this assertion. For instance, the philosopher and theologian Thomas Aquinas argued that the order in nature points to the existence of a transcendent "Orderer," or Creator. Donald D. Evans, however, has suggested a different approach. Basing his remarks on Austin's analysis of performative language, he says, "In the biblical context, religious knowledge is a sort of *doing*. When a man 'knows' God, he acknowledges God; and when God 'knows' a man, He acknowledges the man." Evans had earlier remarked on the importance of the verb "to acknowledge": "The word 'acknowledge' has a *performative* aspect. In saying, 'I acknowledge *x*', I acknowledge *x*, and therein I imply that I have certain intentions or attitudes, and I commit myself to certain behavior." In Austin's terms, these implications are of behabitive and commissive force.

From this perspective, it appears that sentences about God should not be evaluated on a strictly true or false basis, as though they were just descriptions of this peculiar entity. Rather, they should also be evaluated in terms of the sincerity and reasonableness of the commitments and attitudes implied in the acknowledgment. Note, however, that the reasonableness of such commitments may well involve certain factual beliefs. Our point is merely that religious language has other dimensions besides the descriptive.

The following is Psalm 100 from the Old Testament (Revised Standard Version). Keeping in mind the uses of language that Wittgenstein mentioned, Austin's classification of performatives, and Evans's suggestion concerning religious language, see how many different functions of language you can find in this psalm.

Make a joyful noise to the Lord, all the lands!
Serve the Lord with gladness!
  Come into his presence with singing!

Know that the Lord is God!
  It is he that made us, and we are his;
  we are his people, and the sheep of his pasture.

Enter his gates with thanksgiving,
  and his courts with praise!
  Give thanks to him, bless his name!

For the Lord is good;
  his steadfast love endures for ever,
  and his faithfulness to all generations.

Note the use of the word "for" at the beginning of verse 5. "For" often introduces the premise of an argument or the reason or explanation for a statement. Is there an argument present here? What is verse 5 supposed to be a reason for?

In light of your analysis of the language of Psalm 100, in what ways can the utterances made in it be evaluated? Are there statements of fact that may be true or false? Are there commissives that may be sincere or insincere? Are there imperatives that may be reasonable or unreasonable?

Can you find examples from the Bible or from other religious writings that have varied and interesting uses of language?

Inquiry

The Logical Analysis of Arguments

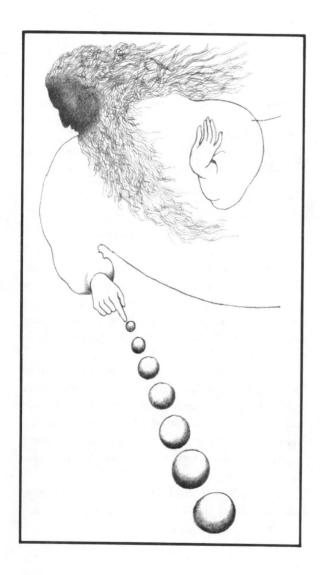

1. In the text, we outlined a method for showing when an argument is valid by justifying a general form of argument (like those listed below) and demonstrating that the particular argument in question has that form. Why are arguments having the forms indicated in this list valid? What particular arguments having these forms can you construct? Justify each form and give at least one example of it. [We have done (*a*) in the text.]
   (*a*) P and Q. Therefore, P.
   (*b*) P and Q. Therefore, Q.
   (*c*) If P, then Q. P. Therefore, Q.
   (*d*) P or Q. It is not the case that P. Therefore, Q.
   (*e*) P. Therefore, P and P.

2. The following arguments are invalid. Prove it by identifying their forms and constructing a counterexample for each one. [We have done (*a*) in the text.]
   (*a*) Ford is President.
   Thus, Ford is President and Rockefeller is Vice-President.
   (*b*) Nixon is President or Ford is President. Therefore, Ford is President.
   (*c*) If Nixon resigned, then Ford is President.
   Ford is President.
   Thus, Nixon resigned.
   (*d*) Snow is white.
   Therefore, God exists.

(e) The earth is round or iron is heavier
than water.

Thus, the earth is round and iron is
heavier than water.

3. The following two arguments are taken
from actual philosophical writings. In each
case, analyze the argument in terms of its
premises and conclusion. Second, note any
other use of language besides argument.
Finally, discuss whether the argument is a
good one or not. Are there places where it
might be attacked? No general procedure
will always tell us when an argument is valid
or when its premises are true, but making
the premises and conclusion explicit should
aid in an evaluation of the argument.

(a) This is the first of St. Thomas Aquinas'
proofs for the existence of God. It is
taken from *Summa Theologica.*

The first and more manifest way is the
argument from motion. It is certain and
evident to our senses that in the world some
things are in motion. Now whatever is
moved is moved by another. [There is here
an argument to establish that.] If that by
which it is moved be itself moved, then this
also must be moved by another, and that by
another again. But this cannot go on to
infinity, because then there would be no
first mover, and, consequently, no other
mover, seeing that subsequent movers
move only inasmuch as they are moved by
the first mover, as the staff moves only
because it is moved by the hand. Therefore
it is necessary to arrive at a first mover,
moved by no other, and this everyone understands to be God.

(b) This argument was formulated by the
Greek philosopher Epicurus: So death,
the most terrifying of ills, is nothing to
us, since so long as we exist, death is
not with us; but when death comes,
then we do not exist. It does not then
concern either the living or the dead,
since for the former it is not, and the
latter are no more.

4. As a project of your own, find some arguments presented in the newspapers, magazines, or books you have read (including,
perhaps, this book) and apply our methods
of analysis to them. The latest words from
politicians of all parties will often contain
interesting and important arguments as well
as other uses of language. The letters to the
editor published in magazines and newspapers also provide examples of good and
bad reasoning. Remember that arguments
frequently have to be expanded somewhat
to be put in the form of explicit premises
and conclusions. As a final suggestion, keep
in mind that political arguments are frequently subject to interesting attempts at
giving counterexamples.

If men cannot refer to a common value, recognized by all as existing in each other, then man is incomprehensible to man.

ALBERT CAMUS

There is nothing either good or bad, but thinking makes it so.

WILLIAM SHAKESPEARE

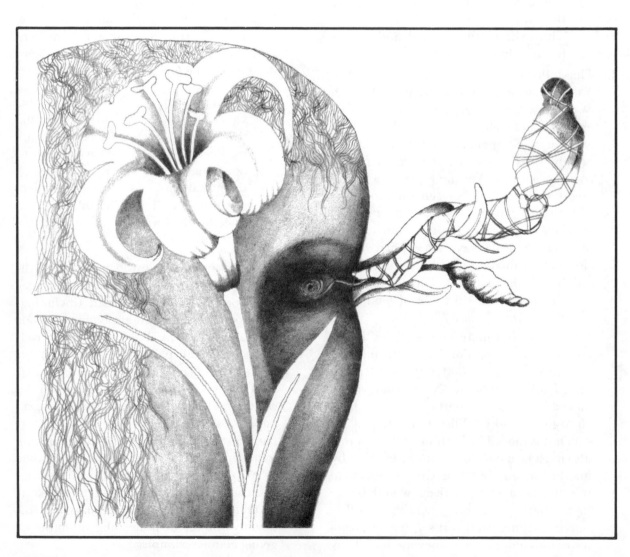

116

VALUE
In Search of the Good Life

Chapter Survey

Friedrich Nietzsche
1844–1900

"The aim is lacking; 'why?' finds no answer."

No modern philosopher has been misinterpreted, misused, and maligned more than Friedrich Nietzsche. Because he became insane late in his life, the brilliant works he wrote before his dramatic collapse on a city street have sometimes been dismissed as the violent and incoherent products of approaching madness. His insanity itself has sometimes been "explained" as the culmination of his philosophical thought.

More seriously still, after his death the Nazis used his name and some of his writings—their sense perverted by grossly dishonest editing—to support their racial theories. In fact, Nietzsche abhorred anti-Semitism. "It is a matter of honor with me," he wrote his sister, "to be absolutely clean and unequivocal regarding anti-Semitism, namely opposed, as I am in my writings." Moreover, he admired the Jews for their contribution to European culture, and he expressly repudiated German nationalism.

Although recent scholarship has established the injustice of many of the charges popularly preferred against him, Nietzsche—the man who announced the death of God, distinguished "master" and "slave" morality, postulated the universal will to power, extolled the "Overman" (or "superman"), and preached the doctrine of eternal recurrence—remains for many misinformed people the legendary mad philosopher of the holocaust.

The will to power and the eternal return of the same things are two themes central to Nietzsche's thought. His intuitive discovery of the will to power provided him with a key to understanding in addition to human relations life itself. In Thus Spoke Zarathustra he wrote, "Where I found the living, there I found the will to power; and even in the

will of those who serve I found the will to be master." He maintained that this notion would account for all purposeful human action: "All events that result from intention," he wrote elsewhere, "are reducible to the intention to increase power." Furthermore, this universal principle would explain all cultural achievements, including art and philosophy, because the will to power can be sublimated, and so it can manifest itself in many different ways. "There is nothing to life that has value," Nietzsche held, "except the degree of power—assuming that life itself is the will to power."

Nietzsche was not glorifying brute force. In fact, he was not glorifying anything at all, although he reported his hypothesis in a poetic and emotionally charged style susceptible to misinterpretation. He held brute force to be primitive, even contemptible; only when reason controls and employs the will to power does it become a creative force. Nietzsche, who scorned militarism, placed the artist and the philosopher at the summit of human achievement.

A second major theme in his work is the doctrine "that all things recur eternally, and we ourselves too; and that we have already existed an eternal number of times, and all things with us." For Nietzsche, whose life was exceptionally lonely, discouraging, and hard, this idea meant a joyous affirmation of both the world and his own existence. It marks an acceptance of grief along with happiness. "Have you ever said Yes to a single joy?" Zarathustra asks. "O my friends, then you said Yes too to all woe."

Nietzsche's impact on contemporary philosophy and literature has been both massive and subtle. Various aspects of his thought not only anticipated but also influenced thinkers and writers as different from one another as Sigmund Freud, George Bernard Shaw, and Jean-Paul Sartre. In addition, his philosophical, psychological, and even prophetic insights were so remarkably penetrating that the student who wants to understand modern times might well turn first to Nietzsche's works.

VALUE

Value and the Quality of Life

What is significant in life? Toward what goals should I strive? How should I conduct myself? These questions, questions about values, have always attracted the attention of philosophers. They may have occurred to you as well, perhaps when you had an important decision to make and didn't know which way to turn because you were not clear about what you really wanted. If you have no clear understanding of what your goals are, how can you decide what course of action to follow to achieve them? You may not lack for advice—your parents may tell you you ought to do one thing, your friends another, and your teachers still another. But how do *you* decide?

"Getting it together" in such circumstances, gaining a clear sense of values and priorities, seems a necessity. Philosophy may be of some help in this regard. Although philosophers can't make our decisions for us, they can help us make choices more systematically and intelligently, and suggest alternatives we may have overlooked.

The branch of philosophy dealing with values is called axiology. Axiologists discuss political rights and duties, aesthetics, what the good life is, and what we ought to do. More generally, they look at what values are, where they come from, how we experience them, and even whether they can be meaningfully talked about at all.

How is a value question philosophical?

Philosophers have always been fascinated by value questions, but since the nineteenth century they seem to have become preoccupied with them. Why has this happened? Two phenomena have greatly contributed to the growing importance of value theory: an increased awareness of how other peoples live and a lack of consensus about values within our own society.

It has often been remarked that questions about values would never arise if everyone agreed about what is important in life and what we ought to do. If you were born in a small village in which everyone had shared the same values for generations and you never learned about ways of life different from your own, you would be unlikely to reflect on your values. It has become increasingly difficult, however, to lead such a provincial life. The growth of social sciences like anthropology and sociology has caused our knowledge of the ways in which people in other times and cultures have dealt with questions of value to be multiplied many times over. The advent of radio, television, and telephones, together with new developments in transportation, has facilitated the dissemination of information about other peoples.

How have social changes since the nineteenth century affected value questions?

The researches of anthropologists, for example, tell us of people who live by widely different customs. Family cohesion is strong in one place and almost nonexistent in another. The ties between mother and child are considered sacred in one culture; in another the father takes prime responsibility for childrearing. Sexual codes vary from strict censures against premarital sex to its encouragement, from polygamy to monogamy. Among the Eskimo, the elderly and sick are left to die in the snow when they are no longer able to contribute to the livelihood of the group. In the United States, on the other hand, medical research is directed toward finding ways to prolong life, even when a person's mind is all but destroyed. Does this difference mean that killing the weak or the sick is good in one place and bad in another?

Viewpoint

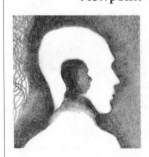

Man's unique position in nature is based upon the predominance of symbols in his life. . . . This, then, indicates the difference between biological and specifically human values. Compared to the biological categories of "useful" or "harmful" for the survival of the individual and the species, what we call human values are essentially symbolic universes that have developed in history. You will find this definition applicable to any field of human activity, be it science, technology, art, morals, or religion. These symbolic universes may be adaptive and utilitarian in the biological sense, as when technology allows man to control nature. They may be indifferent, such as Greek sculpture or Renaissance painting which hardly can be claimed to have contributed toward better adaptation and survival. They may be outright deleterious if the breakdown of his little symbolic universe leads an individual to commit suicide, or the conflict of larger symbolic worlds leads to war and extermination on a large scale.

LUDWIG VON BERTALANFFY, "Human Values in a Changing World," in New Knowledge in Human Values, Abraham Maslow (ed.

There is, of course, an easy solution to the conflicts arising from different views on what's valued. You could just decide that those people in other lands who do not share your scheme of values are "uncivilized," "under-developed," or in some other way inferior to yourself. The easy solution becomes less easy, however, when people in your own society live according to different values, when you yourself may feel torn between conflicting life styles, or when you are confused about what you think is valuable.

Uncertainty, unrest, apathy, conflicting passions, and a lack of a definite value system, it is often said, typify the condition in which we find ourselves. More specifically, people in American society appear to have lost consensus about what is most important in life. They no longer share the same values. Whatever the truth of this assertion—after all, there may not have been much more of a value consensus in our parents' or our grandparents' lifetimes than there is today—it is clear that people in our society do live by different values. The worker and the corporation executive, the suburban housewife, the student, and the person who chooses subsistence farming on a commune, all are likely to evaluate what is important to them differently and have varying reasons for holding the values they do. Some people, for example, sacrifice their friends, their families, their health, and their leisure time to get ahead economically and socially. Others value their friendships over personal advancement and seek the good life in the warmth of a close-knit community. Still others—perhaps most of us—seek both community and individual distinction.

If values are of central concern to modern philosophers, can we just leave the problems to them and go about our business? Does it matter that not everyone agrees about what is valuable? To begin to answer these questions, we'll first try to understand what role values have in our everyday lives. To do this, we'll have to determine just what a value is. Then we'll look at some ways philosophers have said we can learn both the goal of human life and the principles by which to act. The next question is whether freedom of choice implies social responsibility. Finally, we will investigate the relation between values and the community in which we find ourselves.

Values in Our Everyday Experience

Philosophers are certainly not the only people to be concerned with value problems. Everyone becomes involved with the issue each time he or she has a decision to make. Should I quit school and go to work full-time? If I do, I may be able to live more comfortably in the immediate future and become more a part of the "real" world. If I stay in school, my later life might be

How do we acquire values?

How do values change?

more enriched, and I may become more respected by friends and relatives. How do I decide which is better for me to do?

Problems of value permeate our lives and our relations with others. They are integrally related to our self-fulfillment both as individuals and as a species. They are part of the personality unique to each of us and formative of our culture as a whole. Part of what makes us who we are and not someone else are the kinds of things that we feel give our lives meaning, significance, and importance. Are our values purely individual then?

Our values are personal in the sense that we hold them. "I" am the one who experiences a particular thing as valuable to me. Yet we never experience things in complete isolation. Human beings exist in situations and live in both natural and cultural environments. They both influence and are influenced by these situations. The fact that the values we hold are "ours" doesn't necessarily mean that we have created them. We are born into a world full of valuing creatures. Our values may be influenced by many factors—the cultures in which we grow up, the views of those around us, our particular circumstances in life, and the language we speak.

By imitating others and following the dictates of our parents, we first gain a sense of values. It is only later that we can try to make conscious choices about our values and try to weld into a cohesive whole the disparate and often contradictory values we hold. Indeed, some philosophers argue that it is only at this later stage, the stage of reflection in which we make our value choices "freely," that we can call the values we come to hold truly "ours."

When we act on the basis of our values, we affect others. You believe in your personal independence at any cost, so you leave your family. Such an act obviously affects them. Or, you value your own survival over that of others, so in time of danger your friends must fend for themselves. The values on which we act, combined with those of others, determine the texture of society. Can you imagine a community, in any sense of the term, existing if the people who composed it did not value some kind of cooperation? When certain values are no longer shared, change in social institutions is often demanded. The growth of social movements that demand anything from election-law reform to revolution is dependent on groups of people sharing similar sets of values. Gradual changes in social institutions (marriage, for example) reflect changes in value with respect to interpersonal relationships and social customs.

If values play such a large role in our individual lives, what is the relationship between the values we hold and those held by other people? Is it possible to argue about values? How do we decide who is right when disagreements about value arise?

Suppose you're sitting in the cafeteria after class. There's a heated argument over whether or not the food is good. A special menu has been prepared to celebrate the coming holidays. Your friend feels that the chef did an exceptionally fine job. You think the meat is poorly prepared, overcooked, and underseasoned. After ten minutes of arguing, your friend proclaims that the discussion is useless because neither of you will change the other's point of view, and, besides, nothing can be done about it anyway. This last remark sparks your interest. You're convinced (after studying various political institutions in class an hour ago) that if something is unsatisfactory, the system can be altered to change it. If the food is really unacceptable, you can write a letter of protest to the editor of the school newspaper. You can also ask the student government to discuss new arrangements with the college administration. If no changes result, you can organize a demonstration, circulate petitions, and urge others to join you in boycotting the cafeteria.

This experience reveals two things: First, it is not clear whether we can discuss our values meaningfully with one another; second, it is clear that, whether or not we can discuss them, our individual value judgments can have repercussions for others. You may decide the food is good or bad. In

---

Viewpoint

My thesis is, then: we can, in principle, have a descriptive, naturalistic science of human values; that the age-old mutually exclusive contrast between "what is" and "what ought to be" is in part a false one; that we can study the highest values or goals of human beings as we study the values of ants or horses or oak trees, or for the matter, Martians. We can discover (rather than create or invent) which values men trend toward, yearn for, struggle for, as they improve themselves, and which values they lose as they get sick.

But we have seen this can be done fruitfully (at least at this time in history and with the limited techniques at our disposal) only if we differentiate healthy specimens from the rest of the population. We cannot average neurotic yearnings with healthy yearnings and come out with a usable product. . . .

It appears to me that these values are uncovered as well as created or constructed, that they are intrinsic in the structure of human nature itself, that they are biologically and genetically based, as well as culturally developed, that I am describing them rather than inventing them or projecting them, or wishing for them.

ABRAHAM MASLOW, Toward a Psychology of Being

itself, your value judgment will not affect the quality of food in the cafeteria. But value judgments may be expressed by actions as well as by words (and sometimes words are actions too). If you act on your assessment of the food, your action may not only result in better meals for the entire college community but also determine whether the members of the cafeteria staff keep or lose their jobs. And earning a livelihood is obviously an important value to them. Thus, since our values affect others, we can't consider personal and social values in isolation.

What are "norms"?

The problem of reaching an agreement about what's good is usually "settled" by reference to "norms," or to some standard that is considered "normal." It could be that your friend suffers from some kind of salivary dysfunction that affects his sense of taste and that most people you talk to agree with your assessment of the food. One way or the other, as long as the situation does not expand, it probably isn't very important. The issue of what is good or right can involve much more serious controversies— controversies over abortion, capital punishment, equal rights, and so on. Clearly, the issue is not limited to whether each of us has standards or ideals around which we construct our lives. We discover, because we live in a society, that we must also consider whether these standards are compatible or consistent not only with our own goals but also with the goals of others.

Let's begin by trying to discover what kinds of values "normal" people have. Is there some easily established way to identify what they are?

An appeal to the idea of the "average" has frequently been offered to explain what we mean by "normal." Our standard, some argue, should be what occurs naturally or is the usual condition: some kind of statistical median, perhaps. Yet, consider an argument like "if we're all Nazis or most of us are, then being a Nazi must be right." Is this argument acceptable? To advance it could imply it's all right to commit genocide, to exterminate a race of people.

Norms, or what is considered customary and correct, differ from society to society. What we call normal may be more than what we think the standard is; it may also include what we think it ought to be. What we are trying to set up as a measure of existing values may turn out to be a disguised value itself!

The contemporary philosopher Stephen Pepper has suggested that we use what he calls the concept of "selective system," or the natural norm, to think about this complicated issue. He believes that the way we value has a pattern, that there is a process linking the different levels of things we consider valuable. At the same time, it generates and modifies our values. We find out what is considered good or bad at the same time that we find out the criteria by which they are considered so.

Let's say that you are at the beach and want to sift grains of sand of a certain size from pieces of seashell and other grains of sand. You pour handfuls of sand through a sieve that functions as a standard of the value, or "norm," you established. Pepper's point is that the sieve itself doesn't establish that the sand or the shells are either "good" or "bad." Maybe you want sand alone for a sandbox. Maybe you want seashell fragments for decorations. To establish what is "valuable," you have to be able to see not only that sand and seashells are separable according to a certain standard, but also that there is another value that has to be taken into account: what you want to do with what you've separated.

Pepper's suggestion is that establishing what is considered normal and establishing what is good or bad according to the norm both take place by the same process. Our judgments are made on the basis of a process that both generates and modifies our values. Whatever the norm is in any given culture or for any individual, it is not only what the majority thinks or does but also what makes sense as being both meaningful and workable.

A large number of people in America believe liberal democracy to be the correct or right form of government. It just so happens that liberal democracy is the norm in our society; in some sense it holds our way of life together. But the norm, and hence the values, may be different in different

Viewpoint

The value of the moral order is neither intrinsic, absolute, and underived nor to be practiced merely for foreseen benefits. It is obligatory and paramount, not on its own account or for its foreseen consequences but because the creative event in the life of men demands a certain order of interrelatedness among people. It demands this order in the sense that this order releases creative transformation to produce more abundant value in human life than can be produced without it. Also it demands this order in the sense that any impairment of this moral order prevents creativity from operating effectively to deliver man from evils that threaten his existence and his achieved goods. The important consequence of moral conduct is, therefore, the fuller and more effective operation of a nonhuman power creating good and opposing evil in human life. The more power man achieves over subhuman nature and over society, the more dependent he is upon this superhuman creative power to save him from destruction.

HENRY NELSON WIEMAN, The Source of Human Good

countries. Norms, then, do not tell us what is valuable for everyone. A norm is what a particular group finds valuable. As such, it does not tell us what value is in itself.

Some Views on Value

If our values affect our daily decisions and influence the lives of other people, we should try to understand just what these "values" are. Are they feelings? Knowledge? Attitudes? Personal characteristics? Properties? Facts? Where do they come from? Do they describe what is or do they express what ought to be?

Is value the same as fact?

Philosophers have often disagreed about how value should be defined, but they do agree that values and facts, although related, are not the same. Science, as has been pointed out many times, is primarily concerned with giving us facts and describing what *is* the case. For instance, scientists can tell us how to get to the moon and what conditions are like there. Some contemporary philosophers have argued, though, that science can't legitimately go beyond the realm of facts and enter the realm of values. Scientists, speaking as scientists, can't tell us whether or not we should spend millions of dollars to go to the moon. If they do venture such an opinion, then they are not speaking strictly as scientists, but rather as citizens with something to say about a matter of policy. The two functions—one of which is descriptive, the other, evaluative—are different from each other. Values involve facts—we couldn't sensibly debate whether or not we should go to the moon if we couldn't get there—but values aren't simply facts.

The way in which we know values is usually thought to be different from the way in which we know facts. Actually, as we have been describing it, our values are our attitudes or reactions to facts. We accept things as they are or we refuse to accept them; we approve or we disapprove.

It would be interesting, however, and worthwhile, to reach an understanding of facts and values that does justice to the difference between them without separating them completely. Jacob Bronowski, the cultural anthropologist, has argued that values are already implicit in the sciences and scientific method. Honesty, cooperation, and desire for the truth are all assumed in the sciences and are indispensable to them. One could also argue that values are facts (in a sense) because they are in our experience; we can come to know them like other data of experience. And one could argue that in all our knowing judgments of fact depend on judgments of value, not the other way around. "Facts" are not just given to us objectively. The only facts we notice about the world are those that have some importance—some value—for us. Our interests, our theories, our language, and our ways of perceiving decide in advance what facts we will recognize and how we will formulate them.

We can also ask whether our values are "feelings" or whether they refer to some kind of objective truth. When someone says that justice is good or that the late Beethoven quartets are beautiful, are the values expressed merely the opinion and preference of the speaker or are they statements about things that are either true or false? Are we attracted to something, do we desire it because it is valuable? Or is it valuable because we desire it and find it attractive? If the value of a thing does not depend on us, the subject, then values are "objective." If, on the other hand, the value of a thing depends on our attitude toward it, then values are "subjective." Philosophers have proposed each of these positions.

Are values objective or subjective?

Let's look at the objective position first. This position holds that value is something we find or discover in things, persons, or situations themselves. It is a quality of the thing that resides in the object, not in the person or persons viewing it. Objectivists claim that this explains why we can be persuaded to adopt or reject particular values despite our initial preferences. Think how many times you changed your initial judgment of a thing when you realized there was some quality in it you didn't see before.

But if value does reside in the object, how then do we account for the variations in the value people place on it? For objectivists, this is not a problem. The value of a thing doesn't vary, they say, just people's perception of it. Differences in training or environment explain why individuals perceive or don't perceive value in a particular thing. In other words, some individuals can't perceive value in a particular kind of painting in the same way that someone who is blind can't perceive color. The value, like the color, is there even if that particular person doesn't see it.

The second point that objectivists use to support their view is that some things, such as life, seem to be valued by almost all people. If the value of a thing weren't objective, we wouldn't be able to have an experience of it. To support this, objectivists again use the example of perceiving an object; our perception of a picture is not the same as the picture itself. The picture remains objective even though we may see it in only a limited way. We don't create the object when we perceive it; rather, we grasp what the object is through our perception. What is true for objects, the objectivists argue, is also true for values. We only grasp what is there to be valued; we don't create the value itself.

The objectivists have one final argument. Because we often value what does not give us pleasure or even what we do not seem to want, we are forced to recognize that value must exist outside our own preference and desires. Few people would find it pleasurable to risk their own lives to save someone they intensely dislike, for example, but people sometimes do just this because they think it's their duty or obligation. In this situation, an individual dislike is subordinated to a value that doesn't change as individual desires change. Someone might object that doing one's duty really brings a kind of pleasure, perhaps self-esteem. The objectivist would counter that if obligation is the same as what brings us pleasure, then all obligations would be fulfilled.

For almost every point that the objectivists raise, the subjectivists have a countering argument. They believe that values are the creation of the subject rather than a property of the object. How else, they ask, can we account for the fact that people have so many different values? *If* values were objective, people would sooner or later have to agree about them. They haven't, and we continue to disagree.

A second argument the subjectivists propose is that some things seem to be valued for reasons other than clear-cut objective qualities they possess. Remember the bubble-gum trading cards you may have collected years ago? Where did the value of the cards lie? They were obviously not great works of art, beautifully drawn or imaginatively photographed. The paper was of poor quality, and even the information you might have gotten about the world series or RBIs was easily obtained elsewhere. It seems, then, that the cards had value because collectors gave them value. As you grew older and developed interest in other pastimes, the cards "lost" their value.

How do the subjectivists answer the argument that we often value something that does not give us pleasure? The subjectivists respond by claiming that this is not because of any quality that is in the action or object. Instead, it has to do with what different people find pleasurable. Some may find it pleasurable in the long run to save someone they don't like because they find pleasure in the honor and respect others may give them; some may decide it is more pleasurable not to save someone they dislike, in spite of the promise of respect. Trading cards may be desired or not. In either instance it is a personal attraction or its lack that makes the action or object valuable.

Are values relational?

No quick resolution of this debate is in sight. However, another position attempts to find a middle ground between the objectivist and subjectivist views.

The "relationalists," as the name implies, propose that value is neither subjective nor objective but the result of a relationship between persons and actions or objects. In other words, values are neither independently created by us nor the exclusive property of actions or objects. Instead, they have both subjective and objective "aspects."

Confusion over what values are, the relationists say, comes largely from the fact that we have asked questions in the wrong way. We've set up an opposition that forces value to be either subjective or objective. Yet if each of these positions is true in part, an alternative way of understanding the issue must exist. Our experiences, which include desires, interests, and pleasures, are very necessary to an understanding of value, but they are not the only things necessary. To experience an object means that the object has some quality in it to which we react. The relationalists believe that value is the result of interaction between the subject and the object.

To clarify this point, Pepper suggests that we think about whether poisonousness is an "objective" or "subjective" quality. It may at first appear that poisonousness is a clear-cut objective quality, say, of some chemical. But the chemical may cause death in some people although not in others depending on their constitution and the circumstances in which they ingest it. The experience is not purely subjective either because people obviously react to the properties of the chemical. What can be said of a quality like poisonousness can be said of values, the relationalists claim.

Another example may illustrate the differences among the three theories of value we've been discussing. Consider your breakfast this morning. If you were a subjectivist, you would say that its value depended on the pleasure you derived from it. As an objectivist, you would say that the breakfast was valuable whether you liked it or not; it contained proteins and vitamins. If you were a relationalist, you would say that the value of the breakfast depended on how your characteristics meshed with the qualities of the breakfast. If you were sick or allergic to eggs, it wouldn't be a "good" breakfast. If you ate alone or with a friend, in a sunny kitchen or in a crowded and dark cafe, these elements too would have a bearing on the value of the breakfast.

Viewpoint

The ethical problem is the problem of finding a foundation in thought for the fundamental principle of morality. What is the common element of good in the manifold kinds of good which we encounter in our experience? Does such a general notion of the good really exist?

If so, then what is its essential nature, and to what extent is it real and necessary for me? What power does it possess over my opinions and actions? What is the position into which it brings me with regard to the world?

Thought, therefore, must direct its attention to this fundamental moral principle. The mere setting up of lists of virtues and vices is like vamping on the keyboard and calling the ensuing noise music.

ALBERT SCHWEITZER, Civilization and Ethics

Is the difficulty in characterizing value due to language?

Some philosophers, mainly modern ones, think that all three views of value—as objective, subjective, or relational—miss an essential point. You can't consider which position is correct, they say, until you know what you mean when you use terms like "value," "good," "bad," "right," and "wrong." The theories we have so far considered rest on our experience of ourselves, objects and actions, and our relations to these things. Another approach would have us concentrate instead on the terms that we use to describe our experience. This is called the linguistic approach.

According to the linguistic approach, one might be able to shed light on the nature of value by analyzing the individual words that express value judgments and by analyzing the sentences in which these words occur (sentences like "This picture is beautiful" or "This wine is good"). The English philosopher G. E. Moore spent years trying to discover something common to all the uses of the word "good." Other contemporary philosophers have also been concerned with value-judgment statements.

Some linguistic philosophers have argued that the form our value statements often take is misleading. They're put in language that appears to be stating observations about factual things rather than our reaction to the object. Instead of saying "I can't see the point in taking a philosophy class," we say "Philosophy is a waste of time." Instead of saying "I disapprove of lying" or "I enjoy giving," we say "Lying is bad" or "Charity is good." If value statements are misleading in this way, it appears that such judgments may be telling us more about the person who makes the judgment than about the thing evaluated.

A more extreme view on the issue of what value-judgment statements express was presented by the British philosopher A. J. Ayer. He argued that value-judgment statements in general, and ethical propositions in particular, don't tell us anything at all: "The presence of an ethical symbol in a proposition adds nothing to its factual content. Thus if I say to someone 'You acted wrongly in stealing that money,' I am not stating anything more than if I had simply said, 'You stole that money.' " Such value judgments, Ayer concluded, "have no objective validity whatsoever." The subjectivist would argue that value judgments express "facts" about the speaker's feelings; Ayer argued, in contrast, that in making value judgments "I should not be making any statement about my own feelings or about anything else. I should simply be evincing my feelings, which is not at all the same thing as saying that I have them." Those who, following Ayer, believe that value statements merely express emotion are known as emotivists.

R. M. Hare, among others, has taken a more moderate view than Ayer's. He has argued that value judgments are not merely expressions of feeling, but are evaluative and prescriptive statements that often imply our willingness to reason about them. And it certainly seems to be the case that when we make certain value judgments we are doing more than expressing feelings. In a sentence like "Spinach is good," the speaker might be recommending spinach on the basis of its health-giving properties rather than simply expressing emotion or saying that he or she likes spinach.

Strictly speaking, the kinds of distinctions about sentences that many linguistic philosophers make are in the field of linguistics at least as much as in the field of value theory. Values traditionally are concerned with human behavior and choice and not with printed or spoken sentences. Still, the language in which we communicate about value and in which we express value can't be ignored if it helps us understand how we experience value.

We have to rely on a definition of value as a basis for our value judgments. Moral value, one of many kinds of value, has been defined as the good, the useful, the desirable, and even the pleasant. With each of these definitions, however, there is an attempt to determine and describe what is and is not a value as well as the kind of value it is (positive or negative; ethical, aesthetic,

---

Viewpoint

But if the axioms of ethics are not necessary or self-evident truths—what then are they?

The ethical axioms are not necessary truths because they are not truths of any kind. Truth is a predicate of statements; but the linguistic expressions of ethics are not statements. They are directives. A directive cannot be classified as true or false; these predicates do not apply because directive sentences are of a logical nature different from that of indicative sentences, or statements.

An important kind of directive is given by imperatives, which we use for the direction of persons other than ourselves. Consider the command "shut the door." Is this imperative true or false? We need only pronounce the question in order to see that it is nonsensical. The utterance "shut the door" does not inform us about matters of fact; nor does it represent a tautology, that is, a statement of logic. We could not say what would be the case if the utterance "shut the door" were true. An imperative is a linguistic utterance to which the classification true-false does not apply.

What then is an imperative? An imperative is a linguistic utterance which we use with the intention of influencing another person, of making the other person do something we want to be done, or not to do something we want not to be done.

HANS REICHENBACH, The Rise of Scientific Philosophy

or religious). Thinking about the necessary criteria for value choices brings us to our next consideration, our goals in life. Our goals, such as happiness or pleasure, reflect our values. And they also necessitate choosing a means to attain them. How do we choose the correct goal and the proper means?

Moral Value and the Field of Ethics

Rare indeed is the person who performs any significant act without at least considering whether such an act is "legitimate" or, in some way, justified. We often talk about our goals or ends in terms of "good" or "bad," but our discussion of the means to these ends tends to rely on terms like "right" and "wrong." When we ask questions about right and wrong, about our obligations to others, and about how we establish what all human beings ought and ought not to do, we begin to explore the realm of moral value.

When philosophers approach ethical questions such as these, they do not merely describe human conduct (that would be the function of the social sciences like psychology, anthropology, and sociology); they evaluate it. "Normative ethics" is concerned with looking for some unifying principle(s) from which all acts considered right or obligatory can be derived. If an action conforms to the principle, it is judged "right"; if it doesn't conform, it is judged "wrong." Philosophers, however, disagree on what this principle, or "norm," should be. Here we shall discuss some of the most important normative theories.

A number of normative theories, of which Aristotle's is the most famous, propose human well-being as the standard of good action. Among these, however, there is disagreement about what well-being actually is and whose well-being is at stake.

Aristotle believed that everything in nature had some function to fulfill or some "end" to achieve. This he called "the good." "Every act and every scientific inquiry, and similarly every action and purpose," he wrote in the *Nichomachean Ethics,* "may be said to aim at some good. Hence the good has been well defined as that at which all things aim." First, we establish what the person or thing is made *for;* then we can judge if that particular aim is being fulfilled. If it is, then the person or instrument is "good."

It is easy enough to see how this idea applies to things. If a clock doesn't tell time correctly, it is hardly a "good" clock. Establishing the purpose of human beings is a more involved enterprise. Plato had said that the good toward which all humans aim is knowledge of the principle, or, as he called it, the idea of the good. Aristotle objected. He said we could not know such a standard or principle apart from the world of our experience. Rather, the supreme good should be found by careful observation of what people do, in fact, strive for. This, Aristotle believed, was "happiness." Happiness, he argued, was the only quality that was always desired for its own sake and never as a means to something else. The reason there is so much unhappiness is that people do not know what things will really make them happy. For Aristotle, happiness was not a state to be attained, but an activity in conformity with reason and virtue. Here is how he described it in *Nichomachean Ethics:*

> if we define the function of Man as a kind of life, and this life as an activity of soul, or a course of action in conformity with reason, if the function of a good man is such activity or action of a good and noble kind, and if everything is successfully performed when it is performed in accordance with its proper excellence, it follows that the good of Man is an activity of soul in accordance with virtue or, if there are more virtues than one, in accordance with the best and most complete virtue. But it is necessary to add the words "in a complete life." For as one swallow or one day does not make a spring, so one day or a short time does not make a fortunate or happy man.

Another standard for ethical decisions that has been suggested is "pleasure." Aristotle would say that pleasure is a by-product of happiness, of living right. But some theories, called "hedonistic" (from the Greek word for pleasure), say pleasure itself is the ultimate goal. Two variants of this theory—Epicureanism and the highly influential versions of utilitarianism propounded by the nineteenth century English philosophers Jeremy Bentham and John Stuart Mill—are of particular importance.

Epicureanism (after its Greek advocate Epicurus) holds that each person ought to do what increases his or her own pleasure. The psychological assumption that pleasure is the natural end or goal of human action is the basis for this view.

The versions of utilitarianism proposed by Bentham and Mill also suggest pleasure (as opposed to pain) as the standard for human conduct. In utilitarianism, however, it is not one's personal pleasure that is the standard, but that of all people. Mill stated in *Utilitarianism* the general tenet of utilitarianism in this way:

> The creed which accepts as the foundation of morals "utility," or the "greatest happiness principle," holds that actions are right in proportion as they tend to promote happiness; wrong as they tend to produce the reverse of happiness. By happiness is intended pleasure and the absence of pain; by unhappiness, pain and the privation of pleasure.

Bentham believed that pleasure was the only possible object of human desire and that the happiness of society merely consisted in the summation of the personal pleasures of the self-interested individuals who composed it. Pleasures, he argued, were similar in kind and therefore could be quantified and compared mathematically. To determine the morality of an action, one had only to sum up the pleasures and pains produced by it, with each person counting as a unit. If the balance of pleasures exceeded pains, then the action was "good." In Bentham's version of utilitarianism, things had value only insofar as they increased pleasure. "Quantity of pleasure being equal," he once said, "pushpin [a child's game] is as good as poetry."

When Mill reformulated Bentham's utilitarian doctrine he argued that pleasures could not be quantified in the way Bentham supposed. Pleasures are qualitatively different. He also carried the social aspect of utilitarianism further. "The happiness which forms the utilitarian standard of what is right in conduct," he said, "is not the agent's own happiness, but that of all concerned. As between his own happiness and that of others, utilitarianism requires him to be as strictly impartial as a disinterested and benevolent spectator." That people could transcend their immediate self-interest was a possibility that Bentham did not admit.

In the theories we have considered so far, the meaning of "pleasure" or "happiness" remains vague, and there is little discussion of whether acts should be judged according to their immediate or their long-term production of well-being. These theories also judge what we ought to do on the basis of the consequences that an act produces. They are therefore sometimes called "teleological" theories (*telos* meaning "end") because they judge actions right or wrong according to an end.

If the morality of conduct is judged solely by the consequences of an action, then anything is permissible as long as it creates a greater good. In other words, these standards allow that if the end is sufficiently good, the means to it is justified. Most of us, however, would have at least some qualms about murdering a person even if we believed that a greater good for all would most probably result. And if you were the victim rather than the executioner, it might be small consolation to be told that your death would probably result in greater happiness for others.

Another class of theories proposes as a standard of conduct a set of rules that we should always follow, regardless of the consequences for ourselves or others. According to these, there are universal laws that apply to all human beings, and we can make judgments about our actions in the light of them.

Perhaps the most familiar of these theories in the Western tradition is the Judeo-Christian ethical code. Part of the code can be the belief that God has completely revealed once and for all what we ought to do, in the Ten Commandments, for instance. Our values are given us in the word of God, the Bible. Other people believe that it is the spirit behind the religious tradition rather than the letter of the revealed laws that is most important.

One reaction to the rigid interpretation of religious laws has gained some notoriety in recent years. It is embodied in an approach called "situation ethics." Situationists believe that we have to make our moral decisions in a given "situation" and that no set of rules developed in advance can take all the variables into account. We have to rely, instead, on what Joseph Fletcher refers to as "agape," or love. If we can live our lives according to the supreme virtue of love, we will continuously become aware of what we ought to do. "There is only one thing that is always good and right," Fletcher says in *Situation Ethics,* "intrinsically good regardless of the context, and that one thing is love." Actions are right, according to Fletcher, if they increase the amount of love in the world and wrong if they diminish it. We ought to act in a loving way for God's sake, not for our own: "Agape goes out to our neighbors not for our own sakes nor for theirs, really, but for God's." What exactly "love" is remains unclear in Fletcher's account. How it is to be applied depends solely on the individual's interpretation and assessment of the situation. In any case, situation ethics opens options for moral conduct that many feel are inconsistent with other ethical and religious norms.

In the nineteenth century the German philosopher Immanuel Kant proposed a theory quite different from the ones we have considered so far. In contrast to the religious tradition, which claims universal moral laws are given to all of us, Kant argued that moral laws can be discovered by reason alone apart from what is revealed in the Bible. In contrast to the theories of Aristotle, Epicurus, and the utilitarians, Kant argued that simply looking at people's behavior won't tell us how we *should* behave, only how we *do* behave. We can, however, discover what we ought to do, he believed, through the use of our reason, yielding us a general law of morality, a law he called the "categorical imperative." By "categorical imperative" he meant an unconditional command that can be applied universally: We should act as if our actions could become a universal law of nature. Here is how he stated the categorical imperative in *Groundwork of the Metaphysic of Morals: "Act only on that maxim through which you can at the same time will that it should become a universal law."* Kant said this could also be formulated in another way: *"So act as to use humanity, both in your own person and in the person of every other, always at the same time as an end, never merely as a means."* We can use things to achieve our human purposes, but if we use people, we violate and degrade the individual. Kant believed that human beings have worth in themselves (intrinsic value) and are never merely instruments for some other purpose. Regard and reverence for the dignity of the human person is central to his philosophy.

Does everything depend on the situation?

Kant's theory differs in another respect from the ones we have considered. Instead of justifying an action on the basis of what consequences it is likely to have (greatest good for yourself or for the greatest number), Kant argued

Can reason discover an unconditional moral law?

that an action is justified only on the basis of its conformity to the categorical imperative. The morality of an action doesn't come from the end that is expected to be achieved, but from the rule behind it—what we do something for, the basis upon which we act.

All duties, Kant believed, could be deduced from the categorical imperative. The way we can test whether or not an act is moral is by seeing whether we can generalize it into a law that will not be self-contradictory. Two examples will illustrate how Kant thought we ought to apply this principle. Suppose a man is desperately in need of money. He knows that he can't borrow it unless he promises to repay it, but he also knows that he will never be able to keep that promise. Is the man justified in making the promise? Kant's answer is no. Applying his test, he reasons that if everyone in a difficult situation were allowed by moral law to promise whatever he or she pleases with no intention of keeping the promise, then promises would be vain, meaningless, laughable pretenses. No one would ever believe anyone's promises. Thus the person who makes a promise he doesn't intend to keep could not consistently want everyone in his position to adopt the principle that governs his action. And if a certain policy (such as the policy of making promises in bad faith just to get out of a jam) isn't right for everyone, then it isn't right for anyone.

In another example cited by Kant, a man fleeing from a murderer takes refuge in a neighbor's house. The murderer appears at the door and asks whether his victim is there. Should the neighbor lie? Kant's answer again is no, because lying contradicts the categorical imperative. Circumstances are irrelevant. It is precisely against just this sort of interpretation of morality that the situationists rebel. Fletcher, for example, argues that the "loving" and therefore right thing to do in this situation is to lie to the murderer.

Some philosophers have proposed standards that try to combine features of the above theories. They argue that we should try to choose the combination of means and ends that is least harmful and does the most to enhance human rights and happiness. In this view, people ought to be treated as ends in themselves, as Kant suggested, but it must be recognized that there are circumstances in which to do so would be destructive to humanity as a whole. The question "Does the end justify the means?" can't be answered simply yes or no, they say; the answer depends on many variables. In judging the morality of an action, neither its consequences nor its purpose can be ignored.

Are moral values relative?

But what if there is no end or goal in light of which our decisions are made and our actions performed? What if there also is no moral code that is given to us and no universal moral law that we can discover? How do we then go about making moral decisions? This situation concerns philosophers who hold to positions of "relativism" in ethics.

One variant of the relativist position argues that the basic value beliefs of different societies differ and that there is therefore no standard of ethical conduct that can be universally applied. In other words, each society has to be judged on its own terms. What is at issue here is not that different peoples express different values; that is, of course, true (as we saw at the beginning of this chapter). What the relativists argue is that the *basic* values of different peoples vary and would continue to do so under any circumstances.

Although there are obvious differences of opinion on what is considered necessary for the conduct of a good life, the relativist position has by no means been definitively established by anthropologists. In his analyses of the myths and social patterns of many primitive tribes, the French anthropologist Claude Lévi-Strauss, for example, has shown wide variation among human cultures, but he has also suggested some underlying similarities.

Some philosophers, Max Scheler, for one, believe that confusion about the issue of ethical relativity stems from a failure to perceive what does remain the same beneath the surface differences. Scheler believed that in many cases what one culture considers to be strange and evil customs in another may really be similar to its own ways of life. Think, for example, of the human sacrifices of the Incas. How different is that custom from the contemporary one of sending young men off to war? If death is an indirect result, as in the second case, does that make it any the less the taking of life? In both instances, the basic desire is to preserve the group from some grave threat. That this danger is seen to be from some divine source in the first case

Viewpoint

I reduce a principle to a formula. Every naturalism in morality—that is, every healthy morality—is dominated by an instinct of life; some commandment of life is fulfilled by a determinate canon of "shalt" and "shalt not"; some inhibition and hostile element on the path of life is thus removed. Anti-natural *morality—that is, almost every morality which has so far been taught, revered, and preached—turns, conversely,* against *the instincts of life; it is* condemnation *of these instincts, now secret, now outspoken and impudent. When it says, "God looks at the heart," it says No to both the lowest and the highest desires of life, and posits God as the enemy of life. The saint in whom God delights is the ideal eunuch. Life has come to an end where the "kingdom of God" begins.*

FRIEDRICH NIETZSCHE, "Twilight of the Idols," in The Portable Nietzsche,
Walter Kaufmann (ed.)

and from some political enemy in the second does not alter the similarity of the value they both wish to preserve. In the case of the Eskimo tradition that enjoins the death of those unable to assist the maintenance of the group, the preservation of the life of the community as a whole is again the primary goal.

Another variant of the relativist position holds that whatever you think is morally valuable or right for you *is* right, for you if not for others. Still another view, slightly different, holds that ethical statements merely express emotion, whether yours or someone else's.

Whatever may be the truth to the relativist position and whatever the virtues of judging individuals and societies on their own terms, it is important to realize that certain practical problems may arise. The practical difficulty with the views based on any one individual's idea of what's to be valued is that they provide no reasonable means for resolving social conflicts, such as occur, for example, when two people want the same thing

---

Viewpoint

What I refer to as value—not a value—resides in the situation, in the field in which an individual participates. What I have called a value *is a part of the cultural system; what I call* value *resides in the reality that is mediated by culture. According to this view, we experience value when our activity is permeated with satisfaction, when we find meaning in our life, when we feel good, when we act not out of calculating choice and not for extraneous purpose but rather because this is the only way that we, as ourselves, deeply want to act. I believe that value can be experienced only when relatedness with the surround is immediate and, in a sense, active; when the self is not only open to the experience of the other but also, to use Dewey's term, in transaction with the other. To experience the other on the basis of a prior category would be to introduce an interruption into the relationship. According to this view of value, prelabeling, analysis, assessment, calculation, measurement, evaluation, all erect barriers that may diminish or even destroy the value content of a situation.*

The value experience I speak of here has reference to all reality. When the self is in transaction within a social situation, we speak of social value; though the experience itself is personal, it is bound to have value for the transacting other, also.

DOROTHY LEE, "Culture and the Experience of Value," in New Knowledge in Human Values, Abraham Maslow (ed.)

or when one person believes that ill-treating others helps him work out his own problems. In the latter case, would you sit idly by, reasoning that you have no justification for intervening? Have you no responsibility for others?

Freedom and Responsibility

One issue to which we have presupposed an answer is that of freedom and responsibility. Most philosophers believe it doesn't make much sense to talk about morality if everyone's actions are determined completely by a god, a sex drive, a will to power, or by past or present conditions. If we are so determined, how can we be held morally responsible for our actions?

Why is freedom important for moral responsibility?

It is generally held that responsibility for an action presupposes some degree of freedom of choice, or, as it has been succinctly expressed, "I ought implies I can." For example, a promise is a moral obligation that we take on *freely*. A promise isn't really a promise if it is forced. Promises made when we are not aware of the details or we don't understand the circumstances are not made freely and therefore are not usually considered binding. How much responsibility do we have, then, for our own actions and for those of other people?

Among modern existentialist thinkers the issue of freedom and responsibility assumes particular importance. The French philosopher Jean-Paul Sartre, for instance, argues that we create who we are and what our values are through our choices. There is no such thing as "human nature." "Before you come alive life is nothing; it's up to you to give it a meaning, and value is nothing else but the meaning that you choose." We are free to make these choices, but we are not free not to choose. Even not choosing is a choice.

By placing so much emphasis on the freedom of the individual, Sartre has to maintain that each of us is finally and completely responsible for who we are and what we do. He doesn't deny that there are influences on our lives and that we are born into situations not of our own choosing. His point, rather, is that we choose how we are going to respond to these influences and situations. To attempt to shift responsibility for our actions or decisions onto the situation is merely to make excuses and is dishonest. Our freedom is thus a mixed blessing. It is what makes each of us a person instead of an object, and it gives us our human dignity. But it is also a great burden and responsibility because we have nowhere to turn for our justification, no objective or eternal moral code in which to take refuge.

How do we create both ourselves and our values at the same time?

In Sartre's view, we are not only responsible for ourselves but also for others. In making our choices, he argues, we implicitly choose for everyone: "in creating the man that we want to be, there is not a single one of our acts which does not at the same time create an image of man as we think he ought to be. . . . [The person] who realizes that he is not only the person he chooses to be, but also a lawmaker who is, at the same time, choosing all mankind as well as himself, can not help escape the feeling of his total and deep responsibility."

A more concrete sense of what Sartre is saying can be gained by considering the issue of obeying an order when it conflicts with your notions of morality. This issue involves a famous problem in ethics, and it is one that has come to the forefront in the twentieth century with the trials of Nazi war criminals at Nuremberg and the controversy surrounding the American massacre of civilians at My Lai during the Vietnam war. In each of these cases the principals have argued that they were not responsible for their actions because they were merely following the orders of their superiors. Can we ever absolve ourselves of the responsibility to make our own moral decisions by transferring this responsibility to someone else? Sartre's answer is no, because it is we, and we alone, who make the decision to obey orders rather than to follow our conscience. This element of choice always exists. Even if you attempt to transfer your responsibility to someone else, you are the one who makes the decision to attempt this.

Kant argued in a somewhat similar way that we always have to make our own moral decisions because it is we who interpret the law. From the mere fact that a person, a ruler, or God orders us to do something, we cannot conclude that we *ought* to do it. We must make this decision. Note the distinction between the fact that someone orders us to do something and our value judgment that we ought or ought not to do it. In a more general way the Scottish philosopher David Hume stated this when he said that we cannot derive an "ought" simply from an "is." We saw other applications of this principle earlier in the chapter when discussing the distinction between facts and values, a distinction that Sartre carries further than have most philosophers.

If we are responsible for our own decisions, does our responsibility, as Sartre argues, extend to others? Are we obligated to act in a morally responsible way even if the action doesn't return benefit to us? Why, after all, should we do something we don't want to do? One response to these questions is that we obligate ourselves to others through our promises. In Kant's view, for example, human beings are "self-legislative"; that is, they impose, by willing, moral obligations on themselves. The argument says that promising implies the taking on of an obligation. Not to keep that obligation or to deny your right to expect me to keep it contradicts what a promise is. A promise is a commitment and a moral obligation.

This kind of reasoning about the extent of our moral obligations underlies the practices of many American social institutions. Consider loyalty oaths, promises to tell the truth in court, promises to obey the law when obtaining a driver's license, promises to obey orders and serve the country when joining the army, and marriage vows. In each of these cases the idea is to get you to freely promise to do something and thereby obligate you to do it. If you don't fulfill your obligation, then you have broken your own promise.

Despite the different positions on value that we've discussed in this chapter, there may be some goal, some all-encompassing value toward which we all strive: the fulfillment of our human potential. However this is specifically defined—as pleasure, happiness, virtuous activity, the development of reason, or in some other way—the striving for human fulfillment seems to unite differences. We could conclude that persons cannot be reduced to just one quality or one aspect of themselves, but must be seen as complete social beings. To make this goal more clear, we can call on a distinction made by the modern philosopher P. F. Strawson. He argues that a person is not merely a body, for that would be a thing, a particular, a part of what we are. When we have an idea of who *we* are, it's not exhausted in the idea of our body. For this reason Strawson says that the concept of "persons" is "primitive"; that is, persons are not reducible to something that is a part of themselves or anything more basic than themselves. We can make statements about our material bodies that describe an individual, but these statements are not sufficient to identify that individual as a person. In fact, the use of any statements involving "person" implies a recognition of the social element. One has to be able to speak of others as persons in order to apply the term "person" to oneself.

Viewpoint

The concepts of value are profound and difficult exactly because they do two things at once: they join men into societies, and yet they preserve for them a freedom which makes them single men. A philosophy which does not acknowledge both needs cannot evolve values; and indeed cannot allow them. . . .

The problem of values arises only when men try to fit together their need to be social animals with their need to be free men. There is no problem, and there are no values, until men want to do both. If an anarchist wants only freedom, whatever the cost, he will prefer the jungle of man at war with man. And if a tyrant wants only social order, he will create the totalitarian state.

JACOB BRONOWSKI, Science and Human Values

We have seen how difficult it is to establish an individual's moral values without reference to the concrete situations in which human beings exist. It should also be clear how important values are to an understanding of who we are and who we are becoming. We can take our discussion of values even one step further. Values not only determine the individual person; society itself can be defined in terms of values.

Let us reflect a moment on the idea of what a community is. Though there are often differences of opinion and interest within a group of people associated with one another for some particular reason, there is something that they hold in common. Otherwise there would be no reason for their association. There would be no society, no coexistence at all, if two or more people didn't recognize some common value or goal. We may not be consciously aware of just what this common value is, but without at least an inplicit commitment to work together in its pursuit there would be no reason to stay together. The many different values for which people might choose to work account for the wide variety of communities.

Why are values so important to society?

Even the development of our social institutions is determined by values. Banking, electoral politics, marriage, education, and organized sports, along with many other institutions, serve as the means by which individual and social values may be pursued.

Value as it forms us and the world in which we live is related to almost every other philosophic issue we discuss, and it is involved in almost all our relationships in the world. Obviously, the consideration of society, the question of "rights," and the function and purpose of government are directly related to our value system. What form of society would be the most conducive to the realization of our values? Toward what goals should society be oriented? Do we gain rights in society by working in it? Is society obligated to provide us with a decent standard of living and adequate leisure time? Much controversy today surrounds these issues, and indeed, almost all questions of value.

Whenever we as individuals or as a community are faced with the crucial problem of reexamining the values we hold, we are at a turning point that has enormous implications for our definitions of ourselves and our culture. It is precisely because we are in such a situation today that so many philosophers are giving extensive and serious thought to values.

Summary

Values and the Quality of Life: All of us, not only philosophers, are involved in deciding what is most important or valuable in life. Philosophy has a special branch, called axiology, concerned with investigating values, where they come from, how we experience them, and how they can be meaningfully discussed. Value questions have become especially acute since the nineteenth century because we have, due to mass communication and the social sciences, become so aware of the values of other peoples. This has led to a reexamination of our own values.

Values in Our Everyday Experience: We are born into a world in which people share values that provide a sense of community. We thus acquire our sense of what is important in life from our community. But each community has its own set of "norms," or standards, for measuring values. Disagreements on value questions are usually referred to a norm for settlement. Norms do not necessarily tell us what is right for everyone or what value is in itself.

Some Views on Value: Values are not the same as facts. Values reflect what ought to be and facts tell us what is, such as in scientific description. Some thinkers, called objectivists, believe that "ought" resides in the objects of our experience, such as things, persons, and events. Other thinkers, called subjectivists, think that value resides in our responses rather than in an object. Still other philosophers believe values are relational, a position midway between subjectivism and objectivism. Yet another position claims that value questions can't even be considered until we know precisely what terms like "good," "bad," "right," and "wrong" mean.

Moral Value and the Field of Ethics: Normative ethics is concerned with looking for the principles or standards that will tell us what actions are right and obligatory. Different standards have been proposed such as human well-being or happiness, pleasure, revealed truth, and innate moral principle. Some say there is no standard at all and that values are entirely relative.

Freedom and Responsibility: Responsibility for action presupposes a degree of freedom of choice. Some existentialists, Sartre in particular, emphasize our total responsibility for creating who we are through our choices. In creating ourselves we also create our values. Thus freedom is both a blessing and a burden. If we choose well we thank only ourselves, and if we choose badly no one but us will be blamed. The problem that arises from this position is how or if we are responsible to other people since we clearly live in a society. To speak of the individual is to recognize his or her social involvement. This leads us to reflect on what society and the individual have in common and to see that without some common values or goals there could be no society, no coexistence, and perhaps no true individuality.

Suggestions for Further Reading

In the course of developing his own theory of value, Stephen Pepper discusses where we get our values from and how we experience them in *The Source of Value* (Berkeley: University of California Press, 1958).

Henry Nelson Wieman's *The Source of Human Good* (Chicago: The University of Chicago Press, 1946) provides a variety of perspectives on value.

In *Science and Human Values* (New York: Harper & Row, rev. ed., 1965) Jacob Bronowski investigates the relationship between science and value.

A good short introduction to the basic issues, supplemented by his own position, is to be found in William Frankena's *Ethics* (Englewood Cliffs: Prentice-Hall, 2d ed., 1973).

Beginning with Aristotle's view, V. J. McGill's *The Idea of Happiness* is an historical approach to the value issue (New York: Praeger, 1968).

One of the better short surveys of contemporary ethical theory is Mary Warnock's *Ethics Since 1900* (London: Oxford University Press, 1960).

Inquiry

'Of Human Bondage'

How do the issues of value in general and ethics in particular relate to the manner in which we live our lives? In what ways are our decisions, backgrounds, and beliefs intertwined? Through what process do we clarify what's important and significant in our lives?

These issues are frequently of concern in imaginative literature. They're particularly important in novels that deal with the growth and development of the hero or heroine from youth to maturity. *Bildungsroman* is what the Germans call this literary form, the novel of "personality."

W. Somerset Maugham took the title of his novel *Of Human Bondage* from Spinoza's *Ethics*. More than the title is reminiscent of the value questions that we have considered in this chapter. The book traces the life and fortunes of Philip Carey, an orphan forced to deal with a physical deformity, uncertain about the direction of his life.

Philip spends one period of his life as an art student in Paris. There, he makes the acquaintance of Cronshaw, a writer, intellectual, and drunkard. Their conversations are often concerned with their condition and desires in life. In a café on one such occasion they are found discussing moral values.

Cronshaw lives in very squalid conditions, eking out his living by writing art reviews for English newspapers. Knowing Cronshaw's pov-

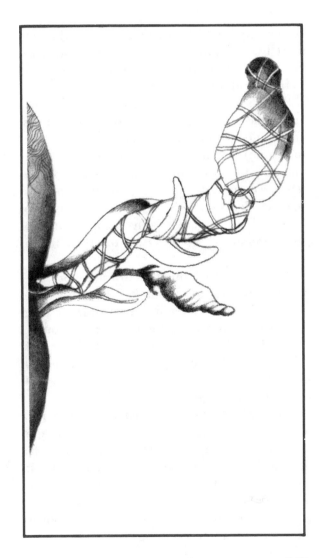

erty, Philip is puzzled by his statement that one must live life rather than write about it. They become involved with the question "what is one in the world for?"

Philip's answer is: "I suppose to do one's duty, and make the best possible use of one's faculties, and avoid hurting other people." He becomes indignant when Cronshaw insists that this amounts to Christianity. Philip considers himself freed from the hollow sanctimoniousness that he identifies with his uncle, the pastor of Blackstable. Not Christianity at all, but "abstract morality," he claims, is the basis for his actions.

There's "no such thing as abstract morality," Cronshaw argues. It makes no difference whether Philip believes in heaven and hell. Even if he has thrown aside the creed, he's retained "the ethic which was based upon it." He tells Philip: "To all intents you are a Christian still, and if there is a God in Heaven you will undoubtedly receive your reward."

Instead of Philip's abstract morality, Cronshaw says that he bases his own actions on something as concrete as fear of the police. This fear, he believes, has had such a long tradition in civilization that it has become second nature to everyone. Philip wonders how one can then account for "honour and virtue and goodness and decency and everything."

Cronshaw claims he has never experienced these values because he's convinced that everything is "inevitable" and that freedom is merely an illusion. Vice and virtue have no meaning for him; he merely accepts what is. He is the center of the world.

Philip can't understand how this can be. If everyone held this view, "things would go to pieces at once." Cronshaw thinks this unlikely because most people already do act on the basis of the rewards they expect to receive. He's selfish, yes, but so is everyone else. "Men seek but one thing in life—their pleasure." Philip cries in protest, "But if all that is true . . . what is the use of anything? If you take away duty and goodness and beauty why are we brought into this world?"

Cronshaw gives no direct answer for their conversation is interrupted by some peddlers selling Persian carpets.

Some months later, Philip develops a plan to investigate the mystery. If, as he has come to hold, there are no absolute values and each man is his own philosopher, then the answers devised in the past are adequate only for those who developed them. Philip came to the conclusion that one had "to discover what one was, and one's system of philosophy would devise itself."

Do you think that Philip is justified in associating Cronshaw's values with his economic situation? If so, what are they? If not, why not?

Is Cronshaw correct in his judgment that even though Philip has rejected the Christian creed, he still maintains a Christian ethic? Do you see any differences in the way in which the two men would understand Christianity and moral values?

Are our moral values the result of civilization or of fear as Cronshaw suggests? Can "virtue" and "vice" have any meaning if there is no freedom? Why or why not?

Does Cronshaw's argument that society won't "go to pieces" even though he makes himself the center of everything convince you or not?

If Cronshaw even lacks many of the bare necessities of life, what do you think he can have in mind by "pleasure"?

How do you think the question of "being" (discovering what one is) is related to the question of "value" (one's system of philosophy)?

Inquiry

The Degrees of Knowledge: Education and Its Values

Values are not only held by atomistic individuals in isolation from one another or in conflict with one another. Commonly, values are also shared by members of societies and communities. And values are incorporated in such social institutions as government, church, and marriage. Institutions may be understood as concrete ways people make their values effective realities, rather than dreams and wishes, in the social world. Institutions "realize" values; without institutions, many values would soon be destroyed or abandoned in the play of power politics. Thus, Amitai Etzioni writes in *The Active Society,* "Values not mediated through concrete social structures tend to become tenuous, frail, and, in the long run, insupportable. Although verbal formulations may remain, authentic commitment is gradually eroded." Etzioni concludes, "there is no escape from erecting edifices if values are to be served."

Unless social changes throw institutions and the values they serve in question, however, people seldom give them much thought. Many people may not perceive the extent to which various social institutions affect their lives or understand the sometimes conflicting values on which those institutions are based. Indeed, it's often difficult to identify accurately the values traditional institutions are built on and to assess the attitudes values foster, especially when their stated aims differ from their practical consequences. Yet values can be freely chosen and institutions designed or reformed to serve them effectively only if the members of a community stop to think critically about them.

Let's look at one institution to which we all belong by virtue of the fact that we're professors and students: higher education. What values do colleges and universities serve? What good are they?

In the mid-nineteenth century, John Henry Cardinal Newman suggested one answer to these questions in his classic work, *The Idea of a University*. What is the use of education? "Such is the constitution of the human mind," Newman wrote, "that any kind of knowledge, if it really be such, is its own reward." Human beings just want to know about things. They have a drive to question and to understand. So knowledge is an end in itself, and by bringing together those who seek the truth in a number of academic disciplines, the college serves as a means to that end. Liberal education, Newman maintained, "is simply the cultivation of the intellect as such, and its object is nothing more or less than intellectual excellence."

Yet although knowledge may be an end in itself, it also has concrete objects and practical applications. Knowledge is always knowledge of something—of oneself, for instance, or others, or the natural world. The physical sciences, like physics, chemistry, and biology, and the social sciences, such as sociology, psychology, political science, and economics, contribute to our understanding of the natural and the human world both as they are and as they might be. These disciplines help us as individuals to see our realities more clearly and to envision our possibilities more intelligently. In addition, the disciplines may also help us as a society to shape and control our own world. Though comparatively impractical, the humanities—art, music, literature, philosophy, and religious studies—also help us explore our horizons, interpret our experience, and express our visions of reality.

Higher education often serves another value as well: vocational training. This is especially important in a rapidly changing world where new jobs requiring new skills are continually created and old occupations just as steadily phased out or transformed. Many educators now argue that the most important contribution colleges can make both to society as a whole and to individual students is to train those students, who might otherwise be unemployable, to compete for jobs in the modern economy.

Clearly, those people who see vocational training as the primary value of higher education are liable to be impatient with those who maintain that knowledge is an end in itself. And those who emphasize the practicality of the physical and social sciences often question the importance of the humanities. Those people who study the humanities, on the other hand, may respond that there's more to life than money and more to education than vocational training: the proper function of the college is neither to manipulate nor to serve the job market. And although art, literature, and philosophy may be considered "useless" from a narrowly pragmatic point of view, they are not "luxuries" at all: they make the world human in a way that the physical and social sciences cannot.

For their part, many students perceive the entire system of higher education as a game. It's a *serious* game, to be sure, in which the competition for scholarships, grades, and diplomas is fierce and bitter, but in the end it's a game with rules and prizes. In students' view, under present conditions what counts is not so much "knowledge" as examinations and not so much "intellectual excellence" as high grades.

These reflections raise a great number of questions. We'll just formulate a few of them; many others will probably occur to you. First, in your view, what social and personal values do colleges and universities serve? And what values

should they serve? What attitudes, personality traits, and patterns of behavior do they encourage and reward among professors and students? Are those attitudes, traits, and patterns of behavior consistent with their ideals and objectives as you understand them?

Second, in your view what value, if any, have the humanities? What place should they have in a college curriculum?

Third, exams and grades are often called "necessary evils." Do you agree that they're necessary? Do you see them as evils? What are their advantages and disadvantages? Do they generally further students' intellectual development, or are they obstacles to genuine education and substitutes for it?

Fourth, how do you view colleges and universities in relation to society and its values? Should they prepare students for life in contemporary society by inculcating its values, to the extent that there's a consensus, or should they teach students to question and to criticize their society's values? And should professors maintain an attitude of distance, objectivity, and detachment, or should they explain to their students what they think about the issues they analyze and discuss in class?

. . . *freedom is not a gift received from a State or a leader but a possession to be won every day by the effort of each and the union of all.*

ALBERT CAMUS

There is a limit to the legitimate interference of collective opinion with individual independence: and to find that limit, and maintain it against encroachment, is as indispensable to a good condition of human affairs, as protection against political despotism.

JOHN STUART MILL

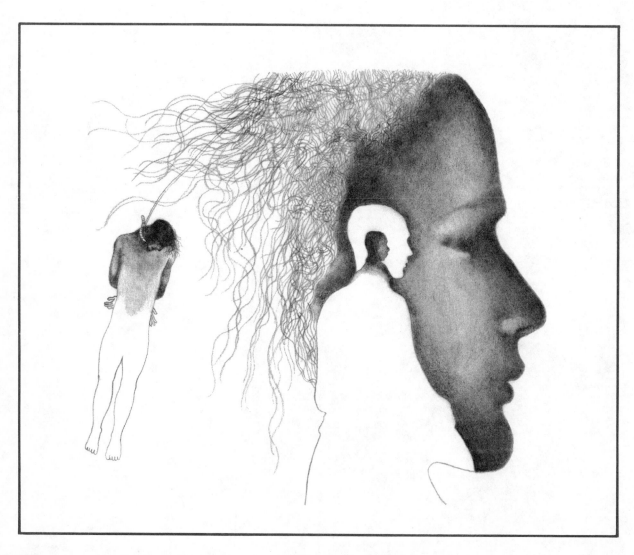

FREEDOM
The Individual in Democratic Society

Chapter Survey

The Social World
Why do social conflicts raise philosophical questions?
How can we make sense of social experience?

The Idea of Democracy
How did the modern Western idea of liberal democracy develop?
Are there alternative ways to understand the idea of democracy?

The Social Contract: Thomas Hobbes and John Locke
Is there a solution to the problems posed by Hobbes' idea of human nature?
Is Locke's solution to the problems posed by his idea of human nature adequate?
What did Hobbes and Locke contribute to modern political thought?

Democracy: The American Dream
What is the Jeffersonian ideal?
How was democracy extended?

Democracy Reconsidered
Why did democracy come under attack?

The Problem of Equality and Freedom: Alexis de Tocqueville
Is there a conflict between equality and freedom?
What kind of psychological threat is posed by the majority?

The Economic Aspect of Freedom: Karl Marx
How can the economy of a country affect individual freedom?
What consequences do Marx's theories have for liberal democratic thought?

The Psychological Aspect of Freedom: Sigmund Freud
Do unconscious processes undermine the efficacy of reason?
Is there a natural harmony between the individual and society?
Are human beings capable of social progress?

Society—An Open Question
Can social problems be resolved?

Jean Jacques Rousseau
1712–1778

"Free peoples, remember this maxim: liberty can be gained, but never regained."

In 1749, Jean Jacques Rousseau boarded a train to visit a friend. On the train, he read a newspaper notice about a question that had been proposed for an essay competition, namely, whether the arts and sciences had contributed to improving morals. In the eighteenth century, when most educated Europeans fervently believed in reason, progress, and their own cultural superiority, the answer was a foregone conclusion: Of course!

But Rousseau's immediate response was different. "If anything ever resembled a sudden inspiration," he wrote later, "it was the emotion which surged up in me while perusing this question. All at once I felt myself dazzled by a thousand lights." Subsequently, in his "first discourse," Rousseau argued that rather than leading people to their moral perfection, civilization had corrupted and enslaved human nature. Society, which is based on inequality, rewards talent, not virtue, and it stresses appearances, not reality. Rousseau demanded, "What good is it to seek our happiness in the opinion of others, if we can't find it in ourselves?"

In particular, Rousseau maintained, European culture had contributed to this corruption and enslavement. "Whereas government and the laws provide for the security and well-being of the men assembled [in society]," he remarked, "the sciences, arts, and letters, less despotic, perhaps, and more powerful, spread garlands of flowers over the iron chains

with which they're burdened." When Rousseau's critical first discourse won the prize, the Geneva philosopher suddenly became a public figure. He would remain at the storm center of philosophical controversies for the rest of his life.

What belongs to human nature, and what's merely due to people's living in

society? In his "second discourse," Rousseau pursued his investigation into the supposed opposition between man's natural and his social, or civil, condition. He admitted that "it's not a light undertaking to sort out what there is that's original and what that's artificial in the current nature of man, and to know well a state which no longer exists, which perhaps never existed at all, and which probably never will exist." But he added that it is, all the same, "necessary to have correct notions [of this hypothetical state of nature] in order properly to judge our present state."

This is how Rousseau pictured man

in the state of nature: "Wandering in the forests, without industry, without word, without domicile, without war and without liaison, without any need for those similar to him as without any desire for their harm . . . the wild man, subject to few passions and sufficing unto himself, had only the sentiments and the lights proper to that state." In his happy isolation, "he felt only his true needs," not the false needs for such things as property and prestige that society would later teach him.

"Man is born free, yet everywhere he is in irons." This famous sentence, with which Rousseau opened the first chapter of the Social Contract, expresses Rousseau's desire not only to analyze society, but also literally to re-form it. Rousseau knew, of course, that there was no question of returning to the state of of nature. In fact, he maintained that it's only in a society governed by law that the person can fully develop as a moral and rational being to attain genuine freedom. However, Rousseau refused to recognize the authority of a government based on coercion or the legitimacy of laws based solely on power: "Force doesn't make right," he maintained, and "one is obliged to obey only legitimate powers." It's not surprising that Rousseau's revolutionary political theories were offensive to many powerful people. When his works were condemned in Paris and Geneva, he fell victim to a persecution complex, and the years before his death were profoundly troubled.

154

FREEDOM

The Social World

The simple word "society" refers to a complex reality. It brings to mind the many different ways individuals are linked to one another. People live together; they share the same neighborhood, city, nation, or planet; and they have things in common. Indeed, to belong to a community means to have things in common with other people.

People need to live together for mutual protection and to satisfy life's material requirements. Tangible things like police, armies, agriculture, and industry help establish social bonds. These things provide the basic necessities and securities without which social life is impossible. Equally important, however, are desires for intangible things such as love, companionship, and prestige.

Such needs and desires are so strong, and the ties of human interdependence so obvious, that you might wonder why individuals are so often unable to understand and live with one another. Conflict-creating issues confront us every day in the newspapers and on radio and television as well as in personal experience. For instance, the energy crisis, environmental problems, inflation and unemployment, affirmative action, and racial questions all lead us to think society could be changed for the better. Conflict has always led some people to imagine how society might be organized to eliminate or minimize social problems. Philosophers have created visions of just and harmonious societies, but it is impossible to point to any period in Western civilization in which the dream of a just, peaceful social order has truly been realized.

Still, the idea, or vision, remains, and the persistence of this idea, however it is formulated, coupled with social unrest, creates dissatisfaction with things as they are. Clearly, what confronts us in everyday life is very far removed from the idea of a just social order. And perception of the great distance between what exists in social reality and what we would like to see exist explains the impulse to think philosophically about social and political questions.

The social and political philosopher attempts to understand how things are: how people live in society and how a given society is organized. And he or she also tries to think of how things ought to be or how society should and might be organized.

For example, many contemporary critics say that the free-enterprise system doesn't really work. They say the present economic situation proves it doesn't work. The critics argue that an economy based on private ownership and personal incentive leads inevitably to confusion and sometimes to disaster. Consider that during a time of high inflation, the government in our free-enterprise system decided to decontrol domestic oil prices. Is this good for the nation? Isn't there something fundamentally wrong with the American system when a small group of oil producers must be bribed into acting for the public interest? And is not the free-enterprise system itself primarily responsible for the growing dangers of air and water pollution, the squalor of the cities, and the despoliation of the land? Some critics are convinced that in a modern industrial society the motive of private greed is a luxury we can no longer afford.

Viewpoint

I had quite an extraordinary dream. . . . A corner of the Greek archipelago; blue, caressing waves, islands and rocks, a foreshore covered in lush vegetation, a magic vista in the distance, a spell-binding sunset—it is impossible to describe it in words. Here was the cradle of European civilization, here were the first scenes from mythology, man's paradise on earth. Here a beautiful race of men had lived. They rose and went to sleep happy and innocent; the woods were filled with their joyful songs, the great over-flow of their untapped energies passed into love and unsophisticated gaiety. The sun shed its rays on these islands and that sea, rejoicing in its beautiful children. A wonderful dream, a sublime illusion! The most incredible dream that has ever been dreamed, but to which all mankind has devoted all its powers during the whole of its existence, for which it has sacrificed everything, for which it has died on the cross and for which its prophets have been killed, without which nations will not live and cannot even die.

FYODOR DOSTOYEVSKY, The Devils

On the other side, defenders of the system argue that free enterprise is not only relatively efficient but also absolutely essential to the individual's dignity. From this point of view, it's a law of human nature that each of us must assume the responsibility for his or her own life. Furthermore, it's a law of society that the pursuit of personal gain ultimately works to everyone's advantage. After all, isn't it a fact that American capitalism, for all its problems, has produced the highest standard of living the world has ever known? Those people who are persuaded by this argument claim that it is impossible to live a truly independent and creative life in any other social system. No other society, they say, leaves so much room for individual choice.

Which of these two views is correct? Is there some truth in both? What does human nature really require in the name of freedom? Is there really a "public good"? If so, how can we determine what it is? And if so, how is it related to individual freedom and welfare? The philosophical questions arise naturally from a consideration of the concrete problems of today's complex economy.

Take the problem of integration. Most people now seem to think that the civil-rights movement is justified. Blacks and other minority-group members are entitled to a fair share of the good things available in our white-dominated society. But as the recent, bitter controversy over school busing indicates, there may be limits to this claim. Some white parents have refused to comply with redistricting and busing plans that inconvenience their children and expose them to physical danger or the possibility of an inferior education. Are these parents right or wrong? And how are we to resolve the question of reverse discrimination? Is it justifiable, for example, for a professional school to refuse to admit a well-qualified white student to make room for a less-qualified black student? Some argue that American society is morally obligated to redress the black citizens' grievances. However, the force of this argument may be lost on the white student, who will understandably feel deprived of an opportunity to which he or she was entitled.

In this kind of situation, what does the idea of equality mean? To what extent does it require sacrificing one person's rights for the enhancement of someone else's? To what extent is individual freedom restricted? Is restriction justified? Again, the general questions naturally arise from a serious consideration of the particular issues.

Satisfactory answers to these fundamental, philosophical questions about society are not easy to find. The problems philosophers have recognized relate to a wide variety of historical circumstances, such as wars, famine, or natural catastrophe. And they touch every aspect of human life. The result has been a multitude of approaches and suggested solutions.

How can we make sense of social experience?

Yet a common thread runs through all philosophical thought about society and politics. From the distant past to the present day, philosophers have wrestled with the same problems—problems like the nature of man, the idea of freedom, and the source and limits of governmental authority. Many thoughtful people are convinced that, despite the widespread belief in progress and in the power of scientific thought, we are no closer to a genuine understanding of the social world than our ancestors were centuries ago.

How can we approach enormously complex social problems? Is it possible to make any sense of social experience? The perceptive contemporary philosopher Karl Jaspers, in *The Future of Mankind,* suggests beginning by considering the individual.

What happens on a large scale is but a symptom of what is done in the privacy of many lives. The man who cannot live in peace with his neighbor, the mischief-maker or secret ill-wisher or slanderer or liar, the adulterer or undutiful son or negligent parent or lawbreaker—by his conduct, which even behind locked doors is never wholly private—keeps peace from the world. He does, in miniature, what on a larger scale makes mankind destroy itself. Nothing that man is and does is quite without political significance.

It would be a mistake to take these words lightly. There's no question here of expecting some sudden, miraculous transformation of human nature. Jaspers' point is that realistic thinking about social problems necessarily involves understanding them from society's point of view as well as from the individual's point of view in concrete, daily existence. In addition, Jasper reminds us that philosophical thought may be futile unless we connect it to our practical concerns in the real world.

In this chapter we'll look at some famous solutions to the problem of how society might be organized to promote social harmony. In doing this, we'll focus on democratic thought and experience to illuminate the problem of individual freedom in modern society. After introducing the idea of democracy, we'll trace the development of liberal thought in the works of two great seventeenth century English philosophers: Thomas Hobbes and John Locke. Both Hobbes and Locke constructed models for the harmonious and just society. Then we'll discuss early American experience, highlighting Thomas Jefferson's ideas. Next we'll turn to the critical analyses offered by Alexis de Tocqueville, Karl Marx, and Sigmund Freud—all of whom recognized different problems with liberal democracy. Finally, we'll close the chapter with some remarks about the question, "Can social problems be resolved?"

The Idea of Democracy

"Democracy" is a word we hear all the time. Have you ever wondered what it really means? Let's begin with the ancient Greeks, who developed the first idea of democracy in Western civilization. By the fifth century B.C., democracy had become to mean "direct rule" (*kratia*) by the "people" (*demos*). The ancient Greeks did not have a complicated system of representation such as we have today in our Congress. The Greeks believed that each citizen should, himself, have the right to propose amendments, vote on proposals, and have a say in literally every kind of governmental decision. Of course, direct participation was easier then because there were fewer people, and the people tended to live in relatively small groups, which the Greeks called city-states.

Democracy in the ancient Greek sense is still an influential idea. However, rule by direct participation in government became unwieldy as the world's population increased, and ever-larger groups of people had to figure out how to live together in mutual harmony. One of the results of this change in population is democracy in the modern sense, which is rule through officials who are elected to represent the people.

Political democracy is also the eventual result of the liberating forces that broke upon Western Europe in the sixteenth and seventeenth centuries. The Renaissance and the Reformation loosened the Catholic church's hold on European thought. And the achievements of great scientific geniuses stimulated the spread of ideas of progress, a belief in the goodness and perfectibility of human nature, and, above all, a faith in reason's power to solve society's problems. These ideas were also important during the American and French revolutions in the eighteenth century. They led people to focus on the importance of the individual and individual freedom.

How did the modern Western idea of liberal democracy develop?

One of the great legacies of the liberal thought of this era is the recognition that the individual's need for liberty inevitably conflicts with society's need for order. For example, during a time of war an individual may because of religious beliefs refuse to be inducted into the armed forces. He may feel a greater responsibility to his religion than to his country. This leads us to question whether it is possible to satisfy completely both the individual and society. In any case, recognition of the importance of the individual and the need to develop harmony between the individual and the society is part of our liberal heritage. It culminates in political democracy as we know it in the twentieth century.

The word "democracy," as you can see, has meant different things to different people. The West has attached the liberal idea of individual freedom to the democratic idea of rule by the people. But the leaders of the great communist nations, such as the People's Republic of China and the

Are there alternative ways to understand the idea of democracy?

Soviet Union, claim that their countries are democratic too, citing, for example, the tremendous progress in combating poverty and disease their people have made under communist rule. Such progress is itself seen as evidence of the existence of a truly democratic spirit. Furthermore, communist leaders contend that the so-called political freedoms such as the right to freedom of speech, assembly, and religion, so much admired in the West, are largely illusory. These freedoms only mask an unceasing struggle for power and wealth in which the few are bound to win and the many are bound to lose. Democracy is considered to be impossible in a society that is always split by a conflict of interest between the wealthy few and the relatively poorer many. Genuine democracy exists only where governmental decisions are made in the best interest of *all* the people. In the West, communist claims are generally regarded as doubtful. Communist governments do not seem to allow the expression of individual or group dissent and are often branded "totalitarian."

The Western conception of democracy is clearly and concisely presented in Abraham Lincoln's Gettysburg Address: It's a "government of the people, by the people, and for the people." The prepositions "of," "by," and "for" suggest different aspects of the democratic ideal. They imply the absence of power and privileges based on social rank or membership in a small political elite. They also imply that decisions will be made in the public interest and that the people will play a vital and continuing role in the governmental process. Thus, in the West, democracy involves such specific freedoms as those guaranteed by the Bill of Rights of the United States. The ideals of liberal democracy are realized, more or less perfectly, in the actual implementation of such rights as the right to vote, the rights to freedom of speech, assembly, and religion, and the right to due process.

The Social Contract: Thomas Hobbes

Try to imagine what it would be like to live without government or laws. Would there be social order of any kind? Would individuals be free to venture outside their dwellings, or would they even be safe in them? Who would try to prevent robbery, murder, and rape? Who would try to protect tradespeople and people in business? In fact, would there be any trades or businesses? Some political philosophers think that your answers to these questions indicate something about your view of human nature.

You may think, along with the philosopher Thomas Hobbes, that individuals are fundamentally selfish. According to Hobbes, without laws or social regulations we would have utter chaos. Or, you may agree with the philosopher John Locke that human beings are by nature peaceful.

According to Locke, without laws people would still be relatively civilized. The political philosopher needs some idea of what people are like in order to determine the kind of society that would be best for them. We'll look at two famous descriptions of human nature. And we'll look at two solutions—called "social-contract" theories—to the problem of how society should be organized for the welfare and peace of everyone involved.

Thomas Hobbes wrote *Leviathan,* his classic work on government, in the middle of the turbulent seventeenth century in response to the urgent problems posed by the English civil war. At this time parliamentary forces challenged monarchical rule. Hobbes thought monarchy was the most stable form of government, and the stated purpose of his argument was to justify the king's absolute rule. We'll see, however, that Hobbes' ideas had clear democratic implications.

The scientific progress of his times also influenced Hobbes. He hoped to clarify political thinking by treating the subject of government rationally and scientifically; that is, he hoped to demonstrate the purpose of government and the principles on which it is based. To do so, Hobbes presented a theory of human nature. To clarify his theory, he postulated what he called a state of nature. The state of nature is the condition in which he imagined human beings to exist before the establishment of government. He thought that imagining how people would act toward one another without governmental coercion would reveal pretty much the essence of human nature. As long as it was reasonable and useful, Hobbes did not especially care about the historical accuracy of his theory of the state of nature. He simply wanted to help people see more clearly what the human situation would be like if there were no government. Then they could see more clearly why government exists.

Hobbes' view of human nature is based on his critical observation of the way people are, not on speculative ideas about how they ought to be. And

Viewpoint

I said: *Until philosophers are kings, or the kings and princes of this world have the spirit and power of philosophy, and political greatness and wisdom meet in one, and those commoner natures who pursue either to the exclusion of the other are compelled to stand aside, cities will never have rest from their evils—no, nor the human race, as I believe,—and then only will this our State have a possibility of life and behold the light of day*

PLATO, The Republic

this view is at the base of his political thought. He wrote, "I put for a general inclination of all mankind, a perpetual and restless desire of power after power, that ceaseth only in death." This selfish quest for power can take many forms: In addition to sheer domination over others, it might mean the pursuit of wealth or recognition. Whatever form it takes, however, the desire for power universally shared by human beings inevitably leads them to compete with one another. And their competition inevitably leads to conflict.

In the state of nature, as Hobbes imagined it, man's passionate desire for power would bring about anarchy. Without government people would be free to take whatever they want, to kill whomever they want to kill. This endless "war of each against all" would be marked by the ever-present threat of violent death. Hobbes wrote, in *Leviathan*,

> *In such condition, there is no place for industry; because the fruit thereof is uncertain: and consequently no culture of the earth; no navigation nor use of the commodities that may be imported by sea; no commodious building; no instruments of moving, and removing, such things as require much force; no knowledge of the face of the earth; no account of time; no arts; no letters; no society; and which is worst of all, continual fear, and danger of violent death; and the life of man, solitary, poor, nasty, brutish, and short.*

Is there a solution to the problems posed by Hobbes' idea of human nature?

In the state of nature individuals are without all social comforts and conveniences. They are alone and afraid—especially afraid of violent death. Hobbes reasoned that individuals would want to end their "miserable condition of war." He thought they would seek peace to guarantee their own preservation and well-being. People are drawn to desire peace and government not because people are innately good but because they are afraid of each other.

Peace cannot be attained in the state of nature, however, because words alone "are too weak to bridle men's ambition, avarice, anger, and other passions, without the fear of some coercive power." Human nature will never obey words that are not backed up by coercion of some kind. It is the primary purpose of the civil state to guarantee the individual's security by enforcing mutual agreements. The state introduces order into human affairs.

The state is the product of an agreement, or pact, theoretically made by each individual with every other individual. According to the terms of this hypothetical "social contract," every person says to every other person, "I will surrender my freedom to such and such a ruler, or ruling body, on the condition that you do the same." The ruler, whom Hobbes called the sovereign, then has absolute power to govern the civil society brought into being by the contract. Hobbes wrote in *Leviathan* that the contract is as if every man should say to every man, *I authorize and give up my right of governing myself, to this man, or to this assembly of men, on this condition, that thou give up thy right to him, and authorize all his actions in like manner.* This done, the multitude so united in one person, is called a COMMONWEALTH . . . to which we owe . . . our peace and defence . . . And in [the sovereign] consisteth the essence of the commonwealth; which, to define it, is *one person, of whose acts a great multitude, by mutual covenants one with another, have made themselves every one the author, to the end he may use the strength and means of them all, as he shall think expedient, for their peace and common defence.*

What is being given up is not freedom as we usually think of it. Individuals agree to give up license to do as they please as long as everyone else agrees to do the same. Then everyone is relatively free from worry. It is a kind of Golden Rule: an agreement to do unto others as you would have them do unto you or an agreement to obey the law if others will too. The social contract explains how we are politically obligated to one another. Furthermore, the social contract is an agreement to allow someone to enforce the obligations and restrictions that make society work.

In Hobbes' theory of the origin, nature, and purpose of government, only one condition limits the sovereign's absolute authority. Since the civil state is based on man's greatest fear, the fear of violent death, the individual retains what Hobbes calls his natural right to resist when the sovereign threatens his life.

Hobbes' purpose was to justify monarchical rule. But in the importance he gave to self-interest and in his attempt to be scientific and impartial, he cleared the way for later liberal thinkers. Hobbes' notions of the state of nature and the social contract involved, for the seventeenth century, radical ideas of individualism and consent. Such ideas became a permanent focus of interest for social and political philosophers.

The Social Contract: John Locke

Like Hobbes, John Locke postulated a state of nature and a social contract. But since the purpose of *his* argument was to show the opposite of what Hobbes tried to show, he gave these ideas a different meaning. Most scholars believe that Locke wrote *Two Treatises of Government* in the late seventeenth century to support the Whig, or Parliamentary, party in its struggle with the Stuart kings. Hobbes wanted to justify absolute rule by a monarch; Locke, in contrast, wanted to establish the people's right to revolt against a tyrannical ruler.

We'll see that Locke's different view of human nature leads to a different picture of how society should be organized. According to Locke, human beings are more rational and less aggressive than Hobbes supposed. Therefore, the state of nature is not a condition of perpetual warfare; rather, it is "a State of Peace, Good Will, Mutual Assistance, and Preservation." Moreover, it is governed by "natural law." Natural law is binding on everyone even though there is no coercive authority behind it. Locke wrote in *Second Treatise of Government,*

> The State of Nature *has a Law of Nature to govern it, which obliges every one: And Reason, which is that Law, teaches all Mankind . . . that being all equal and independent, no one ought to harm another in his Life, Health, Liberty, or Possessions. . . . Every one as he is* bound to preserve himself *. . . so by the like reason when his own Preservation comes not in competition, ought he, as much as he can,* to preserve the rest of Mankind, *and may not unless it be to do Justice on an Offender, take away, or impair the life, or what tends to the Preservation of the Life, Liberty, Health, Limb or Goods of another.*

However, there are noticeable inconveniences in the state of nature. First, though natural law is intuitively clear and understandable, men will not always see it clearly. An individual often doesn't see what is fair for others because of his own interests. Second, there is no impartial judge to make

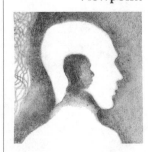

Viewpoint

It has seemed to many philosophers, and it appears to be supported by the convictions of common sense, that we distinguish as a matter of principle between the claims of liberty and right on the one hand and the desirability of increasing aggregate social welfare on the other; and that we give a certain priority, if not absolute weight, to the former. Each member of society is thought to have an inviolability founded on justice or, as some say, on natural right, which even the welfare of every one else cannot override. Justice denies that the loss of freedom for some is made right by a greater good shared by others. The reasoning which balances the gains and losses of different persons as if they were one person is excluded. Therefore in a just society the basic liberties are taken for granted and the rights secured by justice are not subject to political bargaining or to the calculus of social interests.

JOHN RAWLS, A Theory of Justice

decisions when conflicts arise. And third, the person who has been wronged will frequently be unable to gain justice by his own efforts. Therefore, according to Locke, the inconveniences in the state of nature will incline men to establish a civil society.

On Locke's theory, there are two contracts. The first is the social contract itself. This establishes society and requires the consent of all. The second contract requires only the majority's consent. It authorizes certain members of society to form a government. Without the second contract, it would be difficult to conduct the business of government, because every decision would require unanimous consent. This government may rule if it does not violate the natural rights the members of the community have to life, liberty, and property.

Is Locke's solution to the problems posed by his idea of human nature adequate?

Men enter society and establish governments to ensure their well-being. And Locke insisted on the individual's inalienable rights. Under no circumstances will an individual be compelled to give up his or her life. The individual also has the right to such liberty, or freedom, as a just law provides. To have liberty does not mean to be free to kill or steal. Liberty means that individuals have a right to do whatever the law does not forbid. Paradoxically, then, liberty implies some limitations on some freedoms. Again, it is the idea of the Golden Rule we encountered in Hobbes. Individuals also have a right, in Locke's view, to amass as much property as possible. This right created problems, as you might imagine, some of which we'll discuss later. In any case, if a government fails to preserve these rights, it should be overthrown. In *Second Treatise of Government,* Locke wrote,

> *For no Man, or Society of Men, having a Power to deliver up their* Preservation, *or consequently the means of it, to the Absolute Will and arbitrary Dominion of another; whenever any one shall go about to bring them into such a Slavish Condition, they will always have a right to preserve what they have not a Power to part with; and to rid themselves of those who invade this Fundamental, Sacred, and unalterable Law of* Self-Preservation, *for which they enter'd into Society.*

Locke distinguished between society and state. In Hobbes' theory, there was no such distinction. Hobbes assumed that when effective government ceased to exist there was an immediate reversion to the state of nature. But Locke desired to legitimize rebellion in extreme circumstances. And so he was concerned to show that when a government is overthrown it does not necessarily follow that society will disintegrate. But it's difficult to tell whether in any one instance of revolt society will disintegrate, and it's difficult to say whether rebellion can be justified. Hobbes, you'll remember, thought it was never justified.

What did Hobbes and Locke contribute to modern political thought?

Although he stated that decisions ought to be made by the greater number, Locke never clarified an obvious difficulty in his political philosophy. What should be done when a majority tries to subvert the rights of a minority? For example, what if a majority decided to outlaw the Muslim faith in America? Locke believed in the reasonableness of human beings and in the reality and clarity of natural law, so perhaps he did not regard the possibility of this kind of conflict as a serious problem. Locke has been accused of being naïve. He thought the majority would be able to discern what was required by natural law and would want to act on it.

Locke's notion of natural rights has become an essential part of liberal democratic theory. It implies that the citizens' obligation to obey the law is not unqualified. The state itself has a responsibility to follow a higher law in the best interests of the whole society. Hobbes would have regarded this conception of law as an invitation to anarchy. Locke held that revolution was a last resort. It is justified only after a long series of abuses. Locke argued that men weren't as rebellious as Hobbes feared and that the state's recognition of natural rights—including the right ultimately to revolt— would itself reduce the likelihood of revolution.

Democracy: The American Dream

In the course of eighteenth century American history, John Locke was to prove far more influential than Thomas Hobbes. Locke's ideas that all individuals are equal, that they have certain inalienable rights, and that the government is responsible to the people became the cornerstone of American democracy. Thomas Jefferson, whose thought represents the essence of the ideals of American democracy, built on Locke's ideas. And the Declaration of Independence restates the principles of Locke's political philosophy. Equality, natural rights, and government responsibility are there considered "self-evident truths."

What is the Jeffersonian ideal?

Thomas Jefferson also tried to correct some of the negative implications of Locke's ideas. As you will recall, Locke thought people had a right to amass as much property as they could, a policy that, if followed, tends to create vast economic inequalities. Some people end up controlling most of a nation's resources simply because they are clever and aggressive. And as a rule, during Locke's time, the white, male, British middle class owned most of the property. Since they were already rich, they had the best chance of increasing their holdings. These same men were powerful and well represented in Parliament. Locke's philosophy, in part, tried to justify this situation.

Jefferson did not want to see the same injustices perpetrated in America.

In the Declaration's listing of the "inalienable rights" of man, Jefferson substituted the phrase "the pursuit of happiness" for Locke's "property." Jefferson's wording was intended to reflect his belief that government really was, or should be, instituted in order to protect the rights of all people, and not only those of the privileged few.

Jefferson's social and political philosophy cannot be appreciated apart from his concern for the practical realities of American life. His understanding of freedom was bound up with the idea of independent farmers working the land. He'd been born into this kind of environment, and his travels to European cities strengthened his belief in the virtues of farming life. Jefferson saw that economic freedom is essential to political freedom. Since America was primarily agrarian, the interests of the small farmer coincided with those of the large farmer. Legislation enacted on behalf of farming was good for all farmers. Thus, the small landowner could be economically free because legislation benefited him; he could be politically free because his interests were represented along with the interests of the richer landowners.

Viewpoint

The problem is to know what kind of culture is so free in itself that it conceives and begets political freedom as its accompaniment and consequence. What about the state of science and knowledge; of the arts, fine and technological; of friendships and family life; of business and finance; of the attitudes and dispositions created in the give and take of ordinary day by day associations? No matter what is the native make-up of human nature, its working activities, those which respond to institutions and rules and which finally shape the pattern of the latter, are created by the whole body of occupations, interests, skills, beliefs that constitute a given culture. As the latter changes, especially as it grows complex and intricate in the way in which American life has changed since our political organization took shape, new problems take the place of those governing the earlier formation and distribution of political powers. The view that love of freedom is so inherent in man that, if it only has a chance given it by abolition of oppressions exercised by church and state, it will produce and maintain free institutions is no longer adequate. . . . We are now forced to see that positive conditions, forming the prevailing state of culture, are required.

JOHN DEWEY, Freedom and Culture

Jefferson thought local self-government could produce the resourceful, self-reliant individuals democracy required. He dreaded the coming of a complex, capitalist economy. This would create not only a privileged class but also a proletariat, a propertyless working class, which he feared as much as he did aristocracy. Today we have a complex capitalist system with a large number of wage earners. So the relation between economic and political freedom is an entirely different question. We'll consider it in greater detail when we take up Marx.

How was democracy extended?

Because of his views, Jefferson was continually engaged in political struggles with the Federalists who favored business interests and a strong national government. He quarreled with them on behalf of states' rights against the claim of centralized power. He opposed the idea of an independent federal judiciary. He thought it would become a force for the protection of wealthy, minority interests. And it was largely due to the efforts of Jeffersonians that a Bill of Rights was added to the federal Constitution a few years after the original document was ratified.

Later, in the 1820s and 1830s, democratic institutions underwent other important transformations. Property qualifications for voting were gradually eliminated. White, manhood suffrage became the rule. Presidential candidates were nominated at more accessible national conventions rather than in private party caucuses. And, by informal means, the election of presidents came more under the voters' direct influence than the representative electors', and the machinery of government became more responsive to the popular will. The idea of equality for which Jefferson had so long contended was apparently becoming a practical reality.

Democracy Reconsidered

Almost as soon as political democracy had achieved some measure of practical success in the United States, it came under attack. Democracy had made gains, but the idea of equality still was not applicable to everyone. Women and racial minorities lacked many freedoms accorded white, relatively wealthy men, and they were not equal in terms of political opportunity. Neither blacks nor women could vote, for example.

Why did democracy come under attack?

From a philosophical point of view, the key question had to do with the meaning of freedom rather than the idea of equality. People in the eighteenth century had naïvely assumed that liberal democratic political institutions could, by themselves, guarantee substantial freedom for all individuals. Some social philosophers began to think that political democracy was not the answer to all problems. Many people argued that the question of freedom involved society's effects on the individual in even more senses than we've considered so far. Alexis de Tocqueville wrote a book on America in which he described some of the more disturbing implications of what we now call "mass culture." Karl Marx showed how the individual could be controlled by economic conditions. And Sigmund Freud suggested that liberal democracy rests uneasily upon illusion.

The Problem of Equality and Freedom: Alexis de Tocqueville

"Equality" may mean many things. Are we all equal in terms of abilities or gifts? Are we equal in terms of rights, duties, and opportunities? Should we be? We can also speak of equality in a psychological sense. Why do large numbers of people often hold the same opinions and prejudices? Perhaps one reason is that people and customs differing too much from one's own are sometimes a little frightening. It's easy to "do what everyone else is doing" or to "wear what everyone else is wearing." Equality, or similarity, of taste provides a kind of personal identity, because one knows what to expect.

Is there a conflict between equality and freedom?

What happens now when we try to understand what freedom means? We can be free to do things, such as voice opinions. We can be free from things, such as undue governmental coercion. These are political freedoms, guaranteed, ideally, by our Bill of Rights. Freedom can also be discussed in a psychological sense. Do we *feel* free to disagree with our friends or with respected authorities? Do we really feel free to think and act as individuals?

Alexis de Tocqueville had some strong opinions on the subject of freedom. He came to this country in 1831, primarily to study its prisons. His sympathies were clearly aristocratic, but he saw that the democratic tide was irresistible. So he thought it would be wise to gain a firsthand knowledge of democratic society in order to anticipate the future. He then went on to write about the nature and the effects of the American experiment.

Tocqueville's famous book, *Democracy in America,* raises the question we've been considering. The question is still perhaps the central question of democratic theory: Is it possible to reconcile the demands of equality with those of freedom? In Tocqueville's mind there was little doubt that these two ideals conflicted with one another. He was convinced that equality would ultimately prevail over freedom; he thought most differences of opinion would be subtly suppressed by the desire for conformity. The majority would rule not only politically but also psychologically.

Before Tocqueville, the threat posed by the majority was conceived of mostly in political and institutional terms. Some thinkers, for instance, James Madison, saw that a hostile majority could threaten the freedom and rights of individuals and minority groups. If everyone is made equal, then the views of the largest number of people determine the character and laws of the society—for good or ill. Suppose a majority passed a law preventing a minority from attending public schools. Would this be just or right even though most of the people say it is?

Jefferson, like Locke, had not dealt with the threat posed by a hostile majority. Jefferson was an ardent defender of majority rule. With aristocratic Europe in the background, he feared a privileged elite or a monarch more. But the Constitution of the United States is not in harmony with the sentiments of Jeffersonian democracy. It was intended to prevent the formation of monolithic majorities, or "factions," as Madison called them. The founding fathers of our country were afraid of the people, and the machinery of American government was designed to diffuse power so that it could not be used against a minority's legitimate interests.

What kind of psychological threat is posed by the majority?

Tocqueville's concern was not just with politics in this overt sense. He also paid close attention to the underlying psychological reality of American society. He thought that democracy fully released a desire for equality in human beings, and he thought the desire was natural. However, Tocqueville also thought that the idea of equality itself was ambiguous or unclear. He thought it could be "a manly and lawful passion." However, he added in *Democracy in America*:

> there exists also in the human heart a depraved taste for equality which impels the weak to attempt to lower the powerful to their own level, and reduces men to prefer equality in slavery to inequality with freedom. Not that those nations whose social condition is democratic naturally despise liberty; on the contrary, they have an instinctive love of it. But liberty is not the chief and constant object of their desires; equality is their idol; they make rapid and sudden efforts to obtain liberty, and, if they miss their aim, resign themselves to their disappointment; but nothing can satisfy them without equality, and they would rather perish than lose it.

In Tocqueville's view, individuals living in an aristocratic age usually depended on members of an elite to provide standards of value in the arts, sciences, and politics. In a democratic age, however, when the idea of equality is supreme and everyone's opinion carries equal weight, no such superior is acknowledged. Individuals are more inclined to place their trust in the authority of public opinion. At such times, Tocqueville said, "opinion is more than ever the mistress of the world."

To Tocqueville, the democratic ideal meant more than anything else a justification for the idea that the majority is always right. Whatever diversity he found in America seemed to him superficial and meaningless. In the underlying reality of American society, he claimed to discover a disturbing sameness and mediocrity. In contrast to Madison, he did not worry so much about majority rule in a strictly political sense; what concerned him was the greater danger of democratic despotism in a social and psychological sense.

The Economic Aspect of Freedom: Karl Marx

We've looked at freedom from both political and psychological standpoints. We can also ask to what extent the economic system of a country affects the freedom of the individuals living in it. How free is the person who doesn't have enough money for the necessities of life? How free is the person who works long hours for low wages at a job he or she doesn't like? Some philosophers think it's pointless even to discuss the so-called higher freedoms we've been considering. They think we should begin with practical problems.

With the appearance of Karl Marx's writings in the middle of the nineteenth century, liberal thought in the West met its most serious challenge. Marx thought it made no sense to begin with political freedoms like suffrage or freedom of speech. We should look first at the condition of exploited workers. Low-salaried workers are not free; they are enslaved by their employers. The employers in turn are enslaved by the free-enterprise system found in liberal societies. Both worker and employer are enslaved by the economic system. The individuality and freedom of each is destroyed, because each has become inhuman to the other and to himself. Both the worker and the employer have become inhuman by doing unfulfilling work. Workers can enjoy only their leisure time because their work does not develop their creative potentials. The employer is concerned only with profits, not human welfare. What rules human life are miserable jobs and greed rather than human beings themselves. Marx called this situation "alienation." It is the opposite, in his view, of freedom.

How can the economy of a country affect individual freedom?

But Marx did not think that people by nature desire to amass money. (He called it "capital.") In fact, Marx, unlike Hobbes and Locke, did not think we should begin our analysis of social problems by considering the nature of man. Rather, we should begin with the economic structures of society. How a society organizes its economy has a lot to do with how people are and how they behave. For Marx, to talk about the nature of man apart from an economy is to talk about an abstraction.

Perhaps the two central ideas of Marx's social theory are economic determinism and class struggle. Let's begin with economic determinism. Marx thought that the character of a society is determined by how its economy is run. For example, capitalism is characterized by intense competitiveness—basically for money. Capitalism's survival as a system depends on people's trying to acquire as much money as possible. This eventually creates inequalities. Some people end up controlling the land, natural resources, machinery and factories, science and technology. These people, the capitalists, then compete with each other for the "market," or the profits. What happens over a long period is that the vast majority of the population become wage earners with very little control over how the economy is run.

Marx said that social existence determines consciousness. In the context of capitalist society, this means that the competitiveness that characterizes the market rules in all realms of human interaction. We compete for the best grades, the fanciest car, the most prestigious job. Even our ideas of what counts as freedom are affected by the competitiveness of our economic system. That is, we are all "free" to compete with one another. Marx is saying that this attitude is not natural; it is produced by our free-enterprise system.

Marx thought that all societies, past and present, could be understood in terms of their economic structures. Capitalism is just one type of economy, and Marx thought it would develop into socialism. In socialism competitiveness and alienation would disappear because classes would disappear. Let's consider Marx's ideas of the class and class struggle.

Contrary to liberal thought, the class and not the individual is the basic social reality. What human beings feel, think, and do is conditioned not by individual choice but by the class to which they belong. For example, the wealthy factory owners are not likely to see that the poor working class needs labor unions for protection.

Competitiveness in a capitalist society creates class distinctions and antagonisms. It creates distinctions between those who have and those who have not—the rulers and the ruled, the exploiters and the exploited. Marx says that solutions to these basic inequalities are not possible within the framework of the capitalist system. This is because the state is merely an agent of the dominant economic class in society. In other words, the rich run the government or at least make the important decisions. Marx—like Tocqueville—was convinced that claims made on behalf of political democracy are superficial and unrealistic. No member of the working class can escape exploitation by gaining political and legal rights. Gaining these rights does not change the economy or eliminate competitiveness. What is needed is a genuine social revolution as well as a political revolution.

This brings us to another important idea: the idea of the proletariat. Marx's philosophy is more than a theory of the development of society. It is a theory of the development of human consciousness. Marx held that the opportunity for revolution exists only when objective and subjective conditions coincide. That is, genuine social change can occur only when a severe economic crisis is met by a psychological readiness to revolt on the part of the working class, which Marx called the proletariat. The proletariat has the power, once motivated, to set the process of revolution into motion.

Marx contended that the very success of capitalism would ensure its eventual downfall. Periodic crises, for example, depressions or recessions, would arise as an expression of contradictions involved in the capitalist system. Whenever the system produced too many goods and glutted markets, production would have to be brought to a standstill. At such times, there would be vast unemployment because employers couldn't keep paying workers they didn't need. Since workers would have no wages, they would be unable to buy goods. Deprived of markets for their products, many smaller and less efficient capitalists would be unable to survive. These small business people would be forced to join the working class. Marx maintained that the workers' situation would continue to worsen physically and spiritually. Finally, economic crises would become both frequent and severe. The capitalist system itself would be overthrown in a proletarian revolution. At this time classes would disappear, and so would the distinction between rulers and ruled. Marx thought that once the economic source of inequality was removed we would at last fully realize our political freedoms. We could at last be truly equal and human to one another.

Viewpoint

History has no meaning, I contend. But this contention does not imply that all we can do about it is to look aghast at the history of political power, or that we must look on it as a cruel joke. For we can interpret it, with an eye to those problems of power politics whose solution we choose to attempt in our time. We can interpret the history of power politics from the point of view of our fight for the open society, for a rule of reason, for justice, freedom, equality, and for the control of international crime. Although history has no ends, we can impose these ends of ours upon it; and although history has no meaning, we can give it a meaning.

KARL R. POPPER, The Open Society and Its Enemies, vol. II, The High Tide of Prophecy: Hegel, Marx, and the Aftermath, chap. 25, p. 278, Princeton University Press, 5th rev. ed., 1966, Routledge and Kegan Paul, 5th ed., 1966. [Popper's emphasis.]

*What consequences do
Marx's theories have for
liberal democratic thought?*

Let's look at more of the consequences for liberal democratic ideas of the individual and freedom if we take Marx's theories seriously. Perhaps the key belief of liberalism is that human beings are fundamentally free and rational. If this is true, then the social and political institutions Western man has created should have been matters of free choice. They should reflect rationally developed ideas about the best way to organize society. But, as we have seen, Marx says this puts things the wrong way around. Social, political, and economic institutions affect choices without our being entirely aware. In other words, if Marx is correct, the idea of free human beings who observe the world and come to conclusions about what is true all by themselves is a myth. For instance, Marx would say that most advertising undermines our ability to observe independently and choose freely what is best. Similarly, political choices are not rationally made. Sophisticated public relations companies, sponsored by large corporations, tell us who to vote for just as they tell us what to buy. These practices obscure the truth and yet become the bases for important decisions. It's thus difficult for there to be intelligent choices or independent ideas on any issues. Marx held that the economic basis of society conditions its whole social structure, including its religion, its philosophy, its art, and the psychology of its people.

Marx worked out his most original idea—the economic basis of historical development—in great detail with inexhaustible energy. However, political events in the twentieth century may call for some revisions in his theory. First, contrary to Marx's expectations, nationalism has proved a stronger force than class struggle. Second, capitalist systems have so far weathered severe crises. Third, Marx had predicted that communism would come to industrial nations first. But communist ideas have been more influential in the semifeudal societies of the third world than in the countries of the industrialized West. And fourth, because of political reform and the rise of labor unions, the condition of the working class has improved rather than deteriorated.

Despite Marx's apparent errors in his philosophy of history, his ideas have had a powerful influence on the course of events. Marx's insistence on the importance of economic factors is a lasting contribution to social and political thought. Many contemporary social critics owe their inspiration to Marx. And, at the very least, because of Marx it is immensely more difficult for the economically powerful to rationalize their actions.

The Psychological Aspect of Freedom: Sigmund Freud

Are we always rational and entirely aware of what we are thinking and doing? Is there a "natural" harmony between individuals? Between individual and community interests? Are social problems superficial disagreements that would disappear with correct legislation? Are we truly capable of making ourselves better people? Are we capable of social progress? If so, what would that mean?

These questions also lead us back to another familiar question: "What is human nature really like?" As we've seen, this question has many answers. Each answer reveals something about human nature from a new perspective. This question was also Sigmund Freud's lifelong concern, and his answers will lead us back to the questions that introduced this section.

Freud was not primarily a social or political philosopher. He did not concern himself with the possibility of major institutional change. Yet Freud's ideas are vitally important to social and political thought because of his thorough investigation of human nature.

Freud developed the psychoanalytic method. This is a way of approaching psychological problems on an individual basis by talking about them. The problems themselves may have a social basis, but Freud chose to think more about the individual. And as a result of his therapy with individuals, Freud gradually developed theories about human nature in general. We can see that such work is politically conservative since it does not aim directly at social change. It can be argued, however, that this work aims indirectly at social change by aiming at individual change.

The impact of Freud's theories—as of those of Tocqueville and Marx— falls most heavily on thinkers in the tradition of liberal democracy. His ideas challenged three of their most cherished beliefs: first, confidence in the power of human reason; second, the idea of a potential, if not actual, natural harmony between individual and community interests; and third, a belief in progress and the perfectibility of human nature. These three articles of faith correspond roughly to three levels of conflict identified and described by Freud. In other words, it was exactly where liberal philosophy found cause for optimism that Freud could discover nothing but trouble. We'll discuss each challenge.

Since Locke, in the late seventeenth century, the dominant trend of thought in the West had assumed that human nature is basically rational. This implies that individuals, if they try, can be fully aware of and can solve their social problems. Despite the writings of Marx and others, this hopeful view prevailed into the twentieth century. Facts that seemed to indicate the opposite were ordinarily dismissed as exceptional.

Before Freud, then, it had been taken for granted that we are conscious of what goes on in our minds and that there is nothing "hidden" behind our thoughts. Freud's major contribution was to show that, on the contrary, the mind is basically unconscious; conscious processes inform human thought and action only to a limited degree.

Do unconscious processes undermine the efficacy of reason?

In one of his early works, *The Psychopathology of Everyday Life,* Freud demonstrated the existence of the unconscious. This he did through an analysis of slips of the tongue and of errors. He showed how even the most trivial and apparently accidental acts could be understood as symptoms of "repressed" or buried impulses. For instance, Mary addresses her date—whose name is George—as Tom. Unconsciously she probably wishes to be with Tom. Her slip of the tongue reveals her desire. We're all aware of the many times we didn't quite say what we thought we intended. These errors, as well as dreams and feelings, are like boundaries between what we are aware of and what we are not aware of, between the conscious and the unconscious. Freud was the first to try systematically to figure out what it all meant.

One of Freud's discoveries is that there is often tremendous conflict in us between what we are aware of and what we are not aware of. Individuals, he found, tend to repress angry, aggressive thoughts and unpleasant memories. It is sometimes difficult to keep all these things buried if we are in any way reminded of them in the present. Thus we experience conflict. In his clinical work, Freud had discovered that inner conflict characterized not only neurotic behavior but also the behavior of relatively healthy individuals. And the essence of the conflict lies in its not being understood by the individuals themselves.

What challenge does Freud's picture of the enormous influence of unconscious processes present? Freud challenges the liberal belief in the power of reason. Our conscious thoughts reveal only a part of our motives and reasons, since so much of what goes on in us is unconscious. We have far less control over our lives than we think; and our feelings may be just as important in determining our actions as our reason. Perhaps they are even more important. Freud himself expressed better than anyone the effect of psychoanalytic theory in *A General Introduction to Psychoanalysis:*

> man's craving for grandiosity is now suffering the . . . most bitter blow from present-day psychoanalytic research which is endeavoring to prove to the "ego" of each one of us that he is not even master in his own house, but that he must remain content with the veriest scraps of information about what is going on unconsciously in his own mind.

Is there a natural harmony between the individual and society?

Most of Freud's early work deals specifically with clinical research and experimentation. However, he discovered that this approach was inadequate for explaining mental functions and inner conflict, and he turned exclusively to an investigation of interpersonal relationships. In his later books, though, Freud speculated on the relationship between society and the individual. In a sense, his idea of human nature is more disturbing than

Hobbes'. Freud would not have agreed with Hobbes that society or the state is the result of rational calculation on any level. Instead, in Freud's view, human association is largely the result of unconscious processes.

Fundamental to Freud's theory of society is the concept of "libido." Libido is the sexual energy of life. Freud understood the term "sexual" in a very broad sense. Libido can be invested in or directed to other persons, ideas, and things as well as to oneself. Libido is the energy with which one becomes actively interested in something.

The impulses that direct the expenditure of the psychic energy conflict with each other. On one hand, an individual is moved to unite with ever larger groups: the family, small communities, and larger societies. On the other hand, powerful sexual instincts can threaten the stability of such groups. For instance, excessive promiscuity threatens a community. There is little question that Freud assigned enormous importance to the sexual drive. Indeed, the frustration of sexual energy endangers society. In the interest of unity and stability, society requires that this energy be sublimated—or transformed—and redirected into more useful channels. Such energy can be directed toward work or creative activities.

Liberal democracy is based on the assumption of an essential harmony between the individual and society. But Freud pictured Western civilization as a perpetually uneasy balance between society's needs and the powerful, instinctual drives of individuals. He thought, like Hobbes, that society existed to regulate aggression. Freud did not believe this situation could be changed significantly. Obviously, psychoanalytic theory implies that some improvement is possible on the individual level. Human nature, however, is biologically fixed within certain limits. Thus, even a greater degree of self-knowledge will not eliminate the basic conflicts between society and the individual.

In one of his last books, *Civilization and Its Discontents,* Freud described still another source of conflict. He contemplated the cruelty in human history, particularly the horrors of World War I. He was then led to conclude, like Hobbes, that aggression is one of man's primary instincts. This destructiveness, or death drive, as Freud sometimes called it, exists independently of frustrated sexual energy. Freud wrote of it in dramatic language in *Civilization and Its Discontents:*

Are human beings capable of social progress?

> *This instinct of aggression is the derivative and main representative of the death instinct we have found alongside of Eros, sharing his rule over the earth. And now, it seems to me, the meaning of the evolution of culture is no longer a riddle to us. It must present to us the struggle between Eros and Death, between the instincts of life and the instincts of destruction, as it works itself out in the human species. This struggle is what all life essentially consists of and so the*

evolution of civilization may be simply described as the struggle of the human species for existence. And it is this battle of the Titans that our nurses and governesses try to compose with their lullaby-song of Heaven!

Clearly, Freud was not optimistic about social change. If the faithful followers of liberal democracy were unnerved by the Marxist doctrine that individual will counts for little, at least they could derive some solace from Marx's belief that history itself is on man's side. Marx held that exploitation and conflict within society would eventually come to an end. But Freud was unable to provide any assurances at all. Indeed, his speculative work makes the deepest impression at exactly the point where liberalism is most vulnerable: the belief in progress and human perfectibility. The conclusion of Freud's thought is that there can be no guarantees about the future; the issue of man's fate will continue to hang in the balance. From this point of view, the question of freedom is premature: It's the question of survival that takes first place.

Society—An Open Question

Can social problems be resolved?

In a very general way, the history of liberal democratic thought from the seventeenth to the twentieth century can be represented by means of a bell-

---

Viewpoint

. . . even today, whether we know it or not, the question of politics and the fact that man is a being endowed with the gift of action must always be present to our mind when we speak of the problem of freedom; for action and politics, among all the capabilities and potentialities of human life, are the only things of which we could not even conceive without at least assuming that freedom exists, and we can hardly touch a single political issue without, implicitly or explicitly, touching upon an issue of man's liberty. Freedom, moreover, is not only one among the many problems and phenomena of the political realm properly speaking, such as justice, or power, or equality; freedom, which only seldom—in times of crisis or revolution—becomes the direct aim of political action, is actually the reason that men live together in political organization at all. Without it, political life as such would be meaningless.

HANNAH ARENDT, Between Past and Future

shaped curve. From John Locke through the American and French revolutions to the middle of the nineteenth century is the period of the curve's ascendance. Optimism was relatively high, and democratic institutions were widely believed to promise humanity's salvation. But the mid-nineteenth century also marks the point at which the curve starts to descend. As we've seen, social and political philosophers began to criticize democratic ideology in ways too penetrating to be ignored. In the twentieth century, severe economic crises and the two world wars have led some observers to wonder whether the democracies of the West can manage their affairs intelligently. Such catastrophic events make it impossible to maintain the naïve optimism that was perhaps understandable formerly. Though the ideals of liberal democracy are still alive, it's clear that the problem of the good society remains unsolved.

The philosophical problem of the good society is an urgent practical concern. And the great challenges facing twentieth century industrial democracy will not be met merely by hoping for the best or by wishing, no matter how hard, that the situation will improve. First of all, it's necessary to know what the situation actually is and to appreciate its complexity; second, it's essential to reflect on one's goals, to attempt to determine how and to what degree they may be attainable.

If we're aware of the complexity of the problems modern democratic society faces, we may have good reason to be uncomfortable. But, as Socrates was the first to suggest, one of philosophy's methods, if not purposes, is to awaken in us a sense of discomfort. Certainly, we should expect to pay this price if we are to understand the present situation. At a minimum, we should open ourselves to the suspicion that the ideas we thought we had about society, the individual, and freedom were so vague as to be only slogans with little real content, just noises that we were taught to repeat. But perhaps, at this point, the most helpful realization is that questions about the nature and achievable purposes of society are still as open as ever. Unlike scientific knowledge, almost nothing in this area can be regarded as certain.

Summary

The Social World: Specific social problems and a general awareness of the differences between the ideal of a just, harmonious social order and the realities of the social world lead to the philosophical investigation of social life.

The Idea of Democracy: The modern Western idea of democracy originated in the liberalizing movements of the sixteenth and seventeenth centuries. The leaders of communist societies contend that Western political freedoms are largely illusory and that genuine democracy is impossible in a capitalistic system.

The Social Contract: Thomas Hobbes and John Locke: Thomas Hobbes introduced such notions as individualism, consent, and equality. Seeking to justify the right to revolt, John Locke proposed the idea of majority rule and maintained that all men have a natural right to life, liberty, and property.

Democracy: The American Dream: Thomas Jefferson best represents the American democratic ideal. In the early nineteenth century, political democracy expanded in this country.

Democracy Reconsidered: From the mid-nineteenth century, some thinkers attacked liberal democracy's basic principles.

The Problem of Equality and Freedom: Alexis de Tocqueville: Tocqueville believed that equality threatens individual freedom: the majority may rule psychologically as well as politically.

The Economic Aspect of Freedom: Karl Marx: Marx maintained that a society's economic structures determine its social and political institutions.

The Psychological Aspect of Freedom: Sigmund Freud: Freud's ideas contradicted three articles of liberal democratic faith: its confidence in human rationality, its assumption of the harmony of individual and societal interests, and its belief in human perfectibility.

Society—An Open Question: Though the ideals of liberal democracy are still alive, it's clear that the problem of the good society—a philosophical problem which is also an urgent and complex practical concern—remains unsolved.

Suggestions for Further Reading

Hannah Arendt's *The Origins of Totalitarianism* (New York: Meridian, 1958) is a classic in contemporary social thought—a scholarly and intellectually powerful book dealing with the origins, nature, and purposes of totalitarian rule in Nazi Germany and the Soviet Union.

Erich Fromm's work is a sustained attempt to see the potentially bright side of human affairs. Two of his less popular but more important books are *Man for Himself* (Greenwich, CT: Fawcett, 1947) and *Beyond the Chains of Illusion* (New York: Simon and Schuster, 1962). In the first book, Fromm sets forth his idea of humanistic ethics. It is based on his conviction that value judgments are not relative but can be realistically founded in the nature of humanity. In the second book, Fromm describes the influence of Marx and Freud on his own thought.

A. D. Lindsay's *The Modern Democratic State* (New York: Oxford, 1962) is another classic work. This book traces the development of democracy from ancient times to the present. Besides dealing with philosophy, it treats what Lindsay calls the "operative ideals" of democracy, that is, the notions that actually determine developments in a modern, democratic society.

Theodore Lowi's *The End of Liberalism* (New York: Norton, 1969) is an important contemporary book. The author maintains that the problems of modern America necessitate a revival of basic philosophical questions concerning the nature of authority in the public realm.

Karl Popper's *The Open Society and Its Enemies* (Princeton, NJ: Princeton University Press, 5th rev. ed., 2 vols., 1966) is one of the best examples of scientific liberal thought in its defense against the critics of democracy.

Finally, Michael Weinstein's *Philosophy, Theory, and Method in Contemporary Political Thought* (Glenview, IL: Scott, Foresman and Company, 1971) offers a lucid, systematic description of major tendencies in twentieth century social and political philosophy.

Inquiry

Society and Human Life: The Debate over Capital Punishment

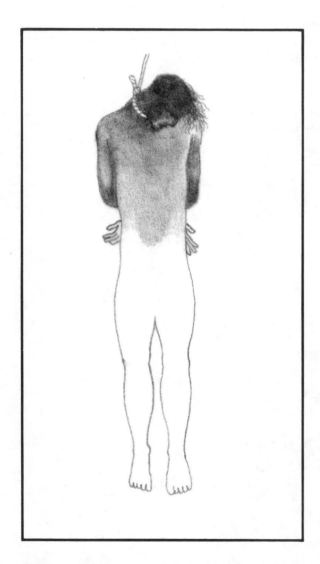

Today there's probably no issue in the law that more clearly touches our deepest beliefs than capital punishment. Disagreement over the morality of executing convicted criminals involves sharply conflicting ideas about such questions as what human dignity means, what justice requires, and what the common good really is.

United States Supreme Court decisions handed down during the 1970s have largely defined public debate over the death penalty in this country. Reviewing the case of Furman vs. Georgia in 1972, a majority of five Supreme Court justices voted to void all statutes providing for the death penalty. In that case, the petitioners had based their argument primarily on the proposition that standards of decency had evolved to the point where capital punishment could no longer be tolerated. However, the court did not rule then that capital punishment was necessarily unconstitutional. Recognizing that blacks had been executed more often than whites convicted of similar offenses, the court ruled only that the laws then on the books were administered "arbitrarily and capriciously" and that in their application these laws thus violated the Eighth Amendment's prohibition against "cruel and unusual punishment." The laws also conflicted with provisions of the Fourteenth Amendment, which reads in part, "No State shall . . . deprive any person of life, liberty, or property, without due process of law; nor deny to any person within its jurisdiction the equal protection of the laws."

Then, ruling four years later on Gregg vs. Georgia and related cases, the Supreme Court reaffirmed in a seven-to-two decision that the death penalty is not unconstitutional in itself and voted to uphold a jury's sentencing a man convicted of a double murder and robbery to death.

Delivering the court's majority opinion on the Gregg case, Justice Stewart cited legal developments that had taken place between 1972 and 1976. Following the Furman decision, the Georgia legislature had enacted new statutes designed to ensure that the death penalty was not imposed in an arbitrary and capricious manner. In the Gregg decision the court ruled that the procedures thus established were sufficient to guard against the social injustices which had previously resulted from the "freakish" execution of convicts. At the same time, the court ruled that laws passed in several other states which made the death penalty mandatory or automatic for certain crimes were unacceptable. Such statutes, the court explained, would impermissibly treat "all persons convicted of a designated offense not as uniquely individual human beings, but as members of a faceless, undifferentiated mass to be subjected to the blind infliction of the death penalty."

Georgia was not alone then in enacting new statutes and establishing new procedures relating to capital punishment between 1972 and 1976: at least thirty-five other states did the same. In addition, in 1974 the United States Congress passed a law providing the death penalty for aircraft piracy resulting in death. In the Gregg decision the Supreme Court took these developments to indicate that contrary to the "standards of decency" argument, "a large proportion of American society continues to regard [capital punishment] as an appropriate and necessary criminal sanction."

However, the court noted that the Eighth Amendment demands more than that a challenged punishment be acceptable to contemporary society: "A penalty must also accord with 'the dignity of man,' which is 'the basic concept underlying the Eighth Amendment.'" If the death penalty results in "the gratuitous infliction of suffering," then it is legally unjustified.

But the court ruled in 1976 that capital punishment is not gratuitous because it may serve two social purposes: retribution and deterrence. First, the court maintained, the death penalty is in part "an expression of society's moral outrage" at particularly offensive crimes. "Indeed, the decision that capital punishment may be the appropriate sanction in extreme cases is an expression of the community's belief that certain crimes are themselves so grievous an affront to humanity that the only adequate response may be the penalty of death." Moreover, the death penalty may serve as a sort of safety valve, preventing people from taking the law into their own hands. Second, even though the court recognized that statistical attempts to evaluate the value of the death penalty in discouraging violent crimes have been contested and remain inconclusive, it held in its majority opinion that for many potential murderers the threat of death may serve as a significant deterrent.

The main arguments against capital punishment today are that the death penalty is not an effective deterrent to crime and that retribution is an unworthy reason for taking a human being's life. A civilized society cannot deliberately kill people without violating its highest ideals. "Reflections on the Guillotine" is Albert Camus' classic statement of passionate moral opposition to capital punishment. In this work Camus maintained that the death penalty "represents a doubtful example and an unsatisfactory justice." He argued that capital punishment denies human solidarity before death. "Compassion does not exclude punishment," Camus wrote, "but it suspends the final condemnation. Compassion loathes the definitive, irreparable measure that does an injustice to mankind as a whole because of failing to take into account the wretchedness of the common condition." Camus held that "the new 'official' murder, far from offering redress for the offense committed against society, adds instead a second defilement to the first."

Dissenting from the Gregg decision, two Supreme Court justices shared Camus' point of view. Justice Brennan argued that "the law has progressed to the point where we should declare that the punishment of death, like punishment on the rack, the screw and the wheel, is no longer morally tolerable in our civilized society." And Justice Marshall restated his view—known as the Marshall hypothesis—that "the American people are largely unaware of the information critical to a judgment on the morality of the death penalty, and . . . if they were better informed they would consider it shocking, unjust, and unacceptable." Justices Brennan and Marshall both maintained that the death penalty is fundamentally and essentially incompatible with human dignity because, as Justice Marshall put it, "such a punishment has as its very basis the total denial of the wrong-doer's dignity and worth."

Thus some people argue that the death penalty denies the value of individual human life (by taking that of the convicted criminal). Other people respond that, on the contrary, the death penalty affirms the value of life: When a person is convicted of murdering someone, then it's right and proper that he or she be put to death. Only then does the punishment fit the crime. It's a matter of simple justice.

It seems that your part in the debate on the death penalty might depend on whom you choose to identify with. Those who favor abolishing capital punishment apparently identify more with the criminal and the executioner. As far as the criminal is concerned, there is certainly great humanity in the assertion "There but for fortune or the grace of God go I." And to picture oneself as the executioner would obviously impress one with the enormity of actually ending another human life. On the other hand, those who favor retention of the death penalty seem to identify more with the victims of horrible crimes and their families. For these people, the ancient standard "an eye for an eye and a tooth for a tooth" strikes a responsive chord. In their minds, the scales of justice are permanently out of balance when the perpetrators of brutal and sadistic acts are not punished in the only ultimate way.

Reviewing these arguments, what do you think? Is society ever justified in executing convicted criminals? If so, when? If not, why not?

In the Gregg decision the Supreme Court countered the argument that "evolving standards of decency" have rendered capital punishment morally unacceptable by citing recent legislation which, the court said, indicates that many if not most Americans find the death penalty "appropriate and necessary" in some cases. If the Marshall hypothesis could be proved, would that invalidate the court's reasoning? Should the Supreme Court merely reflect popular opinion, or should it proceed to define what many would consider higher standards of justice and decency?

Does the idea of retribution justify capital punishment? If it could be shown (after centuries of debate) that the death penalty has a deterrent effect, would that justify its imposition? Finally, is capital punishment compatible with human dignity? In this context, what does "human dignity" mean?

Inquiry

Free Speech and Community Standards:
The Problem of Obscenity
and Censorship

Freedom of speech is clearly among the most important rights belonging to the members of any democratic society. However, it's generally recognized that this right is not absolute; it can be restricted when its exercise is harmful to the public interest.

In the case of obscene material, a difficult question arises. The First Amendment guarantees freedom of speech unless the particular speech in question creates a clear and present danger. Congress, or a state legislature, then has the right to prevent or put a stop to the speech in question. In the case of obscenity, however, it is impossible to show whether or not this standard applies. Lawyers arguing on behalf of the suppression of obscene material contend that it is harmful to children. And, the lawyers say, in adults obscene material is responsible for serious antisocial behavior. Lawyers arguing on the other side deny the existence of any convincing evidence to support this theory.

In 1957 the Supreme Court of the United States attempted to resolve the problem. The Court declared that because obscenity was not historically understood to be covered by free speech, it would be unnecessary to evaluate allegedly obscene material on the basis of the "clear and present danger" standard. The only problem would be to determine whether the material in question actually was obscene or not.

The test used by the Court to make this decision was whether the book, film, magazine, or whatever appealed primarily to a prurient, or lustful, interest in sex.

After some years, it became obvious that this standard was too vague to work. Therefore, in 1973, in a 5-4 decision, the Court's majority agreed to new guidelines that, it hoped, would prove more specific. The purpose was to enable states to enact more precisely defined statutes and thus to resolve the problem of obscene materials once and for all.

The Court's new test would permit states to bar material that "appeals to the prurient interest in sex, which portrays sexual conduct in a patently offensive way, and which, taken as a whole, does not have serious literary, artistic, political or scientific value." The decision stated that the question of what was offensive could be decided according to local and not national standards.

The obscenity issue is an excellent example of the complex problems that confront a democratic society. Many people who are opposed to censorship argue that despite the requirement that legislatures draw up statutes in unmistakably clear language, the new decision is as vague as the preceding ones.

For instance, the phrase "patently offensive" allows for a wide variety of reactions. And if a particular book were found by someone to be offensive, that person would be unlikely to think the book had any serious value. Thus, the language of the decision seems to require negative findings on three separate points. But, in reality, it requires only that certain material be regarded as offensive.

Furthermore, the decision requires that the material have "serious" value. Some lawyers argue that this standard is much too severe. It might result in the suppression of books and films that have only "slight" value but that are still entitled to constitutional protection. In addition, the standard of seriousness raises the question of the burden of proof. Because it's always difficult to demonstrate something's value, this requirement could make it extremely hard for a bookseller or theater owner to win his or her case.

Finally, civil libertarians contend that the community-standards rule is confusing. What is offensive in one community—and it's even difficult to define "community"—may very well be inoffensive in another. Thus, the owner of a theater would have no way of knowing in advance whether or not to show a particular film. If he did, he might run the risk of prosecution; if he didn't, he might deprive himself of legitimate revenue for no reason.

Perhaps the core of the problem here—as with

capital punishment—is that when conflicts arise in society, they're often attended by very strong feelings on both sides. Practical decisions must be made in the absence of sufficient evidence. Those people who are in favor of some kind of censorship or restriction of obscene material take a sensible position in many cases. They are unable to prove that obscene material is in any way harmful, but that doesn't necessarily mean they're wrong in thinking it is so. For instance, it is certainly possible that the easy availability of pornographic literature has harmful effects— particularly on impressionable children. And to say that children needn't be exposed to it is, perhaps, unrealistic: If it's around, they'll get their hands on it. The inability of the Supreme Court to deal effectively with the matter of obscenity suggests the complexity of the issues involved. What is at stake is a question that subtly and importantly affects the quality of life in American society.

In your view, should society outlaw the distribution of pornographic books and films? Or would that be an improper restriction on individual freedom? What arguments would you advance to support or deny society's right and responsibility to censor books and films? If society should act, how can it establish what's obscene? And what about the issue of "redeeming social value," that is, the "serious literary, artistic, political, or scientific value" which might justify obscene works? How could such value be established?

Of all visible things, the world is the greatest; of all invisible, the greatest is God. But, that the world is, we see; that God is, we believe.

SAINT AUGUSTINE

A wise man . . . proportions his belief to the evidence.

DAVID HUME

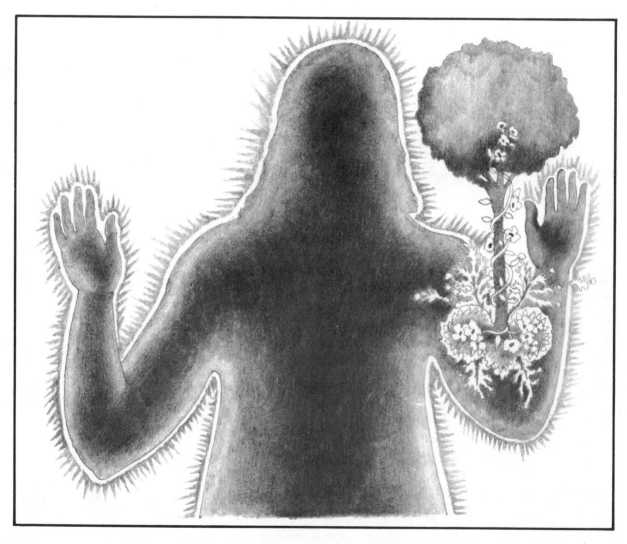

Chapter 6

RELIGION
Insight and Evidence

Chapter Survey

The Philosophy of Religion

What is the distinction between a "problem" and a "mystery"?

Is scientific objectivity possible in the philosophy of religion?

Definitions of Religion

Can religion be defined?

What does religious experience mean?

Does religious experience transcend understanding?

Notions of God

Do all the ways of understanding God have something in common?

Is God in the world or beyond it?

The "Death of God"

Which "God" is absent, and how does it affect modern life?

What kind of God did Nietzsche say had to die?

How do we distinguish between the sacred and the profane?

Three Interpretations of the "Real" God

How is God a projection of human desires, according to Feuerbach?

How, in Tillich's view, is "God above God"?

According to Otto, how is our experience of the divine different from other experiences?

Two Types of Faith and Their Relation to Knowledge

What are Buber's two types of faith?

How does Hick's analysis of significance and interpretation relate to his understanding of faith?

What are Kierkegaard's three stages?

What does Kierkegaard mean by the "leap" of faith?

William James
1842–1910

"The gods we stand by are the gods we need and can use, the gods whose demands on us are reinforcements of our demands on ourselves and on one another."

Although few have done more than he did to shape American thought, William James never conformed to the popular image of a philosophy professor. George Santayana wrote that many people "could not quite swallow a private gentleman who dabbled in hypnotism, frequented mediums, didn't talk like a book and didn't write like a book, except like one of his own. Even his pupils, attached as they invariably were to his person, felt some doubts about the profundity of one who was so very natural, and who after some interruption during a lecture—and he said life was a series of interruptions—would slap his forehead and ask the man in the front row, 'What was I talking about?'" All the same, it's largely due to his popular style that James' "pragmatism" gained currency.

"The whole function of philosophy," James wrote, *"ought to be to find out what definite difference it will make to you and me, at definite instants of our life, if this world-formula or that world-formula be the true one." Pragmatism, in his view, was first of all a method for resolving philosophical disputes by examining the practical consequences of hypothetical options. He described the pragmatic method as* "The attitude of looking away from first things, principles, 'categories,' supposed necessities; and of looking towards last things, fruits, consequences, facts."

Pragmatism, however, was more than just a method. It was also a theory of truth. To the traditional notion of true ideas as copies of reality, James preferred a more dynamic conception. He maintained that pragmatism "converts

the absolutely empty notion of a static relation of 'correspondence' . . . between our minds and reality, into that of a rich and active commerce . . . between particular thoughts of ours, and the great universe of other experiences in which they play their parts and have their uses." For James, true ideas are simply those that "work," that "pay," that respond to practical concerns and resolve practical problems. "The truth of an idea," he insisted, "is not a stagnant property in it. Truth happens *to an idea. It* becomes *true, is* made *true by events."*

James also developed a pragmatic philosophy of religion. In his major

work on this subject, The Varieties of Religious Experience, he investigated the psychology of belief—he was a psychological theorist of unusual penetration—and in his popular essay "The Will to Believe," he proposed "a defense of our right to adopt a believing attitude in religious matters." Although he remained an agnostic and although he recognized that religious belief may offer people a "moral holiday" from the urgent problems of this world, James considered faith to be at least "a genuine option." In its defense he argued that where the intellect could not decide, the will could intervene. Weighing the hope for truth and the fear of error, he wrote, "Dupery for dupery, what proof is there that dupery through hope is so much worse than dupery through fear? . . . If religion be true and the evidence for it be still insufficient, I do not wish . . . to forfeit my sole chance in life of getting upon the winning side—that chance depending, of course, on my willingness to run the risk of acting as if my passional need of taking the world religiously might be prophetic and right."

In his psychological investigation of religious experience as well as in his philosophical analysis of the logical grounds for belief, James was impartial and open-minded. His life and his work both testify, however, to his deep and lasting concern with the religious dimension of human existence.

RELIGION

The Philosophy of Religion

Many people study religion as if it were a problem capable of being fully resolved. If we begin with this idea in mind we soon become involved in gathering facts about what people believe and do. We compare documents and scriptures, and we treat the subject matter (doctrines, rituals, prayers, religious experiences) as if it were just like any other area of study. This is precisely the kind of information that anthropologists, sociologists, psychologists, historians, and other social scientists have gathered about the religions of the world. Because philosophers do not think about questions in a vacuum, they depend on such information to form the foundations for their own explorations. It is the beginning, though, and not the end of questioning.

Philosophers are not content with simply describing what people experience as religious. The sciences of religion do this. Nor are philosophers content with accepting as true what religious people believe just because they believe it. Philosophy cannot accept what has been "revealed" through the scriptures or through tradition as a given without question. Actually, philosophers of religion are in an awkward position. Believers often condemn them for their lack of faith and social scientists, for not sticking to the facts. The issue, however, is whether a philosophic approach to religion can further our understanding of an aspect of human experience. Philosophers say that it can. Indeed, the very subject itself calls for a philosophic understanding.

The French existentialist philosopher Gabriel Marcel has made a distinction that is helpful here. He differentiates between "problem" and "mystery." When we encounter either, our attention is captured, but our powers of understanding and explanation are baffled. Problems, such as those in math, can be complex, but we are convinced that an answer can be found if only we work long enough and hard enough to find it. If we can figure out the best way to ask the question and the best way to look for an

What is the distinction between a "problem" and a "mystery"?

193

answer, we have a good start on finding the solution. But mysteries, such as God, are not explainable at any time—not when they're first encountered and not even in the future. Any reflection on them, and there can be much of that, leads to our being more and more overwhelmed.

Marcel uses the word "mystery" quite differently, then, from the way we would understand the word in the detective novel. Sherlock Holmes and Ellery Queen have only to apply their trained minds to tracking down the clues and piecing them together to be assured of a resolution to the whodunit. If the crime appears insoluble it's because the detective doesn't have enough information. In the popular sense, "mystery" means a lack of knowledge or an insufficient amount of it. In Marcel's sense, "mystery" is the impossibility of ever exhaustively explaining the phenomenon at hand.

As philosophers of religion we must begin with the assumption that some religious issues *may* be mysteries. Our intellect may not be able to contain or comprehend the immensity of all that might be involved. And so what must the philosophy of religion try to do? Our discussion in this chapter will deal with three of the many issues of interest to philosophers of religion. But these three are basic ones: "What is religion?" "Who or what is God?" "What is faith?"

If we were to begin our questions about religion as if it were a "problem," we would immediately be involved in gathering facts. The resulting descriptions of what people believe and do would show how their religion might be viewed by an "outsider." If we approached religion as an "insider," we would adopt a believer's position, accepting what has been revealed. In the latter case, the application of a rational method to the content of faith would result in theology, not in the philosophy of religion. Theology is not identical with religion because, like philosophy, it is theoretical and deals with questions of reason and understanding. If a theologian does not live according to a certain set of commitments and practices, then he is not "religious," even if he has devoted his entire life to understanding what those commitments and practices mean.

The philosophy of religion evaluates all the information it can obtain from both points of view; it explores the relationship between religion and life and puts it together in some pattern. It is open to religious experience, but it does not argue a particular viewpoint on what life is all about from the perspective of any specific religious tradition. The challenge is to make sense of information available through thought, or feeling, or desire, or any other source.

Is scientific objectivity possible in the philosophy of religion?

As an area of philosophic inquiry, religion could be investigated in accordance with any philosophic method. We could analyze religion according to the same criteria we apply in the sciences, trying to remain as objective and detached about the entire matter as we would be in a laboratory. We would then take apart the statements and actions of religious people by relying upon observation and logic. Twentieth century philosophers whose main concerns are with verification and language generally adopt this approach.

We might also contend that objectivity is not realistically possible, especially in religion. This position might lead us to argue, as the existentialists do, that full weight must be given to the subjective side of our experience. Perhaps the commitment of faith is also a kind of knowing, but one different from reason. Perhaps faith provides a kind of "proof" for God's existence that is not available through logic. Philosophy can and does evaluate these claims.

In the following pages we'll consider what religion is, a consideration that will also involve our investigating notions of God, which are the focus of religious experiences and statements, and the relation between faith and knowledge. We'll use insights drawn from the perspectives of both the "outsider" and the "insider." We will give reason and experience and objectivity and subjectivity weight as factors both in religion itself and in our approach to it.

It is interesting to note that despite the differences between the objectivist and the subjectivist approaches to religion (as exemplified in the positivist and the existentialist positions), they agree on one very basic point. This agreement provides a vital clue for beginning to understand what religion is.

Viewpoint

Where the problem aspect prevails one solution follows another: where one ends, the other begins. There is a rectilinear progress of successive mental views or ideal perspectives, of different ways of conceptualizing the object. And if one solution is incomplete, as is always the case, it is replaced *by its successor. It is as when the landscape changes and scene succeeds to scene as the traveler proceeds on his way. Similarly the mind is on the move. Progress of this kind is progress by substitution.*

On the other hand, where the mystery aspect prevails the intellect has to penetrate more and more deeply the same *object. The mind is stationary turning around a fixed point. Or rather it pierces further and further into the same depth. This is progress in the same place, progress by deepening.*

JACQUES MARITAIN, A Preface to Metaphysics

Our concern may be with the object of religious belief or with the subject of religious experience, but it is impossible to think of one without considering the other. Does it make sense to discuss faith without discussing the subject or self who has the faith? Or without discussing the object that the self has faith in?

This suggests an idea that is particularly important for understanding religion—the idea that people define themselves through their relations with those persons and things that concern them. The religious phenomenon makes it clear that, apart from the question whether their claims are true, religious persons are convinced that something is going on *between* themselves and someone or something that is not themselves. Most significant is the *way* in which persons are related to what is important to them, whether it is a vocation, another human being, society, or God. Let's try to define religion. Perhaps then the importance of relatedness will be more clear.

Definitions of Religion

Can religion be defined?

It has often been observed that the word "religion" derives from the Latin *religio,* which means "to bind." A religious person might say that the word implies a union, a completeness, a whole, and without religion we are separated from what makes us fully human. That person might also say an awareness of the sacred is part of being human. Another person might say, however, that "binding" is something confining, trapping, tying us down. All the do's and don'ts of institutional religion limit our freedom.

Can we make such generalizations? Is it possible to talk about "religion" as opposed to discussing specific "religion*s*?" Are the institutional manifestations of religious belief and practice more or less basic to what religion is? But perhaps there is a religious attitude that exists entirely apart from any particular church. Philosophers agree to disagree on one single definition of what religion is; rather, they point to characteristic features and common concerns that may serve to describe religion.

We hesitate to define religion rigidly. If, as philosophers, we begin with a preconceived idea of a particular thing, we might overlook something that does not conform to the preestablished definition, and it may be the very thing we're looking for! Understanding what religion is might become impossible because we would find only what our initial concept allowed us to see. Suppose we began with a definition such as "Religion is a way of life and a body of beliefs centering about the experience of a single deity." This definition would eliminate many of the world's religions. We could also propose definitions that identify religion with faith, reason, feeling, psychological states, or social structure. But focusing on just one possibility could prevent us from seeing what religion is. It seems more sensible to recognize that religion is complex and may involve many factors.

Religion involves thought and ideas, for instance, but it also involves traditions, prayer, ritual, and, in some of its manifestations, institutions. More than just giving intellectual assent to a series of propositions or doctrines, religion involves doing: living and acting in accord with certain convictions, even those convictions that are difficult to express in language. But doing what? Thinking what? Isn't there any basic element we can discover that is held in common by all the particular religions in the history of humanity?

Many attempts have been made to find such a focal point. A feeling of dependence, a sense of moral duty, affirmation of belief in God, observance of ritual and prayer, and fear of the unknown have all been proposed as the essence of religiousness. None has been sufficient because each offers only a particular and partial explanation.

Moreover, religion can be expressed in many ways. Some religions emphasize community; some, the individual. Some emphasize pomp and ritual; some do not. Religion has been used to justify revolution and to maintain the status quo, to restrict and to liberate human potential. No two religions are identical. There simply does not appear to be one characteristic common to all forms of religion. Thus, no rigid, final definition of religion seems possible.

Most attempts by philosophers to identify characteristics that different religions share involve harmonizing two points of view. Some philosophers emphasize experience, the subjective, empirical side of religion. Others emphasize the rational, cognitive side of religion. Recognizing that still others focus on the relation between the two, let's look more closely at these different points of view.

Experience itself is a concept that philosophers have analyzed and debated at length. It has traditionally been associated with empirical

What does religious experience mean?

philosophers like John Locke and David Hume, and, as a result, it is often associated with sense data, observable objects, and the particular thing as opposed to the universal idea. Another option, however, has been proposed by those sometimes called "radical empiricists," first among whom is William James, whose *Varieties of Religious Experience* is a classic study in this field. For such philosophers, experience is not limited to the senses or to the individual object, but is something much more inclusive. It is in fact the relationships that exist between ourselves and all that we encounter in our world. We do not possess it ready-made nor do we discover it in a completed form; it is a process, a happening.

James consequently speaks of religion as experience, but of a special kind. For him, religion is "the feelings, acts, and experiences of individual men in their solitude, so far as they apprehend themselves to stand in relation to whatever they may consider the divine." He continues that since this relation "may be either moral, physical, or ritual, it is evident that out of religion in the sense in which we take it, theologies, philosophies, and ecclesiastical organizations may secondarily grow." Religion as manifested in religious experience is something that evidences a relationship or direction human beings have toward something other than the self.

But those philosophers who emphasize the cognitive, or knowing, aspect of religion have to be heard too. It's all well and good to say that we have religious experiences, but isn't our thinking also part of our human experience? Doesn't it seem to make sense that experience wouldn't be as important for us if we didn't reflect on what it meant? A child may be taught a prayer, which he or she recites at bedtime. This prayer may provide a sense of well-being. And at some point the child may begin thinking about the meaning of the prayer and the responses he or she has to it. We often do things automatically or without being fully aware of what or even why we're doing them. We may never reflect on what we do. But thought can enhance the experience of prayer or it can lead us to question our beliefs.

One way to see how reason has influenced religion is to look at what happened in the ancient world. The peoples living around the Mediterranean had many different gods. The fourth century B.C. historian Xenophon said the ideas of these gods were always based on what an individual culture had accustomed its people to believe. When trade and travel exposed societies to one anothers' beliefs, they began questioning their own. For example, how could all the accounts of the world's creation be true? Which is better, more inclusive, more rational?

In the Christian tradition, some philosophers thought we could do more than simply use our reason to examine and question our beliefs. St. Anselm was one of the medieval theologians who believed we could actually prove God's existence through the use of reason alone. He also believed this was a way to know God more fully. He said that since we possess the concept of God, God must necessarily exist. Anselm reasoned that it makes no sense to discuss a perfect being (God) and then to question its existence. A perfect being, to be perfect, must exist. A nonexistent being certainly wouldn't be perfect, because it would lack something, namely, existence! Many modern philosophers think this argument is circular, that it assumes what it tries to prove. Others question whether "existence" can be considered an attribute like "perfection." The argument does, in any case, represent an attempt to explore the contents of faith rationally.

Given the fact that human beings have minds and think, it is awkward to argue that religion should not make sense, that there should be no pattern or order to it. The real issue, and one that was pointed out as early as Plato, is just how much religion must conform to understanding. If we demand that religion remain consistently rational at all times, then we arbitrarily limit it to what the human mind can structure and comprehend. If by chance it is more than that, there's no way we could explore that possibility because we've already limited what it could be to what we can understand. We can leave open the possibility that the significance and the experience of religion may transcend our understanding, at least in some ways. But then we must confront the question of how we can "know" what our reason can never fully grasp.

Does religious experience transcend understanding?

Religion seems to be, then, a "mystery" in Marcel's sense. It is something we are continually learning more and more about, something we can penetrate more and more deeply, something that holds our interest and concern, but something we haven't and possibly can't exhaust.

But what provides the focal point for religious experience and thought? If we are experiencing or thinking about something other than ourselves, what is it we have experience *of*? What are we thinking *about*? These questions are made more difficult still by the fact that religious language is problematic. Could it be that because our language is a human instrument it is impossible for us to talk about "the other" in any but human terms? We will confront this difficulty as we attempt in the next section to establish what might possibly be meant by the word "God."

Notions of God

There are as many ways to define "God" as there are to define religion. Indeed, it's common to classify actual and historical religions by the number of gods they posit. Thus we have polytheistic religions, which assert the existence of many gods; henotheistic religions, which hold that although there are many gods one is the most important; and monotheistic religions,

Do all the ways of understanding God have something in common?

in which there is only one God. For other students of religion and religions, however, the major point of interest is the kind of being God is. Here we have theism, in which there is a personal God who is the Creator; deism, whose God is so removed from creation that He becomes a kind of abstract principle simply watching over things as they go along on their own; and pantheism, which is just the opposite of deism: God is the all, and everything that exists is God, and God is everything that exists. There's also humanism, in which God is identified with human beings, "God" being merely man's worship of his own ideals; and religious naturalism, in which God is the principle or process responsible for meaning and value in the world. Is there some way to organize these different notions of God so that we can see what they have in common and where they differ?

Notions of God can be analyzed along the same lines as ideas of religion. We can investigate our experiences as well as our conceptions of God. A distinction between two ways of understanding and experiencing the divine may be useful at this point. God may be seen either as "immanent" (meaning "within the world") or as "transcendent" (meaning "beyond or above the world"). If God is conceived of as immanent, the distinction between God and the world or nature seems to disappear. And if God is conceived of as transcendent, then God seems to vanish over the horizon.

Is God in the world or beyond it?

These problems have occupied John Macquarrie, an existentialist philosopher and theologian. He has attempted to organize the approaches of various world religions along a continuum of immanence and transcendence. For instance, Christianity, according to Macquarrie, attempts to keep a balance between the ideas of God's presence (immanence) and God's absence (transcendence) such that the divine is both in and beyond this world. The tension between the two partially explains why Christianity can take on so many different forms. The many different denominations and sects emphasize varying degrees of God's presence or absence or the manner in which this presence or absence is manifested. The two sides to

---

Viewpoint

The first God, the rational God, is the projection to the outward infinite of man as he is by definition—that is to say, of the abstract man, of the man no-man; the other God, the God of feeling and volition, is the projection to the inward infinite of man as he is by life, of the concrete man, the man of flesh and bone.

MIGUEL DE UNAMUNO, Tragic Sense of Life

Christianity are reflected in the strong experiential strain in its mystical tradition and in the equally strong rational strain seen in the elaborate systems of doctrine and dogma in the theologies of the West.

Those forms of religion that lie in the tradition of immanence tend in varying degrees to see the divine as one with nature. If God and nature are identical (as they are in pantheism, where nature is a manifestation of the divine), then to speak of God at all seems superfluous. The only quarrel seems to be over what name you want to give to the "real world." The seventeenth century philosopher Baruch Spinoza has been labeled both an atheist (one who denies the existence of God) *and* a believer. He thought reality was all one "substance," and he called it God or Nature interchangeably. This tendency, to say that nature is all there is and all we can possibly know, often leads to the claim that there is no "super" natural. And even if there were, how could we gain access to it? "God," a useless term, points to nothing beyond the realm of what science can more adequately account for as nature.

Emphasizing the transcendence of God has equally important consequences. If we follow the tradition that claims the divine is wholly other than the natural world, then we must account for the connection between God and the world. How could we ever come in contact with the divine, ever know it, if there were not some connection? The idea of a God-Man, which appears in many religious traditions, is an attempt to resolve just such a difficulty. Such a being is both immanent and transcendent.

Some concepts of "God" we are well rid of, however. Like anything else that can become part of human experience, "God" can be misconstrued. What we have to look at very carefully is which gods are indispensable and which are not as far as the believer is concerned. The god who functions as an explanation for whatever is left unresolved in a philosopher's system surely wouldn't be missed, except, perhaps, by that philosopher. Neither would angry and unpredictable tyrant gods, nor the anthropomorphized white-bearded-father-figure-in-the-sky we are all familiar with. And then there is the crutch god who so readily appears whenever the going gets rough and promptly disappears as soon as things are under control again! Or what about the filling-station god who seems never to run out of whatever spiritual fuel we need to fill up on to get us through whatever needs to be done? However, the disappearance of the "living God," a God alive and present to us is another story. Our concern at this point is more with the believer's experience than with "God" as a troublesome word to be defined. Achieving clarity on how terms are used is an important philosophical activity, but for the believer God is important not as a concept but as a source of salvation or spiritual comfort.

It is because this "living God" is significant to the believer that the cover story in *Time* magazine during Easter week a few years ago caused such a furor. Echoing the nineteenth century German philosopher Friedrich Nietzsche, *Time* proclaimed that "God is dead." If this is the case, why should we bother about God at all? Isn't a postmortem a waste of time?

The "Death of God"

Perhaps an investigation of what is meant by the "death of God" will reveal why some notion of God is central to almost all forms of religion. In the West that God was dead was first proclaimed in the last century. Many still deny that this is so, and why they do is extremely important.

How would the assumption of God's existence or nonexistence affect how we see ourselves? Others? Suffering? Evil? Our goals in life? For some, seeing the world and people as the creation of a divine agency has enhanced the value of human life. Suffering, such as that caused by disease, war, or the loss of loved ones, has variously been understood as part of the divine plan or as a trial to be undergone, a lesson in "making it on our own." Thus, suffering may acquire meaning. Harmonious family and community relations, as well as productive work, have long been sanctioned by religions. To do without God, in Christianity, for example, is to do without the promise of an afterlife or salvation. To proclaim God dead in any religion suggests that this life may have no meaning or justification. We are simply born, we struggle, and then we die. Our suffering seems to have no final validation. Without God we are thus entirely alone. Clearly, whatever we mean by "God" is of central importance to the philosophical investigation of what it means to live with others in the world.

What kind of God did Nietzsche say had to die?

Our culture has been developing the story of how its God died for hundreds of years now. But it was Nietzsche, through his spokesman Zarathustra, who first wrote that God is dead. The problem, as Nietzsche saw it, was that we had lost the meaning and values given to us by some

---

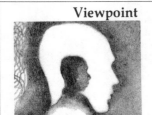

Viewpoint

717. "You can't hear God speak to someone else, you can hear him only if you are being addressed." That is a grammatical remark.

LUDWIG WITTGENSTEIN, *Zettel*

supernatural source, leaving us with the task of creating our own value and meaning. We have to learn to do without the support once provided by the dead religion. But only a very special person, whom Nietzsche called a superman or overman, is able to accomplish this.

A God who made man and gave him values to live by is one too much involved in human affairs. Human beings are prevented from realizing their full potential by themselves. Religion thus keeps us from asking the question "What is the meaning of our lives?" With God out of the way, we must face the terrifying possibility that life is meaningless—and then go on from there. Nietzsche felt that such a God *had* to die, for we had to take "revenge on this witness."

The death of God, then, was no accident. Nietzsche's fictitious prophet, Zarathustra, wondered how it was possible "for one not to have heard of God's death," and by the end of the story he came to realize that the reason his proclamation had not been understood by those who heard him is that the "dreadful occurrence is still on its way." Zarathustra has in fact come "too early."

The idea of the death of God began to acquire momentum for Christianity when Nietzsche wrote of it. His manner of writing philosophy differed from that of the majority of nineteenth century philosophers. Nietzsche did not try to construct a formal system to account for the source, nature, and meaning of the universe and history. Rather, he reacted against this tendency and presented instead issues of passionate concern, such as the meaning of morality and of God. But the idea of the death of God was not entirely original with Nietzsche. It had a long history, integral to the history of religions. God's death has been related in Egyptian, Phrygian, and Syrian religious myths, to mention only a few. But why? What does it mean for a god to die, and why is it so important for the religious mind?

Which "God" is absent, and how does it affect modern life?

John Dunne of the University of Notre Dame suggests that what is common to all stories of God's death is our human fear of death. The only way we can accept death is if we believe that everything, including God, must die. The danger of course is that death itself is worshipped and becomes a "god." Perhaps the Charles Manson cult murders are an example of this. One's attitude toward death has profound implications for the quality of human life, as we shall see later in this book. We human beings are faced with the same questions about the meaning and significance of our existence whether "God" is present or absent!

Since Nietzsche's time, history relates a continuing growth in the human capacity to take charge of everything in our world. We have controlled our environment and influenced the affairs of other nations; we have manipulated the behavior of other human beings. We have, in short, taken over what appears on the surface to have been the function of earlier gods. Yet, many today sense that something has gone amiss. Even Nietzsche was concerned. He believed God's death opened the way for us to affirm life rather than negate it as he saw the Christian tradition having done. But it also meant the advent of wars and the dissolution of distinctions between man and animal. As the culmination of God's creation human beings had enjoyed a special status higher than the animals. Nietzsche asks if we're really any better.

The death of God means man is isolated; God no longer touches our experience. We are no longer "related." In essence, human beings become "alienated." This is not, however, something peculiar to Christian culture. It is basic to religion as a whole. In religious terminology, the word "sin" designates just such separation. Perhaps if we turn to an historian of religion who speaks specifically of this topic we can understand more fully what is at stake.

How do we distinguish between the sacred and the profane?

In his classic study, *The Sacred and the Profane,* Mircea Eliade examines and contrasts the experience of religious and secular human beings. Both live in the world, but they perceive this world very differently. The "profane" world, in Eliade's understanding, is one in which we are in control of objects. It is the "natural world." Even though the objects and things in our experience might resist us, we can in the end manipulate them and influence what happens in the world. It is just such a world, he feels, that modern people live in: a desacralized universe. It is a world of strip mines, oil rigs, and life-prolonging devices. In such a situation no "true orientation is possible, for the fixed point no longer enjoys a unique ontological status," a special place in the order of being.

The sacred world, on the contrary, presents us with things we do not control, things that produce a response of wonder or awe. It is the manifestation of a different order from the "natural" order. Eliade explains that "by manifesting the sacred, any object becomes *something else,* yet it continues to remain *itself.*" In the Bible, no one thought of mowing down the "burning bush" in which the angel of the Lord appeared to Moses. The bush came to represent something more than itself. Nature can represent the divine, and thus it is "never only natural" for the religious person.

Eliade's study suggests a way of talking about both this world and what is not this world, a distinction that avoids making us choose between the two. We can live in the world as alienated beings or we can have an open relationship to it. The basic presupposition of Eliade's approach is that neither we as subjects nor what is not us (the object, or what demands our attention) are necessarily religious or sacred. Rather, it is the way subjects and objects are related that counts because the "way" is either sacred or profane.

Events and objects of our experience can be sacred, then, depending on our relation to them. But how do we identify the sacred in the midst of the profane? Eliade maintained that religious images and symbols help us locate the sacred. They provide models for organizing experience.

Through religious symbols we can arrange things, or our perceptions of things, so they acquire meaning. Some primitive cultures see generation and childbirth as human versions of what takes place as seeds germinate in the earth or as trees flower. Human events can thus become sacred, can become symbols, of a larger divine process.

The kind of control implied in this function of symbols is not, however, like that of technology. It seeks not to manipulate but to liberate. Symbols

---

Viewpoint

His form stanzas hang like hives in hell
Or what hell was, since now both heaven and hell
Are one, and here, O terra infidel.

The fault lies with an over-human god,
Who by sympathy has made himself a man
And is not to be distinguished, when we cry

Because we suffer, our oldest parent, peer
Of the populace of the heart, the reddest lord,
Who has gone before us in experience.

If only he would not pity us so much,
Weaken our fate, relieve us of woe both great
And small, a constant fellow of destiny,

A too, too human god, self-pity's kin
And uncourageous genesis . . . It seems
As if the health of the world might be enough.

It seems as if the honey of common summer
Might be enough, as if the golden combs
Were part of a sustenance itself enough,

As if hell, so modified, had disappeared,
As if pain, no longer satanic mimicry,
Could be borne, as if we were sure to find our way.

WALLACE STEVENS, "Esthétique de Mal"

mark an attempt to let the thing or event reveal itself and reveal our relation to a transcendent order.

What does this tell us about the "irrelevance" of God in modern thought and modern life? John Warwick Montgomery argues that the difficulty is a case of the wrong corpse. It is man, not God, who is dead. Human beings have become manipulated by what they manipulate. We're mourning our own failure to do what we felt God did not do: give meaning and significance to life. In making God too immanent, too closely identified with the secular, we are left with only our own isolation and loneliness, with only the secular world. By emphasizing our own powers of understanding, by assuming we can know everything, we have made God seem superfluous. "Religion," in the sense we have been using the term here, exists only as some vital living dimension between ourselves and the divine. It would be impossible without positing some relationship between subjects.

Three Interpretations of the "Real" God

How is God a projection of human desires, according to Feuerbach?

A number of philosophers represent the view that God is really man in exaggerated form. Auguste Comte's positivism was surely one of the most significant influences on the development of this idea. But the nineteenth century philosopher Ludwig Feuerbach articulated the view in great detail in *The Essence of Christianity*. Feuerbach was born about forty years before Nietzsche, and religious problems remained a central concern for him throughout his philosophic career. Like Nietzsche later, Feuerbach disliked the emphasis in the philosophy of his time on constructing grand systems to account for the origin and structure of reality. He wanted philosophy to become associated with the empirical sciences and to return to the everyday world. Because he believed the world is human-centered, he argued that philosophy should be based on anthropology and physiology.

As the most perfect being in creation, man becomes Feuerbach's ideal. Beginning with this perspective, religion subsequently becomes just one form of human thought and activity. But it is the one responsible for raising man above the animals. Religion is, then, "the dream of the human mind." Human beings are conscious not of a limited nature, but of an infinite one. By means of our thought process we are "self-transcending"; we can project all kinds of ideas of what we might become. Nothing, then, is really supernatural because everything is basically a human affair.

In Feuerbach's view God thus becomes identical with human beings. We "project" our own ideas, ideals, values, and aspirations—righteousness, justice, love, knowledge—onto the object of worship. The projected ideal human image becomes the subject of religion. As Feuerbach puts it, "What man himself is not and would like to be he imagines as existing in his gods; divinities are human desires, imagined as if they had been realized and transformed into real beings."

What Feuerbach attempted to do in *The Essence of Christianity* was "unmask" Christian belief. Philosophy's duty is to destroy illusions. The symbols, doctrines, myths, and rituals of religion actually tell us more about human beings, he held, than about some object or person that humans worship. If all the good qualities in human beings are "projected" to become "God," as Feuerbach maintained, then human beings must be alienated from themselves. If people were at one with themselves and fulfilled, the projection would not be necessary. Those who reject the unqualified thesis that God is dead argue that it is "God-as-projected-man" who has died.

Human reason led Feuerbach to his conclusion that God is a projection of human desires. But does this mean that reason has no place in "real" religion, that we must rely solely on "religious experiences" as self-validating? Philosophers would be loathe to entertain such an idea. After all, both reason and experience are part of what it means to be human, and both have a role to play in religious life. It is also true that when subjectivity is overemphasized, man becomes everything; when objectivity is over-emphasized, technology becomes important, and things manipulate us as much as we manipulate them. In either case, we are guilty of philosophical dishonesty.

Philosophers have emphasized personal experience since the nineteenth century. By examining its relationship to religion and religious knowledge, we will be led, before long, into considerations of the traditional function of reason in religion. We will ask whether reason can be a way of "knowing" God.

Religious people are often challenged by doubters to substantiate their views of life and their belief in God. They frequently respond the way most of us would if we were asked to verify statements such as, "The sky is blue." To determine the truth or falsity of this statement we turn to the testimony of experience. But is the experience we have of the sacred the same kind we have of a stone, say, or a book, or a blue sky? That question has prompted the work of many thinkers; we'll consider two of them here. Paul Tillich argued that our experience of God is the experience of just what is most basic and fundamental to all our existence. When we are experiencing an "ultimate concern," we are experiencing "the gound of being," or God. Rudolph Otto argues that religious experience is unlike any other experi-ence. It is an encounter with something entirely "other" than the everyday realm. And both thinkers, in spite of their differences, hold that religious experience can't be verified the same way as our experience of skies, stones, or books. We can't observe or touch the object of religious experience and

How, in Tillich's view, is "God above God"?

cognition. Religion thus does not and cannot have the same status as science; we cannot use the same procedures to "prove" what is "known."

Tillich elaborates his view of religious experience or concern by explaining how people characterize their God. Knowing God as an ultimate concern is a state experienced by all human beings, "whatever the content of the concern might be." The individual who worships the idea of the nation, for instance, or social standing and material possessions, evidences an ultimate concern, however far away from correctly viewing God that individual may be.

In *Systematic Theology,* Tillich organizes the possible conceptions of God into three basic types. For him, the confusion we experience today about the meaning of God is due to the religious tradition that has viewed God as a being; it "separates God as a being, the highest being, from all other beings, alongside and above which he has his existence." This results in turning God into an object that can be manipulated (as in magic), or talked to, or even killed. The first type of God is theistic, a transcendent, personal Creator. It easily becomes anthropomorphic, and we attribute human characteristics to it, seeing it as a larger, more powerful human being.

The second conception identifies God with the universe, "with its essence or with special powers within it." Here God is immanent and is often viewed as being manifested in the natural and material world. Neither of these meanings is appropriate, in Tillich's view. He proposes a third.

For Tillich, God really is the "ground of being" rather than nature or one particular being. As the ground of being, God "infinitely transcends that of which he is the ground." God also transcends all imagery we use to characterize Him. For example, a big stumbling block for our understanding of God, Tillich holds, is the spatial imagery theism and naturalism use. Both employ the prepositions "in" and "above," and these preclude the possibility of expressing the true relation between the world and God, which "certainly is not spatial."

Since God is "being itself," we could never properly speak of God as "in" or "above" the world. However, God is "nearer" to things and to us than we are to ourselves. "He is their creative ground, here and now, always and everywhere." Thus we avoid the difficulties of either an immanentist or a transcendent view because God is neither a subject nor an object but the basis and ground for both. We also avoid the difficulties of trying to "prove" God's existence because God is being itself, and it seems unnecessary to establish that being exists. Whether or not this argument is circular, we can come to know the "God above God," who is beyond any definition or limit that human beings have made ever since they began to wonder who or what their "ultimate concerns" were all about.

For Rudolph Otto, our experience of the sacred is unique. Our other concerns are not reflections of it, nor are they related to it. But how do we recognize it, never having had any experience of the same kind? Furthermore, how can any knowledge gained in and through such an experience be communicated to anyone else? How can it be integrated into our minds and our lives if to compare it to anything in the everyday realm is to falsify it?

According to Otto, how is our experience of the Divine different from other experiences?

Perhaps a distinction made here will help us understand some of these questions. We can say there are two ways of talking about religious experience. Most of us are familiar with the first, the feeling or emotion that an individual claims is inspired by a divine source. It is something "given" to individuals that they may have prepared themselves to receive but cannot make happen. Under this heading might come what Otto calls the *mysterium tremendum* and the *mysterium fascinans.* The sense of the first results in a feeling of fear and awe. The second results in a feeling of being fascinated by and drawn toward what is encountered, what Otto calls "the numinous." The second has to do with the cognitive aspect of the experience. It's not so much what we feel as what we come to understand and know. In the experience something that we did not know before is revealed, opened up, unveiled to us.

Usually when we think of knowing something we have in mind the possibility at least of being able to check it, to verify it, or test it by some means. If we can test something, we call the results "objective." They do not depend on our personal, "subjective" feelings or reactions. The word "objective" qualifies something outside ourselves, something external, some reality independent of us. "Subjective," on the other hand, refers to something within us, internalized, personal. It does not point to something separate from ourselves.

Viewpoint

Suppose you are walking along the beach and cut your foot on a broken shell. Your senses can verify that your discomfort results from an object different from you. It is objective. Suppose you are at the same beach, this time sitting on a breakwater watching the waves and listening to the roar of the ocean. You begin to hear a rustling behind you and to get an overwhelming sense that someone is about to push you off the breakwater. You turn around and no one is there. The "person" is purely subjective, never having existed outside your imagination. In fact, the person never was "real" apart from your own mind.

Usually we can decide if things are subjective or objective by observing. We check our imagination with our senses. But what happens if we can't see, hear, or touch something but know it's there? This problem doesn't occur exclusively in religious experience. How do psychologists observe motivation? Astronomers, the origin of the universe? Biologists, the evolutionary principle? Or physicists, electricity? In such instances, however, there is some consensus. Scientists can agree that particular standards and criteria of human behavior be applied. This ensures that personal factors (like differences in visual ability) and social factors (like assumptions prevalent in a given culture about why people act as they do) are ruled out. In short, the scientific approach ensures "objectivity."

The reason many critics feel that religion is subjective is because it does not easily or obviously lend itself to the kind of objectivity we are describing. Religions don't seem to agree on what specifically is there; just consider the many conceptions of God we have examined. The critics suggest that the subjectivity of religion makes agreement impossible from the start.

These criticisms pose a serious problem for the philosopher of religion. To accept them would mean accepting that religious experience has no objective cognitive content. The other option is to develop a different way of understanding objectivity and subjectivity. Perhaps scientific objectivity is not the only kind of objectivity. All this has immense importance for the question of whether religious experience yields "knowledge." It is central to how we understand the relation between knowledge and faith.

Two Types of Faith and Their Relation to Knowledge

The question of whether or not there is a God is different from the questions of whether or not, or how, or why people believe there is. Let us now turn our attention to the issue of "faith." How is this phenomenon related to religious experience in particular and human experience in general? How, especially, is it like or unlike our ordinary ways of knowing and believing?

In his book *Two Types of Faith* the Jewish existentialist Martin Buber distinguishes two uses of the term "faith." He argues that the term can denote a cognitive act, an act of knowledge. But it can also refer to an attitude of trust, maintained even when all the "evidence" seems to indicate that such an attitude toward the divine is unfounded. The first use suggests that faith might be directly related to our ordinary experiences of knowing and believing. It also includes the possibility of *not* being able to know, where knowledge remains the most important criteria. The second use is more encompassing and is associated with religious experience.

What are Buber's two types of faith?

The cognitive use of the term "faith" predominated until modern times. Until relatively recently most people argued that "faith" referred to intellectual assent to such propositions as "I believe in . . ." or "I believe that . . ." With the turn to the subjective that characterizes so much modern thought, the emphasis changed. Faith was no longer viewed so much *cognitively* as *conatively*. It became an affair of attitude, feeling, experience, and concern rather than of intellectual assent.

To try to discover the relationship between faith and knowledge, we will look at philosophers who discuss the issue from both the cognitive and the conative points of view. We will ask how each use of the term "faith" relates to other experiences in our everyday life: how cognitive faith relates to how we reason in all areas, not merely about religious questions; and how conative faith relates to how and what we desire in general. Our discussion will focus on the modern philosopher John Hick as an example of the

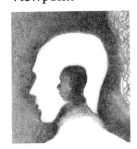

Viewpoint

So we see religious commitment as a total *commitment to the whole universe; something in relation to which argument has only a very odd function; its purpose being to tell such a tale as evokes the "insight," the "discernment" from which the commitment follows as a response. Further, religious commitment is something bound up with key words whose logic no doubt resembles that of the words which characterize personal loyalty as well as that of the axioms of mathematics, and somehow combines features of both, being what might be called "specially resistant" posits, "final" endpoints of explanation, key words suited to the whole job of living— "apex" words.*

IAN T. RAMSEY, Religious Language: An Empirical Placing of Theological Phrases

How does Hick's analysis of significance and interpretation relate to his understanding of faith?

cognitive position. The religious thought of Søren Kierkegaard, a nine-teenth century philosopher, will provide an example of the conative position.

In *Faith and Knowledge,* John Hick attempts to explain how our awareness of God is related to our other cognitions. He remarks that we become conscious of anything in our experience either by experiencing it ourselves or by inferring it from what we have experienced. In other words, we use both experience and reason to become aware. For the believer, however, God is viewed not as someone or something that has been inferred or reasoned to (although rational arguments may be used to support the believer's position) but as a reality that has been experienced in and of itself, something that has entered into the person's life in a concrete way. In Hick's terminology, our knowledge of the divine is "mediated" knowledge. It comes to us in and through our involvement in the world of people and things, the world of everyday life.

Hick argues that such mediated knowledge is something we are all familiar with because it is the way we know everything. It includes two aspects, "significance" and "interpretation," that are interdependent, always occurring together when we are conscious of anything at all in our experience.

What does Hick mean by "significance"? All of us at some point in our lives have had moments when we felt that things were settled, made sense, fit into some whole. We somehow understood what it was all about or we felt there was a comfortable order to our lives. Hick calls this response to living "significance." It's "that fundamental and all-pervasive characteristic of our conscious experience which de facto constitutes it for us as the experience of a 'world' and not of a mere empty void or churning chaos." In fact, when we are conscious of something, we are conscious of significance.

We think of the world, of others, and of the divine as what is familiar to us and what we "know" in some sense. Without being acquainted this way we probably would not be fully attentive to the world or others around us; we would be "spaced out," in a state of psychological disorientation.

But what about the wide diversity of orientations and "significances" that people have toward the world and their place in it? Hick seeks to answer this question with his concept of "interpretation." We couldn't have interpretation if different accounts of what is weren't possible. This does not, however, mean that one position is right and the other wrong. And interpretations can include other interpretations, yet not be identical with them. Take, for example, what you're doing right now, trying to understand the philosophical concepts presented in this book. Because you can read the language you can interpret the content of the book as a discussion on the subject of philosophy. If you could not read English, you might not be able to know what thoughts are in the book, but you would be able to decide what the object is and what it is for. If you had never seen anything written in your entire life, you would have no comprehension of what the object is, or what it is for, much less what it might be about. Still, you could probably guess that it was something man-made.

The significance of the event (reading) and the object (book) is interpreted differently in each of the three examples. None is wrong. The first is simply more adequate or more comprehensive than the second, and the second, more than the third. The most comprehensive interpretation of the significance of what you're doing includes and presupposes the other two. We can say that there are different orders, or layers, of significance, and in each case we have selected what fits in with the world as we experience it at the time.

Hick proposes three main orders of significance that we interpret. These correspond to the realms of nature (or the world), man (or the social order), and God (or the divine). In the physical world we encounter an objective environment to which we have to be related correctly in order to survive. It is significant for us for that reason. The personal human world is one of moral significance where we are "responsible agents, subject to moral obligation" in a realm of relationships. The natural world thus becomes a "stage" for the personal world. Being moral agents entails a specific relation to the natural world. Our sense of right and wrong influences such things as farming, mining, or manufacturing. The same holds true for the divine order. For the religious person, the most encompassing situation of all is that of the relation to God or being in the presence of the divine. It does not exclude our being in the world or our being with others; it is superimposed on them. The first two orders of significance take on a broader meaning by virtue of their being within the all-inclusive order of God's presence. Our relation to the divine influences our sense of right and wrong and our understanding of the natural world.

But is interpretation merely an intellectual process? Hick argues that significance is essentially related to action. No situation or object is really significant if it doesn't make a practical difference to us. For instance, judging from innate ability and past learning experiences, we suspect we can learn to drive a car, or dance, or perhaps even become a surgeon. But we don't find out until we try. It is necessary to act on our interpretations, or evaluate past actions, to determine which are real possibilities.

The big question is how Hick's discussion of the way we acquire a sense of form or meaning in our experience relates to the question of faith and knowledge. After explaining how we come to know the orders of nature and persons, he suggests a further application of the paradigm "of one order of significance superimposed upon and mediated through another." That application is to religious significance, which for the believer is the "total interpretation" necessary to make the most sense of our experience. The believer would maintain that only by interpreting the world and others as mediating a divine presence and purpose do we acquire a complete picture of what is really going on. We gain a perspective that was lacking in the other two levels of significance. A river, for example, does not exist simply as drinking water, or as a means of transportation, or as a source of energy. The religious person may recognize the importance of the river but also see in its beauty the craft of a divine artisan.

Hick implies that what we commonly call "faith" might be a natural extension of how we attribute significance to anything in our experience. It amounts to a "religious perception, or basic act of religious interpretation," a way of seeing not unrelated to other ways of seeing but in a different perspective. It is not something inferred, or a reasoned conclusion, or even a hunch that the divine is there. It is part of our experience itself, including both an encounter with the divine and our consciousness of it. Religion, then, is "not only a way of cognizing but also and no less vitally, a way of living."

In Hick's view, there is similar structure between our "basic convictions in relation to the world, moral responsibility, and divine existence." He does *not* prove that God exists. But if the Divine exists Hick is telling us how it might be known and how our knowledge of it ties in with our other knowledge.

While Hick investigated the cognitive side of faith, Søren Kierkegaard focused on faith as lived experience. Many nineteenth century philosophers were preoccupied with the power of reason and cognition, with the development of philosophy as a science, or with natural and scientific laws—all emphases that have continued to be strong in twentieth-century philosophy. But there was another voice, one speaking with the accents of modern existentialism. Kierkegaard was concerned with concrete, individual experience as opposed to generalities, feeling as opposed to reason, and faith rather than knowledge.

Like his contemporary Feuerbach, Kierkegaard tried to discover the significance of God for human life. But what each saw was very different. Where Feuerbach argued that God was merely a projection of human desires, Kierkegaard argued that the fullness of our humanity could not be understood apart from our relationship to the divine.

Truth, Kierkegaard proposed, was "subjectivity," and this has little to do with analyzing concepts. It is also impossible to make the important decisions in life on the basis of some criterion external to oneself. How could my choice to become a doctor, lawyer, or Christian be made by anyone but me or by anyone else's standards? It is ultimately I who make the decision and take the risk. There is no way to know the "right" thing by referring to some external standard. Nor is there even an internal standard. I must remain "objectively uncertain," yet continue to act. To do otherwise is to lead an inauthentic existence, to be untrue to myself.

Our crucial decisions are necessarily subjective and indeed reveal our uniqueness. We make ourselves into what we are by choosing our way of life at every moment. Kierkegaard says we must be actors in life—taking risks—rather than spectators. And we must accept the uncertainty we live in that causes the "fear and trembling" in which we must work out our salvation. Uncertainty cannot be eliminated; it is part of being finite.

Viewpoint

. . . if the man who asserts that he is seeing God is merely asserting that he is experiencing a peculiar kind of sense-content, then we do not for a moment deny that his assertion may be true. But, ordinarily, the man who says that he is seeing God is saying not merely that he is experiencing a religious emotion, but also that there exists a transcendent being who is the object of this emotion; just as the man who says that he sees a yellow patch is ordinarily saying not merely that his visual sense-field contains a yellow sense-content, but also that there exists a yellow object to which the sense-content belongs. And it is not irrational to be prepared to believe a man when he asserts the existence of a yellow object and to refuse to believe him when he asserts the existence of a transcendent god. For whereas the sentence "There exists here a yellow-coloured material thing" expresses a genuine synthetic proposition which could be empirically verified, the sentence "There exists a transcendent god" has, as we have seen, no literal significance.

We conclude, therefore, that the argument from religious experience is altogether fallacious. The fact that people have religious experiences is interesting from the psychological point of view, but it does not in any way imply that there is such a thing as religious knowledge, any more than our having moral experience implies that there is such a thing as moral knowledge. The theist, like the moralist, may believe that his experiences are cognitive experiences, but, unless he can formulate his "knowledge" in propositions that are empirically verifiable, we may be sure that he is deceiving himself.

A. J. AYER, Language, Truth, and Logic

Focusing on the risk involved in having to make such momentous decisions on an uncertain base, Kierkegaard shows how the absurd and the paradoxical are central to his argument. Faith can't be objectively certain because if it were it would be like scientific knowledge. Real faith has nothing to do with knowledge; it is not cognitive. In fact, it is the opposite of knowledge because it is a belief in something we can never really know. To will unconditionally to believe, in the face of the unknown, thus is a tremendous act of courage.

Our attitude in believing is all important, as is the way we choose and act. It is like the difference between "believing in" and "believing that," a difference that H. H. Price has noted. We would react differently to someone's saying he believed that Joe would be elected student body president and the same person's saying he believed in Joe. The first statement indicates that the individual probably has some statistical information indicating that Joe has a good chance of obtaining the office. It refers to an issue that can be limited and investigated, in other words, a problem. The second statement, believing in Joe, conveys the sense of a trust or a hope in Joe as an individual, a person. Perhaps the speaker is referring to qualities in his personality such as honesty and intelligence that would make him a good leader. Perhaps others do not even see Joe as possessing those qualities at the present time. The speaker may feel that such capacities are there and will be realized. In fact, one may never be able to define and describe precisely what it is about Joe that the speaker believes in because much of that is as yet undeveloped. Joe is something of a mystery.

Human existence is always developing, is always a mystery, for Kierkegaard. He discusses the tension in our lived experience between the infinite and the finite against this background. Human beings are in fact, he proposes, a synthesis of the finite and the infinite. To be finite means to have a limited view of things, and it also means we will someday die. But we are also aware of something infinite, something beyond all our understanding, yet part of the experience of being human. What we are helps explain the paradox and anxiety in our lives. We are continually trying to escape from the transient world to that of eternity, and it is in religion that this longing is most clearly evidenced. Fanatical commitments to social reform and excessive, morbid fantasizing also express our desire to escape, but engaging in such activities is like trying to create a false eternity rather than face the anguish of being human. Such attempts to escape frustrate us because eventually we see how limited we are.

What are Kierkegaard's three stages?

Fundamentally, human beings react to this frustration and tension in three ways. Kierkegaard's accounting provides the rationale behind his schema of the three stages on life's way: the aesthetic, the ethical, and the religious. The only way for us to deal with our anxiety about our finitude, the paradox that is our essential being, is to make an act of personal commit ment: to choose, to will, rather than to reason. There are, however, various ways and things to which we can commit ourselves. Some represent a flight from reality; others, a choice of authenticity.

On the first level, the aesthetic, we are influenced largely by the senses, by our impulses and our desires. Our imagination takes over, and we live in the realm of possibilities. We pursue pleasure and novelty. Our life is never settled because things are always changing. There are no moral standards. Kierkegaard's paradigm for the "aesthetic person" is Don Juan, the lover who refuses to commit himself to a particular woman, or indeed to anything at all. He hungers for one experience after another, but none provides satisfaction. The Don Juan type attempts to escape facing the need to commit himself to any one person or thing. But he may decide that life should be more than a series of disconnected experiences void of ethical standards. It is possible to move to what Kierkegaard calls "the ethical stage."

In the ethical stage we have a sense of responsibility lacking in the aesthetic stage. There are rules of behavior and appropriate actions. One accepts the limitations, which are self-imposed, and acts with a sense of obligation. Kierkegaard's paradigm is Judge William, who leads an upright life, who values continuity and acting according to rational principles. But the ethical stage is not entirely adequate from a religious point of view. Kierkegaard holds that it is based on general moral laws and thus cannot necessarily say what is best for every individual. The authentic individual must *be* individual and personal. Eventually, the ethical person recognizes that he must make choices not always sanctioned by moral law. There is again a moment of choice: to remain in the ethical stage or to act, to make the "leap of faith" to the religious stage.

There is no rational way to move from the ethical to the religious stage. To illustrate his idea of faith, Kierkegaard interprets a Biblical story. The Old Testament figure Abraham is asked by God to sacrifice his only son Isaac. According to moral law, this is murder, abhorrent and forbidden. But God has requested the sacrifice, and Kierkegaard says this makes a difference. Does Abraham have a greater obligation to obey the law or to maintain his faith and trust in God? Abraham must make a decision, but he has no standard by which to make it. He has only an anguished uncertainty and his sorely tested faith. God must have some reason that he, Abraham, cannot fathom.

The leap involves making a commitment, being willing to take a risk and not knowing what will come of the act. After the trial of faith, God did spare Isaac; but Abraham could not anticipate this. Only when a relationship between the divine and the human is established through this commitment

What does Kierkegaard mean by the "leap" of faith?

is knowledge possible. Commitment also means living differently from the way we lived before. Kierkegaard thought that being a person necessarily involved having a relation to God, but being a person also means we are free to ignore this essential aspect of ourselves. Only faith can bring us to the third stage; only here can we become most fully ourselves. We are drawn on to the precipice and forced to take the risk of faith our particular situation demands, in the hope of meeting the eternal with all the anxiety this hope entails. Or we do not take the leap, and hide our relation to the eternal. By default we become less than what we could be.

Kierkegaard was a committed Christian as well as a philosopher. This raises an interesting question about the possibilities and limitations of the philosopher's discussion of religious questions, the nature of God, and the experience of faith. If the philosopher has not had religious experiences can he or she discuss the questions raised in this chapter with any insight into what they really mean in human experience? If the philosopher is in addition a believer, can he or she overcome the preconceptions and biases in a particular religious position and discuss the questions objectively?

Many believers have found that a philosophical investigation of religious questions has either strengthened their position or led them to change it. Many of those who remained "outside" religion have either had their skepticism reinforced or been drawn "inside." Whatever the outcome, it is important to approach the philosophy of religion, as all other areas of philosophy, with an open mind and to be willing to listen closely, even sympathetically, to all positions. If we are to make decisions of our own with respect to belief in God, we first must have some understanding of the issues involved and the positions available. No less is at stake than how we will live our lives.

Summary

The Philosophy of Religion: Religion contains an element that cannot be adequately described by the social sciences. Gabriel Marcel describes the object of religious belief as a mystery rather than a problem; our finite minds will never fully understand it no matter how much we learn about it. Philosophy of religion attempts to arrive at a more critical understanding of such things as the nature of religion, notions of God, religious experience, and faith. It differs from theology because the philosopher as philosopher makes no commitment to the doctrines of any particular historical religion.

Definitions of Religion: We can point to a number of characteristics and concerns held in common by most religions, but it is neither easy nor perhaps desirable to "define" religion. Two of its most basic elements are experience and belief. Both are manifested in such expressions of religious awareness as ritual, myth, prayer, and doctrine.

Notions of God: We can classify religions in terms of how many gods there are and what kind of being God is or the gods are. We can locate various ideas of God along a continuum ranging from the immanent (that which is present within the world) to the transcendent (that which is beyond and remote from the world).

The "Death of God":   Nietzsche announced that God is dead because belief in the God of Christianity had so dwindled that there was no meaning left Christianity, could create. Commentators on the "death of God" position argue that the God who is gone was a false one anyway; what we are mourning is our own human isolation. We live in a "profane" as opposed to a "sacred" world, where the difference between the two is in our attitude.

Three Interpretations of the "Real" God: For Feuerbach, who proposed a religion of "humanism," God is really the projection of our own human ideals; He does exist but is identical with humanity. Paul Tillich states that rather than the God of traditional theism or of naturalism we must look to a "God above God." This God is "being itself" and what concerns us ultimately. In Rudolph Otto's view, God is anything *but* what is within our ordinary human experience. "The numinous" is completely "other," and our encounter with it both terrifies and fascinates us.

Two Types of Faith and Their Relation to Knowledge: Martin Buber speaks of "faith" in both a cognitive sense (faith as knowledge) and a conative sense (faith as willing). The first involves reason, and the second, experience. These interpretations are related to the difference between believing "that" and believing "in."

John Hick argues that all our knowledge is "mediated" through what we are familiar with (our levels of significance). Faith, in the view of a believer, is simply the most complete interpretation of experience or the most comprehensive level of significance.

Kierkegaard proposed that faith is unlike objective knowledge, for "truth is subjectivity." We may progress from the aesthetic to the moral to the religious stage of life. The last demands the risk of a leap into the unknown.

Suggestions for Further Reading

Readable and thorough, Malcolm L. Diamond's *Contemporary Philosophy and Religious Thought: An Introduction to the Philosophy of Religion* (New York:

McGraw-Hill, 1974) provides discussion of individual thinkers as well as exploration of the issues with which they are concerned.

More personal but no less philosophical in approach is Simone Weil's *Waiting for God* (New York: Harper Torchbooks, 1973). This is a collection of letters and essays that evidence the French philosopher's concern with both the intellectual and experiential aspects of religion.

John Hick's *Faith and Knowledge* (Ithaca, NY: Cornell University Press, 1966) discusses what we mean by knowledge in religion and how it is related to the nature of faith.

For a classic collection of over fifty essays dealing with a wide variety of philosophers and their thoughts about God, see *Philosophers Speak of God* (Chicago: University of Chicago Press, 1953), edited by Charles Hartshorne and William Reese.

In *Belief and Unbelief* (New York: Macmillan, 1965), the American Catholic philosopher Michael Novak argues, "Belief is opposed to unbelief as one radical interpretation of human destiny to another." Writing from a viewpoint that he identifies as "intelligent subjectivity," Novak finds that belief is rooted in the human drive to question.

Inquiry

The Book of Job and the Problem of Evil

One of the most persistent and troubling issues in Western religious thought is the problem of evil: Why must the good suffer? In the Judeo-Christian tradition, the classic statement of the problem is to be found in the Old Testament Book of Job. The story of Job is divided into three parts: an introductory section, in prose, which presents the situation; the long middle section, in poetry, which is comprised of conversations between Job and his friends about his plight; and the last few concluding verses, also in prose, which show Job restored to his former position.

The basic premise of the story is that Job is a just man, "perfect and upright." He is, indeed, the kind of person the Lord loves and the model of integrity. God recognizes Job as such. Then in a series of scenes that take place both in Heaven and on earth, we see that God allows Satan to test Job. Job first loses everything he owns; then his family is taken away; and finally his health is destroyed. He is in complete misery, an outcast from society. Through all this Job remains faithful to God and does not "sin with his lips."

The story then turns to the poetic conversations between Job and a number of his friends, of whom Eliphaz, Bildad, and Zophar are the most important. Job laments his wretched condition. Eliphaz responds by telling him that all men are sinners in God's eyes and that God has

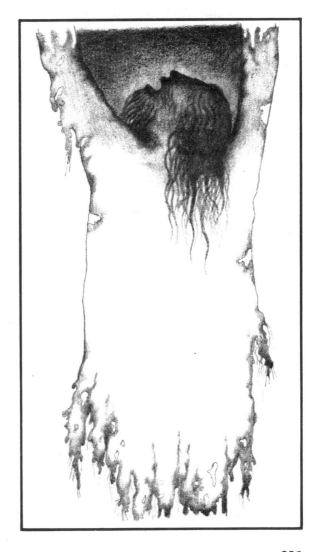

always been just. All that human beings can do is simply *accept* their lot and continue to bless the Lord. In the end, God will make all things right. While Eliphaz's comments are based on the wisdom of Biblical tradition, Job doesn't feel that they address *his* case adequately. He restates his agony and asks simply to be allowed to die.

When Job is overcome with his suffering and asks God why he should be so put upon, Bildad is infuriated. He says God is all-knowing and all-powerful. But Job says that this is exactly the problem: He has no recourse for his own defense and is baffled that God appears to be destroying the good along with the bad. He asks God why, if God made him, He's trying so hard to destroy him.

Zophar responds violently and accuses Job of opposing and blaspheming God. Job, he cries, is a plain fool, and if he knew what was good for him he would put away his sins. Job is obviously a terrible sinner or he wouldn't be suffering so.

None of his friends' stock arguments resolve Job's dilemma. He knows he's just, and he therefore questions what appears to be an unjust use of power on God's part. Job rails at his friends, telling them talking is easy and words cheap. They couldn't possibly see his situation fairly since they have not been made to suffer.

In desperation, Job turns again to God and presents his "case," almost in a legal form. He begs for a decision, but none is forthcoming. In desperate straits, Job asserts his belief that he will ultimately be saved and vindicated. Finally, the Lord appears. God's response, however, is not directed to Job's situation; rather, it is a presentation of His providential ordering of nature.

The final verses relate Job's response to God. He says that all along he didn't really know what he was saying or even what he was talking about because he'd only heard of God. Now he has seen God and is comforted. His peace is not due to any understanding of his situation, for that is hidden from him in God's mysterious glory, but rather he's at peace because, having seen, he can place his trust in God even without understanding. In the last few lines, God restores Job's good fortune and grants him a full and happy life.

The concerns raised in the Biblical narrative are substantial and certainly not easily resolved. We will address only a few of them here. First, how would you phrase the resolution to the problem of evil as it appears in the Book of Job? Do you feel that you can accept that resolution? Why or why not?

Biblical scholars have noted that portions of the book were composed at different periods in history. The first two chapters, the prose narrative outlining the situation, are the oldest, composed before a long period of trials suffered by the Israelites. Its theme, the suffering of the good as a test of faith that, if endured, will result in a faith still stronger, is much more optimistic than the middle section of the book. Does this imply that the traditional religious answer to the problem of evil—namely, that suffering patiently endured reinforces faith—would be acceptable only to those who have not themselves suffered greatly?

Biblical scholars have also noted that the short prose conclusion showing Job restored to his health, wealth, and family dates from a different period than the poetic section. If this conclusion had been left out, would the resolution of the problem have been changed? If so, how?

The long middle section dealing with the dialogues presents a different Job from the introductory section. There, Job was primarily a man of faith committed to God. In the middle section, Job is seen as abandoned by this God and even breaking into violent outbursts. Does this contrast indicate anything to you about the various dimensions of the nature of "faith?" If so, what and how?

Consider these other possible options for resolving the problem of evil. Examine each one to determine its strengths and weaknesses, whether or not you agree or disagree with it, and in what ways each is consistent or inconsistent with the Biblical story:

1. There really is not a God.
2. God does exist, but He is responsible for evil and therefore not good.
3. God does exist and is good but is helpless to prevent suffering in the world and therefore is not all-powerful.
4. God exists and is both good and powerful; it is Job who is guilty. In this option, consider also by what standards Job could be judged guilty and by whom.
5. There is no meaning; the suffering of the good in the world is completely arbitrary.

Inquiry

Does God Exist?
The Argument
from Design

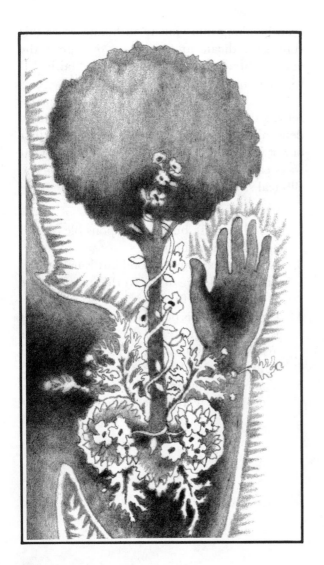

Design, or the order of the universe, is perhaps the evidence cited most often to substantiate the existence of God. Proponents of this view say that it is obvious in the experience of any one of us who looks at the world closely. You don't have to be a "philosopher" to see its force.

According to this argument, it is impossible to conceive of an orderly, harmonious universe without reference to some intelligence, force, or purpose responsible for the order. It seems absurd that the balance and intricacy of nature could have happened simply by chance. The life forms on earth are too intricate and complex; the motion of the heavenly bodies is too well organized; and the interdependence of life forms and environment is too tight for it all to have been some fortunate congruence of circumstance. Looking at all this around us, we have "proof" of a God, an eternal designer, the intelligence or power within and behind nature.

Philosophers are still interested in the subtleties of this argument. Among modern thinkers, John Wisdom points out its ambiguities by telling a parable in his well-known essay, "Gods," about an "invisible gardener." Wisdom's parable goes something like this.

Two individuals return home after a long absence. They find that despite the weeds in their garden some of the old plants are doing beautifully. One claims that some gardener must have been taking care of them. None of their neighbors, however, has seen anyone. The first person concludes that the gardener must have come when everyone was sleeping. The second doesn't think so because someone would probably have heard him. And furthermore, why would a gardener who cared about the plants not have done something about all the weeds?

The first speaker feels that this isn't a good objection. Just look at how the weeds are arranged in the garden; they reflect "purpose and a sense for beauty." If the two of them just look, he thinks, they will discover evidence for "someone invisible to mortal eyes" who comes to the garden. They look very carefully at everything.

After their exploration, the first still feels there is an invisible gardener, and the second, there isn't. Both have the same information. Their different conclusions reflect "no difference as to what they have found in the garden." Wisdom concludes that the two differ in what they say about the gardener, that he exists, or that he doesn't; and that with this first difference comes a second difference in what they feel about and how they perceive the garden. Neither, however, expects anything of the garden that the other doesn't. What Wisdom wants to know is whether this is all the difference between the two, and if so, can we still ask which one is "right" and "reasonable"?

The argument from design presents us with some interesting philosophical questions. Wisdom's parable emphasizes some of them. It seems that we can all agree on "facts," but very often we can differ in the interpretation of them such that we arrive at different conclusions. Is this the case with any attempt at "proof," scientific or otherwise? How would an attempt to "prove" the existence of "God" be the same or different from a scientific proof? How important are evaluation and interpretation? More important here than in scientific proof?

Sometimes we can resolve a difference by redoing our "calculations" or by reordering our facts. It is possible that we have made a mistake either in observing or in figuring things out. Do you think the question of the existence of God can be resolved by another look at the facts? Why or why not?

The empiricist philosopher David Hume responded to the design argument. He claimed that things may appear to be ordered but the appearance doesn't necessarily imply a conscious plan. It's entirely feasible in his view that given enough time and enough variables, the apparent "order" of the universe could simply result from chance. Do you think that his objection is valid?

Immanuel Kant suggests another possibility. The order or design that exists may exist not in the things themselves, which we couldn't know anyway, but in our own minds, in the way we perceive things to be. Is this possible? If so, how could reason alone ever come up with an argument for God's existence?

The secret of the human universe is that there is no equilibrium between man and the surrounding forces of nature, which infinitely exceed him when in inaction; there is only equilibrium in action by which man recreates his own life through work.

SIMONE WEIL

But from the moment one man began to stand in need of the help of another; from the moment it appeared advantageous to any one man to have enough provisions for two, equality disappeared, property was introduced, work became indispensable, and vast forests became smiling fields, which man had to water with the sweat of his brow, and where slavery and misery were soon seen to germinate and grow up with the crops.

JEAN JACQUES ROUSSEAU

226

Chapter 7

WORK
Achievement and Alienation

Chapter Survey

The Philosophy of Work
How does work involve the social world?
What are the paradoxes of work?
How does Herbert Marcuse view advanced industrial society?

Man and Work in Recent Thought
What does work mean in modern philosophy?
What are the characteristics of Homo faber?

The Work Ethic
Why do people work harder than they have to?
Is the work ethic still important in American life?

Alienation
What does "alienation" mean?
What are the human costs of technological progress?
What are the positive aspects of work?

Work and Society
What is the relationship between the working person and society?
Is work the problem, or is leisure the problem?

Albert Camus
1913–1960

"Beginning to think is beginning to be undermined."

"On summer evenings," Albert Camus recalled, "the workingmen sit on their balconies. . . . There was the street, the ice-cream vendor next door, the cafés across the way, and the noise of children running from door to door." Fatherless and impoverished, Camus grew up in a hard Algiers neighborhood; his mother was a cleaning woman. Despite some family resistance to his "wasting his time," he went to the university, where he majored in philosophy. A partial scholarship helped him get by, but to continue his studies he had to take a number of jobs. Among other things, he sold spare parts for cars, worked for a shipping firm, and acted in plays before becoming a journalist. His writing gave him a chance to travel, but Camus never forgot—indeed, did not want to forget—his early experience. For the rest of his life, he remained sensitive to the problems and the dignity of working people.

Camus' first important philosophical study was The Myth of Sisyphus. There, confronting what struck him as the world's unreasonableness, he addressed the possibility of suicide. "It happens," Camus wrote, "that the stage sets collapse. Rising, streetcar, four hours in the office or factory, meal, streetcar, four hours of work, meal, sleep, and Monday Tuesday Wednesday Thursday Friday and Saturday according to the same rhythm—this path is easily followed most of the time. But one day the 'why' arises." This "why," this "impulse of consciousness," leads to the

feeling of the absurd: the contradiction between the human mind, which desires rational unity, and the inhuman world, which remains irrational and fragmented.

Defining the absurd as "that divorce between the mind that desires and the

world that disappoints," Camus wrote, "There can be no question of masking the evidence, of suppressing the absurd by denying one of the terms of its equation. It is essential to know whether one can live with it or whether, on the other hand, logic commands one to die of it." He added, "I am not interested in philosophical suicide, but rather in plain suicide. I merely wish to purge it of its emotional content and know its logic and its integrity."

If the why finds no satisfactory answer—if the world is stubbornly irrational and one's life apparently meaningless—then is suicide the logical conclusion? Following his "absurd rea-

soning" to the end, Camus said no, because committing suicide would amount to escaping the problem or denying one of its terms rather than resolving it. Instead, he argued, the only honest stance is one of sustained revolt against the world's meaninglessness. "That revolt," he maintained, "gives life its value." In The Myth of Sisyphus, Camus celebrated the capacity of people to go on living "without appeal" in a world that doesn't make any sense.

In 1951 Camus, who had courageously edited a clandestine resistance newspaper in France during World War II, published The Rebel, a major philosophical work in which he turned from the problem of suicide to the problem of murder. "It is incumbent upon us," he wrote, ". . . to give a definite answer to the question implicit in the blood and strife of this century." Murder, he affirmed, is no more justifiable than suicide: "From the moment that life is recognized as good, it becomes good for all men."

This affirmation of life and this deep sense of human solidarity distinguish Camus' philosophy. In essays, plays, and short stories, as well as in such novels as The Stranger and The Plague, he explored the human condition in the twentieth century, but he summarized his work in these terms: "If I have tried to define something, it is . . . simply the common existence of history and of man, everyday life with the most possible light thrown upon it, the dogged struggle against one's own degradation and that of others."

Chapter 7

WORK

The Philosophy of Work

Surprisingly, work is one subject that philosophers don't ordinarily talk about. Yet most of us have to work for a living, and the job you have will probably determine how you spend a large part of your time. It may determine a lot more than that, too, like where and how you live, and what your "place" in society is, and who your friends are. Your work may be an unpleasant necessity, tedious, boring, deadening, and alienating or it may be creative, fascinating, and fulfilling, but in either case it's bound to be a big part of your life.

In this chapter we'll investigate philosophically relevant aspects of work. First, to introduce the philosophy of work, we'll look at some of work's social and political implications and consider three of its paradoxes. Then we'll discuss the modern image of man as a worker before examining the work ethic. Finally, after analyzing the various forms in which alienation supposedly appears in the modern world, we'll close with additional remarks on work and society.

The economic and political organization of a society always involves value choices. To establish a communistic society, at one extreme, or a highly individualistic society, at the other, is to make fundamental decisions about whether the group's welfare or the individual's matters more and about who gets what. These decisions express the society's commitments to and understanding of values such as freedom, justice, equality, and human dignity. The society's institutions, laws, customs, and economy then function, more or less adequately, to realize those values. Since work is a social reality and since the values of a given society determine who gets what for doing this or that, work involves us in philosophical questions.

In the world of work, acute social and political problems surround the complex question of the person's independence from and interdependence with other persons. For instance, individualism has long been recognized as a distinctive American trait. The word "individualism" was introduced into

How does work involve the social world?

the English language by the first translator of Alexis de Tocqueville's *Democracy in America.* It became an ideal that such native writers as Emerson and Whitman celebrated in the nineteenth century.

Historically, in this country's economic life, individualism has been manifested in the people's active resistance to governmental regulation. In *America's Frontier Heritage,* the prominent historian Ray Allen Billington affirms, "From colonial days when merchants defied Britain's trade regulations to the late nineteenth century when business titans preached the gospel of 'rugged American individualism,' the people demanded freedom from government as well as freedom under government." And in his recent article "Why Regulation Fails," Peter H. Schuck argues that

> *government regulation is fundamentally at variance with the philosophical assumptions underlying the American political system. We are a liberal society, rooted in utilitarian ideas about the relation between citizen and state. The primary notion holds that the individual is the sole judge of his own interest and welfare. . . . In this view, voluntary exchanges of value between individuals, as in a market transaction, are socially beneficial.*

Many would respond that today such individualism is outmoded. The massive social, economic, and ecological problems facing advanced industrial societies like ours can be resolved only by massive governmental intervention. What one company does in our times can affect the quality of life for many individuals. For instance, the use of many cancer-causing chemicals in manufacturing seems to call for careful government scrutiny. Others think as Schuck does that governmental regulation of business is already too extensive and that the government's bureaucratic agencies are both inefficient and harmful.

This political issue clearly involves value choices, and it bears on the world of work. So, more directly, do such historical developments as the government's abolition of child labor, its determination of individual and corporate tax schedules, its establishment of a minimum wage, its institution of unemployment and workmen's compensation programs, and its setting up of the Occupational Safety and Health Administration. These are political and legal developments, but they rest upon arguable philosophical notions about the individual's relationship to society.

There's another, more immediate sense in which work implies social interdependence. Although small businesses and individual craftsmanship remain important, most people today work for and with other people. Individualism still means a great deal to many Americans, but life in an advanced industrial society means extensive and complicated networks of social and economic interdependence. Work is necessarily a social experience. If philosophy is taken to mean critical reflection on experience, then this primary social dimension of work will be philosophically relevant.

In *Philosophy of Labor,* Remy Kwant, a contemporary Dutch-American philosopher, presents a thoughtful argument on the philosophical interest of work. He supports it by citing a number of paradoxes, or apparent contradictions, peculiar to what he calls the world of labor.

What are the paradoxes of work?

One of them is the paradox of freedom and restraint. Labor makes us free because it creates and maintains a human world. Things such as buildings, cars, televisions, chairs, and pencils are "worked," that is, made by human ingenuity and effort. To take another example, work transforms trees into coffee tables and books. In this sense, work makes the natural world a human world.

What's more, this world is one in which we're free, both negatively (free from) and positively (free to or free for). To cite some negative freedoms, our buildings free us from having to live and work outside, our cars free us from having to walk everywhere, and our pencils free us from having to remember everything. The division of labor and the increasing specialization of tasks further free us from having to do things for ourselves. For instance, we don't have to make our own shoes or grow our own food; we can spend our working time doing something else, buying these things from others with the money we earn. In fact, it's this social organization of work that's made possible the mass production of all the more sophisticated things we use every day, like typewriters, telephones, and refrigerators.

Positively, we're free to do what we want in this familiar, worked world whose cars and airplanes allow us to travel easily and whose books and televisions offer us the chance to stay home and still travel. Work and its products allow us a greater freedom for human development.

However, the same work that gives us such freedom in the human world also increasingly restricts our freedom. For obvious reasons, all these manufactured things require cooperative efforts if they're to be made widely available. From the worker's point of view, in the modern, industrial world cooperative efforts have meant such restrictive things as factories, assembly lines, production quotas, time cards, efficiency experts, and rules and regulations.

Even leisure time may be said to belong to the world of work. The coffee break and the one- or two-week vacation are commonly called "time off" or "free time," that is, time off from work or time free from work. Some writers have even suggested that these regularly scheduled leisure periods are good for people, not simply because it's pleasant to take a break and drink a cup of coffee and to pass a few days in the mountains, but because they enable people to work better!

Toward the end of the nineteenth century, the German philosopher Friedrich Nietzsche lamented the joylessness of modern society. He said people are so unfree and so much given over to working that they're unable to relax with an easy conscience, unable to do *nothing* without finding some excuse for it. "Oh, the restrictions on joy among our people," he wrote, "educated and uneducated! All clear conscience stands on the side of work: any disposition toward joy calls itself need for recuperation, and begins to be ashamed of itself. It is necessary to preserve one's health—such is the excuse if one is discovered on a jaunt in the country." Nietzsche saw this attitude that glorifies work as a threat to high culture and philosophical thought, which are possible only if leisure time is valued. It "might soon reach the point," he warned, "that no one could give in to a disposition to the [contemplative life] without self-reproach and a bad conscience."

Freedom is an abstract concept, but it's also a practical social and political problem. In Kwant's terms, this first paradox, the paradox of freedom and restraint, means that work both liberates us and enslaves us. It

Viewpoint

Clinging to immense slopes are rails, pick-up trucks, cranes, and miniature railways. . . . Through whistles, dust, and smoke, toylike locomotives twist around vast blocks of stone under a devouring sun. Night and day a nation of ants swarms over the smoking carcass of the mountain. Scores of men, hanging from the same rope against the cliff face, their bellies pressed to the handles of pneumatic drills, quiver day after day in mid-air, unloosing whole patches of stone that crash down in a roar of dust. Further along, trucks dump their loads from the top of the slopes, and the rocks, suddenly launched toward the sea, roll and dive into the water, each heavy block followed by a shower of lighter stones. At regular intervals, in the dead of night or in the middle of the day, explosions shake the whole mountain and raise the very sea itself.

What man is doing with these excavations is launching a head-on attack against stone. And if we could for a moment forget the harsh slavery that makes this work possible, we would be filled with admiration. These stones, wrenched from the mountain, help man in his designs. They pile up beneath the first waves, gradually emerge, and finally take shape as a jetty that will soon be covered with men and machines daily moving further out to sea.

ALBERT CAMUS, "The Minotaur, or Stopping in Oran"

raises a thorny question: "How can we maintain the world we built without becoming its victims?"

Another paradox is that of availability. Our work, especially now with the development of mass production and distribution networks, makes things easily available to us. In fact, more things are more available today than ever before. The book you're reading now is a good example. During the Middle Ages, laboriously copied manuscripts were chained to their stands in monastery libraries because there were so few of them. Now, it's possible for two teachers to collaborate on a book, using airplanes, typewriters, the postal system, and the telephone—all of which are themselves the products of others people's work—to meet and communicate with each other. Furthermore, it's possible for their book to be reproduced in large numbers and distributed to college bookstores all over the country, where it's made available to students like you. Similarly, it's work that makes all the things we use available to us.

In Kwant's words, this is the paradox of availability: "Man enjoys an available world, but the more his world becomes available, the more he himself must be available. His availability dominates his life." As a practical matter, people have to live within commuting distance of the place they work. Every year, in fact, countless American families pack up and move from one city to another because of a promotion, a transfer, or a new job. Such moves demand that they start all over in a new community. For this reason, our society has been described as mobile and rootless.

In addition, many people who work have to be on call much of the time. The physician's case offers an extreme example. On television, the surgeon's lunch is always being interrupted by the insistent beeping that comes from the radio he wears on his belt. But medical doctors are not the only ones who remain on call. So do many plumbers, members of the National Guard, attorneys, locksmiths, ambulance attendants, maintenance workers, counselors, mechanics, and firemen. A lot of people have telephone answering services so that they can receive messages when they're not available; many others request unlisted telephone numbers precisely so that they can limit their availability.

There's another sense in which we have to be available to work: To survive in the modern economy, we have to learn the skills to do the jobs that are open. In this sense, availability may mean employability. To sum up, work makes things available to us, but it also requires that we ourselves be available.

A third paradox involves the riches and the poverty of modern work. It is undeniable that modern labor techniques have increased our human capacities tremendously, but many social critics argue that because of them we've also become one-sided. Our lives are entirely given over to producing and consuming. There are signs of change, especially among young people, but working to produce more and more consumer goods faster and faster has become part of our way of life, just as consuming more and faster has. Work and its products have enriched our possibilities for living full, rewarding lives. But that same work and those same products may also have led to an intellectual and emotional impoverishment. Concern for producing and consuming, for making money and having expensive things, may take up all one's time. A person may lose the power to relax and enjoy ideas and people.

There's another, more obvious way in which modern labor techniques, whose products have liberated us and enriched our world, have also enslaved and impoverished us. Specialization and mechanization have increased our capacity to make and to do things, but as a result many of us are compelled to perform the same operation over and over all day long.

How does Marcuse view advanced industrial society?

The controversial social philosopher Herbert Marcuse has focused on another, closely related aspect of modern life in developing his radical critique of advanced industrial society. Marcuse describes "the new forms of control" in *One-Dimensional Man.* He argues, "Independence of thought, autonomy, and the right to political opposition are being deprived of their basic critical function in a society which seems increasingly capable of satisfying the needs of the individuals through the way in which it is organized."

Marcuse maintains that the extension of affluence produces servitude: Freedom from material want neutralizes working individuals' impulses to criticize the prevailing system. And the perpetual creation of new, "false" needs confirms them in their pursuit of material satisfaction. He asserts that "The only needs that have an unqualified claim for satisfaction are the vital ones—nourishment, clothing, lodging at the attainable level of culture." The satisfaction of these vital needs is the precondition for the satisfaction of spiritual needs. By contrast, Marcuse, in *One-Dimensional Man,* defines false needs as

> those which are superimposed upon the individual by particular social interests in his repression: the needs which perpetuate toil, aggressiveness, misery and injustice. . . . Most of the prevailing needs to relax, to have fun, to behave and consume in accordance with the advertisements, to love and hate what others love and hate, belong to this category of false needs.

In brief, Marcuse says we are told what we need by advertising and public relations agencies. Our "needs" for a new car every year or a certain brand of cigarettes are thus dictated to us in part by the interests of large corporations. And Marcuse holds, "The capabilities (intellectual and material) of contemporary society are immeasurably greater than ever before—which means that the scope of society's domination over the individual is immeasurably greater than ever before." False needs are treated as though they are vital needs.

In the modern world, economic advances have meant both freedom and repression, physical comfort and spiritual poverty: "With technical progress as its instrument, unfreedom—in the sense of man's subjection to his productive apparatus—is perpetuated and intensified in the form of many liberties and comforts." We have freedom of speech, which is carefully supervised. And we have freedom of the press, which is carefully controlled. We also have comforts provided by such things as tranquilizers, which in Marcuse's view, probably prevent us from being aware of our true needs. Television may perform much the same function as a tranquilizer, and in one state at least a television is considered to be a necessity—it cannot be repossessed.

Marcuse's critique of contemporary society may be countered by the objections that it's impossible to distinguish between true and false needs (especially when the individuals themselves perceive what Marcuse would consider false needs as true ones). And if advanced industrial society has succeeded in extending affluence to members of the working class, then perhaps workers should find little to criticize. All the same, Marcuse has identified some noteworthy features of modern life.

Work presents other contradictions, but the three paradoxes we've mentioned—the paradox of freedom and restraint, the paradox of availability, and the paradox of the riches and poverty of modern work—establish that this everyday dimension of our human condition and our individual lives does pose philosophical as well as practical problems. That's not surprising. Philosophical reflection is the effort we make to understand our practical experience and our ordinary lives, and working is certainly a significant part of our experience and our lives. Simple arithmetic shows that if we work forty hours a week fifty weeks a year for forty years, then we'll have spent 80,000 hours of our life on the job—and each of us presumably has only one life to "spend"!

Man and Work in Recent Thought

Perceptions of labor and work vary, but it's safe to say that in modern philosophical thought, at least, these human activities are frequently seen in a positive light. A widely shared modern view has it that persons freely and creatively define themselves and realize their human values in their productive lives. This perception of human reality is significantly different from earlier Western views. Work—in the specific, limited sense of philo-

What does work mean in modern philosophy?

sophical reflection, scholarly research, and artistic creation—has always been held in high esteem by Western thinkers. But labor—the physical exertion required to meet life's economic necessities—was long scorned.

For the classical Greeks, labor was what slaves did, and free men were free to the extent that their slaves freed them from the need to labor. The classical idea that having to labor for a living is essentially incompatible with freedom and the person's full humanity still prevailed in Charlemagne's time (the ninth century). The French historian Marc Bloch has suggested that it never completely disappeared during the Middle Ages in Europe.

It's only in our own times, within the last few centuries, that labor has become respectable. In *The Human Condition,* Hannah Arendt has traced this change to early modern times:

> *The sudden, spectacular rise of labor from the lowest, most despised position to the highest rank, as the most esteemed of all human activities, began when Locke discovered [in the seventeenth century] that labor is the source of all property. It followed its course when Adam Smith asserted that labor was the source of all wealth and found its climax [during the nineteenth century] in Marx's "system of labor," where labor became the source of all productivity and the expression of the very humanity of man.*

Perhaps the most prevalent image of man today is that of *Homo faber.* Literally, this Latin phrase means "man the maker," but more generally it refers to human beings as workers or world builders. (By "man" in this context we mean *all* human beings.) This is not to suggest that there is a single, typically modern image of human nature; like perceptions of work, perceptions of human nature vary tremendously. In addition, many philosophers maintain that it's inappropriate to speak about "human nature" at all, since to do so means to treat a "who" like a "what," or persons like objects. They prefer to speak of the human condition. However, we might justifiably propose the image of man the maker as one popular approach to the problem of contemporary identity.

What are the characteristics of Homo faber?

In his *Apology for Wonder,* Sam Keen, a contemporary American religious philosopher, indicates characteristics peculiar to man the maker. First, in this view, man is the animal who makes and uses tools. Second, the human mind, like the human hand, is a toolmaking and tool-using faculty. Third, man is his own chief product.

Like his ability to use language, man the maker's ability to make tools and to use them sets him apart from other animals. Karl Popper recently distinguished animal evolution and human evolution in these terms. Animal evolution proceeds largely by the modification of organs and behavior or by the emergence of new organs and new patterns of behavior. By contrast, Popper says, human evolution proceeds largely by our developing new organs outside our bodies. "These new organs are tools," Popper explains, "or weapons, or machines, or houses," and "instead of growing better brains and memories, we grow paper, pens, pencils, typewriters, dictaphones, the printing press, and libraries." One of the more recent evolutionary developments, of course, is the growth of computers. In this connection, it's interesting to note that in the language of computer specialists themselves, the development of computers is proceeding by generations. Each generation of computers is more complex, more efficient, and more useful than the preceding one.

Man the maker's second characteristic is that his mind, no less than his hand, is a toolmaking and tool-using faculty. The American pragmatists, among whom figured such remarkable philosophers as Charles Sanders Peirce, William James, and John Dewey, found this instrumental view of human intelligence especially satisfying. It explains the mind's function, and it also corresponds to our common sense ideas about our own intellectual abilities. Earlier in this century, John Dewey wrote that the "function of intelligence is . . . not that of copying the objects of the environment [that is, mentally representing them to ourselves], but rather of taking account of the way in which more effective and more profitable relations with these objects may be established in the future."

This signals a practical orientation. For Dewey, human intelligence, the product of evolution, is useful because it can effectively guide our future actions in the world, enabling us to achieve better working relations with the objects that surround us. This is the way we ordinarily understand intelligence too. Dewey wrote in *Philosophy and Civilization* that

> *Common sense regards intelligence as having a purpose, and knowledge as amounting to something. . . . Popularly, good judgment is judgment as to the relative values of things: good sense is horse sense, ability to take hold of things right end up, to fit an instrument to an obstacle, to select resources apt for a task. . . . Intelligence, in its ordinary use, is a practical term; ability to size up matters with respect to the needs and possibilities of the various situations in which one is called to do something . . .*

This popular notion of the mind as a toolmaking, tool-using faculty has important and far-reaching consequences. Its tools are symbolic concepts. In this view, such scientific concepts as "cause" and "effect," such psychological concepts as "id," "Oedipal complex," and "conditioning," and such political concepts as "power" and "fascism" are all man-made tools the purpose of which is to organize and explain our experience. In everyday life and conversation, as well as in the physical sciences and social sciences, we continually use concepts to make sense of the world. The concepts employed by common sense and by science are instrumental, functional, or operational; like tools, they have practical uses in different situations. They allow us to define and to resolve problems.

The pragmatists did not see the mind as a machine, but others have made this comparison. In fact, it's become fairly commonplace to compare the human mind to a computer. In *Mechanical Man,* the American physicist Dean E. Wooldridge wrote that "there is good reason to suspect that brains and computers employ similar operating principles." Except for such practical problems as the complexity of design and equipment required, he argues, it should be theoretically possible to develop a computer that would, "among other things, be able to direct the muscles of the fingers to write, and those of the throat to speak, all the details of the theory of relativity that Einstein did in fact write and speak during his lifetime." According to those who urge such comparisons between human and artificial intelligence, the brain is like a sophisticated computer. This position, which some scientists and mathematicians have argued very carefully, has important implications for one's view of human beings.

Some science fiction writers and film producers have made more fanciful comparisons between people and machines. A classic example is Stanley Kubrick's film *2001,* in which the computer HAL develops individuality. Such stories are immensely entertaining, and their power to capture the twentieth century imagination probably says something about our culture. But their premises—that mechanisms could learn human emotional re-

Viewpoint

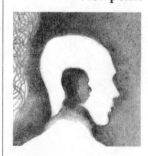

The trouble with the leading and most powerful symbol in American culture [the tool] is that it leads a man to think of himself as an object on which tools are to be used, or as a tool to be used on other objects. Such a symbol makes human value depend on a man's usefulness; the ascription of intrinsic worth becomes impossible. It also excludes too much reality— excludes experiences of honesty, courage, freedom and community that are not adequately expressed in the language of tools and functions. It is for this reason that the political struggle in America today does not concern power and interests merely, but new perceptions of what is real.

MICHAEL NOVAK, The Experience of Nothingness

sponses and could creatively initiate action—are dubious. More realistic, and more significant for a philosophical anthropology, is the popular view that the human mind operates like a computer, at least in solving certain kinds of problems.

In popular thought, this way of thinking about human beings has had considerable impact. If the human mind is like a computer both in how it works and in what it does—solve problems—then speed and accuracy are the best measures of intelligence. Logic and objectivity are more valuable than intuition or feeling. And the mind's purpose, correctly understood, is not to appreciate the world but to use it, to work it, and to transform it.

Lately, some thinkers have argued that this view of the human mind, its operations, and its use, is both inhuman and dehumanizing. It has devalued sensitivity, spontaneity, creativity, our capacity for aesthetic, moral, and religious experience, and the very planet on which we live. It has impelled us to create such things as freeways and airports, assembly lines and productivity quotas, and nuclear bombs and nerve gas. Whether or not such charges may be justified, they underline the fact that our philosophical views of human nature have practical consequences. How we understand ourselves and our relations to nature and other persons will influence how we act in the world. To see man as a maker, for instance, may have a decisive effect on the lives we lead and on the earth we inhabit.

A third characteristic of man the maker is that he makes himself. He's his own chief product. He creates his own identity and forms his own destiny. This has also been an important theme in twentieth century thought, one you've probably heard many times in one form or another. The counter-cultural exhortation "Do your own thing" gives popular expression to this idea, for instance. The European existentialists like Jean-Paul Sartre and Albert Camus wrote philosophical essays, plays, and novels during and after World War II. In these works, they made this idea of personal responsibility for one's own life central to their humanistic philosophy.

Sartre wrote that "existence precedes essence," which means that we first simply find ourselves existing in the world and then must make ourselves what we essentially are. We must define our own identity. There is no such thing as a human nature given in advance, Sartre held, and nobody is "born" anything. If a person becomes a hero or a coward, a patriot or a traitor, it's because he or she has chosen to become that. Our freedom implies that we're responsible for what we do and what we become. There are no excuses. For the existentialists, it's through their own freely chosen projects that persons create themselves. Authentic human existence, is, then, a personal responsibility and an ideal always in the future. The past can provide models for us, but it does not determine our present actions.

The existentialist notion of the "project" also reflects the practical orientation of recent thought. Sartre sees in the project an active way of knowing and being in relation with the human environment. It "lights our way," he said, "and gives its meaning to the situation, but reciprocally, it is nothing but a certain way of understanding it." The concrete projects we choose to undertake might include circulating a petition, or writing a philosophy paper, or just about anything else. But in general, Sartre writes, our project is ourself: "Through its light our relation to the world becomes specified, the ends and the means appear which reflect to us, at the same time, the hostility of things [which resist us] and our own objective."

In *Apology for Wonder,* Keen notes a fourth characteristic of man the maker. "If at best *homo faber* is purely creative," he writes, "at worst he is compulsively active." That is, he creates "busy work." "Under the impact of the techniques of mass production, creativity has been increasingly identified with work, and work with productive activity." "To discover the influence of the image of *homo faber,*" Keen advises, "we must look at the significance work has for personal identity in contemporary society."

The Work Ethic

What does work really mean to working people? To a great extent, of course, the answer to that question depends on the individual person and the specific situation. For instance, one writer contrasts a female convict sewing in a prison workshop with an expectant mother who's sewing a layette for her unborn child. They're both working; in fact, they're occupied with similar tasks and solving similar technical problems. However, there's likely a world of difference between them.

In general, we might distinguish two basic meanings work has for people. In its normal usage in everyday language, the word "work" signifies, on the one hand, misery and toil and, on the other, accomplishment. Accordingly, although they generally hold in common the idea that work is the person's most specifically human activity, recent thinkers have offered two very different views of these experiences. One of them is the view that the conditions of work in capitalistic society are alienating, the other, the view that whatever its nature and whatever the conditions under which it's performed, work—even long, hard hours of work—is a good thing. Let's look at the second one first.

In the United States, at least until quite recently, people have generally emphasized the personal and social importance of work. Reviewing the accounts of American life and character written by European observers during the eighteenth and nineteenth centuries, Billington reports in *America's Frontier Heritage* that in their eyes *the American differed from his European contemporaries . . . in his belief in the universal obligation of all persons to work endlessly in their eternal pursuit of material gain. . . . The progress of society demanded that all labor at top speed with no time wasted on frivolity. . . . This nose-to-the-grindstone philosophy, linked with the "go-ahead" spirit that permeated nineteenth-century enterprise, endowed the people with certain characteristics: an acceptance of materialism with a corresponding mistrust of esthetic and intellectual pursuits, a dislike of a leisure class, and an inability to enjoy recreation or luxuriate in indolence. Americans even played games with a grim determination to win rather than for pure sport.*

Historically, Americans have been imbued with the spirit of the Protestant ethic, or the work ethic. The economic realities and possibilities of this country fostered a positive attitude toward work, but we might look deeper to discover the sources of the work ethic. A number of outstanding social scientists have offered theories to explain this drive to work. Most of them

Why do people work harder than they have to?

Viewpoint

. . . the extraordinary productivity of American agriculture could never have been achieved by the availability of fertile soil alone, even in infinite amount; it was accomplished by the specialization of labor, by scientific agriculture, and most of all by the mechanization of farm operations. Thus it is safe to say that the American standard of living is a resultant much less of natural resources than of the increase in capacity to produce and that this was the result, directly, of human endeavor—the ventures and struggles of the pioneer, the exertions of the workman, the ingenuity of the inventor, the drive of the enterpriser, and the economic efficiency of all kinds of Americans, who shared a notorious addiction to hard work. These activities may themselves be the product of deterministic forces, and no implication of superior merit is necessarily involved; but, at least, one important point emerges—namely, that American abundance is a condition which has been achieved in the same way that other goals have been achieved by other men at other times throughout history, and it is not a mere matter of getting into the path of blind luck. Though based upon a primary environment, abundance is realized through the creation by society of a secondary environment, and it should be regarded accordingly.

DAVID M. POTTER, People of Plenty: Economic Abundance and the American Character introduce philosophical ideas about salvation, culture, or death, that is, philosophical notions about lived human reality. This is, once again, the philosophical dimension of everyday life. It appears that to ask about the meaning work has had in different times and places will unavoidably lead us to inquire about such things as the human condition, the place of human beings in the universe, and the meaning, value, and purpose of human existence itself.

It's to the German sociologist Max Weber that we owe the familiar notion of the Protestant ethic. Weber noticed that after the Reformation capitalism flourished in areas of Europe largely controlled by the followers of John Calvin. Since Calvinism focuses on salvation, not on worldly pursuits, Weber tried to understand and to explain how these people reconciled their religious commitments and their economic interests. The answer, he proposed, lay in the surprising psychological effect that the Calvinist doctrine of "election" had upon its adherents.

In a popular interpretation, the doctrine of election meant that a person's salvation could only be a totally undeserved gift of divine grace. Calvinists couldn't know for sure if they'd be saved or damned, and they couldn't do anything to influence the decision. That's a state of affairs which can become emotionally intolerable for believers, however, so they tended to look for signs of their election in this world. Weber suggested that certain Calvinist groups wound up believing their members' economic success provided the proof that God had chosen these individual members. In other words, individuals were driven to work for success in this world to surmount the anguish of not knowing whether they were eternally saved or damned.

The British historian R. H. Tawney proposed a similar analysis of the impact certain religious beliefs had on the developing secular spirit of early modern times. Consider the old maxim "To work is to pray." Tawney argued in *Religion and the Rise of Capitalism* that for the seventeenth century Puritan this maxim assumed a new and more intense meaning:

> *The labor which [the Puritan moralist] idealizes is not simply a requirement imposed by nature, or a punishment for the sin of Adam. . . . It is itself . . . a discipline imposed by the will of God. . . . [Moreover, it's] not merely an economic means, to be laid aside when physical needs have been satisfied. It is a spiritual end, for in labor alone can the soul find health, and it must be continued as an ethical duty long after it has ceased to be a material necessity.*

In other words, for the Puritans work was not merely a necessary evil; it was good discipline, and people had an ethical obligation to work hard.

In *Earthwalk,* Philip Slater has offered another, more provocative explanation for the value so many contemporary men, at least, place on hard work and success. It's a value peculiar to what he calls our "Oedipal" culture. "Successful men," he writes,

are brought up by mothers who make certain they reject and transcend [that is, surpass] their fathers. The son in such a family is encouraged to break out of his temporal setting and become a being who belongs to no place and no time. He has hitched his wagon to a star and ceases to pay emotional heed to the here-and-now. He is out of synchrony with his environment, living only for achievements that will make him worthy of a maternal ideal that can only be possessed in some beyond-space outside of time.

This is a "rather bizarre notion," Slater concludes, "yet such individuals, whose lives are sacrificed to an almost hallucinatory vision, are accounted the most sane and superior beings in our society (except, perhaps, by those closest to them)." Slater's account is harsh, but some people might recognize themselves in it. It does have the advantage of explaining why we put so much emphasis on work and achievement in our male-dominated, youth-oriented culture, where the son's relationship to his mother is, at least in middle-class society, so much more intense than it is in some other cultures.

Other philosophers and social scientists have linked the modern individual's extraordinary motivation to work to the universal human condition of mortality. Many people work, they claim, in order to overcome or to escape their fear of death. Arendt remarks in *The Human Condition* that work and its product, the artifact, bestow "a measure of permanence and durability upon the futility of mortal life." And Alfred Schütz has called the anticipation of death our "basic experience" and our "fundamental anxiety." We all know we'll die, and we're all afraid of dying. "From the fundamental anxiety," Schütz claims, "spring the many interrelated systems of hopes and fears, of wants and satisfactions, of chances and risks which incite man . . . to attempt the mastery of the world, to overcome obstacles, to draft projects, and to realize them." Schütz describes the anxiety relating to death as a part of our existence as human beings "within the paramount reality of daily life." He says it orients us toward achievement "within the world of working."

Similarly, David Cole Gordon has commented that many people work "to the exclusion of everything else, including love, play, creativity, human relationships, and even . . . the things they like to do most." This may be comprehensible, he suggests, in terms of their fear of death, whether or not that fear is a conscious one. Such people might be seeking to forget their mortality or to deny it as a practical matter of fact. They may even be trying to achieve a sort of synthetic immortality through their work, which might survive them.

How much of the work ethic survives today in America? In *People of Paradox,* the American historian Michael Kammen notes that the work ethic seems to have lost much of its appeal for younger people. "For a considerable period of time now," he writes,

> *middle-class children in America have been pulled by conflicting forces within the Protestant ethos: to obey moral rules and precepts of brotherhood while adjusting to forces of social mobility pushing children to compete strenuously against their playmates and peers. Many of the "cynical young idealists" who face difficult decisions about professional careers condemn what Kenneth Keniston labels "the failure of success." The world lies before them, but they reject it.*

At the same time, many people continue to work very long, hard hours, even though they could get by comfortably on a reduced income. In fact, "workaholism" is a new word that appears more and more frequently in newspaper and magazine articles. As the term suggests, those people to whom it might apply probably aren't motivated to overwork by religious concerns or even by the understandable desire to achieve economic security. They may, rather, depend on their work for the satisfactions it affords them—the sense of purpose and meaning it lends their lives—or they may work hard to overcome, or banish, personal problems.

The work ethic is only one modern view of work. It has unquestionably had a great impact on American culture, and for many people it apparently continues to define a life style. Another, less optimistic, view of work under modern capitalism has also proved important in recent philosophical thought. This view, to which we'll now turn, has it that in contemporary society working people are alienated—estranged from themselves, the world, and others.

Alienation

The word "alienation," as we use it here, means experiencing oneself, the world, and other persons as foreign things. Being alienated is the opposite of belonging. Alienated persons don't see themselves as centers of creative activity living with others in the world; instead, all their relations are disconnective. The person is a stranger, existing like a thing among other things in a hostile environment.

Karl Marx was the first to apply the concept of alienation specifically to the practical world of work. He recognized that work shouldn't be merely a means for staying alive. It should be what a contemporary philosopher might call the human being's existential activity. It should provide the individual with a sense of meaning and importance. However, focusing upon work's real, lived meaning in the nineteenth century's emerging capitalistic and industrial society, Marx found that working people were in a passive rather than active relationship with their world. Under the prevailing social and economic conditions, labor's product, the salable commodity, determined the very nature of human relations. The worked or man-made things intended to serve human life had come to rule over it.

This state of affairs suggested to Marx that the exploited members of the laboring class were alienated. Erich Fromm explains in *The Sane Society,* "Alienation (or 'estrangement') means, for Marx, that man does *not* experience himself as the acting agent in his grasp of the world, but that the world (nature, others, and he himself) remain alien to him. They stand above and against him as objects, even though they may be objects of his own creation. Alienation is essentially experiencing the world and oneself passively."

In the first place, according to Marx, the modern worker is alienated from himself. He's forced to sell himself like an object. What he sells isn't the product of his work, but his work itself—his "labor power," or his time and energy. "Instead of developing his free physical and mental energies," Marx wrote, "he mortifies his body and ruins his mind. He therefore first feels he is with himself when he is free from work and apart from himself when he is at work. He is at home [in the world] when he does not work and not at home when he does."

Viewpoint

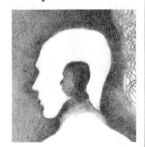

Easy as it was to mow the wet, soft grass, it was hard work going up and down the steep sides of the ravine. But this did not trouble the old man. Swinging his scythe just as usual, and moving his feet in their big bast shoes with firm little steps, he climbed slowly up the steep place, and though his breeches were hanging out below his smock, and his whole frame trembled with effort, he did not miss one blade of grass or one mushroom on his way, and kept making jokes with the peasants and Levin. Levin walked after him, thinking often that he would fall any minute, as he climbed with a scythe up a steep cliff where it would have been hard work to climb even without anything. But he climbed up and did what he had to do. He felt as though some external force was moving him.

LEO TOLSTOY, Anna Karenina

In the second place, the modern worker is alienated from his product. There is no personal relationship to products, no pride in craftsmanship. He's cut off from the things he makes because he surrenders them for money, and what he produces becomes independent of him. In fact, Marx argued that "the more the worker toils, the more powerful becomes the alien world of objects he produces to oppose him [as a worker without capital], and the poorer he himself becomes."

Finally, according to Marx, the modern person is alienated from other people because his relations to them are economically defined. Outside the family, money is what links people to one another; money—and the pursuit of it—is also what keeps them apart from one another. In general, Marx suggested, people don't meet each other as persons in our times, but rather as competitors, producers, and consumers.

Aside from its economic and political implications, yet another aspect of modern, "alienated" life is philosophically important. It has to do with the nature and the quality of human life in our times. Many critical observers in addition to Marx have suggested that man has tragically created an inhuman world. It's a world in which what Marcuse calls false needs govern human life—sex-appeal toothpastes, color televisions, and cars that can travel at 100 miles per hour. The urgency of false needs fills the emptiness created by alienated labor. It's a world in which many dreams have not only

Viewpoint

The ordinary city-dweller knows nothing of the earth's productivity; he does not know the sunrise and rarely notices when the sun sets; ask him in what phase the moon is, or when the tide in the harbor is high, or even how high the average tide runs, and likely as not he cannot answer you. Seedtime and harvest are nothing to him. If he has never witnessed an earthquake, a great flood, or a hurricane, he probably does not feel the power of nature as a reality surrounding his life at all. His realities are the motors that run elevators, subway trains, and cars, the steady feed of water and gas through the mains and of electricity over the wires, the crates of food-stuff that arrive by night and are spread for his inspection before his day begins, the concrete and brick, bright steel and dingy woodwork that take the place of earth and waterside and sheltering roof for him.

SUSANNE K. LANGER, Philosophy in a New Key: A Study in the Symbolism of
Reason, Rite and Art

been realized, but have assumed an independent reality, so that they determine how people live. Supermarkets, supertankers, supersonic jets—all these things that human beings have created govern the lives of individual persons.

According to some thinkers, modern persons are cut off from the world of things in which they live in another sense. José Ortega y Gasset wrote in *The Revolt of the Masses* that modern persons are basically primitive persons who are out of place in this world and who don't really understand their own times. The modern world is as mysterious for the ordinary modern person as the primitive world was for the primitive person. As Ortega expressed it, "the world is a civilized one, its inhabitant is not; he does not see the civilization of the world around him, but he uses it as if it were a natural force. The new man wants his motor-car, and enjoys it, but he believes that it is the spontaneous fruit of an Edenic tree."

What are the human costs of technological progress?

More recently still, Erich Fromm wrote to the same effect in *The Sane Society* that the "telephone, radio, phonograph, and all other complicated machines are almost as mysterious to us as they would be to a man from a primitive culture; we know how to use them, that is, we know which button to turn, but we do not know on what principle they function, except in the vaguest terms of something we once learned in school." And it's not only these sophisticated products of technology that we don't really understand; it's the simpler, more basic things, too, like how our water is purified, how our clothes are manufactured, how our glass and steel and rubber are produced, and how our bread is made. "We consume," Fromm continues, "as we produce, without any concrete relatedness to the objects with which we deal; we live in a world of things, and our only connection with them is that we know how to manipulate or to consume them."

Many modern writers emphasize the irony of this state of affairs: Through our technical inventiveness we've created a dehumanized world. Machinery was first introduced to make the hostile natural environment a familiar world in which people could find themselves at home. It has resulted in an alien world fit only for objects and more machines. Moreover, it's forced many people to adjust to the machines they operate, while others have had to "adjust" to chronic unemployment. Because of the machines we've made, some argue, we've had to become machines ourselves. In *The Fate of Man in the Modern World*, Nicholas Berdyaev wrote,

> *Dehumanization is, first of all, the mechanization of human life, turning man into a machine. The power of the machine shatters the integrity of the human image. Economic life is seen to be completely separated from spiritual life. . . . The machine was intended to liberate man from slavery to nature, to lighten his burden of labor, but instead of that it has [both] enslaved man anew and cursed him with unemployment.*

Marx's critical analysis of the worker's position in modern society led him to investigate both political economics and history, concerns that lie beyond our immediate interest. It seems, however, that his word "alienating" is not inappropriate to describe much of the work that goes on in factories and offices today. In the factory, tools, which were once the link between craftsmen and their artifacts, have largely been replaced by machines to whose deadening, deafening rhythms operators must conform. In bureaucratic offices, some people encode computer cards they can't decipher, others run copying machines, and others type page after page of technical correspondence that they don't really understand and that doesn't interest them anyway. For the factory worker and the typist, as for many others, working is likely to be tedious and unrewarding. It would be inappropriate, in fact, to speak of such jobs as vocations or to describe such work as the realization of the person's values and human possibilities and as his or her existential project. Work may mean accomplishment to some, but for many, the only meaningful accomplishment is either making it through another workday or getting to the weekend.

Yet it remains true that not all work is alienating; some work, at least under some conditions, has positive aspects. Indeed, if so many modern thinkers are critical of the "dehumanizing" effects of work in advanced industrial societies, it's because work *can* be a fulfilling and rewarding experience. We have already mentioned this ideal: In a popular modern view, people freely and creatively define their values and realize their possibilities through the projects they undertake. This view is perhaps best exemplified by the work of creative writers and artists.

The Greek philosopher Aristotle distinguished between *poiein* ("to make") and *prattein* ("to do"). The work of a "poet," and by extension the work of writers and artists generally, is not "practical." In theory, it isn't primarily geared toward making a living.

Nonetheless, creative work is hard work; it requires discipline and it presupposes a commitment to excellence. Nor is the discipline merely the "will power" that keeps writers at their desks or artists in their studios on a sunny day when the work is going badly. It's much more than that: It implies structure, control, technical mastery, and self-criticism. In artistic work (and truly in all work), discipline and excellence go together.

This is not by any means to suggest that only writers, artists, designers, architects, and the like can fully commit themselves to their work and grow and "become themselves." That would be misleading (if not simply false). For one thing, even the most creative people—especially the most creative people—frequently doubt the value of their own work. If they have authentically dedicated their lives to the pursuit of excellence, they run the risk of failure and existential (profound) disappointment. For another, many people genuinely enjoy work that is not "creative" but "practical." Self-fulfillment is not reserved for the leisure class alone. And excellence is not merely an aesthetic ideal; it is a moral quality, a quality of the person, whatever he or she does in life.

These reflections raise once again the question of the meaning of human existence. Karl Britton remarks succinctly, "It can be that a man finds the point of his life in his work; many do not. . . . For many people there is no choice of worthwhile work"; that is, "for many, no choice; for some, no work." But this does not necessarily mean that those who are unemployed and those whose jobs seem pointless are condemned to lead meaningless lives. In Britton's words, "life may have a meaning even if one has work without meaning; certainly it may have a meaning for those whose work has come to nothing."

Work and Society

Basically, we work to earn money to satisfy our physical needs. If we didn't have bodies, we wouldn't have to work, although we might want to. We do have bodies, however, which require nourishment, clothing, and shelter, and to survive as individuals we have to take care of them. This doesn't mean that working is merely a matter of ensuring our individual survival, of course; we've already seen that when earning a living becomes the only reason for working at tedious jobs, the result is liable to be a feeling of alienation. When we work only to maintain our lives, work loses its human meaning. For Marx, such work is labor, and in theory we then have to realize ourselves—our freedom and our creativity—apart from it. In practice, "Man feels himself acting freely only in his animal functions like eating, drinking, and begetting . . . whereas in his human functions he is nothing but [a laboring] animal. The animal becomes the human and the human the animal." The fact remains, however, that most of us work to live; we don't live to work.

We don't usually work alone. In fact, the division of labor and job specialization are at the very heart of social organization. Arendt defines society as "the form in which the fact of mutual dependence for the sake of life . . . assumes public significance and where the activities connected with sheer survival . . . appear in public." In other words, society is the public organization and expression of our interdependence.

What is the relationship between the working person and society?

Despite the advantages it clearly offers, living in society poses serious problems for the individual. One of them is the problem of personal freedom. The contemporary French philosopher Eric Weil has formulated the conflict between individual and social interests this way: For the individual, the problem is society's demand that he work; for society, the problem is the individual's need for leisure time. "Man works in order to have free time—man ought to have free time in order to work well: these are the two [problems] brought down to their simplest terms. . . . The 'leisure problem' is the form in which the individual's problem becomes a problem for the society."

This situation may be changing. It's not the philosopher's job to prophesy, but if, as many social scientists expect, people are required to spend less of their time working in the future, then the individual's relationship to society will change significantly. The expectation is not utopian. It's not an unrealistic hope. The liberation from the need to work has always been one of humanity's fondest dreams, but such liberation would not necessarily mark the arrival of a new paradise. Rather, we'd be faced with new problems, not the least of which would be what to do with all our free time.

Boredom both on and off the job is already a serious problem for many people. Arendt is pessimistic. In her view, the threat that Nietzsche recognized at the end of the nineteenth century has come to pass in the twentieth. The modern attitude that glorifies work has resulted in many people's losing the capacity to use their free time creatively. It's "a society of laborers which is about to be liberated from the fetters of labor," she writes, "and this society does no longer know of those other higher and more meaningful activities for the sake of which this freedom would deserve to be won." We might well disagree with her assessment of modern society, but she has at least identified a potential problem.

In any case, Arendt is clearly right to link work with culture. Yves Simon remarked that culture originally referred to the cultivating of the soil, labor in its most primitive sense. By extension, then, "what we mean by culture is not something produced by nature but something superadded to the effects of nature by the agency of human will and reason." In other words, cultural objects are artifacts, man-made or worked things.

Work also involves another series of problems that should be mentioned, although they're entirely too complex to discuss adequately here. We may refer to this set of problems as those of social justice. It's apparent to the most casual observer that what a person does for a living determines not only his or her social standing but also how much of the society's goods and honors he or she will enjoy. It's equally apparent that the rewards, monetary and otherwise, that society gives to people in different lines of work don't always correspond to how much those people contribute to that society. The rewards often don't even relate to how much people work. Finally, it's undeniable that some have been (and some still are, in this last quarter of the twentieth century) denied work, or denied certain kinds of work, or underpaid for their work for reasons that have nothing to do with their qualifications, abilities, or performance, reasons like age, sex, or race. These injustices aren't peculiar to our society, of course, and in recent years Americans have generally become more conscious of human rights, but such discriminatory and exploitative practices continue to exist, and they do conflict with the democratic ideals of fairness and equal opportunity. "Whatever one's philosophical or even theological position," Maurice Merleau-Ponty wrote, "society is not the temple of value-idols that figure on the front of its monuments or in its constitutional scrolls; the value of a society is the value it places upon man's relation to man." Certainly hiring practices and working conditions involve our relations with one another.

Summary

The Philosophy of Work: Because work is a social reality, it raises acute social and political problems. These problems, which generally include those of freedom, justice, and equality, involve value choices and arguable philosophical ideas about the individual's relation to society. Work also presents some paradoxes. The paradox of freedom and restraint is that the products of our work liberate us, but our work itself enslaves us. The paradox of availability is that our work makes the things of the world available to us, but we ourselves must be available to work. The paradox of the riches and poverty of work is that modern labor techniques, which have increased our human capabilities and whose products have enriched our world, have impoverished us intellectually and emotionally.

Man and Work in Recent Thought: A prevalent modern image of human nature represents man as *Homo faber,* a maker or worker who freely and creatively defines himself through his activity, realizing his values and human possibilities. These characteristics typify him: He is the animal who makes and uses tools; his mind is a toolmaking and tool-using faculty; and he creates his own identity.

The Work Ethic: Social theorists have offered several explanations to account for the sources of the modern drive to work. In one theory, economic success can be seen as a sign of God's favor; in another, people work in order to deny that they are mortal.

Alienation: Alienation means passively experiencing oneself, the world, and others as foreign things. According to Marx and others, in capitalistic, industrial society man is alienated from himself because he has to sell his time and energy; from his products because he has to sell them; and from others because he meets them as producers and consumers. Some philosophers also argue that man's technology has alienated him from nature. Not all work, however, seems alienating, and many modern thinkers stress the positive side of work as creativity.

Work and Society: For the individual, the problem is society's demand that he or she work; for society, the problem is the individual's need for leisure. Liberation from work would not necessarily mark the establishment of a new paradise. Finally, as a social reality, work raises the complex and acute problems of social justice.

Suggestions for Further Reading

Although it is not easy reading, Hannah Arendt's *The Human Condition* (New York: Doubleday, 1959) is one of the most important and rewarding contemporary studies of the nature of work and its meaning for human existence.

Erich Fromm discusses alienation in the modern world in "Man in Capitalistic Society" (chap. 5), *The Sane Society* (Greenwich, CT: Fawcett, 1955).

Herbert Marcuse examines Karl Marx's notion of alienated labor in *Reason and Revolution: Hegel and the Rise of Social Theory* (Boston: Beacon Press, 1941). Two of Marcuse's most important essays in social thought, both critical of contemporary society, are *One-Dimensional Man* (Boston: Beacon Press, 1964) and *An Essay on Liberation* (Boston: Beacon Press, 1969).

Sam Keen sketches and criticizes the modern image of man the maker in "The Travail of Homo Faber," chap. 5 of his readable book *Apology for Wonder* (New York: Harper & Row, 1969).

John J. McDermott has brought together selections from John Dewey's works in an excellent two-volume set, *The Philosophy of John Dewey* (New York: Putnam, 1973). His introductory essay is well written and informative.

The phenomenologist Remy Kwant's *Philosophy of Labor* (Pittsburgh: Duquesne University Press, 1960) is an extended, insightful study of work as a philosophical problem. Its first chapter is especially good.

Work in America (Cambridge: M.I.T., 1973) is the report of a special task force to the United States secretary of health, education, and welfare. Its authors describe the realities of work in our times and present their policy recommendations for humanizing it. Certainly one of the most extensive and important reports on working conditions, it is also interesting reading.

Technology and Civilization: "Progress" toward What?

Do the technological advances of our times—the new products that unquestionably extend our human capacities and make our lives easier—clearly spell progress for humanity?

Some contemporary philosophers have serious doubts. José Ortega y Gasset, for instance, wrote in "Man the Technician" that the popular belief and confidence in the superiority of modern technology poses a threat to our culture. What is precisely our culture's greatest achievement might destroy it! We're too secure, Ortega thought, and "it is just this feeling of security which is endangering Western civilization. The belief in progress, the conviction that on this level of history a major setback can no longer happen and the world will mechanically go the full length of prosperity, has loosened the rivets of human caution and flung open the gates for a new invasion of barbarism."

Why is that? "Since present-day man, as soon as he opens his eyes to life, finds himself surrounded by a superabundance of technical objects and procedures forming an artificial environment of such compactness that primordial nature is hidden behind it," Ortega explains, "he will tend to believe that all these things are there in the same way as nature itself is there without further effort on his part: that aspirin and automobiles grow on trees like apples." This would signal a return to the "primi-

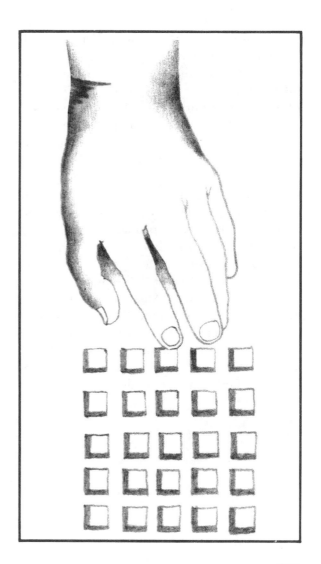

tive attitude" of the "natural man." The modern person "may easily lose sight of technology and of the conditions—the moral conditions, for example—under which it is produced, and return to the primitive attitude of taking it for the gift of nature which is simply there."

What are the "moral conditions" of scientific culture to which Ortega refers? In his view of Western history, the single most important value is the "nobility" that characterizes those exceptional persons who make great demands upon themselves—those people who expect a lot from themselves. In what Ortega describes in *The Revolt of the Masses* as our own "self-satisfied age," most people live the "life of inertia," rather than the "noble life." "Mass man" wants to do as little as possible. Ironically, it's technology and its products (which can be invented, produced, and maintained only through study and sacrifice) that are partially responsible for this state of affairs. They've made our lives so easy that we're no longer inclined to make the effort to do anything at all!

Ortega's spirited critique of mass society raises a number of questions. Do you think he's right, that what he calls "inertia" (and what we might call laziness or apathy) poses a threat to our scientific culture? How do his ideas compare to Arendt's when she identifies leisure as a potential problem for our society?

Does technology pose any other dangers for modern individuals and society?

In your opinion, what are the advantages and disadvantages of living and working in a technological society, where such things as cars, telephones, electronic surveillance devices, and computers are available?

Despite the fact that human beings created technology, some thinkers apparently blame it for "dehumanizing" the world. Are they right to do so? Why or why not?

One of their favorite games was "just before she swallows." They'd wait until one of the younger children, or one of the aged persons, had chewed her food, and then they'd pry her jaws open to take it from her. They did this to the old men too. Sometimes they'd just pretend they were going to do it since it was amusing for the children to see their playmates, and the adults their parents and grandparents, gulp down their food in a panic and choke on it.

When someone died, his or her next of kin did their best to keep it a secret, for two good reasons: First, tribal custom demanded that they provide a funeral feast for the village; second, as long as they could conceal the death from the government, they could collect the dead one's famine relief (such as it was). They never directly engineered one another's death (they weren't given to that sort of murderous violence), but sons and daughters would deprive their mothers and fathers of food and shelter, and parents would throw their children out to take care of themselves when they were three years old.

They didn't know love, or generosity, or friendship beyond the bonds of indebtedness, and although it had not always been that way "goodness" meant "a full belly." If someone fell down or otherwise injured himself or herself, they laughed; and when they went out together

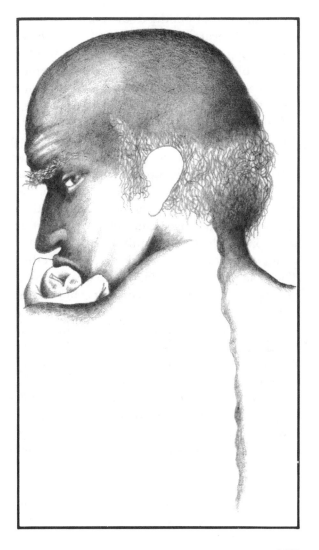

to unwind vines from the trees in order to make twine, it appeared that "the only motive for working in [one another's] company . . . was the pleasurable prospect of being able to enjoy someone else's misfortune" when a "good" vine broke.

In *The Mountain People,* the American anthropologist Colin M. Turnbull describes the social life of the Ik, a hunting-and-gathering tribe that faced extinction when the Ugandan government resettled it on barren farmland. In better times, when tribe members had lived their nomadic life, they had been a closely knit group who apparently valued family and clan loyalties and who presumably worked well together. They had practiced two kinds of hunting: In the grasslands, they hunted with nets, but in the hills, where they were most at home, they used spears and bows and arrows. "Each technique of hunting," Turnbull remarks, "called for the formation of different kinds of groups, but the essential was always cooperativeness." The same, of course, is true of gathering. But when they were removed from their mountains, and forced to abandon the life they'd known there, the spirit of cooperation withered, as did, eventually, all the other social values.

"In such a fluid society of hunters," Turnbull explains, "the environment invariably provides the central theme that holds them together, that gives them a sense of common identity; it is the hub around which their life revolves. . . . It is not just that the Ik would not know how to live, to hunt or to farm, in the flat, arid plateau below them, because they are as intelligent as any and a good deal sharper, quicker to learn and more adaptable than many. But with regard to the mountains it is different. . . . The Ik, without their mountains, would no longer be the Ik."

When drought and famine struck northern Uganda, the situation worsened for the former mountain people. Finally, nothing mattered but their survival as individuals. There were no other "human" values; "society" became a "survival system," where there was no room for personal affection or loyalty. "If people went off in hunting or gathering parties," Turnbull writes, "for the mutual protection of numbers or for necessary cooperation, such goodwill as might have been engendered by the companionship and cooperation was quickly dispelled by the acrimony involved in division of the spoils, if they were communally acquired, or by the sheer envy of seeing anyone else eating food even if it was acquired by his own solitary effort."

At the close of his study, Turnbull offers two conclusions. The first is that such "basic" and "human" qualities and values as family, cooperative sociality, belief, love, and hope are luxuries, if not illusions: "Man is not the social animal he has always thought himself to be, and . . . he is perfectly capable of associating for purposes of survival without being social," that is, without respecting and caring for those with whom he lives. The second is this: Through their extreme individualism, the Ik "have made of a world that was alive a world that is dead, a cold, dispassionate world that is without ugliness because it is without beauty, without hate because it is without love. . . . *And the symptoms of change in our own society indicate that we are heading in precisely the same direction"* (emphasis added). "The Ik have relinquished all luxury in the name of individual survival," Turnbull insists, "and the result is that they live on as a people without life, without passion, beyond humanity. We pursue those trivial, idiotic technological encumbrances and imagine *them* to be the luxuries that make life worth living, and all the time we are losing our potential for social rather than individual survival."

Are such things as love, cooperation, generosity, and respect for one another "luxuries" and "illusions," as Turnbull's study of Icien life suggests? Are they possible only when a society has achieved a certain level of prosperity and economic stability? Are they merely conditional human possibilities rather than the mark of man's essential moral superiority over other forms of animal life?

Is Turnbull justified in suggesting parallels between Icien and American life? Is he right that the "individualism that is preached with a curious fanaticism, heightened by our ever growing emphasis on competitive sports, the more violent the better, and suicidal recreations, is . . . at direct variance with our still proclaimed social ideals" such as brotherhood and community?

In effect, what is a game, if not an activity whose first origin is man, whose principles man himself poses and which can have consequences only according to the principles posed? As soon as a man grasps himself as free and wants to exercise his freedom, whatever his anguish may be, his activity is a game.

JEAN-PAUL SARTRE

In order to define art correctly, it is necessary first of all to cease to consider it as a means to pleasure, and to consider it as one of the conditions of human life.

LEO TOLSTOY

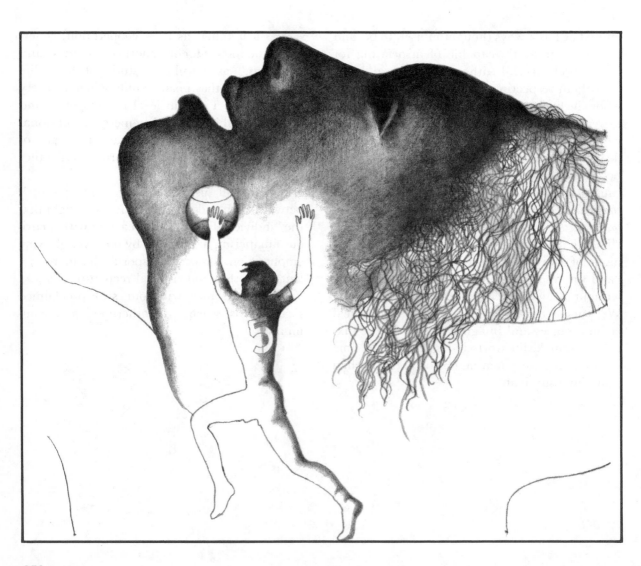

ORDER AND ILLUSION
The Problems of Play and Art

Chapter Survey

Philosophy, Play, and Games
Is philosophy a game?
What is play, and what are games?

The Paradoxes of Play and Games
Is play fun or serious?
Is the play world illusion or reality?
Is play free or necessary?

The Concept of Games
What do games have in common?

Games and Their Rules
What is the significance of rules for games?
What meaning have rules for society?

Play and Culture
Is play related to ritual?
Is play related to music, dance, and drama?

Philosophy and Art
What is art?
What is aesthetic experience?

Art, Religion, and Science
Is art comparable to religion?
Can art be compared to science?

Expression and Imitation
Is art the artist's expression of subjective feeling?
Is art the artist's representation of objective reality?

Art—An Open Concept
Is it possible and desirable to define art?

Susanne Langer
1895–

"What we need today is not primarily a rebirth of good will, or a return to some ancient order of life; we need a generation of vigorous thinkers."

"Every age in the history of philosophy," Susanne Langer wrote, *"has its own preoccupation."* One of America's most vigorous twentieth century thinkers, Langer identified the problems of symbolism and meaning as the dominant philosophical concerns of this age. In her view, language marks the difference between human beings and animals. It is the capacity to use symbols for ideas that allows us to transform our natural environment into a world of relations or facts. "The profound difference," Langer wrote in Philosophical Sketches,

between speech-gifted beings and speechless ones is due to the power of words to set forth relations, which cannot be seen and touched, yet are the bonds among our sensations that create "facts." Our world of facts is shot through and through with concepts comprehended symbolically; "nature" is far more a language-made affair than people generally realize—made not only for sense, but for understanding, and prone to collapse into chaos if ideation fails.

Born in New York City, for fifteen years Susanne Knauth Langer taught philosophy at Radcliffe, where she herself had earned the bachelor's, master's, and doctor's degrees. Although she published some early work in logic, Lang-

er's first truly original philosophical study was Philosophy in a New Key. Aptly entitled, it focused on music to present the theory of art she would later develop in Feeling and Form and other works.

In Philosophy in a New Key, Langer explained, "The general theory of symbolism here set forth, which distinguishes between two symbolic modes rather than restricting intelligence to discursive forms and relegating all other conception to some irrational realm of feeling and instinct, has the great advantage of assimilating all mental activity to reason. . . . It accounts for imagination and dream, myth and ritual as well as for practical intelligence." In particular, her theory would permit her to develop a rational theory of art, which she defined in Problems of Art as "the

creation of perceptible forms expressive of human feeling." Although language serves well to describe and analyze external reality, she maintained, art conceptualizes the inner life. "What discursive symbolism—language in its literal use—does for our awareness of things about us and our own relation to them," she wrote, "the arts do for our awareness of subjective reality, feeling and emotion; they give form to inward experiences and thus make them conceivable."

These ideas suggest the cultural importance of art. Its primary function (one that the different arts accomplish in significantly different ways) is to objectify feeling so that we can contemplate and understand it. Moreover, Langer claimed, the arts actually form our emotive experience: They "mold our actual life of feeling." This assertion partially explains why art, which she described in Philosophical Sketches as "the spearhead of human development, social and individual," arises not late in a society's cultural history, but at its very beginning. It has a practical consequence too. In any culture, art is the people's "school of feeling, and their defense against outer and inner chaos." For that reason, Langer repeatedly warned that the society which neglects art education and vulgarizes art gives itself up to formless emotion.

ORDER AND ILLUSION

Philosophy, Play, and Games

Play and games, which are very much a part of our everyday lives, pose philosophical problems and invite philosophical analysis. In fact, some thinkers have suggested that philosophy itself is a game, and not just in the trivial sense that philosophers play with ideas. For instance, Johan Huizinga, the contemporary Dutch historian who wrote *Homo Ludens* ("Playing Man" or "Man at Play"), emphasized the competitive side of philosophical activity. According to Huizinga, philosophy gradually evolved from what, in the remote past, were sacred riddle-guessing contests. Those riddle games were both rituals and forms of entertainment. Even today there remain what Huizinga would call philosophical play-forms. Philosophical debates are no longer the public, festive, and sometimes fiercely competitive affairs they once were. But philosophers continue to contest one another's ideas at conventions, in seminars, and through the pages of scholarly journals, just as you challenge each other in class.

Is philosophy a game?

Philosophy may also be considered a game from another point of view. It is governed by certain conventional rules: the rules of logic. No argument that breaks such universally recognized logical rules as the one outlawing contradiction is a valid argument. Huizinga noted that "the process of reasoning is itself marked by play-rules." And he supposed, rather naively, that when we debate we always have a tacit understanding with one another to take the validity of the terms and the concepts we use for granted, just as we do the pieces on a chessboard. Similarly, although much more critically, the contemporary Austrian philosopher Ludwig Wittgenstein thought that the ways we use language are so many different games. These games are played according to more or less clearly defined rules.

What is play, and what are games? In our everyday speech, we use both words in a number of ways. For instance, among the more common meanings of the word "play," taken as a verb are "to engage in sport or

What is play, and what are games?

recreation," "to gamble," "to act the part of a theatrical character," "to perform on a musical instrument," and "to move or function freely within limits." The same word, "play," could be taken as a noun. Then the meanings roughly corresponding to some of these different uses of the verb are "sport or recreation," as in "They're at play"; "a theatrical production," as in "They're at a play"; and "the more or less acceptable give in a piece of machinery," as in "The steering wheel has too much play in it." There are also other, less common uses of the word, as a glance at a dictionary will show you.

The meanings of the word "game," which is most frequently used as a noun, are somewhat less diverse. In general, but not always, "games" are "rule-governed, competitive affairs whose primary purpose is recreational." Later in this chapter, when we analyze the notion of games, we'll see that it's difficult and maybe impossible to specify the situations and activities this word might fit.

Obviously, "play" and "games" are not the same thing. We do play games, however, and as long as we remember that the terms "play" and "game" are not interchangeable, we may consider the activities to which they refer as being closely related to one another.

In this chapter we'll discuss some philosophically pertinent aspects of play and games before turning to the problems of art. First, looking at three paradoxes peculiar to play and games, we'll focus on the relationship between these human activities and society's definition of what is real and valuable. Then we'll examine the notion of games to see what, if anything, they all have in common. In the following section, turning again from the play world to the social world, we'll discuss the significance of rules. Finally, we'll close the first part of this chapter by suggesting the relationships between play and games, on the one hand, and such cultural forms as ritual, music, dance, and theater, on the other. Thus, thinking about play will lead us to the second part of the chapter: a consideration of art forms and the major philosophical questions surrounding them. We'll investigate the questions "What is art?" and "What is aesthetic experience?" And we'll try to decide whether it's even possible to define art. But now let's look at the paradoxes of play and games.

The Paradoxes of Play and Games

Is play fun or serious?

Like work, play and games present some paradoxes or apparent contradictions. For instance, playing a game suggests having fun. This element of fun seems, in fact, to be play's most primitive or fundamental characteristic. Have you ever tried to explain the fun of playing a game, though? Have you ever tried to make someone who doesn't share your interest and enthusiasm understand why you find a certain game fun to play? It's not always easy to do!

Still, playing a game is fun. On the face of it, it's certainly not serious. But when you were young, how often did your parents and teachers remind you that it was "only a game"? They frequently *had* to remind you that playing a game is not a consequential matter because children tend to take their games very seriously indeed—and so do adults.

All kinds of games, including football, tennis, and chess, are played in profound seriousness. The players don't have any inclination to laugh. If you want to convince yourself of this, just watch how a bridge, canasta, Monopoly, or poker game can involve the most even-tempered people in heated arguments. Even in parlor games like these, if a player's attention wanders and he makes an innocent mistake, he might provoke his opponents' or his partner's anger. Players are not the only ones who take their game seriously and their losses hard. Spectators at competitive events always take sides too, and the team's record frequently becomes a matter of intense interest. Play is simply fun, then, but paradoxically it has a serious side.

Closely related to the first paradox, a second paradox is that of play's illusory reality. Play doesn't belong to ordinary life in the real world; it usually has a space and a time all its own. For example, when you play football or tennis, bridge or chess, you play on the field or the court, the table

Is the play world illusion or reality?

Play interrupts *the continuity and purposive structure of our lives; it remains at a distance from our usual mode of existence. But while seeming to be unrelated to our normal life, it relates to it in a very meaningful way, namely in its mode of representation. If we define play in the usual manner by contrasting it with work, reality, seriousness and authenticity, we falsely juxtapose it with other existential phenomena. Play is a basic existential phenomenon, just as primordial and autonomous as death, love, work and struggle for power, but it is* not *bound to these phenomena in a common ultimate purpose. Play, so to speak, confronts them all—it absorbs them by representing them. We play at being serious, we play truth, we play reality, we play work and struggle, we play love and death—and we even play play itself.*

Viewpoint

EUGEN FINK, The Oasis of Happiness: Toward an Ontology of Play

or the board. Artificial spatial boundaries are agreed on. And even when time is not especially broken up, say, into quarters for the game's duration, you may experience and think of playtime as different from worktime. It doesn't drag. It flies. Play seems extraordinary and unreal when compared to everyday activities such as getting up and going to work. It's set apart spatially, and it's outside the ordinary flow of time in the real world.

The play world is not the real world, but play paradoxically involves us in another reality. We play in the real world, though usually in special places, and we use real objects in our play. But while playing, we create an artificial world whose reality is open to question. As children we may have played in the living room with dolls and toy trucks made of plastic; now we may use footballs made of leather and tennis rackets made of wood or aluminum to play games in areas set aside for these activities. But while we're playing with real things in the real world, we create a fragile, illusory world that assumes a certain reality of its own. Play is a creative activity. It produces a sphere of illusion, an imaginary but possible and deeply involving realm. It's as if we spectators and players were willing to suspend our disbelief in the world of play for a while. We *know* it *is* only make-believe, it's only a game, it's not serious, it's not real, but we *act* as if it *were* real, and its outcome, vitally important.

Let's turn from play to the theater for an example that might make this difficult idea more clear. You may remember the scene in James Barrie's *Peter Pan* in which Peter turns to the audience and asks them to clap their hands, expressing their belief in fairies, to save Tinkerbelle's life. Most children respond enthusiastically to this request. In appealing to them, Peter offers them the chance to do something, rather than simply watch in helpless dismay while Tinkerbelle dies. For the children in the audience, Never-Never Land, the play's make-believe world, is very real, and what happens there is very important. They clap their hands desperately, and they cheer when Tinkerbelle recovers.

This "as-if" reality that the world of play assumes is fragile, however, as this same example may show. Susanne K. Langer, who uses the example to make another point in another context, reports that when as a child she first saw Barrie's play, Peter's appeal to the audience made her acutely miserable. She claims that since Peter's action destroys the illusion, it is a moment "when most children would like to slink out of the theater and not a few cry—not because Tinkerbelle may die, but because the magic is gone." George Dickie points out that it's doubtful many children would respond that way. But, in any case, for Langer, at least, the spell was broken, and her experience shows that the play world's reality is at every moment open to question.

Although they're both forms of play, there's a great difference between fantasy and competitive games. To varying degrees, however, while the play is going on both fantasy and games assume a reality and an importance that might later seem odd to us. In everyday life, when we're concerned about getting by or getting ahead—gaining power and possessions—we make a distinction between the real world of responsibilities and work and the unreal world of freedom and play. This distinction between what is real and important and what isn't is so widely shared and seems so fundamental that we may well consider those who fail to make it the same way we do abnormal because they've "lost contact with reality." It's immature and irresponsible to play when there's work to be done and deals to be made, and it's insane to consider the play world more real and more important than the world of work.

In a critical essay on Huizinga's book, though, Jacques Ehrmann insists that this common sense distinction between the real world of work and the unreal world of play is misconceived. He asserts, "there is no 'reality' (ordinary or extraordinary!) outside of, or prior to, the manifestations of the culture that expresses it. . . . The problem of play is therefore not *linked* to the problem of 'reality,' itself linked to the problem of culture. It is one and the same problem." What Ehrmann means is that the problem of defining play, or deciding what qualifies as play in a given culture, and the problem of defining reality, or deciding what qualifies as real in a given culture, are one and the same problem. Moreover, since what might merely be make-believe in one culture might be considered real in another, the problem of defining play is also the problem of defining culture. "To define play," Ehrmann writes, "is *at the same time* and *in the same movement* to define reality and to define culture."

Clearly, then, the question we've posed, "What is play?", is not an innocent or casual question. It's not an inconsequential matter. Where and how we mark off the boundaries between work and play and between the serious and the frivolous involves what we are willing to recognize as real. And thus it also involves what we recognize as valuable.

Many modern philosophers and social scientists have pointed out that perceptions and definitions of reality and value can differ from one person and one culture to another. For people who fit into their society, share its assumptions, and function well, the questions of reality and value have largely been settled. What their culture says is real is unquestionably real; what their society values is certainly valuable. It's all a matter of common sense. But what's simply a matter of common sense in one society may seem very strange in another.

It's possible to imagine a society in which people would perceive as hard work what we consider play. Even within our own culture, we could conceivably disagree with one another, not so much perhaps about what's

Is play free or necessary?

real and important, but certainly about what's work and what's play. For the professional athlete, for instance, play may be work; for someone who's good at his job and really enjoys it, work may be play. If we can accept this, can't we also imagine a society that considers, say, the academic world or the business world an illusion and the play world real? Or a society that values play more than work, games more than possessions, and leisure more than income?

So far, we've looked at two interrelated paradoxes: first, play and games are both fun and serious; second, the world of play is both illusory and real. A third paradox, which is in its turn related to the first two, might further clarify the important idea that our notions of work and play, seriousness and fun, and reality and illusion are socially defined and culture-bound. This third paradox is that of the freedom and the necessity of play in the modern world.

Play is spontaneous, voluntary, and gratuitous. Its source is spring fever, the overflowing of high spirits and youthful energy; it's free, it is in fact the

---

Viewpoint

To say that play "implies leisure" is to set forth the problem while placing oneself in an ethnocentric perspective that falsifies the basic data to be analyzed: it is to oppose the notion of work to that of leisure (an opposition which carries with it all the others we have already noted: utility-gratuitousness, seriousness-play, etc.). Such an opposition may be valid in our society (and even there, less and less), but it certainly cannot be generalized to include cultures other than our own. . . .

Clearly, the opposition leisure-work (science) corresponds to a conception of culture limited to the industrial phase of our civilization. It seems to give rise only to rudimentary and simplistic Marxist analyses. In point of fact, alienation in and through work can no longer be automatically opposed to leisure-freedom in a society—our society—where leisure is being industrialized and work is being automated.

The value attributed to accumulation, to capitalization through work and science is thus part of this same utilitarian and materialist attitude toward culture (time lost as opposed to time well spent) whose ethnocentric position . . . entails the expulsion of play into the exterior of gratuitousness and futility, where it becomes the utopian complement of seriousness.

JACQUES EHRMANN, *"Homo Ludens* Revisited"

model and expression of human freedom. It isn't productive, it doesn't belong to the world of work at all, and it hasn't anything to do with physical necessity, individual survival, or the serious business of making a living.

Yet, right or wrong, we frequently talk as if play does serve a purpose and have a function in the world of work. We commonly subordinate play to work, ascribing to it a certain usefulness in relation to work. Indeed, in Western thought, this view of play has a long history. In his *Laws,* for example, Plato expressed it mythologically:

> *The gods . . . took pity on the human race, born to suffer as it was, and gave it relief in the form of religious festivals to serve as periods of rest from their labours. They gave us the Muses, with Apollo their leader, and Dionysus; by having these gods to share their holidays, men were to be made whole again, and thanks to them, we find refreshment in the celebration of these festivals.*

In our times, much more than in Plato's, if we contrast work and play, it's usually to justify play in terms of work: Physically and emotionally, we working people have to play sometimes. We arrive, then, at the third paradox: Play is the expression of our freedom from necessity and work, but it is necessary if we're to work efficiently. We need vacations and weekends, play and games, in order to recharge our batteries for work.

Against this utilitarian view of play, Eugen Fink, a contemporary German philosopher, protests, "Whenever we play 'for the sake of' physical fitness, military training, or health, play has been perverted and has become merely a means to an end." He implies that play should be an end in itself. But the fact remains that in our society we do ordinarily think and talk about play in these functional, utilitarian terms, and that fact may say something about our society.

It appears, then, that in modern Western society, at least, play and games have these three paradoxical aspects. First, they are fun, but they are also serious. Second, the world of play and games is illusory, but it also has a certain reality, if only for the play's duration. And third, play and games are free, but they are also necessary. Let's now examine the notion of games to see what, if anything, games have in common and what the social significance of their rules might be.

The Concept of Games

What is a game? When you think of all the different activities we call games, it's hard to say just what they might have in common with one another.

What do games have in common?

Hopscotch, football, solitaire, and chess are all games people play, but they're very different from one another.

Ludwig Wittgenstein, in his effort to understand how we use language, criticized philosophers for trying "to say more than we can know." We all have a "craving for generality," a tendency to look for a shared feature that identifies a whole class of things. Many philosophers make this pursuit their business. An example of it is seeking something common to all the different things referred to by the single, general term "games." "We are inclined to think that there must be something in common to all games, say, and that this common property is the justification for applying the general term 'game' to the various games." Otherwise, why would we call all of them games?

Wittgenstein's advice is not to speculate about how these very different activities logically must share a common feature, but to examine them, instead, to see if in fact they do. As a result of the craving for generality, we may not investigate individual instances carefully enough. Look at "the proceedings we call 'games,'" Wittgenstein said. "I mean board-games, card-games, ball-games, Olympic games, and so on. What is common to them all?—Don't say: 'There *must* be something common, or they would not be called "games"'—but *look and see* whether there is anything common to *all.*"

Such an examination of games would reveal, Wittgenstein argued, not that there is a single feature common to all games, but rather that there is "a complicated network of similarities overlapping and criss-crossing; sometimes overall similarities, sometimes similarities of detail." Wittgenstein called these similarities "family resemblances" because "the various resemblances between members of a family: build, features, colour of eyes, gait, temperament, *etc., etc.,* overlap and criss-cross in the same way."

A contemporary analytic philosopher, Renford Bambrough, has explained Wittgenstein's useful notion of family resemblances this way. Suppose, he suggests, that we are told to classify a set of objects according to whether or not they have the features A, B, C, D, and E. It could occur that five objects (e, d, c, b, and a) each have four of the properties in question but lack the fifth and that the missing feature is different in each case. Here's how that might look:

e	d	c	b	a
ABCD	ABCE	ABDE	ACDE	BCDE

"Here we can already see how natural and how proper it might be," Bambrough concludes from his illustration, "to apply the same word to a number of objects between which there is no common feature."

What is a game, then? What might hopscotch, football, solitaire, and chess have in common? It may not, in fact, be possible to establish a definition that would isolate one criterion, one thing common to all games and peculiar to them. But we may very well succeed in pointing out significant features, or family resemblances, that would generally distinguish games from other activities. After all, we use the concept "game" all the time, and we only rarely have disagreements about what this general term means and whether or not it applies in a particular case.

For instance, although their objects vary, it seems that most games are competitive. In a race, the object is ordinarily to get somewhere faster than your opponents, though it can also be to break a previously established record, even your own. In ball games and in many board games the object is to score more points than your opponents. Winning may not be everything, but people who play games ordinarily play to win, and anyone who deliberately tried to lose a game would most likely be accused of not playing the game at all. At first glance, then, this competitive aspect appears to be one feature generally shared by games.

Not all games are competitive, however. For instance, solitaire, which is a game you can win, is not a competitive game. Many children's games, such as "house" and "cowboys and Indians," are simply make-believe. They're rainy-day, role-playing games: "Let's pretend that I'm the pilot, and you're the control tower. . . ."

Moreover, competition is not peculiar to games. Sometimes in school or business we contend for important prizes. Students compete for the top grades in high school, and for scholarships in college; after graduation they compete for desirable jobs. Architects and builders bid for contracts. Shopkeepers compete with one another, as do salespersons—"Competition is good for business"—and reporters vie with one another to get the facts first. These competitive situations are not games.

We might conclude two things. First, although many games have a competitive aspect, not all games are competitions and not all competitions are games. It does not seem that we can use the terms "competition" and "contest" to define the concept of games. We could only if we were willing at one and the same time to *restrict* our use of the term "game" to include only competitive games and to *extend* our use of the term "game" to include competitive activities that are not generally considered games. Second, we might yet discover some quality or feature that all games, and games only, have in common with one another, and this would then serve as a criterion for deciding whether or not a certain activity is a game. But chances are that the concept of games is an open concept. There may be family resemblances among games, rather than a single feature that would allow us mechanically to distinguish games from nongames.

Games seem generally to share another significant feature: They have rules. In the next section we'll discuss the importance of rules not only for the games we play but also for the language we use and the society in which we live.

Games and Their Rules

What is the significance of rules for games?

To judge from the way we ordinarily use the term "games," not all rule-governed activities are games, but all games have rules. We can *play* without rules, but we can't play *games* without them. For a philosophical understanding of games, this fact is more promising than the fact that many of them are competitive. In practical terms, it means that we cannot simply define games as "the set of all rule-governed activities." But neither can we understand the concept of games without understanding the concept of rules, nor can we explain particular games without explaining their rules. In recent years, some philosophers of language have given their attention to the notion of rules; by considering some of their ideas about our uses of language, which are also rule-governed activities, we may learn something about games.

"Language-game" is an expression Ludwig Wittgenstein employed in his later philosophical works, where he maintained that the many ways we use language in our everyday life are comparable to games whose rules can be defined and explained more or less clearly. In *Philosophical Investigations,* Wittgenstein emphasized the conventional nature of rules. They're agreements we make with one another: "The word 'agreement' and the word 'rule' are *related* to one another," Wittgenstein asserted, "they are cousins. If I teach anyone the use of the one word, he learns the use of the other with it." In *Remarks on the Foundations of Mathematics,* Wittgenstein even suggested that the concept of rules is logically more primitive or more fundamental than the idea of an agreement. "One does not learn to obey a rule by first learning the use of the word 'agreement.' Rather, one learns the meaning of 'agreement' by learning to follow a rule." To say that rules are agreements and, indeed, to suggest that we learn what an agreement is by learning to follow a rule is to identify rules as arbitrary conventions.

Rules, or conventions, are agreements we make in society. They are public affairs. And since the games we play are rule-governed, they are social activities. We play games with and against one another in the social world according to rules we agree to observe. From this perspective, even games like puzzles and solitaire presuppose a social background. When questions arise, how do you decide whether you've solved a puzzle properly or completed a game of solitaire according to the rules? By referring to established standards. But you can't establish standards in complete isolation from other people, because for standards to serve their purpose they have to provide an objective check on your actions. Wittgenstein argued that "it is not possible to obey a rule 'privately': otherwise, thinking one was obeying the rule would be the same thing as [actually] obeying it."

Fundamentally, then, following a rule is not a private but a public affair. Playing a game is a social activity. And so is using a language. The American logician Willard Van Orman Quine remarked that the person who learns to use the word "square"—or any other word—"has to take his chances with the rest of society, and he ends up using the word to suit."

A contemporary American philosopher of language, John Searle, has also discussed the notion of rules. In *Speech Acts*, Searle distinguished two sorts of rules, and his explanation of them introduces their social dimension.

What meaning have rules for society?

Viewpoint

Consider the following parable. In the land of Erewhon, there are, returning travelers say, no games as we know them, governed by fixed rules of play freely accepted. But while the Erewhonians abhor the idea of being fettered in their amusements by arbitrary regulations, they love to play. *This leads to foreseeable complications. When friends meet to "play at cards," each comes with his own pack, some marked with symbols we should recognize, others inscribed with representations of flowers, animals, or whatever pleases the individual fancy. Endless time is wasted, before play can begin, in arguing* how *to play and what is to count as "winning" for the particular occasion. And even if agreement is reached, the level of skill is deplorably low, for with constantly shifting conventions, there is no chance for theories of strategy to emerge.*

Contrast now this babel with the position of anybody in the Western world invited to an evening's bridge. The very definition of the game guarantees that the play will proceed according to predetermined rules and conventions, known to all the players and accepted by all of them as binding. . . . The existence and acceptance of the rules of bridge make possible the game as we know it and all the subsidiary activities of theorizing about *the game, inventing strategies, teaching, and learning it. The game is partly constituted by the rules,* i.e., *in the absence of rules it would not be what we understand by a* game.

MAX BLACK, The Labyrinth of Language

Constitutive rules establish or institute new forms of meaningful behavior in the social world; regulative rules govern previously existing, logically independent forms of meaningful behavior.

Searle suggests some examples that might make these definitions more clear. Regulative rules regulate forms of behavior that already exist in the social world. Rules of etiquette are regulative rules. They govern interpersonal relationships that would still exist apart from any such norms of behavior or standards of politeness. Constitutive rules, however, do not merely regulate behavior. They create new forms of behavior and new possibilities for intelligent action. The rules of particular games, like football, for instance, or chess, are constitutive rules. They don't just govern the way we play those games, but create the very possibility of playing them.

If game rules are constitutive, then it's clear not only that games are social activities but also that their rules are not incidental to them. On the contrary, the rules are foundational.

This analysis suggests some interesting similarities, and perhaps relationships, between games and other aspects of social life. Because they have rules, games introduce order into the play world, just as our customs and laws introduce order into the social world. Huizinga writes of play that "it creates order, *is* order. Into an imperfect world and into the confusion of life it brings a temporary, a limited perfection." The rules of games introduce order by governing our action on the playing field as customs and laws govern our behavior off the field.

Moreover, because their rules are constitutive, games are comparable to social institutions like courts and colleges, whose rules establish the possibility of certain forms of orderly behavior. In football games, players score touchdowns, and in chess games, players check their opponents; in courts, lawyers argue cases, and in colleges students take examinations. These are all activities that make sense within their respective institutional contexts. As rule-governed activities, then, games create order and "introduce a limited perfection into an imperfect world" by establishing and regulating forms of behavior. Game rules institute activities and define what, in the game situation, is appropriate and acceptable behavior. For this reason, games may be considered model institutions.

In this connection, it deserves mention that the concept of rules is crucial to the social sciences since their effort is to understand human behavior in the social world. Peter Winch argues cogently in *The Idea of a Social Science* that "all behaviour which is meaningful (therefore all specifically human behaviour) is [by that very fact] rule-governed"—it's meaningful and understandable *because* it follows rules—so "the analysis of meaningful behaviour must allot a central role to the notion of a rule."

Of course, the concept of rules has importance beyond the social sciences.

It's important to society itself. In a perceptive and influential essay on play, Roger Caillois, a contemporary French thinker, maintains with good reason that there's "no civilization without play and rules of fair play, without conventions consciously established and freely respected." Social life would be impossible without rules like those that govern the games we play.

We've now seen that the concept of games is an open concept which evidently can't be simply and clearly defined once and for all. But games have rules, and in this respect they are comparable both to the ways we use language for different purposes in different situations and to social institutions. In the next section we'll consider the relationship between play and culture, focusing on the points of contact between play and ritual, music, dance, and theater.

Play and Culture

What, if anything, do play and games have to do with culture, with such forms of expression as music, dance, and drama? Philosophers agree only that the answer isn't simple. As you might have concluded from our discussion of games, rules, and meaningful behavior in the social world, play isn't as unimportant and inconsequential as most people probably think. It may not be just an accident or a coincidence that we say, for instance, "He's learning to play the piano," or "She's going to see a play at the theater this evening." Although his ideas have been criticized, Huizinga may intuitively have been right to hold that "culture arises in the form of play."

Some philosophers have investigated the possibility of a relationship between play, games, and culture. These philosophers have called attention to the fact that play is similar to religious ritual, and they have suggested a connection between them. Play has at least some formal characteristics that might lend support to the idea. For instance, as we've already seen, play usually has a place and a time of its own. Huizinga saw in the simple fact that we set playgrounds aside for ourselves a significant point of comparison between play and ritual. He claimed, in *Homo Ludens,*

Is play related to ritual?

> *Formally speaking, there is no distinction whatever between marking out a space for a sacred purpose and marking it out for purposes of sheer play. The turf, the tennis-court, the chess-board and pavement-hopscotch cannot formally be distinguished from the temple or the magic circle.*

Similarly, Louis Dupré, a contemporary American philosopher of religion, has focused on the time of play. "The verb *to celebrate* which we apply to acts of worship is also the proper term for 'having a good time,'"

Dupré remarks. "By their festive nature religious rites are related to the exuberant activity of playing."

As we've just seen, another formal characteristic of games is that they are governed by rules, and so they introduce a certain order into the world. Rituals are also ceremonially rule-governed, and in a sense they too symbolically order the world.

There is, however, a crucial difference between play, or at least competitive games, and religious rituals. Socially, they have the opposite effect. Claude Lévi-Strauss, the contemporary French anthropologist, points out that the game is disjunctive, or divisive, since it results in the social distinction between winners and losers. The ritual, by contrast, is conjunctive, since it issues in a heightened sense of community involvement. For instance, passage rites or transitional rites—the ceremonies surrounding birth, adulthood, marriage, and death—accentuate the individual's mem-

Viewpoint

What we ask is: Is the original function of play in giving basic structure to existence different from that of ritual? That both are instrumental in the discovery of such elementary distinctions as the one between the sacred and the profane seems to me beyond doubt. The only question is: Did they contribute to it in the same way or in a different way?

Whatever the answer may be, once man becomes reflectively conscious of the nature of the sacred, his attitude with respect to ritual (including ritual games) evidently differs from his play attitude. Man considers himself the inventor and creator of the game: he determines the rules and sets the stakes. In the religious universe, on the contrary, man feels at the mercy of powers which entirely surpass him. Nor can man ever completely relax in ritual as he can in play. Much as the sacred reality fascinates him, he experiences it nevertheless as a dangerous force which must be kept at bay. The dread of the sacred maintains in him an anguished tension that is absent from a genuine game. Finally, the attitude with respect to ordinary reality differs. While the player is unconcerned about it to the point of oblivion, religious man remains constantly aware of its existence. It is present to him, not merely as that which he must leave but as that for which he is somehow held responsible and which he eventually must integrate with the sacred.

LOUIS DUPRÉ, The Other Dimension: A Search for the Meaning of Religious Attitudes

bership in a community by giving the private events of that person's life a public character. If play is somehow related to ritual, then, it's because of its potentially symbolic, representational, or make-believe character and not because of its competitive aspect.

Not everyone agrees, of course, that play and ritual should be linked to each other. And it certainly would not be correct to move from the recognition of formal, or abstract, similarities between play and ritual to the affirmation that they are actually related to each other in any given culture (much less in all cultures). Although he admits the formal similarities between play and ritual, Roger Caillois, for one, insists in *Man and the Sacred* that in a religious ceremony the participants' attitude is not playful:

> *I know that [the sacred] is separated from the routine world, that all acts performed there are regulated and symbolic, that the priest dons ceremonial vestments and plays a role, and finally I know that the entire liturgy is something of a game. However, if one considers not merely its forms, but the intimate attitudes of the officiant and the faithful, I also see that sacrifice and communion are involved, that one is then fully in the sacred, and as far removed from play as is conceivable.*

Not only for a philosophical understanding of culture, then, but for a philosophy of religion as well, the differences between play and ritual are as important and instructive as their similarities.

What about music? Are play and music significantly comparable? Both these activities are primarily nonutilitarian; that is, they don't enter into the categories of means and ends that order our moral, political, and economic lives. Except in the case of professional athletes and musicians, play and music have nothing to do with necessity and responsibility. More positively, music, like play, is enchanting, and it has its own time; when we're absorbed by a symphony, or a game, we're not aware of the passing minutes.

Is play related to music, dance, and drama?

Music is closely related to dancing; in a sense, to listen attentively to the music is to refrain from dancing. And dancing is, like music, playful. Huizinga goes so far as to call dancing the purest and most perfect form of play there is! Of course, in its exuberance dance is also linked to religious ritual. Langer remarks that "the magic circle around the altar or the totem pole, the holy space inside the Kiwa or the temple, is the natural dance floor." The theologian and historian Hugo Rahner has also called attention to the fact that "dance is a sacral form of play," although in *Man at Play* he focuses not on the exuberance of dance but on its expressive power.

Plato said our ability to appreciate rhythm and harmony is a divine gift that sets human play apart from animal play. All young creatures are active. They find it impossible to keep their bodies still and their mouths quiet.

Although "animals have no sense of order and disorder in movement ('rhythm' and 'harmony,' as we call it), we human beings have been made sensitive to both and can enjoy them." This, he said, is "the gift of the same gods whom we said were given to us as companions in dancing." In Plato's thought, then, play, music, dancing, and religious festivals were all linked to one another.

In much the same way, the formal similarities between play and the theater are readily apparent: Whether it's comic or tragic, the play's make-believe action goes on in its own illusory space and time. Plays involve us just as play itself does, so that in both cases the play world, imagination's product, assumes a certain reality for us. And think about how much role playing we do in real life!

We've talked about how play is a creative activity and also about how it produces a sphere of illusion and enchantment. Many philosophers have focused on these characteristics of play, comparing the activity of play to the creation of art. And perhaps the play of childhood—or adulthood—is a stepping-stone to the mixture of seriousness and playfulness that creates the arts.

However, the view that derives culture and art in general from play has limits. For one thing, play seems to be much closer to the performing arts, music, dance, and drama, than to the plastic arts like painting and sculpture (except possibly in execution). For another, the artistic imagination should be distinguished from the kind of imagination that typifies our play activity, as Ernst Cassirer argues in *An Essay on Man*. "Play gives us illusory images; art gives us a new kind of truth—a truth not of empirical things but of pure forms," he writes. "The child plays with *things,* the artist plays with *forms,* with lines and designs, rhythms, and melodies." Cassirer's remarks may remind us that to reduce art to play would indeed "indicate a very meager conception of its character and task." Finally, even if play is at the very

Viewpoint

587. A child learns to walk, to crawl, to play. It does not learn to play voluntarily and involuntarily. But what makes its movements in play into voluntary movements?—What would it be like if they were involuntary?— Equally, I might ask: what makes this movement into a game?—Its character and its surroundings.

LUDWIG WITTGENSTEIN, Zettel

source of culture, it would not be correct to suggest that all our cultural activities and artistic achievements are merely games!

The thesis that activities apparently as disparate as those we've considered—play, ritual, music, dance, and theater—are comparable to one another and may indeed have a common source is a thesis that betrays the philosopher's "craving for generality." Cultural anthropologists studying particular societies might find the hypothesis that play is more or less directly related to other activities interesting. But even if it proved useful they could establish its validity only by scrutinizing specific, concrete cases, with one eye always open for counterexamples and better explanations. In another context, the contemporary English philosophers H. P. Grice and P. F. Strawson wrote, "On the whole, it seems that philosophers are prone to make too few distinctions, rather than too many. It is their assimilations, rather than their distinctions, which tend to be spurious." Their caution is certainly not inappropriate here.

There remain problems to analyze and issues to debate, but these remarks conclude our discussion of play and games and our discussion of the possible similarities and differences between play and the arts. In the remaining pages of this chapter, we shall turn to the problems of defining art and aesthetic experience.

Philosophy and Art

"All human life," Leo Tolstoy wrote, "is filled with works of art of every kind—from cradle-song, jest, mimicry, the ornamentation of houses, dress, and utensils, to church services, buildings, monuments and triumphal processions. It is all artistic activity." Tolstoy's remarks are valuable because they call our attention to the fact that art is not just a special activity that a special kind of person does. It is a familiar human activity that enters into many aspects of our everyday lives.

What is art?

However, this view that art is not something extraordinary and exceptional also poses a problem: If art is such a large part of human life, then why do we ordinarily restrict our use of the term to relatively unusual activities, experiences, and objects like dance, music, drama, paintings, sculptures, and novels? "We are accustomed," Tolstoy affirmed, "to understand art to be only what we hear and see in theaters, concerts, and exhibitions; together with buildings, statues, poems, and novels." We ordinarily use the word "art" in this more limited sense, and we ordinarily understand it that way too. For some reason, we attach special importance to those extraordinary things for which we reserve the term "art."

What is art? This problem of definition has divided philosophers for centuries. It would appear, in fact, that the word "art" may be very much like the word "game." We all know how to use the word in meaningful sentences, but we'd be hard put to name one feature or set of features that all artistic activities and experiences, or that all works of art, have in common and that sets them apart from other things.

In an effort to explain what art is, some philosophers have given their attention to "aesthetic experience." Derived from the Greek *aisthesis,* meaning "perception" or "sensation," the adjective "aesthetic" relates to the beautiful; an aesthetic experience is an experience of the beautiful. If we could describe aesthetic experience, then we might be able to decide whether or not any given object is a work of art, and we might further be justified in saying that a particular work of art is "good" or "bad." In terms of aesthetic experience, we might succeed not only in defining art but also in evaluating works of art.

What might characterize aesthetic experience? What might distinguish aesthetic experience from ordinary experience? Is there, for example, a specific way to perceive a painting that is significantly different from the way we perceive coffee cups and ashtrays?

Some contemporary philosophers have suggested that perception itself is, like art, a creative integration of the elements of our experience. In a certain sense, they hold, all our acts of perceiving are artistic. Our perception of the external world is not a passive affair; we don't simply observe objects and record events. Rather, in perceiving, we have an active relationship with the objects of our environment. Perception is selective: We focus on particular aspects of the phenomena we encounter. Accordingly, the French philosopher Maurice Merleau-Ponty argued that "being" is "that which demands of us creation in order that we might have experience of it." The American philosopher John Dewey said very nearly the same thing, namely, that "to perceive, a beholder must *create* his own experience."

Nonetheless, our perception of works of art seems to differ from our perception of other objects. It seems somehow to be the case that we don't see paintings, for instance, the same way that we see sledgehammers, and we don't hear music the same way we hear the horn of an oncoming car. Those philosophers of art who stress the notion of aesthetic experience generally hold that the appreciative person's attitude toward a work of art is "disinterested." When we attend to a work of art, we are not interested in its usefulness as a means to some end; rather, we contemplate it for its own sake.

It's possible, of course, that the difference between aesthetic and ordinary experience has to do not so much with *how* as with *what* we perceive. Aesthetic experience might simply be the experience of aesthetic objects, or works of art. Even if it were not an instance of circular reasoning, however, this suggestion would reintroduce rather than resolve the problem of definition. What is an aesthetic object? What is a work of art? It clearly won't do just to repeat that works of art are things like musical scores, dramatic scripts, poems, novels, paintings, and sculptures. This definition is not satisfactory because it does not provide us with a rule for continuing the series. We cannot legitimately decide what else to consider "things like these." Moreover, we sometimes refer to things apparently quite unlike these as works of art. We might say, for instance, that a certain natural rock formation or a certain piece of driftwood is a work of art.

In the following sections of this chapter we'll attempt to reach a better understanding of art by examining aesthetic experience. First we'll compare art to religion and science; then we'll discuss whether art is an expression of subjective feeling or an imitation of objective reality. Finally, returning to the notion of aesthetic objects, we'll conclude with some further remarks on the concept of art.

Art, Religion, and Science

How does art compare to other approaches to the world, or other ways of relating to it, such as religion and science? Some thinkers have proposed that art, like religion and science, is an effort to make sense of the world. In this view, reality is not meaningful in itself; on the contrary, it's chaotic, absurd, and pointless. The human mind intervenes to lend meaning to reality by constructing religious systems and scientific models; similarly, the artist creates works of art—such as sculptures, paintings, plays, novels, and poems—that give a certain imaginative order and coherence to the world. In each case, the religious believer, the scientist, and the creative artist are impelled to build their theories about the world by the fact that it doesn't seem to make any sense at all. Art, in this respect like religion and science, introduces order into the world of human experience. This theory is similar to Huizinga's thesis that games introduce a certain, limited perfection into "an imperfect world and the confusion of life."

Is art comparable to religion?

To appreciate more fully the suggestion that art and religion serve similar functions, compare the following passages. The first presents a capsule theory of the origin and the purpose of religion; the second, a similar account of art, or at least of the novelist's art.

Cited by the contemporary British philosopher Bertrand Russell in his essay, "A Free Man's Worship," the imaginative theory of religion comes from Goethe's *Faust*. There, the devil named Mephistopheles presents his own version of the creation and history of the world—and, incidentally, of the source and the function of religious belief. In Mephistopheles' account, existence is a play God has staged for his own amusement.

And Man saw that all is passing in this mad, monstrous world, that all is struggling to snatch, at any cost, a few brief moments of life before Death's inexorable decree. And Man said: "There is a hidden purpose, could we but fathom it, and the purpose is good; for we must reverence something, and in the visible world there is nothing worthy of reverence." And Man stood aside from the struggle, resolving that God intended harmony to come out of chaos by human efforts. And when he followed the instincts which God had transmitted to him from his ancestry of beasts of prey, he called it Sin, and asked God to forgive him. But he doubted whether he could be justly forgiven, until he invented a divine Plan by which God's wrath was to have been appeased.

According to the demon Mephistopheles, then, religion is a human invention that postulates a "hidden purpose" and a "divine plan" behind the blind struggle for existence. An arbitrary construct, in this view religion gives order, purpose, and meaning to an existence that would otherwise seem chaotic, pointless, and meaningless.

In his novel *I Thought of Daisy,* the American critic Edmund Wilson offers a parallel explanation of art. Focusing on imaginative literature, the story's narrator presents a theory of art that is, in fact, strikingly similar to Mephistopheles' theory of religion:

A work of art was, then, an imposture. But the reader, himself balked and bewildered [by reality], received naïvely the artist's picture as a true diagram of the world. The artist who had been disconcerted and spurred to compose a work of art by his failure to discover in the universe either harmony or logic, supplied the logic and harmony himself; and the reader, who had also been hungering for harmony and logic, accepted with joyful reassurance what the artist gave him, and assumed that the artist's makeshift was certified revelation, and the artist a kind of oracle.

In this popular view, art serves to make sense of the world. However, the comparison we've suggested between art and religion—a comparison that these passages from Goethe's and Wilson's works highlight—is valid only if religion does not express revealed truths about God, human beings, and the world, but is, rather, just a fiction.

Can art be compared to science?

Is art similarly comparable to science? Any response, whether affirmative or negative, will depend on one's view of both art and science, but if art and science do represent our effort to explain the world, to make things intelligible, then in a general way they might be considered similar to one another. Clearly, scientific theories do offer coherent explanations of the natural world, just as works of art, in this view, offer explanations of the human world.

The primary function of scientific theories becomes clearer when we ask, "Why do we accept one theory in preference to others?" In *The Logic of Scientific Discovery*, Karl Popper writes, "We choose the theory which best holds its own in competition with other theories. . . . A theory is a tool which we test by applying it, and which we judge as to its fitness by the results of its applications." In other words, when two competing theories offer different explanations for the same thing, we test them and choose the one that works better.

However, many contemporary philosophers argue that art differs fundamentally from science. Ernst Cassirer points out that it's "characteristic of the nature of man that he is not limited to one specific and single approach to reality but can choose his point of view." Cassirer suggests that whereas science gives us order in our thoughts, art gives us order in our perception of things. "Language and science," he writes, "are abbreviations of reality; art is an intensification of reality. Language and science depend upon one and the same process of abstraction; art may be described as a continuous process of concretion."

These remarks suggest that even though both art and science are in some sense explorations of reality, the artist expresses his discoveries about the world in a concrete form (a painting, for instance, or a novel), but the

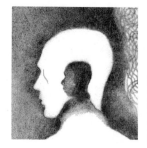

Viewpoint

. . . if modern tendencies are justified in putting art and creation first, then the implications of this position should be avowed and carried through. It would then be seen that science is an art, that art is practice, and that the only distinction worth drawing is not between practice and theory, but between those modes of practice that are not intelligent, not inherently and immediately enjoyable, and those which are full of enjoyed meanings. When this perception dawns, it will be a commonplace that art—the mode of activity that is charged with meanings capable of immediately enjoyed possession—is the complete culmination of nature, and that "science" is properly a handmaiden that conducts natural events to this happy issue. Thus would disappear the separations that trouble present thinking: division of everything into nature and experience, of experience into practice and theory, art and science, of art into useful and fine, menial and free.

JOHN DEWEY, Experience and Nature

scientist expresses his conclusions about the world in an abstract form (a law or a formula). Cassirer also writes in *An Essay on Man:*

> *A single formula, like the Newtonian law of gravitation, seems to comprise and explain the whole structure of our material universe. It would seem as though reality were not only accessible to our scientific abstractions but exhaustible by them. But as soon as we approach the field of art this proves to be an illusion. For the aspects of things are innumerable, and they vary from one moment to another. Any attempt to comprehend them within a simple formula would be in vain. Heraclitus' saying that the sun is new every day is true for the sun of the artist if not for the sun of the scientist.*

According to Cassirer then, taken as approaches to reality, art and science are thoroughly different from each other. It's instructive to contrast them, but it would be misleading, or simply incorrect, to compare them to each other.

Indeed, there are limits to the comparative interpretation of art, religion, and science we've proposed. Many contemporary philosophers would be sharply dissatisfied with any philosophy of culture that suggested similarities between such different perspectives on the objects and events of our experience. Peter Winch, for one, objects in *The Idea of a Social Science:*

> *There is just as much point in saying that science, art, religion, and philosophy are all concerned with making things intelligible as there is in saying that football, chess, patience and skipping are all games. But just as it would be foolish to say that all these activities are part of one supergame, if only we were clever enough to learn how to play it, so is it foolish to suppose that the results of all those other activities should all add up to one grand theory of reality (as some philosophers have imagined: with the corollary that it was their job to discover it).*

It seems that we may consider art, religion, and science to be similar to one another in their purposes and functions only as long as we think about them in terms sufficiently general and abstract to transcend their practical differences. As soon as we stop to examine them more carefully, however, their similarities vanish, and we become aware of their distinctiveness.

What is it that distinguishes the aesthetic point of view from other approaches to the world? What is aesthetic experience? In the next section, centering on art alone, we'll discuss a philosophical problem whose resolution is crucial for a definition of art, if such a definition is indeed possible. It is also crucial for an understanding of aesthetic experience: Is a work of art the artist's expression of subjective feelings, or is it his representation of objective reality?

Have you ever been baffled by a work of art? Have you ever stood before a modern sculpture or an abstract painting and wondered what it meant and what you should say about it? Many artists, critics, and philosophers have developed theories to explain what works of art express or represent. In the past some theorists maintained that the artist should remain detached from the scene; in their works, they insist, artists should then imitate or represent the world as it appears to them. Others have stressed the artists' personal involvement in the scenes they're symbolically recreating (if there's any sense in which they're "recreating scenes" to begin with); they hold that artists should give expression to their ideas and emotional responses through language, form, and color. Today, the philosophical debate over the relative importance one should accord the subjective and the objective poles of aesthetic experience continues to divide those who consider the problems of art.

In passing, did you notice that the word "should" occurs in the last paragraph? Generally, definitions of art are not merely descriptive, but normative or evaluative too. This is so because definitions are restrictive: When we define a concept, we establish the limits of its applicability. Defining what art is, is also defining what art is not (or what is not art). To take an extreme case as an illustration, if you were to define art as the photographic representation of a scene, then nonrepresentational works would not qualify as works of art. Your definition would not admit most modern entries, including the paintings of Gauguin, Picasso, Dali, and Miro, as works of art. Assuming it's possible and desirable to define art, saying what art is amounts to saying what art should be.

One popular and influential theory of art, advanced by the modern Russian novelist and philosopher Leo Tolstoy among others, has it that art is an emotionally expressive form of communication. Through their works, artists express their feelings and communicate them to others. Art is possible because we can understand and share one another's emotional responses. In *What Is Art?* Tolstoy affirmed, "it is on this capacity of man to receive another man's expression of feeling and to experience those feelings himself, that the activity of art is based."

Is art the artist's expression of subjective feeling?

In line with his emphasis on feeling and communication, Tolstoy formulated this concise definition of art: *"Art is a human activity consisting in this, that one man consciously by means of certain external signs, hands on to others feelings he has lived through, and that others are infected by these feelings and also experience them."*

Tolstoy also established certain criteria for identifying and evaluating works of art. Specifically, he cited three features essential to good, or successful, works of art. First, a work of art should express a particular feeling, such as grief or joy. Second, it should express that feeling clearly. Third, the artist should sincerely desire to express his or her emotion. Summarizing these criteria, Tolstoy wrote, "If the work does not transmit the artist's peculiarity of feeling and is therefore not individual, if it is unintelligibly expressed, or if it has not proceeded from the author's inner need for expression—it is not a work of art."

It's possible to maintain that art is emotionally expressive without subscribing to Tolstoy's remarkable criteria. However, these criteria do throw some light on the subjective theory of art. The third criterion, the one that refers to the artist's intentions, is especially illuminating. If works of art express their creators' sincere feelings, then it would not be possible for a composer to write a melancholic song while he was elated or for a painter to paint a bright, festive picture while she was depressed. That conclusion, however, is doubtful. And must creative writers actually experience the emotional responses they attribute to fictional or dramatic characters? It appears that works of art may very well express the artist's actual feelings at the time of their composition but that they also may very well not.

Is art the artist's representation of objective reality?

If works of art do not necessarily express the artist's own subjective feelings, then do they "imitate" or represent objective reality? The twentieth century Spanish thinker José Ortega y Gasset figures among the many philosophers who have suggested as much. The critical theory Ortega developed in *The Dehumanization of Art* not only provides an alternate account of artistic activity but also clarifies another aspect of aesthetic experience. Ortega argues that the artist properly puts a certain psychical or emotional distance between himself and the object or the scene he's representing. Ortega outlines in *The Dehumanization of Art* a simple dramatic situation to illustrate how the artistic perspective on reality differs from other approaches:

> *A great man is dying. His wife is by his bedside. A doctor takes the dying man's pulse. In the background two more persons are discovered: a reporter who is present for professional reasons, and a painter whom mere chance has brought here. Wife, doctor, reporter, and painter witness one and the same event. Nonetheless, this identical event—a man's death—impresses each of them in a different way. . . . What this scene means to the wife who is all grief has so little to do with what it means to the painter who looks on impassively that it seems doubtful whether the two can be said to be present at the same event.*

If we think about this situation, Ortega remarks, it becomes clear that a single reality (a man's dying) may split into many different realities when it's considered from different points of view. He suggests that we might best distinguish these realities and these points of view by measuring the emotional distance between each person and the event at which they all are present.

The dying man's wife is so intensely involved in her husband's struggle for life that she's part of the scene. This is significant, Ortega argues, because we can observe an event only when we have separated ourselves from it. For this reason, the man's wife is not simply present at the end; she does not just *witness* the scene. She *lives* it.

By comparison, the doctor is detached. Although he's responsible for attending the suffering man, his interest and involvement in the scene is not emotional but professional and practical. He lives the event too, but much less intensely.

The reporter, of course, is still less involved in the situation. Since the great man's death is a newsworthy event, the reporter is, like the doctor, present for professional reasons and not out of his own emotional involvement. But Ortega points out that although the doctor's profession requires him to interfere, the reporter's requires him to stand back and look on. Thus, he doesn't live the scene, he observes it, although he has a practical interest in it. He wants to describe it to his readers in such a way as to involve them.

Finally, the painter, whose presence is fortuitous, remains completely unconcerned. He does nothing but keep his eyes open, and the event's "tragic inner meaning" escapes his attention. He is interested only in forms, colors, lights, and shadows. Ortega concludes, "In the painter, we find a maximum of distance and a minimum of feeling intervention."

In sketching this scene, Ortega suggests a scale of emotional distances between what we might call perceiving subjects and their perceived realities. He writes:

> *In this scale, the degree of closeness is equivalent to the degree of feeling participation; the degree of remoteness, on the other hand, marks the degree to which we have freed ourselves from the real event, thus objectifying it and turning it into a theme of pure observation. At one end of the scale the world—persons, things, situations—is given to us in the aspect of "lived" reality; at the other end we see everything in the aspect of "observed" reality.*

Precisely because he puts himself at a certain emotional distance from the scene he witnesses (precisely because he witnesses, rather than lives, the scene), the artist can paint it. The aesthetic attitude is one of noninvolvement; aesthetic experience is disinterested. However, in the scale Ortega proposes, the lived or human reality has a primacy that compels us to see it as *the* reality. If the painter does commit this scene to a canvas, then his painting is meaningful because of its reference or links to the situation's lived or human reality. "A painting or a poem without any vestiges of 'lived' forms," Ortega asserts, "would be unintelligible, i.e., nothing—as a discourse is nothing whose every word is emptied of its customary meaning."

Is Ortega's theory of art satisfactory? His conclusion apparently doesn't admit pure, abstract, or nonrepresentational paintings and sculptures as legitimate and possibly good works of art. The modern artist, he writes, "is brazenly set on deforming reality, shattering its human aspect, dehumanizing it." His works are "unintelligible." Clearly, any theory that favors traditional work to the very point of disallowing modern art is at best inadequate. Any definition that does not admit a large part of what we ordinarily recognize as art is simply too restrictive.

What may we conclude from this analysis? Is art the expression of subjective feelings or is it the representation of objective reality? Neither exclusively. Both in part. Neither Tolstoy nor Ortega has adequately explained art, but each has illuminated important aspects of aesthetic experience. Is it possible, then, to define art? Is it desirable to do so?

Art—An Open Concept

Is it possible and desirable to define art?

In his article "The Role of Theory in Aesthetics," Morris Weitz, a contemporary American philosopher of art, wrote that "aesthetic theory is a logically vain attempt to define what cannot be defined." Recalling Wittgenstein's analysis of the concept of games and his notion of family resemblances, Weitz suggested that as we use it in ordinary language the concept of art is similarly open. "If we actually look and see what it is that we call 'art,'" he wrote, "we will . . . find no common properties—only strands of similarities."

In Weitz's view, it is not possible to define the concept of art because the diverse things that we commonly call works of art—things like paintings,

---

Viewpoint

What does art seek to express? . . . I think every work of art expresses, more or less purely, more or less subtly, not feelings and emotions which the artist has, *but feelings and emotions which the artist* knows; *his* insight *into the nature of sentience, his picture of vital experience, physical and emotive and fantastic.*

SUSANNE LANGER, Problems of Art: Ten Philosophical Lectures

sculptures, poems, plays, collages, mobiles, and novels—do not seem to have any common feature or set of features that might serve as a criterion. Furthermore, it is not desirable to define art because any definition (delimitation) would rule out new art forms in advance. Weitz explains his position:

> *What I am arguing . . . is that the very expansive, adventurous character of art, its ever-present changes and novel creations, makes it logically impossible to ensure any set of defining properties. We can, of course, choose to close the concept. But to do this . . . is ludicrous since it forecloses on the very conditions of creativity in the arts.*

Weitz's argument is compelling. Art is not a game, but the problem of the nature of art is very much like the problem of the nature of games. And from a logical point of view the concept of art we use all the time is very much like our open concept of games.

Summary

Philosophy, Play, and Games: Philosophy might be considered a game, primarily because philosophers contest one another's arguments; moreover, those arguments are governed by logical rules. "Play" and "games" are not synonymous, but they are closely related to each other and may be considered together.

The Paradoxes of Play and Games: Play has these paradoxical aspects: it's fun, but it's also serious; it's illusory, but it has a certain reality; and it's an activity freely undertaken, but it's frequently said to serve a necessary function. Where and how we mark off the boundaries between work and play involves our culture and its definition of what is real and valuable.

The Concept of Games: Since games don't have a common defining feature, or set of features, the concept of games is open.

Games and Their Rules: Since rules are public matters, and games have rules, games are social activities. Game rules, like customs, laws, and institutions, introduce order into human affairs.

Play and Culture: Play might be closely related to other cultural forms, such as ritual, music, dance, and drama. However, this theory of culture has limits.

Philosophy and Art: Some philosophers consider the problematic notion of aesthetic experience the key to an understanding of art.

Art, Religion, and Science: Some thinkers have proposed that art, like religion and science, is an effort to make things intelligible. Others stress the differences among these perspectives on the world.

Expression and Imitation: Theorists also disagree as to the relative importance of the subjective and the objective sides of aesthetic experience. Some hold that art is the artist's creative expression of his or her own feelings; others argue that art should represent the world as it appears to the artist.

Art—An Open Concept: Like the concept of games, the concept of art as we ordinarily use it cannot be defined by referring to a common feature or set of features. Any definition would preclude new art forms.

Suggestions for Further Reading

The classic philosophical and historical inquiry into the significance of play is Johan Huizinga's *Homo Ludens: A Study of the Play Element in Culture* (Boston: Beacon Press, 1955). More recently, Michael Novak has made a fine contribution to the philosophical study of sports in American culture by writing *The Joy of Sports: End Zones, Bases, Baskets, Balls, and the Consecration of the American Spirit* (New York: Basic Books, 1976). Novak argues that "sports flow outward into action from a deep natural impulse that is radically religious: an impulse of freedom, respect for ritual limits, a zest for symbolic meaning and a longing for perfection."

In "Deep Play: Notes on the Balinese Cockfight," Clifford Geertz, a philosophically minded cultural anthropologist, presents a sensitive and illuminating study of the functions of one form of play in one society. He argues that in Bali what the cockfight does "is what, for other peoples with other temperaments and other conventions, *Lear* and *Crime and Punishment* do; it catches up these themes—death, masculinity, rage, pride, loss, beneficence, chance—and, ordering them into an encompassing structure, presents them in such a way as to throw into relief a particular view of their essential nature." "Deep Play" is included in Clifford Geertz (ed.), *Myth, Symbol, and Culture* (New York: Norton, 1971).

Roger Caillois' essay "Play and the Sacred" was published as an appendix to his book *Man and the Sacred,* trans. Meyer Barash (New York: Free Press, 1959).

Peter Winch maintains that "any worthwhile study of society must be philosophical in character and any worthwhile philosophy must be concerned with the nature of human society" in *The Idea of a Social Science and Its Relation to Philosophy,* (London: Routledge, 1958). In developing his argument, he presents and discusses Wittgenstein's notion of rules.

One of the best introductory studies of the philosophical problems surrounding art is George Dickie's *Aesthetics: An Introduction* (New York: Pegasus, 1971). Also excellent is Virgil C. Aldrich's *Philosophy of Art* (Englewood Cliffs, NJ: Prentice-Hall, Foundations of Philosophy Series, 1963).

Inquiry

Sports:
Big Money and
High Drama

In *The Astonished Muse,* the contemporary sociologist Reuel Denney observes that for "the American culture as a whole, no sharp line exists between work and play." Denney was talking about the role of sports in our mass culture, and surely no area of modern life is more ambiguous. Here the paradoxes of play are fully visible, especially its serious and its fun sides. Pro football, hockey, basketball, tennis, and baseball have all become part of the entertainment industry, and their stars play well for fabulous salaries while millions of fans watch with what almost amounts to religious enthusiasm. What's the role of sports in American life? What do they mean for the players and the fan?

For both, the game presents an opportunity to make a total commitment to one side. Indeed, the sports ethic and the media encourage such commitments, so that good and evil are clearly defined, at least on Sunday afternoon. Winning is good. Losing is evil. Playing fair is good; cheating is evil. Sports may be the only area of modern life where values can be defined in black and white and where unqualified and unreserved commitments can be made. But even here, disputes arise as to whether or not a rule has been broken or a play successfully completed, and umpires and referees frequently have to make judgment calls to decide unclear cases.

The classical notion of drama can also be

applied to sports. In this point of view the game may be seen as a tragic conflict. Examining Thucydides' notion of the unpredictable fortunes of war, the classical scholar Francis Cornford noted that for the Greeks "not only the sudden fall from prosperity, but equally the sudden rise from adversity, was a part of the tragic fact." The jump from one state to another is the tragic reversal, and it can come about either through human pride, blindness, and failure, or through the gods' fateful intervention. It's this element of chance that makes the competitive game exciting. We can speculate and gamble on its outcome, but until it's over we can't know for sure how the game will end. To enter a game, then, is to take one's chances with the unpredictable fortunes of war and to play out one's tragic destiny.

Aristotle's notion of *katharsis* is interesting in this context. Although it's been interpreted in different ways, this Greek word is usually taken to refer to the emotional release that dramatic action affords the spectator. In the traditional interpretation, the spectator at a tragic play fearfully shares the hero's destiny and sympathetically experiences his reversal; he leaves the theater and returns to the real world emotionally drained but pleased (perhaps ennobled) by the conflict's resolution. Monroe Beardsley explains, "The general theory attributed to Aristotle, then, would be that tragedy, by arousing these emotions [namely, fear and pity], has some sort of therapeutic effect upon the audience's mental health, giving a pleasurable sense of relief—'in calm of mind, all passion spent' (as Milton echoes this view in *Samson Agonistes*)." Since the sports fan commonly identifies with the team he supports and shares its fortunes (witness the sense of community involvement when the home team enters the playoffs), it's quite possible that the game does allow him such release.

This tragic interpretation doesn't exhaust the meaning of sports, though; a number of critical questions suggest themselves for analysis and discussion. These are just a few of them:

In your opinion, why do so many people follow sports with such avid interest? What satisfactions do they find in watching athletic contests, either in the stands or on television? Are sports merely entertainment, or do games actually dramatize and represent other facets of life, such as the struggle for success, the dread of failure, and the role of fate in human affairs?

Some thinkers have suggested that sports may be a form of religion. Is there any merit in this proposal? In formulating your response, define what you mean by religion, and specify what aspects of sports, if any, strike you as having a religious dimension.

Noting that violence is discouraged on the street but encouraged in the stadium (where it's controlled by the game's rules), other people have suggested that sports offer both the player and the spectator a socially acceptable way of expressing their aggressive impulses and feelings. Is this the case? If so, are human beings naturally and instinctively violent, or do they *learn* to behave aggressively?

Team sports also demand discipline and cooperative action. What other social and psychological functions (apart from *katharsis* and the channeling of aggression) might sports serve?

Religion and Literature:
Faith, Fact, and Fiction

What meaning does literature have for you? What do short stories, for example, and novels have to do with the ways we live and the ways we understand our lives? What's the relationship between the novel's imaginary world and our real world?

Giles Gunn has noted that since literary situations are imagined, they require the readers' assent to their possibility. The author would not gain our assent, though, if his imagined situations and his characters were not plausible and did not address our "sense of ourselves."

Through his imagined situations, or (what amounts to the same thing) through his "possibilities," the creative writer presents a view of the world; intentionally or not, he makes a philosophical notion of reality concrete. As Gunn expresses it, "every writer draws from the common fund of human experience which has been bequeathed to us by history, society, and, as it were, blood. But his procedure is to select from that common fund some single assumption or interrelated series of assumptions about the way things are, or can be, or should be, and then order his entire work in terms of it."

These remarks suggest an answer to the question we asked about the link between our real world and the novel's fictitious world: "literature is neither totally immersed in the world of everyday experience nor completely divorced

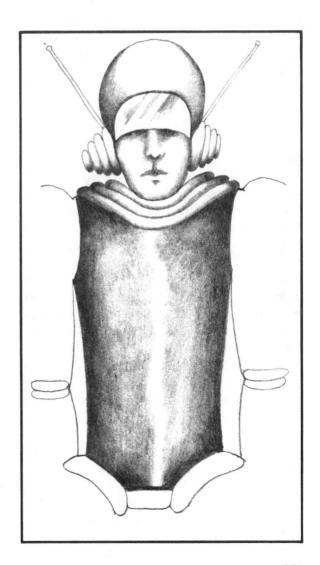

from it." While literature belongs, not to the realm of fact (the real world in which we live), but to the realm of hypothesis (the possible world of the novel), there is "a circuit of belief and desire" between the two. If the novel is well written, then while we're reading it we gladly allow ourselves to believe its world is real.

Citing Dorothy Van Ghent's study, *The English Novel,* Gunn reasons that "literature's value and significance for us 'lies less in confirming and interpreting the known' than in compelling us to suppose, indeed at least for a time to believe, *'that something else might be the case.'* " Literature, in this view, is more an imaginative exploration of human possibilities than a description of human reality. When we read what fictional characters do and say in situations different from our own, we can imagine ourselves in their places, and we can understand their responses even if we don't always agree with them or approve of them. Any novel that describes possible human responses to imagined situations (in short, any novel) may be seen as an inquiry into human possibilities; probably the most extreme examples are science fiction novels.

Building on this understanding of literature's meaning and value, Gunn proposes for it a religious interpretation. In his view, three elements of literature have religious significance. The first is simply that every literary work presupposes a commitment to "vital possibility," which "represents that half-conscious, half-unconscious faith in all that lies beyond the range of our immediate perception." Every novel assumes our willingness as readers to believe in its world and its characters as if they might exist. Second, literature invokes our deepest sense of ourselves, so that "in responding to every work of literature we are—if we are bringing the whole of ourselves to that response— responding with whatever for us is the religious center of our being." And third, as we've seen, every work is based on some assumption about what might constitute the "ground of experience," and this "primal intuition" acts as the organizing principle for the work's hypothetical reconstruction of the world. "Call it what you will," Gunn writes, "the informing or presiding assumption, the shaping cause, the concrete universal, the embodied vision, or the metaphysic—every meaningfully coherent work of literature has such an executive principle, and it functions analogously to the notion of ultimacy in religious experience." Generally, this executive principle is the author's conscious or unconscious assumption about what is ultimately real—God, for instance, or the will to live, or the will to die, or the drive to create, or the drive to destroy—whatever is the key to the novelist's world.

Gunn does not mean to argue, of course, that approaches to literature other than his religious interpretation are invalid or uninteresting; nor does he suggest that works possessing these elements are necessarily religious. What he does maintain is that the existence of these features justifies our taking the possibility that a given work has religious meaning at least as seriously as we do its potential psychological, political, or social meaning.

These difficult and provocative ideas suggest several philosophical questions:

How does Gunn's interpretation of literature compare with the theory Edmund Wilson offered in his Novel *I Thought of Daisy?* (We presented Wilson's theory in the art, religion, and science section of this chapter.)

Is Gunn's explanation of the relationship between our everyday world (what he calls the realm of facts) and the novel's imaginary world (what he calls the realm of hypothesis) correct? Is his appreciation of literature's meaning and value correct?

Peter Jones holds that to classify something as a work of art, for instance, to call a book a novel, is to assume a certain freedom to interpret it for oneself. "All interpretations are takings," he writes, "and all are from viewpoints." It's precisely because works of art call on us for creative responses that we can legitimately disagree with one another about their meaning, and "artists can make artists of us all." How does Gunn's religious interpretation of literature allow for our personal, creative response to the novel?

This freedom to interpret a work of art is a limited freedom; in any given case, it's possible and meaningful to say of somebody's interpretation that it's wrong. What limits our freedom to interpret novels creatively?

Gunn evidently would agree with Maurice Merleau-Ponty: "The work of a great novelist is always borne by two or three philosophical ideas." Creative writers, however, are not primarily concerned with developing philosophical arguments to resolve philosophical problems or with expressing a philosophical world view; their work is simply to tell stories. Is it the case then that the authors of literary works generally do make philosophical ideas concrete? If so, how? In formulating an answer to this question, you might refer specifically to a novel you've read recently, or you might review Chapter 1's Inquiry on William Golding's *Lord of the Flies,* Chapter 4's Inquiry on W. Somerset Maugham's *Of Human Bondage,* or Chapter 10's Inquiry on Edward Bellamy's *Looking Backward.* Whatever novel you choose to consider, develop a narrative situation and describe the characters' responses to it. In doing this, try to show how the author has given concrete expression to a philosophical idea about human nature, for instance, or morality, or social justice. If you take the opposite view, that philosophical ideas do not generally enter into literary works, explain and justify your position.

Death comes to all, not as a scourge or punishment, but as the culmination and fulfillment of life.

DAVID COLE GORDON

Nevertheless Death is never an entirely welcome guest.

JOHANN WOLFGANG VON GOETHE

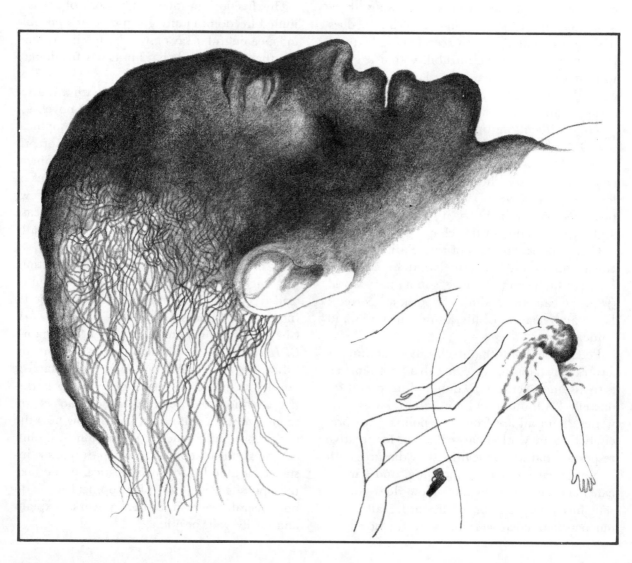

296

DEATH
The Unwelcome Fulfillment of Life

Chapter Survey

Philosophy and Death
Why think about death?
How does our view of death relate to our perspective on life?

The Nature of Death
How is death perceived in the contemporary West?
What philosophical and practical consequences does the modern scientific view of death have?

Death and the Self
Why is death frightening?
Is death an experience?

Death and the Meaning of Life
Why does death throw the meaning of life into question?
Can work or love constitute the meaning of an individual's life?

The Problem of Immortality
What is the problem of immortality?
How did Plato argue for personal immortality?
What grounds for belief did Kant propose?

Death in America
How do contemporary Americans perceive and manage death?
Why is death a forbidden subject in American culture?

Immanuel Kant
1724–1804

"... the hope of a future life has chiefly rested on that peculiar character of human nature, never to be satisfied by what is merely temporal."

From the day he was born to the day he died, Immanuel Kant lived in the East Prussian city of Königsberg (now Kaliningrad in the Soviet Union). He rarely ventured outside the city limits. And, just as his travels were limited, so his habits were inflexible. The regularity of his life is legendary. Heinrich Heine reported, "Rising from bed, coffee-drinking, writing, lecturing, eating, walking, everything had its fixed time." But Kant pursued his philosophical studies with inexhaustible energy. His life's work was an uncompromising effort to answer three fundamental questions: What can I know? What should I do? And what may I hope?

Kant first addressed himself systematically to these questions in the Critique of Pure Reason. His inquiry into the limits of knowledge—What can I know?—was prompted by his dissatisfaction with metaphysical dogmatism on the one hand and empirical skepticism on the other hand. The former presupposes that we can know God exists, that we have free wills, and that our souls are immortal; the latter assumes we cannot know anything beyond our immediate experience. But Kant complained that dogmatism "teaches us nothing," and skepticism "doesn't even promise us anything."

To determine what we can and cannot legitimately claim to know, Kant set out to investigate the conditions under which knowledge is possible. The complex and subtle theory of knowledge he consequently developed in the Critique of

Pure Reason rests upon a revolutionary hypothesis. Earlier philosophers had taken it for granted that if we're to know anything, our minds have to conform to the object of our inquiry. But Kant postulated that objects, to be known, have to meet conditions set by our minds. In presenting his theory, Kant examined our use of the concepts of space and time;

looked into common sense notions of causality and the self; and analyzed traditional arguments for and against God, freedom, and immortality. Kant concluded that metaphysical knowledge is impossible. It lies beyond the limits of pure reason.

What should I do? And what may I hope? A prolific writer, Kant turned his attention to the second and third questions in such analytically powerful works as the Groundwork of the Metaphysics of Morals and the Critique of Practical Reason. He explained that his purpose in the Groundwork was "to seek out and establish the supreme principle of morality." Stressing the importance of "good will," Kant maintained

that from an ethical point of view what counts is not the consequences of an action but our intention in doing it. To determine the moral worth of a certain action, Kant held, we should ask ourselves if we could honestly want the principle governing our action to govern the actions of everyone in our position. In its first form—Kant proposed five—the "categorical imperative" or unconditional law of morality is: "Act only on that maxim through which you can at the same time will that it should become a universal law."

But moral law is possible only if we are free to choose one action over another. Moreover, God and immortality constitute the highest good, which the good will acting in accordance with moral law seeks. In the Critique of Practical Reason, then, Kant argued that although we can't know that God exists, that we're free, or that our souls will live forever, we can reasonably suppose that these propositions are true.

In the Introduction to Five Types of Ethical Theory, the contemporary British philosopher C. D. Broad wrote,

> *There is no important problem in any branch of philosophy which is not treated by Kant, and he never treated a problem without saying something illuminating and original about it. He was certainly wrong on many points of detail, and he may well be wrong in his fundamental principles; but, when all criticisms have been made, it seems to me that Kant's failures are more important than most men's successes.*

DEATH

Philosophy and Death

Why think about death at all? The questions surrounding death are disturbing, and most people would rather change the subject than dwell on it. Even our everyday language reflects this reluctance to confront death. When we speak of those who have died, we commonly use phrases ranging from the polite "She passed away" to the callous "He's pushing up daisies." We try to avoid the hard, brutal reality of death or to make a joke of it even when we do think and talk about it.

Why think about death?

What is more, most people find it almost impossible to take their own deaths seriously or really to believe what they have known since they were eight or ten years old—that they too will die. This psychological oddity partly accounts for adolescents' harmlessly imagining themselves present at their own funerals, listening in while others both praise them and lament that they never really appreciated them. A scene in Mark Twain's *Adventures of Tom Sawyer* builds on this daydream. In this scene Tom, Huckleberry Finn, and Joe Harper have returned from their island hideout to eavesdrop on their premature funeral service. "As the service proceeded, the clergyman drew such pictures of the graces, the winning ways, and the rare promise of the lost lads that every soul there, thinking he recognized these pictures, felt a pang."

More seriously, this apparently widespread inability to believe in their own mortality might explain why desperately unhappy people commit suicide to punish others, as if they will be around afterward to enjoy their revenge. It might also explain why normally sensible people continue to smoke two or three packs of cigarettes every day, despite the well-established and well-publicized threat to their health. Other people die. When we picture ourselves dead, we picture ourselves as other people.

When they're so often confronted by the immediate and incontrovertible evidence of others' deaths, why do so many people apparently refuse to believe that they too are mortal? Denying their own eventual deaths might

How does our view of death relate to our perspective on life?

simply be one way in which they try to cope with the awareness of their mortality. However, many modern thinkers hold that refusing to believe what you know very well to be the case is bad faith. It's an inauthentic or dishonest way of being in the world.

Furthermore, the way you see death involves the way you see life. For instance, the effort to deny the reality of death or to avoid facing it might lead you to place a high value on some aspect of your individual life, such as physical pleasure, personal relationships, or work. Admitting the practical certainty of death, in contrast, might lead you to conclude that life is absurd. There are, of course, other possibilities. The point is that your perception of death is bound to influence your perception of life and vice versa although perhaps in very subtle ways. To say that some things are more important than others or that nothing matters at all is to take a philosophical stand. How you see it has to do with how you understand the meaning, value, and purpose of life. And this is a philosophical problem.

Indeed, many philosophers, both classical and modern, have seen the inevitable experience of death as the single most important event in life. They've given the problem of death a central place in their thinking. Some persons have always reflected on death because they think that philosophy might help them, if not to reconcile themselves to its awful inevitability, then at least to make some sense of it.

Viewpoint

And the true philosophers, Simmias, are always occupied in the practice of dying, wherefore also to them least of all men is death terrible. Look at the matter thus: if they have been in every way the enemies of the body, and are wanting to be alone with the soul, when this desire of theirs is granted, how inconsistent would they be if they trembled and repined, instead of rejoicing at their departure to that place where, when they arrive, they hope to gain that which in life they desired—and this was wisdom—and at the same time to be rid of the company of their enemy. Many a man has been willing to go to the world below animated by the hope of seeing there an earthly love, or wife, or son, and conversing with them. And will he who is a true lover of wisdom, and is strongly persuaded in like manner that only in the world below he can worthily enjoy her, still repine at death? Will he not depart with joy? Surely he will, O my friend, if he be a true philosopher.

PLATO, Phaedo

In this chapter we'll first discuss death in modern thought. Then, after reviewing the reasons why people generally fear their deaths, we'll consider the experience of death itself (if there is, in fact, any sense in which death is an experience). Thinking about the experience of death will lead to a discussion of the problem of the meaning of life. Then we'll examine the grounds for belief in personal immortality. Finally, focusing upon contemporary American attitudes, we'll consider the relationship between death and culture.

The Nature of Death

Contemporary philosophers disagree on the nature of death. For instance, the German thinker Martin Heidegger describes human existence as "being-toward-death." In Heidegger's view, authentic human reality is oriented toward death as its natural, although fearsome, culmination. If a person wants to be an artist, for example, and fully realizes the limitation on time ensured by finitude, that person will throw himself or herself into the meaningful activity. Authentic human existence demands a fearful confrontation with one's own death, one's own limitation. Only after this is it possible genuinely to commit oneself and stop allowing trivial everyday concerns to take up all one's time.

How is death perceived in the contemporary West?

Emmanuel Levinas, a student of Heidegger's thought, has a different view. He sees death as completely alien to life. For Heidegger, death is an act that one can freely embrace and an event that one can welcome because if we face it, it tells us the meaning of our lives. For Levinas, death is an experience of pure passivity, something that comes uninvited and unwanted to do violence to the individual. For instance, death does violence to the artist; after his or her death, there is no longer a person who creates.

In our scientific culture the common sense view is that apart from heart attacks, murders, suicides, and the like, living *is* dying. Aging is life's natural running down. Death is in life itself, and life is oriented toward death. Although there is no consensus, this view—that death is continuous with life and so its natural end—predominates in contemporary philosophical thought.

What might this way of seeing death not as something that happens to the living but as something that grows in life itself mean for us? For instance, could this modern, scientific view of death as a natural process help us to accept it? Could it reconcile us to our mortality?

What philosophical and practical consequences does the modern scientific view of death have?

From a philosophical point of view, it appears that if death is natural, then it's unnatural for us not to welcome it. However, we might propose several objections to this facile consolation. In the first place, very few persons could achieve such a distant, impersonal view of their own lives that the inevitability of death would become a matter of indifference to them or its naturalness a source of comfort. Death may be the natural end of life, even the culmination of life, but in most cases it is an unwelcome presence for the person who has to die.

In the second place, for many people death is an affront to life because it makes living seem pointless. It's not much solace to say that death itself is the point of life. As we've indicated, the understanding of death as a natural process is, at base, scientific, and the scientific view of man's place in the universe has failed to make human existence more meaningful for many people. On the contrary, it has made human life seem insignificant. In *Death and Modern Man,* Jacques Choron, a contemporary historian of ideas, remarks that science can "preach the sweet reasonableness of acceptance of mortality," but that is "the best it can do." He argues:

> *Science here is not only totally incapable of giving help, but on the contrary has contributed to man's intellectual and emotional helplessness vis-à-vis death, and this not so much because of its reaffirmation of the common-sense conclusion that death is total annihilation of the individual, as because in the view of the world that science presents human existence is irrelevant and man but another animal species destined to eventual disappearance.*

The position is extreme, but it may not be entirely wrong. It's important however, in assessing the human implications of the scientific world view, not to neglect or to minimize the life-saving and life-serving technical advances it has rendered possible. Practical considerations may recommend the prevalent modern view of death as a natural process. Not only does the scientific view explain death in relation to life, and so make it appear somewhat less alien; but it also allows further human intervention to postpone the end. Physicians have identified a number of external factors, such as occupation, exercise, and heredity, that apparently affect the individual's life expectancy. If they also succeed in identifying the internal causes of aging, then—barring diseases, accidents, murders, and suicides—it might be possible to extend the human life span indefinitely. On a planet that is rapidly becoming overpopulated, such a development may or may not be desirable, but in any case it's clear that to see dying as a winding down of the person's biological clock has both philosophical and practical implications.

With these brief remarks on what seems to be the modern, secular understanding of death, we'll turn to a consideration of the anticipation and the experience of death. Death has always been viewed as a fearsome experience, but the widespread loss of traditional religious faith as well as the development of a scientific world view have produced changes not only in the experience but also in the fear of death. Why do most people fear death today? And what is the experience of death? In the next two sections we'll discuss these questions.

Death and the Self

For almost everyone who admits and faces death rather than denying it, death is a frightening prospect. Indeed, as we've already suggested, it's precisely because the inevitability of death is so disturbing that people generally prefer not to think about it, instead acting as if their own lives will go on forever. Mortality is an aspect of the human condition that people in the modern West find deeply disturbing. Out of fear, they tend to deny and avoid it much more than people in earlier times and in other cultures.

Why is death frightening?

In the past, the fear of death seems to have centered on what would follow it, that is, what would come "after the end." Some dreaded physical decomposition; others, eternal damnation. Whatever their real effectiveness, however, the now common practices of embalming the dead and burying them in airtight metal caskets have largely dispelled the fear of decomposition. An increasingly general disbelief (at least, a practical disbelief) in the existence of God and the immortality of the soul have also made the fear of hell much less widespread and urgent than it once was in Western Europe and the United States. Today, when people think about it at all, many are apparently most concerned that *nothing* will happen to them after they die. Dying itself would be the last occurrence. There would be no one to whom anything could happen anyway: Death would not be transition to another life but the absolute end of life. Indeed, in this view the very notion of immortality—"life after death"—is a contradiction in terms.

The idea that death is the utter end of personal existence has important philosophical and psychological consequences. For most people who endorse this view, the fear of death is actually a fear for the loss of their selves. But what does this mean? The self, obviously, is not simply the body. You *aren't* just your body; you *have* a body. Beyond that, the concept of the self is surprisingly elusive. Many contemporary philosophers think that the self is merely a convenient grammatical fiction, that it doesn't really exist the way things exist.

Just the same, we speak of the self all the time, even if we don't stop to analyze how we use the word. Lately, for instance, people talk a lot about "getting in touch with themselves," in the sense of coming to understand and be comfortable with a hidden, inner reality. In psychology and popular thought, a distinction is commonly drawn between the "public," "outer," or "false" self and the "private," "inner," or "true" self, where the former emerges in response to others' expectations. You are, or at least you may pretend to be, what others think you are, and to a large extent you act as they expect you to.

However, even your real self—your true personal identity—is a social reality. It may be defined primarily by your relations with other people. In fact, the self is constantly shifting in response to new social situations. As the contemporary American psychologist David Cole Gordon affirms, "what most of us regard as our self is nothing permanent, but is merely a constellation of changing thoughts orbiting around a physical body and relating to a certain number of people with whom we are in contact and involved. . . ."

It appears, then, that those who fear death because they dread losing their present self (that is, the personality which they take at the moment to be their essential identity) are worried about not being anyone at all after they die. They perceive death as the absolute obliteration of the self, total nonexistence.

It's interesting to note in this connection that some contemporary Christian theologians have proposed a sort of conditional immortality. According to one version of this theory, God will grant immortality to the good while reserving complete nonexistence for the wicked. The latter simply will not be resurrected at the end of the world. According to another, subtly different version, God will allow those who choose evil and refuse to live in His world to pass out of existence.

For many, the fear of death has another side. Those who are apparently indifferent to their own deaths often fear the deaths of those others who matter to them. Indeed, "your death" has joined if not replaced "my death" as a dominant theme in Western thought. Although some people never think of their own deaths, as though they didn't believe they would actually die, they worry about the deaths of their parents, spouses, or children. This doesn't necessarily mean that they are unusually insecure either or even that deep down they actually desire the deaths of these others. In fact, fearing that another person will die can be perfectly normal. It's in the nature of love to desire the loved one's welfare. And people generally consider life to be one of the greatest values because it is the condition for all the other things they value. To wish someone a long life is to wish that person well. Conversely, to fear someone's death is not necessarily just to dread one's own loss; it may be genuinely to fear that person's being deprived of the fundamental good, which is life itself.

Is death an experience? If there is nothing after death, can death properly be called an experience? Dying evidently can, but death? Ludwig Wittgenstein thought not. "Death," he wrote, "is not an event in life: we do not live to experience death." Epicurus, a Greek philosopher, went further, saying that death is "nothing to us, since so long as we exist death is not with us, but when death comes, then we do not exist." So there's nothing to be afraid of!

This line of reasoning may not offer much consolation. It might be reassuring for those who fear what may happen after death, but for those who fear the extinction of their self, it simply underscores the threat death poses to the individual. In *The Politics of Experience,* R. D. Laing writes: " 'There's nothing to be afraid of.' The ultimate reassurance and the ultimate terror."

"Nothing," of course, is hard to picture. Close your eyes in a darkened room and "see" the blackness. Then, try to imagine yourself not even there to see nothing, and nowhere else, either. Can you do it? Not really. If you could, you'd probably have an idea of the nothingness that might follow death. But as the contemporary Spanish philosopher Miguel de Unamuno remarks in *Tragic Sense of Life,* "It is impossible for us, in effect, to conceive of ourselves as not existing, and no effort is capable of enabling consciousness to realize absolute unconsciousness, its own annihilation."

If Unamuno's right, as logically he must be, and it's impossible for us to imagine the experience of absolutely nothing, then can we meaningfully speak of it? Many contemporary philosophers argue that experience can only be experience *of something,* and that we can't coherently speak of an experience of nothing.

However, the language of nothingness is more poetic than logical: We may use it to express more than we can fully understand or explain. Wittgenstein criticized Gottlob Frege, another contemporary philosopher, for comparing a concept to an area and saying that "an area with vague boundaries cannot be called an area at all." A concept that cannot be precisely defined, or delimited, doesn't deserve to be called a "concept" at all. Wittgenstein objected, "is it senseless to say: 'Stand roughly there?'" To speak of nothing might, in fact, be to point in a general direction.

Is death an experience then? We can witness somebody else's passing on, but properly speaking we can't experience it. Martin Heidegger maintains that "The dying of Others is not something which we experience in a genuine sense; at most we are always just 'there alongside' [of them]." It may not be correct to speak of one's own death as an experience, either, since experience is always experience of something, and death, perhaps, is nothing. Experience is lived, and death is beyond, or outside, life; and experience presupposes the existence of an "experiencer," a conscious self who experiences, and death may mean the loss of consciousness and one's self. But it may make sense to speak of death as nothingness, or nonbeing, as long as we remember that such phrases are poetic and indicate more than we can really know or say.

If death is the end—if it means, as it does to so many twentieth century persons, the complete annihilation of the conscious personality—then what is the meaning, the purpose, and the value of life? Jacques Choron presses this demand for meaning in *Death and Modern Man:*

> *Caught between, on the one hand, a philosophy of history that sees in the historical process only the working of blind chance (or, even more pessimistically, inevitable doom) and, on the other hand, the scientific image of man as an insignificant speck on a minor planet in a remote corner of an indifferent universe, what can modern man answer to this question?*

Death and the Meaning of Life

Why does death throw the meaning of life into question?

If there is no God and no immortality of the soul (which is, of course, far from certain), death makes the problem of the meaning of human life especially urgent. Death throws into question the value of activity. If we're

---

Viewpoint

Some existentialists have suggested that the mark of authenticity is the ability to face up to one's own dread of death. But all their tedious talk of dread and death has not made them authentic. . . . The dread of death is not universal and . . . an autonomous individual will not fear death. Nor need the road to autonomy lead through such fear. What makes people inauthentic (and what makes their talk of food and clothes and petty failures and successes so utterly pathetic) is not that they have forgotten that they must die before long. It is that they have forgotten that they are survivors.

Thinking only of oneself can never generate an ethic; nor will it ever lead to autonomy. Neither dread nor courage in the face of death need keep anyone from seeking trivial satisfactions in his final days or years. What makes such pursuits seem inappropriate, if not outrageous, is a vivid sense that one is a survivor. What is needed is some sense of solidarity with others—not necessarily or even usually all others, but some. . . . Solzhenitsyn's unique moral force is inseparable from the fact that he has never forgotten that he is a survivor.

WALTER KAUFMANN, Without Guilt and Justice: From Decidophobia to Autonomy sure to die in the end, what's the use of doing anything at all? Even people's most remarkable accomplishments seem futile when death destroys them and time overcomes their works, erases their memories, and wipes them out as if they'd never existed at all. What is more, for the individual, death, so understood, means not only the disintegration of a center of consciousness and activity—the self—but also the obliteration of the world.

To put it in the first person, when I die, I will no longer exist, and the world will no longer exist for me, although it will, of course, continue to exist for others. The awareness of this fact probably accounts for the resentment the dying frequently feel toward those around them, even toward those they love, who will be the most saddened by their death. If I'm bound to die, then, and if this world in which I've struggled to live will disappear with me, what's the use in struggling? Moreover, if I'm certain to die, and if this world in which I've known pleasure and happiness will be destroyed with me (as far as I'm concerned), then even those transitory pleasures and that passing happiness seem pointless.

Although the realization that someday we will die does not prevent most of us from enjoying life (and may spur some of us to live better), these thoughts about the meaning, purpose, and value of life probably occur to everyone at one point or another. Death is a universal dimension of the human condition. Along with the capacity to think (about death, among other things) and to communicate one's thoughts, the fact of one's mortality must enter any definition of what it is to be a person. To come to terms with death, then, means in the largest sense to come to terms with life. But is that possible? How?

It should be recognized from the beginning that the familiar complaints about the meaninglessness, purposelessness, and sheer futility of a life that leads only to death and nothingness have led some thinkers into logical inconsistencies. Many pessimistic philosophers have started by recognizing the horror of death and finished by claiming that death is preferable to the life it supposedly renders futile! In *Tragic Sense of Life,* Unamuno has traced this line of reasoning:

> *"If it is true that I am to die utterly,"* we say to ourselves, *"then once I am annihilated the world has ended so far as I am concerned—it is finished. Why, then, should it not end forthwith, so that no new consciousnesses, doomed to suffer the tormenting illusion of a transient and apparential existence, may come into being? If, the illusion of living being shattered, living for the mere sake of living or for the sake of others who are likewise doomed to die, does not satisfy the soul, what is the good of living? Our best remedy is death."*

It should also be recognized that the word "meaning" is used in at least two ways in this context. As Paul Edwards has suggested, it may be taken in a "cosmic," or global, sense. This is how we use it when we ask if there is a meaning to life in general: "Does any life have meaning?" But it may also be taken in a "terrestrial," or mundane, sense, as when we ask ourselves, "Does my life have any meaning?" Answering the first question might involve us in philosophical speculation about the order and purpose of the universe. An answer to the second, however, might involve such ordinary, everyday concerns as the individual's work, hobbies, devotion to a political cause, or love for others. A satisfactory answer to this second question—"What is meaningful *in my life?*"—will not necessarily be an intellectually and emotionally satisfying response to the more general first question—"What is the meaning *of life?*"

Furthermore, it's significant that this first, fundamental, abstract question about the meaning of life is usually taken to involve its value and its purpose. To inquire about the value and, especially, the purpose of something is to introduce the distinction between means (or methods) and ends (or goals). Thus, the primary purpose (one is tempted to say, "the point") of a pencil is to write on paper; the purpose of a piece of chalk, to write on a blackboard. The pencil and the chalk are valuable as means to a specific end, namely, communicating with others through written words and symbols. This purpose confers on them a meaning: Their point is to serve as instruments for communication among different persons, or, more abstractly, to function in a system of verbal and symbolic behavior. But what, in terms of means and ends, is the meaning, value, or purpose of life?

Viewpoint

Buddha told a parable in a sutra:

"A man traveling across a field encountered a tiger. He fled, the tiger after him. Coming to a precipice, he caught hold of the root of a wild vine and swung himself down over the edge. The tiger sniffed at him from above. Trembling, the man looked down to where, far below, another tiger was waiting to eat him. Only the vine sustained him.

"Two mice, one white and one black, little by little started to gnaw away the vine. The man saw a luscious strawberry near him. Grasping the vine with one hand, he plucked the strawberry with the other. How sweet it tasted!"

No. 18, "A Parable," from PAUL REPS, compilator, *Zen Flesh, Zen Bones: A Collection of Zen and Pre-Zen Writings*

Popular wisdom and common sense reply that the meaning of life is life itself, but this rough-and-ready answer is clearly inadequate. It begs the question. But it does suggest an idea important in Western thought, namely, that individual life is good in itself and is not merely a means to some other end. Objects and symbols *have* meanings, however; they are not the meanings themselves. And it seems that death itself is the only "end" of life, that is, both its finish and its goal. The end of life is its annihilation, that is, nothing at all.

Does death imply, though, that life has no meaning? Not necessarily. Philosophers have struggled with the problem of the meaning of mortal existence for centuries. Among the many solutions Western thinkers have proposed to the mystery of life in the face of death, two stand out, although they have been formulated in many different ways. The first is the idea that a person's work can lend meaning, value, and purpose to his or her life; the second is that love is what counts.

Can work or love constitute the meaning of an individual's life?

In one form, the salvific value of work is a fairly modern idea, and it may mark a reversal of the earlier order of things. Many people seem to live to work, rather than working to live. This argument has another form. In this form it is creative work, art, that makes life meaningful, gives it purpose, and assigns it a value. This is seen to be so not only because for many persons beauty has been, and remains, a transcendent goal, but also because art structures the chaotic reality of our experience. It gives our lives an order and a coherence that we might otherwise not discover.

In addition, many artists and writers, from ancient times to the present, have sought a sort of synthetic immortality in their works. Homer, who lived in the ninth century B.C., called his epic poem the *Odyssey,* "a monument more lasting than bronze." Many other creative writers and artists have also survived their own deaths, if only in the sense that we remember them, and the works they've left us still solicit our attention.

It's clear, however, that the argument that work lends meaning to life is not entirely satisfactory. In its first and simplest form, the idealistic notion that people's work can give them a reason for living, a sense of meaning and purpose in life, is compromised by the realities of their jobs. Millions of human beings, perhaps the majority, find their jobs unrewarding at best and more often tedious, boring, and frustrating. There are not very many creative artists and writers, and fewer still are successful. Can they alone enjoy meaningful lives? And even the "immortality" these few earn is questionable. Their works sometimes survive them, it's true, but their continued existence depends on a number of external conditions, including the physical integrity of the materials with which they work (paper, canvas, wood, and so on). In any case, why should such remembrance be a guarantee that their lives were meaningful?

Work, then, is not necessarily meaningful and valuable. And because of this, it cannot provide an adequate and universally valid answer to the question, "What is the meaning of life?"

Another answer to the question of life's meaning is that love is what matters. In loving others and being loved by them, people can find themselves, their place, and their purpose in the social world. Love entails the responsibility to care for the beloved; this responsibility, freely accepted, can give the one who loves a sense of purpose in life and a reason for being, a reason not to die.

There is a scene in Henrik Ibsen's play *A Doll's House* that illustrates the idea. Mrs. Linde has just arrived to visit her childhood friend Nora, and they exchange these words:

> MRS. LINDE: . . . The last three years have seemed like one long working day, with no rest. Now it is at an end, Nora. My poor mother needs me no more, for she is gone; and the boys do not need me either; they have got situations and can shift for themselves.
> NORA: What a relief you must feel it.
> MRS. LINDE: No indeed; I only feel my life unspeakably empty. No one to live for any more.

Describing one of the terminally ill patients interviewed in her study *On Death and Dying,* Elisabeth Kübler-Ross presents a situation significantly different from Mrs. Linde's, but it points to the same conclusion:

> *Mrs. C. [a leukemia victim] is . . . a middle-aged woman for whom death approaches in the midst of a life of responsibilities, caring for a number of dependent people. She has a father-in-law who is eighty-one and who recently had a heart attack, a mother with Parkinson's disease who is seventy-six, a twelve-year-old girl who still needs her mother and may have to grow up "too quickly" . . . and a twenty-two-year-old [retarded] son who goes in and out of state hospitals, for whom she both fears and cares. [Mrs. C. worries that she] has to leave all these dependent people now at a time when they need her the most.*

Ibsen's character feels she has no one to live for anymore, but Kübler-Ross' patient fears death because it will deprive her of the further possibility of caring for those whom she loves. Both situations, the fictional and the real, testify to the importance of love not only for a person's sense of self but also for a sense of meaning and purpose in life.

In this context, we might mention in passing another idea about the meaning of life. This one combines the ideas of work and love by suggesting that people can give their lives meaning by devoting themselves to social or political causes. It should be recognized, however, that others can easily betray such causes after the particular person's death and misinterpret that person's life work and intentions to support their own ends.

Some thinkers have suggested that parental love can eventuate in a sort of biological immortality: Those who have families can live on in their children. Psychologically, this idea might account for the importance many people attach to seeing their family names continue. We might well ask, though, how much of a person really survives in his or her children. We might also ask if in this theory those who have no children are condemned to lead meaningless lives. And what about the deaths of young children? If we settle for biological immortality as the answer to the meaning of life, we are left with too many meaningless deaths.

Unamuno's remarks in *Tragic Sense of Life* may be unnecessarily polemical, but they are very much to the point:

> *All this talk of a man surviving in his children, or in his works, or in the universal consciousness, is but vague verbiage which satisfies only those who suffer from affective stupidity, and who, for the rest, may be persons of a certain cerebral distinction. For it is possible to possess great talent . . . and yet to be stupid as regards the feelings.*

Unamuno held that the synthetic immortality people might achieve through work or love was at best a poor substitute for the real thing, which is true immortality, eternal life, the personal survival of the person after physical death. But what is the evidence and what are the arguments for immortality?

The Problem of Immortality

It seems the possibility of some form of continued personal existence after death has always fascinated human beings. However, the problem of immortality remains philosophically controversial. Indeed, the very fact that so many have longed for immortality and sought to prove through rational argument that the soul does survive the body's death has itself been cited as evidence both that the soul *is* immortal and that it *isn't!*

What is the problem of immortality?

Writing of the possibility of belief in personal immortality during an age of disbelief, William James remarked that there are two kinds of people: those "whom we find indulging to their heart's content in the prospects of immortality; and [those] who experience the greatest difficulty in making such a notion seem real to themselves at all." The former would be inclined to say that since people, as though by nature, have always desired immortality, it must be the case that the individual lives on spiritually after he or she has died physically. As John Stuart Mill commented in *Nature*,

we often hear it maintained that every wish which it is supposed to be natural to entertain must have a corresponding provision in the order of the universe for its gratification; insomuch (for instance) that the desire of an indefinite prolongation of existence is believed by many to be in itself a sufficient proof of the reality of a future life.

Those who are disinclined to believe in immortality would be likely to respond that the widespread belief in personal survival, although admittedly issuing from deep-rooted "natural" desires, is merely a sort of wishful thinking.

Actually, of course, both would be wrong in drawing conclusions. The first argument is based on a debatable premise, namely, that men and women naturally desire immortality. Some claim to find the prospect of infinite existence infinitely tiresome. George Bernard Shaw gave imaginative expression to this opinion in the third act of his play *Man and Superman*, better known as "Don Juan in Hell." There, Don Juan complains that hell bores him "beyond description, beyond belief" and that "men get tired of everything, of heaven no less than of hell." More fundamentally, even if the desire for immortality is natural—and universal, despite the exemptions claimed by some—belief might still be unjustified. Unamuno tacitly admits this when he writes, "'Tis a tragic fate, without a doubt, to have to base the affirmation of immortality upon the insecure and slippery foundation of the desire for immortality."

The second argument is equally dubious. The fact that many have craved

---

Viewpoint

The fact that the belief in immortality is practically coextensive with the human race does not, unfortunately, prove that the belief is well founded, but it does prove that the desire for a life beyond this life is universal, and that, in turn, may be used to show that individualism is one of the most fundamental human traits, since the desire for immortality is an expression of the human protest against the scheme of nature which takes so little account of man and his demands.

JOSEPH WOOD KRUTCH, The Modern Temper

and affirmed immortality doesn't make it true that the soul survives the body, but it doesn't necessarily make it false either.

What does immortality mean? Perhaps its most familiar meaning in twentieth century Western thought is defined by the traditional Christian teaching that, depending on how people live on earth, their souls will go to heaven, where they will know eternal happiness in God's presence, or to hell, where, cut off from God, they will forever endure the most unspeakable torments. Some people believe in another sort of immortality: the soul's transmigration to another body, or its reincarnation in another physical form. (Still others believe that the soul, or the separative ego, will merge with universal consciousness—the world mind—at the individual's death. This belief posits that the person will not survive death as a person, that the individual will not retain his or her identity. We shall restrict our discussion to the more usual understanding of immortality as personal survival.)

Clearly, establishing the fact of personal immortality would finally resolve the question of life's meaning in the face of death. For Christians, given the existence of God and the immortality of the soul, this short life is merely a preparation for another, eternal life. Death has no sting. On the contrary, for the faithful person who has lived a good life according to Christian precepts, death means liberation from this earthly domain. For those who believe in reincarnation, individuals participate in the cosmic process of cyclical recurrence: for some, the circle of eternal return; for others, the long, difficult way through many lives toward eventual release from the bonds of physical existence.

In Western thought, perhaps the two most famous arguments in support of the doctrine of immortality are those formulated by the classical Greek philosopher Plato and the modern German philosopher Immanuel Kant.

In *Phaedo*, one of Plato's finest dialogues, a companion of Socrates' named Phaedo recounts a discussion the imprisoned philosopher had with friends as he awaited his execution. One of the company insisted that "he who is confident about death has but a foolish confidence, unless he is able to prove that the soul is altogether immortal and imperishable." He appealed to Socrates for philosophical reassurance. "Socrates," he said, "you must argue us out of our fears—and yet, strictly speaking, they are not our fears, but there is a child within us to whom death is a sort of hobgoblin: him too we must persuade not to be afraid when he is alone in the dark."

How did Plato argue for personal immortality?

As Plato represents their discussion, Socrates developed several arguments in response to his friend's request that he prove the soul immortal. All depend on the premise that human beings have souls that exist independently of the body. Reduced to its simplest terms, this argument may be the best: Since death is decomposition and since the soul is absolutely simple, it is logically impossible for the soul to die. To decompose is to break down into parts; the soul may have different faculties, or capabilities, but it has no parts. In other words, only physical or material things, which have parts, can die; spiritual or immaterial things, which have no parts, cannot. So the soul, a spiritual thing, must be imperishable or immortal.

Plato's classic proof has been reformulated many times in the history of Western thought. In the seventeenth century, the French Catholic philosopher René Descartes asserted in *Discourse on Method*,

> *Our soul is in its nature entirely independent of the body, and in consequence . . . it is not liable to die with it. And then, inasmuch as we observe no other causes capable of destroying it, we are naturally inclined to judge that it is immortal.*

In our own century, Jacques Maritain, another French Catholic philosopher, has likewise argued, in *Man's Destiny in Eternity,* that the human soul

> *cannot be corrupted, since it has no matter, it cannot be disintegrated, since it has no substantial parts, it cannot lose its individual unity, since it is self-subsisting, nor its internal energy, since it contains within itself all the sources of its energies. The human soul cannot die. Once existing, it cannot disappear, it will necessarily exist always, endure without end.*

It's evident, however, that Plato's proof rests on a certain idea of the soul that many thinkers would refuse today. Alfred North Whitehead, a contemporary English philosopher, identified the popular opinion that minds, like souls, exist in the manner of objects as an instance of "the fallacy of misplaced concreteness." In his view, in its contemporary form this prevalent but erroneous belief is a by-product of modern scientific thought as it took shape during the seventeenth century. In *Science and the Modern World,* Whitehead explains:

> *The enormous success of the scientific abstractions yielding on the one hand matter* with its *simple location* in space and time, on the other hand *mind, perceiving, suffering, reasoning, but not interfering, has foisted onto philosophy the task of accepting them as the most concrete rendering of fact.*

But, Whitehead argues, minds don't exist concretely—any more than thoughts or feelings do. There is no mental "thing" that might, for instance, continue to exist on its own after the body has died. In light of Whitehead's analysis, the common sense notion of the mind as an immaterial reality, a mental thing, seems misconceived. So does Plato's logically similar concept of "soul."

In the eighteenth century, Immanuel Kant argued, as Plato had, that the soul must be immortal. In the *Critique of Pure Reason,* Kant did, it is true, maintain the impossibility of affirming or denying that the soul is immortal. He held that we can't know for sure that it is or that it is not. We cannot say with complete certainty that God does or does not exist, either, or that man is or is not free. These things are beyond the limits of human reason. However, in his later work, the *Critique of Practical Reason,* Kant claimed that he had achieved practical or moral certainty, as opposed to logical certainty, about them. He felt confident that God does exist, that man is free, and that the human soul is immortal, even though he could not claim to know for sure.

In Kant's philosophical system, "practical reason" is the faculty by which we know the universal imperatives of moral law. To establish the immortality of the human soul, which he offered as a postulate of pure practical reason, he formulated this argument: Moral law requires that we become perfect. What moral law requires must, in principle, be possible. (Kant maintained that "if you should, you can.") But it would be possible for us to become perfect only if our souls were immortal. Unending progress toward moral perfection, or holiness, would be possible only if our individual lives were themselves endless. "Thus," Kant concluded, "the highest good [moral perfection, or holiness] is practically possible only on the supposition of the immortality of the soul, and the latter, as inseparably bound to the moral law, is a postulate of pure practical reason." He went on to explain, "By a postulate of pure practical reason, I understand a theoretical proposition which is not as such demonstrable, but which is an inseparable corollary of an a priori unconditionally valid practical law."

To Plato's dubious premises that human beings have souls and that their souls are independent of their bodies, Kant's remarkable argument adds a third: a supposed obligation to become perfect. Unlike Plato's argument Kant's doesn't pretend to offer proof human souls are immortal: It offers only "a theoretical proposition which is not as such demonstrable." A valid proof would lead to logical certainty. And logical certainty is very different from the elusive "moral certainty" at which Kant arrived but of which, as James remarked, some are simply incapable. There is a big difference between a logical must ("The answer to that arithmetic problem must be 12") and a moral must ("You must not do that"). So when Kant urges that the soul "must" survive the body, it's important to recognize how he uses the word. In effect, his argument amounts to making demands on the universe— "nature," he wrote, "cannot lure us on by deceitful promises and in the end betray us"—and to assuming that what he presumably wanted to be true was true.

What grounds for belief did Kant propose?

Unamuno has offered an insightful psychological explanation for Kant's later work:

> *Kant reconstructed with the heart that which with the head he had overthrown. And we know . . . that the man Kant, the more or less selfish old bachelor who professed philosophy at Königsberg at the end of the century of the Encyclopedia and the goddess of Reason, was a man much preoccupied with the problem—I mean with the only real vital problem, the problem that strikes at the very root of our being, the problem of our individual and personal destiny, of the immortality of the soul. The man Kant was not resigned to die utterly. And because he was not resigned to die utterly he made that leap . . . from the one Critique to the other.*

Maritain, too, recognized the opposition of the heart and the head when it comes to discussing immortality. Like so many other philosophers, he maintained that "there is in man a natural, an instinctive knowledge of his immortality." Reason might deny it; yet, Maritain wrote,

> *when the intellect of a man denies immortality, this man continues living, despite his rational convictions, on the basis of an unconscious and, so to speak, biological assumption of this very immortality—though it is rationally denied.*

Our concern, however, is with reasons. Apart from the more or less satisfactory arguments from immortality we've examined, what empirical evidence is there that human beings have souls and that their souls live on after their physical death? People have cited both scientific experiments and personal experiences as evidence that death is not the end of life. The inconclusive experiments, most of which were conducted early in this century, usually involved attempts to establish through photography the existence of a soul that leaves the body at the moment of death. The personal experiences are familiar to everybody who reads in the daily newspaper accounts of haunted houses, previous existences, and communications from the dead. It's probably the case that many of these "supernatural" occurrences and reported experiences of psychic phenomena are fraudulent, that many more are hallucinatory, and that the rest could be explained in terms of natural causes. Indeed, the single most compelling argument against immortality is that mental activity is bound up with the brain, and mental life dependent upon physical existence.

However, it seems plausible to some that these incidents are not always susceptible to ordinary scientific explanations. Still less easily dismissed are the accounts of those who are said to have "died" for a few moments but were then restored to life by medical science and the strenuous exertions of doctors and nurses. These people often report "out of body" experiences during which they observed what was happening. In addition, they frequently recall a sense of peace and calm, and they sometimes express their annoyance at having been saved. "Immortality" may not, after all, be the correct explanation of these things, but the hypothesis that the human soul or mind survives the death of the human body, at least for a limited time, merits consideration.

In the next section, focusing on what one writer has called "the American way of death," we'll consider the relationship between culture and the perception of death.

Death in America

Attitudes toward dying and death have varied widely from one age and one society to another. David Cole Gordon argues, however, that there is a causal relationship between humanity's fear of death and its cultural achievements. In *Overcoming the Fear of Death,* Gordon writes, "Everything man does, builds, or creates is in large measure designed to assuage his conscious or unconscious fear of oblivion." In this view, which has much to recommend it, it is human beings' anguished awareness of their mortality, or finitude, that renders the meaning of life and death doubtful and impels them to act and to create.

How do contemporary Americans perceive death? In the United States dying is a rather "dehumanized" affair, and death was, at least until quite recently, a forbidden subject. We've already mentioned that our "death talk," the euphemistic expressions we use when we talk about death, is almost a code that avoids the very subject it presents. For instance, the death certificate is frequently called a "vital statistics form," and a cemetery, "a memorial park." And people don't die; they expire, pass on, or join the majority.

How do contemporary Americans perceive and manage death?

Of course, it's not only our way of talking that conveys, or betrays, our attitudes toward death. In addition to using euphemisms, we also do our best to shield children from witnessing a death in the family or from perceiving the anxiety and turmoil that death occasions. Today, this is not too difficult, since most people die not at home but more conveniently in the hospital. And in many cases we decide not to inform dying persons that they are dying. We may later take comfort in the fact that they apparently never knew the end was at hand.

These practices mark a reversal of attitudes toward death: During the Middle Ages, family members and neighbors would crowd into the dying person's room, where that person would preside over his or her death;

today's customs deny the one who is about to die even this limited mastery of death. Contrasting the twentieth century with earlier times in the Western world, the French historian Philippe Ariès writes, in "The Reversal of Death," "Today nothing remains either of the sense that everyone has or should have of his impending death, or of the public solemnity surrounding the moment of death. What used to be appreciated is now hidden; what used to be solemn is now avoided."

After someone has died, we turn the funeral arrangements over to professional funeral directors; with chemicals and cosmetics, they contrive to make the dead person look as if he or she were merely sleeping. The funeral home then serves as an acceptable compromise between the hospital, which is too impersonal a place for the wake, and the family home, which is too personal. At the funeral home, the dead person can, as it were, receive his or her relatives and acquaintances one last time. Finally, where burial is preferred to cremation, we escort the dead person—the corpse, actually—to a cemetery that looks like a park. In fact, parks look like cemeteries: The nineteenth century "rural cemetery" movement gave impetus to the later establishment of municipal parks in this country.

After the funeral, we discourage mourning. Just as the dying person had to overcome his or her anxiety, follow orders, and die in quiet dignity, so the survivors have to hide their grief and go on with their social lives and their work. Because death is unpleasant, and because it rends the social fabric, those who cannot suppress their grief are shunned in much the same way as deviants and misfits are.

Both our language and our behavior appear to confirm what many social scientists have recently suggested: In the twentieth century, death has replaced sex as the principal taboo. It mustn't be brought up in public.

Why is death a forbidden subject in American culture?

Why has death become a forbidden subject? There are several theories. Kübler-Ross indicates that, although there are probably many reasons for the flight from death, one of the most pertinent facts is that due to medical and technical advances, dying is ironically more gruesome now than it ever was before: "more lonely, mechanical, and dehumanized." Ariès, however, in *Western Attitudes toward Death,* identifies the cause of the ban on mentioning death as "the need for happiness—the moral duty and the social obligation to contribute to the collective happiness by avoiding any cause for sadness or boredom, by appearing to be always happy, even if in the depths of despair."

Another explanation is still more specific to twentieth century American culture. Sam Keen describes death as an affront to modern man's image of himself as the lord of nature and an obstacle to his hopes for the future. Mortality sets a limit to modern man's visions of a utopian environment free from the negativities that terrified people in earlier times. Keen maintains in

Apology for Wonder, "It is not accidental that the repression of the awareness of death is to the twentieth century what the repression of sex was to the nineteenth. A culture animated by technological hopes is unable to face the problem of death because it throws into question the values and goals for which it strives."

Whatever the reasons for this prevalent attitude, it should be clear that to ignore death is unrealistic. As Choron remarked in *Death and Western Thought,* "not 'bothering' with the problem of death is equivalent to divorcing philosophy from the profoundest theme which has troubled, mystified and haunted mankind from the beginning of time." Denying death amounts to giving up the quest for a human understanding of human existence.

Summary

Philosophy and Death: One's view of death involves one's perspective on life; coming to terms with death amounts to defining a personal philosophy.
The Nature of Death: In contemporary scientific culture, many thinkers see death not as a catastrophic event but as a natural process. However, the scientific world view has not unequivocally made man's place in the universe seem more meaningful.
Death and the Self: A common reason why people fear death is their dread of nothingness or nonbeing, the complete obliteration of their conscious selves. However, the concept of self is philosophically problematic. If death means nothingness, then it may not be correct to anticipate one's own death as an experience.
Death and the Meaning of Life: Death renders the problem of the meaning, value, and purpose of human life especially urgent. Among the many solutions that have been proposed are that work and art give life its value and that love is what makes life worth living.
The Problem of Immortality: Among many others, Plato and Kant proposed arguments intended to establish that the human soul is immortal. Plato held that the soul, which is a simple, immaterial entity, must be imperishable; Kant maintained that moral law requires perfection, which is possible only if individual lives are in fact endless. Their premises, and so their conclusions, are debatable.
Death in America: In contemporary American culture, death seems to have replaced sex as the principal forbidden subject. The dehumanization of death, the modern emphasis on happiness, and the utopian hopes that animate technological culture might account for this denial of death.

Suggestions for Further Reading

Jacques Choron has written three serious books on death. The most popular is *Death and Modern Man* (New York: Macmillan, 1964). His scholarly history of philosophical reflection on mortality, *Death and Western Thought* (New York: Macmillan, 1963), deserves attention as a reference work. Finally, his very readable *Suicide* (New York: Scribner, 1972) is one of the most balanced and comprehensive studies of that subject currently available.

Although their philosophical approaches and styles differ tremendously, two leading twentieth century Catholic thinkers have addressed the problem of immortality in their works. One of them is Miguel de Unamuno, the Spanish philosopher of life whose passionate writing is the model of contemporary irrationalism; see especially his major work, *Tragic Sense of Life,* trans. J. E. Crawford Flitch (New York: Dover, 1954). The other is Jacques Maritain, a French philosopher whose voluminous and brilliant works on epistemology, metaphysics, moral philosophy, social philosophy, and aesthetics have made him one of the preeminent intellectuals of our times. In the present context, see especially *The Range of Reason* (New York: Scribner, 1962) and *Man's Destiny in Eternity* (Boston: Beacon Press, 1949).

Hywel D. Lewis' *The Self and Immortality* (New York: Seabury, 1973) also deserves mention. Although the author identifies his aim as "a modest one of indicating how we must think of persons in the context that is most relevant to Christian and related affirmations of a positive expectation of a life beyond the grave," he offers a balanced view of the mind-body problem in contemporary thought as well as a critical examination of the notion of reincarnation.

One of the finest short studies of the history of death is Philippe Ariès' *Western Attitudes toward Death: From the Middle Ages to the Present,* trans. Patricia M. Ranum (Baltimore: Johns Hopkins, 1974). In four brief sections, Ariès distinguishes different, culturally defined attitudes toward death from the millenium to the twentieth century.

Edited by David E. Stannard, *Death in America* (Philadelphia: University of Pennsylvania Press, 1975) is an excellent selection of historical essays. In addition to Stannard's "Death and the Puritan Child," this collection includes studies of nineteenth century American consolation literature and the "rural cemetery" movement as well as a good translation of Philippe Ariès' 1967 article "The Reversal of Death; Changes in Attitudes toward Death in Western Societies." For a critical view of contemporary American customs, see Jessica Mitford's now classic study of the funeral industry, *The American Way of Death* (New York: Simon and Schuster, 1963).

Inquiry

Easy Death: The Problem of Euthanasia

In Dalton Trumbo's controversial novel *Johnny Got His Gun,* the hero, Joe Bonham, was a war victim who had no face, no arms, and no legs. Almost totally paralyzed, he had spent six years in a military hospital—six lonely, tortured years during which he reflected on fragmentary visions of his former life and the senselessness of war. Time and again he had tried desperately to communicate with his nurse by banging his head against the railing of his bed. Although he'd never been deeply religious, he prayed feverishly while he tapped a message, saying, "oh please god make her understand what I'm trying to tell her. I've been alone so long god I've been here for years and years suffocating smothering dead while alive like a man who has been buried in a casket deep in the ground and awakens and screams I'm alive I'm alive I'm alive." When the nurse finally understood that he was signaling her, she called an attendant who rapped out an overwhelming question in Morse code on Joe's forehead: What do you want? "Let me out he thought that's all I want. I've been lying here for years and years in a room in a bed in a little covering of skin. Now I want out. I've got to get out."

Mary Cooper's mother had lung cancer. There was no question about the diagnosis; she was terminally ill. When the disease entered its final stages, she was admitted to a private hospi-

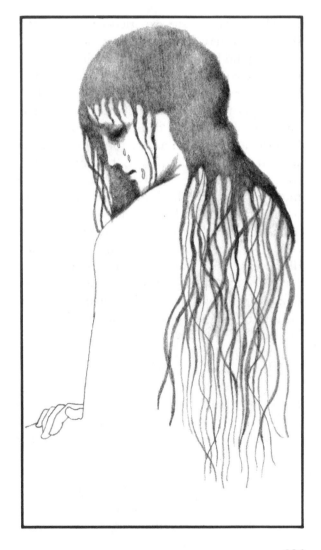

tal where, though she experienced awful pain, she survived day after day. Mary took an indefinite, unpaid leave of absence from her job in an insurance company's secretarial pool to be with her mother as much as possible, although it hurt her deeply to see her suffer so; her mother had always been a strong and optimistic woman. Jim Cooper, a foundryman, felt sorry for both his wife and his mother-in-law, but he resented Mary's missing work—all the more since her mother's medical bills had almost taken all the money they'd saved over the years for their teenage son's college education. One evening he called her physician to complain about his handling of the case. "Make her comfortable, Doctor. Give her all the drugs she needs, so she doesn't feel anything. But let her die—give her an injection, if you have to, but let her go. For her and for us." Dr. Malloy was sympathetic, but he reminded Jim that what he was suggesting was against the law. Jim didn't tell Mary about that conversation, but he didn't have to. She knew what he was thinking, and sometimes (although she felt guilty about it) she too prayed that the end would come soon. Still, her mother lingered.

"Euthanasia" means "easy death"; to administer it—many would say, to commit it—would be knowingly to interrupt medical treatment or deliberately to take lethal measures to release the incurably ill painlessly from their suffering. For centuries, it has been condemned by religion and law. In our times, however, technological advances have changed the situation for those who clearly can't be restored to an active, rewarding life because of an illness or an accident. Because of this, many serious students of bioethics (the ethics of the biological sciences and medicine) have called for a critical and compassionate review of the pros and cons relating to euthanasia. In some cases, they argue, it is both morally and medically correct to administer an easy death.

In general, the two most extreme arguments for and against euthanasia are these: Those who oppose it maintain that it's against God's will ("Thou shalt not kill") and that it violates not only the doctor's oath but also, more fundamentally, the patient's right to live. Moreover, it might open the door to the further extension of such murderous practices. If euthanasia is administered to the incurably ill today, they argue, it might be exercised on the mentally retarded, for instance, or the aged tomorrow. And who but God has the right to decide that another person shouldn't live or has already lived long enough?

Those who support it argue that both "negative," or "passive," euthanasia (stopping treatment that will keep the patient alive) and "positive," or "active," euthanasia (applying measures that will cause the patient to die) should be administered as often as it's justified. The approval of the patient himself, if he's conscious, and his family and physician should be obtained. A compassionate and just God would not condemn euthanasia when it's performed for the greater good not only of the patient and his family but of society too. Because of technological and medical progress— because, that is, of the recent invention of life-prolonging machines and the development of new therapeutic methods—it's now possible to keep patients like Joe Bonham alive almost indefinitely. But this is expensive; the machines cost a lot to build and to run, and the highly trained paramedical specialists who operate them have to be paid too, just like the doctors and the nurses. When one considers that the machines, the technicians' skills, the nurses' time, and even the hospital room might all be put to better use, and when one also considers the patient's suffering, both physical and emotional, then the cost to the patient, to his or her family, and to society is not justified. Proponents of euthanasia hold that in such cases allowing the patient to die easily and painlessly is not merely morally defensible but positively good. It's the merciful thing to do. Mary Cooper's mother would be better off dead.

In your view, is euthanasia justified in Joe Bonham's case? In Mary Cooper's mother's case? What's the difference, if any, between the two cases? If euthanasia were legal, and they were your next of kin, so that you were personally involved if not responsible for making the decision, what would you do? Why?

Ethically, is there any difference between negative euthanasia and positive euthanasia?

Among the social costs of maintaining the incurably ill, those who advocate the controlled exercise of euthanasia sometimes cite the danger of overpopulation. Would this be a valid argument to justify "terminating" a patient?

Assuming that administering an easy death is the right thing to do in some cases and assuming its legality, what general criteria would you establish to control euthanasia? For instance, would it be enough that the patient still has the capacity to think, or should he or she also be able to contribute something to others to justify his or her continued existence? And who should make the final decision?

Inquiry

Untimely Death:
The Problem
of Suicide

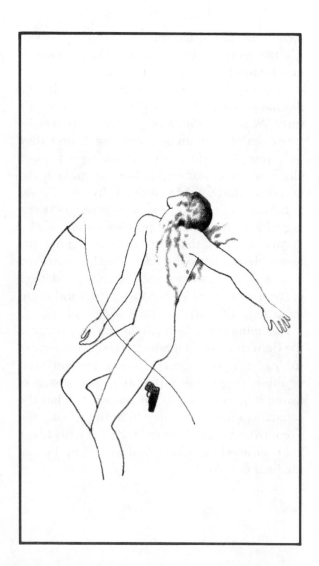

Why do people kill themselves? There are probably as many reasons as there are suicide attempts, but some psychologists and sociologists have proposed general theoretical explanations involving philosophical views of individual life and death. Among these theorists, the Austrian psychologist Sigmund Freud and the French sociologist Émile Durkheim are the most thoughtful. Their theories may not be entirely correct, but they have introduced some provocative ideas and valuable insights.

Freud asserted that there's a natural "death drive" pushing all people toward suicide. The source of man's aggressive tendencies, this supposed death drive, or death instinct, would function in opposition to the sex drive, pleasure principle, or life instinct. Thus, Freud wrote, "We recognize two fundamental instincts and ascribe to each of them its own aim": The one, Eros, is an expression of the will to live; the other, Thanatos, is a will to die. When the life instinct blocks the death drive the self-destructive tendency is turned outward against the world and other people. Suicide and murder, according to this theory, come from the same dark center, a desire for nothingness hidden deep within the primitive unconscious.

David Cole Gordon has taken Freud's death-drive theory further. He contests that suicide is a negative act of self-destruction. In his view of life and death, "man's basic drive is for unification, for merging with himself, others, and the entire world or nature." Death may seem to be the ultimate experience of such peaceful unification with oneself, others, and nature. Gordon writes in *Self-Love:*

> *In this state [the individual's] mind is totally and permanently stilled, his alienation and mind-body split are repaired, and he is one with all. The Eros and Thanatos, or life and death instincts, are not the contradictory and opposed drives that Freud postulated, but are both part of the same drive or instinct, man's desire for unification.*

Obviously, proving the effective existence of a death instinct would go a long way not only toward explaining otherwise unintelligible suicides and, more generally, human aggression in this century of unprecedented violence but also toward reconciling man to death. Death wouldn't just be natural; it would be desirable.

On the basis of their clinical observations, however, many other psychologists have contested these ideas. There simply is no unequivocal evidence to support the theory that a death drive impels human beings to destroy themselves and one another. Schopenhauer may have been much closer to the truth when he wrote

that the suicidal person "wills life, and is dissatisfied only with the conditions under which it has presented itself to him"; that is, the person who seriously considers suicide may not want to die; he or she may just be unwilling to go on living in circumstances that have become intolerable and that don't promise to improve.

Relating suicide to the social environment, Durkheim made some useful distinctions. There are, he maintained, three kinds of suicide. The first, which he called egoistic, is the most common; it occurs because individuals are not sufficiently integrated into their communities. They have no strong ties to other people. In a passage that recalls an idea we discussed earlier in this chapter—that a person's relationship to others may constitute the meaning of his or her life—Durkheim wrote, "Life is said to be intolerable unless some reason for existing is involved, some purpose justifying life's trials. The individual alone is not a sufficient end for his activity. He is too little." People need other people.

The second kind of suicide, which Durkheim called "anomic" because it reflects a disordered state of society, results from the person's inability to cope with rapid social change. Durkheim maintained that society ordinarily imposes upon the individual "a conscience superior to his own," but "when society is disturbed by some painful crisis or . . . by abrupt transitions, it is momentarily incapable of exercising this influence; thence come the sudden rises in the curve of suicides."

Finally, Durkheim recognized that altruistic or other-directed suicides happen when the group's authority over the individual is so complete and so compelling that he loses his sense of personal identity and subordinates his life to the group's ends. Heroic but fatal actions under battlefield conditions such as a soldier's throwing himself on a hand grenade in order to shield others are altruistic suicides.

Durkheim's classification marked the first serious attempt to relate suicide attempts to larger social forces. More recent sociological studies have tended to confirm his thesis, at least in its outlines, although there is no consensus on the question.

Philosophical discussions of suicide usually center on the related questions of its rationality and its morality. Among the more specific reasons for suicide generally cited by those social scientists who have studied the problem are sharp disappointments like the failure of a business, overwhelming griefs like the death of someone close, and difficult situations like prolonged unemployment, ill health, or imprisonment. However, many people suffer grievous disappointments and face discouraging, worrisome situations without resorting to suicide. May we conclude that those who decide to end their lives are insane?

That depends, of course, on how you define "insanity." If you take it to mean nothing more than an emotionally confused and depressed frame of mind, then clearly many suicide victims are insane. But in many other cases persons who are apparently stable and well adjusted have taken their lives after weighing the advantages and disadvantages of continuing to live in what seems to be a senseless world or an impossible situation. Not all suicidal persons act irrationally. For practical reasons, this is an important point. The suicide prevention centers recently established in some sections of this country have been modestly successful because it's often possible to discuss suicide rationally with those who are considering it.

Is suicide morally defensible? The ethical justifiability or blameworthiness of suicide is a complex and emotionally charged question. Those who oppose suicide in principle have variously argued that God forbids it, that it is contrary to natural law, and that it is harmful to society. However, the first argument—that God forbids suicide—presupposes that God exists, that He has revealed to human beings a moral code that condemns the taking of human life, even one's own, and that He takes an interest in the actions of men and women. Today, although many people would endorse this argument, others would find it more quaint than compelling. The second argument—that suicide is contrary to natural law—might be rebutted by counterexamples: Generosity and chastity, generally deemed desirable, also seem rather unnatural. The third argument—that suicide is harmful to society—is somewhat more cogent, but in fact many suicides make very little difference to "society" at all, and some seem positively beneficial.

In the view of many contemporary secular thinkers, suicide is not always clearly wrong. It may very well be a tragic decision, and in a particular case it may indeed be ethically indefensible, but in this view it is not necessarily an immoral action. A brief comparison of different cases might serve at least to illustrate the problem's complexity. Society may properly condemn the person whose suicide is unquestionably a flight from responsibility toward others, but it might condone the accident victim's decision to terminate his life rather than burden his family by depending on machines for continued existence, and it might praise the driver who hits a tree instead of a pedestrian when her brakes fail. Accordingly, some philosophers argue that it is not correct to condemn all suicides in principle.

Albert Camus wrote, "There is but one truly serious philosophical problem, and that is suicide. Judging whether life is or is not worth living amounts to answering the fundamental question of philosophy." And E. M. Cioran has written, "Why don't I kill myself? If I knew *exactly* what keeps me from doing so, I should have no more questions to ask myself, since I should have answered them all." In your view, what implications does the "fundamental question" of suicide have for an understanding of the purpose, meaning, and value of human existence?

From your perspective, is suicide morally wrong? Always? Why? What arguments can you present to support this position? And if it's not wrong or not always wrong, then when is it justifiable and why?

In a well-written and carefully reasoned article "The Morality and Rationality of Suicide," Richard B. Brandt poses the question, "What are the moral obligations of other persons toward those who are contemplating suicide?" Brandt urges that since people who consider suicide a genuine option are usually depressed and so may not see things in perspective, those to whom they apply for advice and assistance should at least help them to see whatever alternative courses of action are available, so that they can make an intelligent decision. Suppose a friend contemplating suicide turned to you for guidance. What questions would you ask? What advice might you give?

If after discussing the situation with you your friend freely made a rational decision to commit suicide, would you have a moral obligation to prevent it by frustrating his or her plan? If so, does your response imply that people cannot decide freely and rationally to commit suicide—that such decisions are irrational? Would you then have a responsibility to see that your friend received psychiatric counseling? Or would you prevent him or her from committing suicide, not because the decision to do so is irrational, but simply because it's wrong?

Suppose you decided that in your friend's case suicide was neither wrong nor irrational, and your friend asked you to help—for instance, by providing sleeping pills—what would you do?

THE DEVIL: *Have you walked up and down upon the earth lately? I have; and I have examined Man's wonderful inventions. And I tell you that in the arts of life man invents nothing; but in the arts of death he outdoes Nature herself, and produces by chemistry and machinery all the slaughter of plague, pestilence, and famine.*

GEORGE BERNARD SHAW

I decline to accept the end of man. It is easy enough to say that man is immortal simply because he will endure: that when the last ding-dong of doom has clanged and faded from the last worthless rock hanging tideless in the last red and dying evening, that even then there will still be one more sound: that of his puny inexhaustible voice, still talking. I refuse to accept this. I believe that man will not merely endure: he will prevail.

WILLIAM FAULKNER

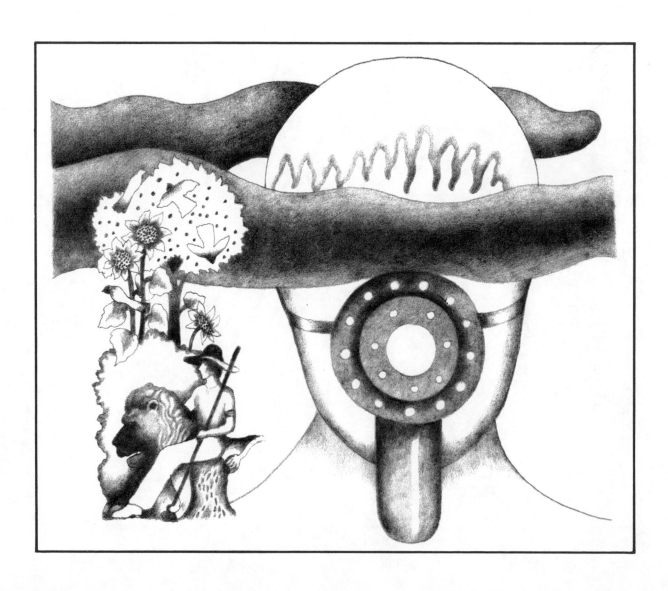

Chapter 10

HORIZONS
Nature and Civilization in a New Age

Chapter Survey

Toward the Twenty-First Century

What are our prospects?

How can we respond to new demands in a new age?

Religion and Science in the West

What is the relationship between people and nature in Western religious and scientific thought?

How have these traditions influenced the formation of modern values?

Nature and Civilization in American Life

How has the American intellectual past shaped present American reality?

What was Thoreau's philosophy of life?

What values underlie the American response to nature?

Some Personal and Societal Options

What are society's alternatives?

What are the individual's options?

Bertrand Russell
1872–1970

"We want to stand upon our own feet and look fair and square at the world—its good facts, its bad facts, its beauties and its ugliness; see the world as it is and be not afraid of it."

In the tongue-in-cheek obituary he composed for himself thirty-three years before he died, Lord Bertrand Russell wrote, "His principles were curious, but, such as they were, they governed his actions." During the course of his long life, those "curious principles"—which did indeed govern his actions—made him a controversial figure on more than one occasion. His extraordinary contributions to twentieth century thought made him a great philosopher, however, and his enduring commitment to world peace made him a great man.

Although his books, essays, and lectures on moral, social, and political questions understandably received more public attention than his technical works, Russell was not only a social critic but also one of the founders of modern mathematical logic. In the 1910s, he collaborated with Alfred North Whitehead on Principia Mathematica. In that work, Russell and Whitehead attempted to show that all of pure mathematics could be logically constructed, using no undefined terms or unproved propositions other than those generally required in logic. Although their attempt to present mathematics as an extension of logic has been criticized on a number of points, they did identify and analyze some important problems,

and their seminal study of the logical foundations of mathematics is now a classic in that field.

Russell's unorthodox ethical views were famous (or infamous). In 1940, he

was barred by a celebrated court decision from teaching philosophy at New York's City College because, the judge ruled, his appointment would establish "a chair of indecency." However, his cogently reasoned opinions about ethical problems and about such traditions as the institution of marriage certainly merit consideration.

Generally, Russell maintained that value judgments express not truths, but tastes. He recognized, of course, that according to any such "subjectivist" theory, ethical disputes could not be resolved. However, he made an interesting critical distinction between "personal" and "impersonal" desires—one's

personal desire for, say, something to eat differs significantly from one's impersonal desire for universal justice—and he always attempted to support his own particular moral judgments by rational argument.

Russell's open rejection of religious belief, which he explained and defended in Why I Am Not a Christian, was equally notorious. He held that religious belief is harmful because, not being based upon the rational assessment of evidence, it leads to intolerance. Essentially, his condemnation of religion was ethically motivated.

Addressing the question why we should "waste time" with philosophy's "insoluble problems," Russell proposed two complementary answers in the introduction to his History of Western Philosophy. One is historical, and the other, more personal; together, they reflect both the philosopher's desire to understand not only past times but his own too and his willingness to live, if necessary, with ambiguity. "To understand an age or a nation," he wrote, "we must understand its philosophy, and to understand its philosophy we must ourselves be in some degree philosophers." And, he suggested, philosophy can teach us "how to live without certainty, and yet without being paralyzed by hesitation."

HORIZONS

Toward the Twenty-First Century

During the winter of 1973 to 1974, a gasoline shortage disrupted the lives of many people in this country. Provoked by the boycott some Mideast oil-producing countries imposed on Western nations, that shortage may also have been exaggerated by American oil companies to excuse or justify substantial price increases over and above the price of crude. For many individuals who relied on their cars to get to school, work, and the stores, however, the shortage was a real problem. It varied in both duration and intensity from one section of the country to another, but in the New England states, where it was the worst, drivers would line up at the pumps at dawn and wait, sometimes for hours, to get their tanks filled. Some states adopted a simple rationing plan: Cars whose license plates ended in even numbers were to be serviced only on even-numbered days of the month, and cars whose last plate number was odd would be given gas only on odd-numbered days. Plate swapping was common. Many service stations went out of business; those that remained open kept shorter hours. To discourage anxious drivers from topping off their tanks at every opportunity, most service station managers posted a notice of the minimum amount of gas they'd sell to any driver. And along with the price of gas, the sales of siphon hoses and gas-tank locks increased dramatically.

What are our prospects?

Whether or not that shortage was contrived, the fact remains that the world's oil reserves are limited. So, indeed, are the reserves of many other nonrenewable natural resources on which our industrialized civilization depends. In the experience of that first shortage, many observers caught a glimpse of the future.

The rapid depletion of nonrenewable resources is not the only danger confronting us in this last quarter of the twentieth century. Before long, increasing population—and consequently increasing demand for space and food—may also mean overcrowding and, probably, mass starvation in many areas.

These global dangers are already realities in some of the world's underdeveloped countries, where widespread illiteracy and disease also affect the quality of life. Since those third-world nations may soon have nuclear weapons with which to bargain for a massive redistribution of wealth, the problems of resource depletion, overcrowding, and starvation pose the most serious threats to world peace.

In addition, overwhelming environmental pollution may seriously disturb the earth's ecological balance, endangering not only plant and animal life but human life as well. The smog over some cities and the oil spills that have befouled California beaches on several occasions are well-known instances of environmental pollution. However, other ecological disruptions, less visible but no less insidious, threaten all forms of life.

If the ecologists have taught us anything at all about the natural order, it's that there are no isolated problems; if recent history has taught us anything about the human order, it's that we can't always count on enlightened diplomacy to resolve conflicts. In 1950 one political philosopher observed, "On the level of historical insight and political thought, there prevails an ill-defined, general agreement that the essential structure of all civilizations is at the breaking point." Today, many share the same opinion, fully expecting social disorders to precede the inevitable environmental collapse. This dreaded culmination of our amazing economic growth and technological progress over the last few centuries would indeed be ironic if it weren't so awful.

How can we respond to new demands in a new age?

What can we do to resolve such complex, interrelated problems and to avert such tragedies? In his pessimistic *Inquiry into the Human Prospect,* Robert L. Heilbroner underscores some of the difficulties we face in responding creatively and effectively to these worldwide problems. We have compromised our capacities through our loss of confidence in ourselves and our future, our dissatisfaction with traditional value systems (such as the work ethic), and a certain "civilizational malaise." He suggests that this malaise, or uneasiness, "reflects the inability of a civilization directed to material improvement—higher incomes, better diets, miracles of medicine, triumphs of applied physics and chemistry—to satisfy the human spirit."

Heilbroner's observations are perceptive, and the authors of this textbook are convinced that if the attitudes he described lead to a mass "cop-out," or evasion of responsibility, that is, if they bring us to accept a fatalistic withdrawal from social and political action, then there is probably no hope. Those who say that the problems we face can't be resolved may be right. This is not because the problems can't be resolved but because these people begin with negative attitudes that preclude a search for solutions. If, however, these attitudes lead us critically to examine our civilization's values, then there may be grounds for restrained optimism.

Primary among the forces that have worked together to shape the modern world are science and industrialization. The one, when applied to the conquest of matter, is oriented toward continual technical progress; the other is oriented toward continual economic growth. In effect, the products of applied science, such as airplanes, cars, television, computers, hospital equipment, and the machines with which we make them, have profoundly affected modern life and the character of modern people. Today technology conditions human reality. It involves our understanding of ourselves, and it does at least influence, and perhaps determine, our relations with both the natural environment and other persons. Since the development of modern technology has had such a profound impact on the way we live, it's important to think philosophically about it. The crises we face today have their historical roots in our culture's values and achievements. And since their resolution will demand value choices, it's important to think philosophically about them too.

Of course, philosophical reflection alone won't resolve any problems we face. It may, however, allow us to act more intelligently and more compassionately. It may give us a better understanding of those problems and a deeper appreciation of our relations to nature and one another. Our action and our inaction—what we do and what we refuse or simply fail to do—involve us in value judgments affecting the quality of our lives and others', including others not yet born. Philosophy won't provide us with any new facts, and it may, indeed, make the choices more difficult for us, precisely by making us aware of their complexity. But it may help us to develop the relational wisdom that will allow us not only to survive on earth but also to live well together.

We'll look critically at the contributions Western religion and Western science have presumably made in shaping our current attitudes toward the natural world. Then, focusing on Henry David Thoreau's life and thought, we will discuss the way American experience has been shaped by its intellectual past. Finally, after having tried to grasp how we got where we are, we'll close this chapter by suggesting some directions in which realistic and healthy alternatives to our present dangerous course can be conceived. If we submit to our technology's predominance over us, and if we seek only to increase our material possessions, then we'll have no one else to blame for our feelings of loneliness, impotence, and boredom. We'll have no one else to blame for environmental catastrophes, either. But we may attempt to reconcile the civilized state we've achieved largely through our technology— for technology is, after all, a *human* achievement—with a certain ecological harmony and a certain respect for nature. Then we may move toward a world in which we stimulate and celebrate the full creative capacity of our humanity.

Religion and Science in the West

What is the relationship between people and nature in Western religious and scientific thought?

A cursory examination of the ways we commonly use the word "man" reveals that the concept of man is ambiguous. In *Man's Place in Nature,* Max Scheler, a contemporary German philosopher, pointed out that this word has two radically different meanings; indeed, he suggested, it would be difficult to find another word in our ordinary language quite as ambiguous as this one. Contrasting the two meanings of "man," he wrote:

> *In one sense, it signifies the particular . . . characteristics of man as a subclass of the vertebrates and mammals. It is perfectly clear that . . . the living being described as man is not only subordinate to the concept "animal," but occupies a*

Viewpoint

Self-awareness, reason and imagination disrupt the "harmony" which characterizes animal existence. Their emergence has made man into an anomaly, into the freak of the universe. He is part of nature, subject to her physical laws and unable to change them, yet he transcends the rest of nature. He is set apart while being a part; he is homeless, yet chained to the home he shares with all creatures. Cast into this world at an accidental place and time, he is forced out of it, again accidentally. Being aware of himself, he realizes his powerlessness and the limitations of his existence. He visualizes his own end: death. Never is he free from the dichotomy of his existence: he cannot rid himself of his mind, even if he should want to; he cannot rid himself of his body as long as he is alive— and his body makes him want to be alive.

Reason, man's blessing, is also his curse; it forces him to cope everlastingly with the task of solving an insoluble dichotomy. Human existence is different in this respect from that of all other organisms; it is in a state of constant and unavoidable disequilibrium. Man's life cannot "be lived" by repeating the pattern of his species; he must live. Man is the only animal that can be bored, that can feel evicted from paradise. Man is the only animal that finds his own existence a problem which he has to solve and from which he cannot escape. He cannot go back to the prehuman state of harmony with nature; he must proceed to develop his reason until he becomes the master of nature, and of himself.

ERICH FROMM, The Sane Society

relatively very small corner of the animal kingdom. . . . The word "man," in the second sense, [however,] signifies a set of characteristics which must be sharply distinguished from the concept "animal"—including all mammals and vertebrates.

Used one way, then, the word "man" connotes the characteristics proper to human beings seen as members of the animal world; used the other way, it serves to distinguish human beings from animals.

It's evident that, corresponding to these two very different senses of the word, there are in general two conflicting ways to see man (that is, human beings, male and female alike) in relation to nature. Both these concepts of man have been important in modern Western thought. The first, which has prevailed in our recent scientific tradition, sees *man as a part of nature;* the second, fostered by our Judeo-Christian religious tradition, sets *man apart from nature.*

These statements, of course, present a simplified, extreme, or ideal typification of the two perspectives on human nature. However, sharply distinguishing these two conceptions of the relationship between the human and the natural orders may prove useful.

The difference between these two perspectives on man's relation to nature is not just a matter of words. Both have important philosophical consequences. To set man against nature or to maintain that the human world is not continuous with the animal world but radically different from it is to emphasize man's distinctiveness. This view accentuates not only human rationality and creativity but also human freedom. Man's capacity to respond rationally and creatively to his environment liberates him from being totally determined by it. However, this position may also support an unwarranted philosophical world view that places man at the center of the universe. Such a view might be used as justification for considering human beings more important than the rest of nature or the universe.

To consider man a part of nature—even the highest form of natural life— is to stress the continuity of the human, animal, and plant worlds and perhaps the inorganic world as well. It further suggests that human behavior may be studied and explained in much the same way as other domains of nature. However, the distinctiveness of human life might be overlooked. It appears that these extreme views both have philosophical implications. As we'll indicate, they also have practical consequences for the way we live in the natural world.

The religious view of the world and man's place in it rests upon the fundamental distinctions between God, the Creator, and nature, God's creation, on the one hand, and between man and nature, on the other. Although created by God, like all things, man is a unique creature because in addition to a physical body he also has a rational soul. Man is different in kind from everything else God has created. He belongs to two worlds: As a creature he's a natural being, so he belongs to the realm of matter; as a special creature, one made in the very image of God, he's also a supernatural being, so he also belongs to the realm of spirit.

How have these traditions influenced the formation of modern values?

This dualistic view of man's created nature seems to have ecological implications. Man's special relation to the Creator evidently implies that he has a special relation to other creatures. He has dominion over them, signified in the Judeo-Christian tradition by the Biblical claim that Adam gave their names to all the other animals.

In contrast, the scientific view—the view that man is not apart from but rather a part of nature—has it that man isn't unique, at least not because he has an extraordinary faculty no other creature has. Instead, man is just one animal among many other animals from which he differs not in kind, but in degree. Since reason itself is an evolutionary product, man differs from the other animals only by the degree to which he is capable of exercising reason.

Paradoxically, then, it seems that the religious view of man rather than the scientific view is more compatible with our conquest and manipulation of nature! It's this religious understanding that presents man as a stranger to the natural world—a sojourner whose true home is elsewhere. And it's this view too that accords him a certain dominion or rule over nature, which was, after all, created for his use and enjoyment. The scientific view, in contrast, is apparently more sensitive to man's dependence on the earth and interdependence with other living things.

Lynn White, Jr., the contemporary American historian whose controversial work reflects his lively interest in technology, focused on the Judeo-Christian view of man in his much debated article "The Historical Roots of Our Ecologic Crisis." White remarks there, "What people do about their ecology depends on what they think about themselves in relation to things around them. Human ecology is deeply conditioned by beliefs about our nature and destiny—that is, by religion." White argues that Christianity, in particular, has shaped the modern Western disposition toward the earth. As an historian, then, sensitive to the force of an idea, White contends:

> *Our science and technology have grown out of Christian attitudes toward man's relation to nature which are almost universally held not only by Christians and neo-Christians but also by those who fondly regard themselves as post-Christians. . . . More science and more technology are not going to get us out of the present ecologic crisis until we find a new religion, or rethink our old one. . . . Since the roots of our trouble are so largely religious, the remedy must also be essentially religious, whether we call it that or not.*

Noting that there have indeed been countertendencies in the history of Western religious thought, White suggests that St. Francis of Assisi would serve well as a model for contemporary Christians, since he loved and respected all God's creatures. This suggestion may well be interesting for those who would want to "rethink our old religion" rather than "find a new one," that is, for those who would want to reinterpret the relationship between the individual and nature within the philosophical and theological framework provided by the Judeo-Christian tradition.

St. Francis spoke of the sun, the moon, and the wind, of fire and water, and of plants and animals as "brothers" and "sisters." In celebrating nature, he didn't degrade the person, but his appreciation of nature wasn't man-centered either. Rather, he saw God's beauty in nature, and this insight filled him with joy and gratitude. (His sun song conveys his attitude toward God and nature.)

St. Francis did not merely see religious symbols in nature. He experienced a direct, living relationship with his co-creatures, both animate and inanimate. In *The Nature of Sympathy,* Max Scheler explains:

> *what is really new and unusual in St. Francis' emotional relationship to Nature, is that natural objects and processes take on an expressive significance of* their own, *without any parabolic reference to man or to human relationships generally. Thus sun, moon, wind, and so on, which have no need whatever of benevolent or compassionate love, are greeted in heartfelt recognition as brother and sister. All created things are taken in their metaphysical contiguity (man being also included), to be* immediately *related to their Creator and Father as self-subsistent beings having, even in relation to man, a* quite intrinsic value of their own.

Other contemporary scholars besides White have investigated other ways of rethinking the traditional Judeo-Christian view of the relationship between human beings and the natural world. Proposing another model, the American biologist René Dubos suggests that "ecologists should select St. Benedict as a much truer symbol of the human condition than Francis of Assisi." What's involved in this debate, he explains, are two contrasting attitudes toward nature, and to the Franciscan attitude of "passive worship" he prefers the Benedictine attitude of "creative intervention." Stressing prayer and labor, the Benedictine monks learned to manage the land so that it would support them while retaining its productive capacity. Moreover, one order of Benedictine monks generally established its monasteries in unhealthy, malaria-ridden lowlands and swamps; as a result, the monks had to develop the technological skills that would allow them to render these lands habitable and productive. Dubos remarks in "A Theology of the Earth" that "monastic labor, skill, and intelligence converted these dismal swamps into productive agricultural areas, many of which have become centers for [European] civilization. They demonstrate that transforming of the land, when intelligently carried out, is not destructive, but, instead, can be a creative art."

It appears, then, that the Judeo-Christian heritage does not necessarily imply a disdainful attitude toward the physical world. It can, indeed, lead us to a renewed respect for our natural environment. And it may even allow us to see ourselves as limited co-creators to whom God has confided the world. Historically, though, Christianity has emphasized the spiritual dimension of our humanity and deemphasized our physical nature. Such

---

Viewpoint

The pivot round which the religious life . . . revolves, is the interest of the individual in his private personal destiny. Religion, in short, is a monumental chapter in the history of human egotism. The gods believed in—whether by crude savages or by men disciplined intellectually—agree with one another in recognizing personal calls. Religious thought is carried on in terms of personality, this being, in the world of religion, the one fundamental fact. Today, quite as much as at any previous age, the religious individual tells you that the divine meets him on the basis of his personal concerns.

Science, on the other hand, has ended by utterly repudiating the personal point of view. She catalogues her elements and records her laws indifferent as to what purpose may be shown forth by them, and constructs her theories quite careless of their bearing on human anxieties and fates. Though the scientist may individually nourish a religion and be a theist in his irresponsible hours, the days are over when it could be said that for Science herself the heavens declare the glory of God and the firmament showeth his handiwork. Our solar system, with its harmonies, is seen now as but one passing case of a certain sort of moving equilibrium in the heavens, realized by a local accident in an appalling wilderness of worlds where no life can exist. In a span of time which as a cosmic interval will count but as an hour, it will have ceased to be. . . . It is impossible, in the present temper of the scientific imagination, to find in the driftings of the cosmic atoms . . . anything but a kind of aimless weather, doing and undoing, achieving no proper history, and leaving no result. Nature has no one distinguishable tendency with which it is possible to feel a sympathy.

WILLIAM JAMES, The Varieties of Religious Experience: A Study in Human Nature

Christian doctrines as those certifying the soul's immortality and the consequent possibility of our finding happiness in another world after our physical death may have made it easier for us to devalue and abuse this world.

Still, it remains true that it isn't our Western religious heritage but our development of applied science and our use of its products that now threatens the ecological balance. Some religious philosophers have argued, in fact, that it's precisely the "desacralization" or "profanation" of nature effected by science itself which has allowed us to conquer and manipulate matter. Science tries to understand and to explain the natural world in terms of natural causes. Scientific theories do not recognize, or at least do not introduce, the notions of divine order and intervention in nature. The scientific world is a secular, or nonreligious, world. As Conrad Bonifazi writes in *A Theology of Things,* the desacralization of nature in Western civilization

> released forces of enquiry which have not ceased to drive us along unpredictable ways of scientific advancement, so that immense technological structures now rest upon a secular *view* of the world. The world is now a field of human exploration and endeavour from which the gods have been sealed off. All the consequences of the secularizing of nature have not yet reached fruition, but the judgement that matter may be utilized without consideration for the fate of mankind and the earth as a whole is . . . fraught with extreme hazard. Nature had to be desacralized, or "disenchanted," in order to advance the humanisation of man and his physical environment.

Written from a theological perspective, Bonifazi's remarks may hold the key for a balanced appraisal of the scientific approach to reality. Nature, he suggests, had to be disenchanted or demystified to allow us to humanize our surroundings, to transform a hostile environment peopled with demons into a familiar world in which we are at home. Scientific rationality refused to ascribe to physical events a supernatural agency. It sought causal explanations for natural phenomena and contributed immensely to that demystification. In modern times, science and its technological applications have literally changed the face of the earth.

But, Bonifazi notes, the practical judgment that we can use matter without taking into account the earth as a whole and the rest of mankind is a dangerous one. Ignoring our involvement in and dependence on the ecosystem and denying our responsibility to other people could result in environmental and social chaos of a magnitude difficult to imagine. Unless we appreciate our interrelatedness with nature and other persons, the scientific advances that have made the world more human—that have, in effect, made the world a more pleasant place to live—might very well end up "dehumanizing" us. And in the process they may make the earth a very unpleasant place indeed.

Our ways of thinking, our everyday philosophies, more or less clearly and consistently articulated, can't be separated from our ways of living. This is true whatever your assessment of the influence traditional Western religious and scientific ideas about man and nature may have had in forming contemporary attitudes toward our physical environment. The fact that we're living in the United States in the twentieth century isn't irrelevant either because what we might call the American experience has also contributed to our understanding of ourselves in relation to our physical environment. Our national history has shaped our culture, and our culture, like our language, influences the way we think, and feel, and act. To understand the development of this country's conflicting attitudes toward nature, in the next section we'll discuss the ideas of Henry David Thoreau, the nineteenth century American philosopher who preferred independence to industry.

Nature and Civilization in American Life

How has the American intellectual past shaped present American reality?

Philosophers and historians of thought have traced the origins of the present ecological crisis to the development, especially during the nineteenth century, of conflicting modes of thought that haven't yet been reconciled. H. Paul Santmire, for instance, asserts that "When we contemplate and manipulate nature today in America, we are heirs of the nineteenth century much more than we usually realize." Examining the ecological "schizophrenia," or split personality, that we've presumably inherited, he writes in "Historical Dimensions of the American Crisis":

> On the one hand, we Americans venerate nature passionately, camping, hiking, sailing, surfing, and fighting for conservation whenever we can find the time. On the other hand, no less passionately, we venerate the Gross National Product as a criterion of national health and virtue, when increasing production regularly means the exhaustion and pollution of nature.

Santmire argues that "we will not be able to solve our ecological crisis unless we have first resolved our ecological schizophrenia." In the United States, the question of the relationship between man and nature—a question that every culture confronts—is complicated by our paradoxical ability to devastate the natural world and at the same time to mourn its passing. We long for the wilderness even as we "develop" it.

How did these conflicting attitudes develop? The question is extremely complex, of course, and we can give only some indications here. Partially because of the works of two popular and influential eighteenth century men, Michel de Crèvecoeur and Thomas Jefferson, this country already had a pastoral, or rustic, literary tradition before its industry made great advances in the following century. Then, however, the times changed. Cities grew more populous, and factories thrived. By 1845, the year Henry David Thoreau left the village of Concord, Massachusetts to move to a cabin on Ralph Waldo Emerson's wooded property at Walden Pond, the railroad had invaded the countryside.

Thoreau's decision to undertake his famous Walden experiment was prompted by his sharp dissatisfaction with the Concord economy, which rested on the work ethic, and by his desire to simplify his life further. He energetically expressed his critique of nineteenth century industry and industriousness in his essays, addresses, and journals as well as in *Walden,* his report on his two-year stay at the pond. These works have become classics in American philosophical literature. What's most remarkable about Thoreau is that he didn't just write down his ideas about the good life; he attempted personally to realize them by living well. In *The Machine in the Garden,* Leo Marx comments:

What was Thoreau's philosophy of life?

> *The effect of the American environment . . . was to break down common-sense distinctions between art and life. No one understood this more clearly than Henry Thoreau; skilled in the national art of disguising art, in* Walden *he succeeds in obscuring the traditional, literary character of the pastoral withdrawal. Instead of writing about it—or* merely *writing about it—he tries it.*

Thoreau's thought and action, his philosophy and his life, formed an exemplary unity. Moreover, the personal qualities he respected and that others respected in him were independence, simplicity, and common sense. Emerson said, "No truer American existed than Thoreau." For these reasons, his works may be valuable not only for those who want to understand our national experience but also for those who seek viable alternatives to urban life.

"The mass of men," Thoreau wrote in *Walden,* "lead lives of quiet desperation." And, he added, "What is called resignation is confirmed desperation." Most people are desperate, or resigned, because of their exclusive concern for their material well-being. This concern prevents them from enjoying life, leisure, and neighborly relations with other people. In today's language, most people are alienated by their work from themselves and their community. "Actually," Thoreau wrote, "the laboring man has not leisure for a true integrity day by day; he cannot afford the manliest relations to men [that is, authentic human relations with other persons]; his labor would be depreciated in the market. He has no time to be any thing but a machine." In another passage of the same work, he wrote that "men have become the tools of their tools." Several years later, Thoreau was to return to this theme in his short essay *Life without Principle*, where he deplored his contemporaries' lost capacity to enjoy their lives:

> *This world is a place of business. What an infinite bustle! I am awakened almost every night by the panting of the locomotive. It interrupts my dreams. . . . It would be glorious to see mankind at leisure for once. It is nothing but work, work, work. I cannot easily buy a blank-book to write thoughts in; they are commonly ruled for dollars and cents.*

"Machines" and "tools of their tools" people are alienated not only from themselves and their neighbors; they're also alienated from nature. Economic and moral pressures combine to force them to *use* the wilderness rather than to *enjoy* it. Thoreau wrote in *Life without Principle:*

Viewpoint

Well, the night got gray and ruther thick, which is the next meanest thing to fog. You can't tell the shape of the river, and you can't see no distance. It got to be very late and still, and then along comes a steamboat up the river. . . . We could hear her pounding along, but we didn't see her good till she was close. She aimed right for us. Often they do that and try to see how close they can come without touching; sometimes the wheel bites off a sweep, and then the pilot sticks his head out and laughs, and thinks he's mighty smart. Well, here she comes, and we said she was going to try and shave us; but she didn't seem to be sheering off a bit. She was a big one, and she was coming in a hurry, too, looking like a black cloud with rows of glow-worms around it; but all of a sudden she bulged out, big and scary, with a long row of wide-open furnace doors shining like red-hot teeth, and her monstrous bows and guards hanging right over us. There was a yell at us, and a jingling of bells to stop the engines, a powwow of cussing, and whistling of steam—and as Jim went overboard on one side and I on the other, she come smashing straight through the raft.

MARK TWAIN, The Adventures of Huckleberry Finn

If a man walk in the woods for love of them half of each day, he is in danger of being regarded as a loafer; but if he spends his whole day as a speculator, shearing off those woods and making earth bald before her time, he is esteemed an industrious and enterprising citizen. As if a town had no interest in its forests but to cut them down!

Most of Thoreau's Concord neighbors, of course, thought him eccentric, and even Emerson, his closest friend, admitted that his virtues "sometimes ran into extremes." He added, "I cannot help counting it a fault in him that he had no ambition." Thoreau made it clear, though, through both his speaking and his writing, that his primary purpose in moving to Walden Pond, where he built his own cabin, was to simplify his life. Leaving the village meant leaving the business community in order, as he put it in *Walden*, to "transact some private business with the fewest obstacles." He further explained:

I went to the woods because I wished to live deliberately, to front only the essential facts of life, and see if I could not learn what it had to teach, and not, when I came to die, discover that I had not lived. I did not wish to live what was not life, living is so dear, nor did I wish to practise resignation, unless it was quite necessary. I wanted to live deep and suck out all the marrow of life, to live so sturdily and Spartan-like as to put to rout all that was not life . . . to drive life into a corner, and reduce it to its lowest terms. . . .

In one of the passages from *Life without Principle* we've already cited, Thoreau complained that in Concord the railroad's whistle awakened him every night. "It interrupts my dreams," he said. But the sound reached the shores of Walden Pond too. Sitting at his window on a summer afternoon, hearkening to the wood sounds, Thoreau remarked in *Walden* on the distant "rattle of the railroad cars, now dying away and then reviving like the beat of a partridge, conveying travelers from Boston to the country." Later, though, Thoreau wrote not of that distant rattle, as pacific as "the beat of a partridge," but of the locomotive's penetrating whistle that continually violated the stillness of his woods, "sounding like the scream of a hawk."

The whistle of the locomotive penetrates my woods summer and winter, sounding like the scream of a hawk sailing over some farmer's yard, informing me that many restless city merchants are arriving within the circle of the town, or adventurous country traders from the other side. . . . Up comes the cotton, down goes the woven cloth; up comes the silk, down goes the woolen; up come the books, but down goes the wit that writes them.

As Leo Marx explains, this episode shows that "the Walden site cannot provide a refuge, in any literal sense, from the forces of change." Moreover, Thoreau's attitude toward the railroad, a popular symbol of those forces of change, was surprisingly ambivalent. He did not value commerce, and he did not welcome the "restless city merchants," but the railroad itself and the sheer mechanical power it represented fascinated him, as it did most nineteenth century people. He wrote:

> when I hear the iron horse make the hills echo with his snort like thunder, shaking the earth with his feet, and breathing fire and smoke from his nostrils, (what kind of winged horse or fiery dragon they will put into the new Mythology I don't know,) it seems as if the earth had got a race now worthy to inhabit it. If all were as it seems, and men made the elements their servants for noble ends!

It seems that even Thoreau suffered from the ecological schizophrenia that Santmore says we've inherited from the last century. In the same chapter of *Walden*, though, Thoreau did unquestionably reaffirm his withdrawal from industrial society despite its inevitable expansion. "So is your pastoral life whirled past and away," he wrote. "But the bell rings, and I must get off the track and let the cars go by." And of the railroad train itself he said defiantly, "I will not have my eyes put out and my ears spoiled by its smoke and steam and hissing."

Thoreau's preference for pastoral solitude rather than city life orders his social and political thought too. In fact, Santmire argues that what he calls "the nineteenth-century religion of nature," best expressed, perhaps, in Thoreau's writings, was "permeated with a conservative social ideology." The love of nature implied an ethic of withdrawal from the town (witness Thoreau's actual retreat from Concord to Walden Pond); "the result of that, as a matter of course, was that lovers of nature consistently refused to participate in movements for social, political, and economic betterment in the town." This Thoreauvian ethic of withdrawal from social and political life generally eventuated, then, "in a tacit but firm acceptance of the urban status quo."

Although Thoreau ardently endorsed and publicly defended the abolitionist John Brown in his fatal 1859 raid on Harper's Ferry, many passages of his social and political writings lend support to Santmire's interpretation. An individualist who took pride in his self-reliance, Thoreau was naturally conservative. Thoreau's famous essay *Civil Disobedience* opens with an endorsement of the first principle of political conservatism. "I heartily accept the motto, 'That government is best which governs least,' " Thoreau asserted there, "and I should like to see it acted up to more rapidly and systematically." Indeed, he went further: "Carried out," he wrote, "it finally amounts to this, which I also believe,—'That government is best which governs not at all'; and when men are prepared for it, that will be the kind of government which they will have."

Thoreau's ethic was one of disengagement. He wrote succinctly in *Civil Disobedience*, "What I have to do is to see . . . that I do not lend myself to the wrong which I condemn." Beyond that, though, he did not consider it his personal responsibility to struggle for the good or to fight against evil:

It is not a man's duty, as a matter of course, to devote himself to the eradication of any, even the most enormous, wrong; he may still properly have other concerns to engage him; but it is his duty, at least, to wash his hands of it, and, if he gives it no thought longer, not to give it practically his support.

Viewpoint

The greatest delight which the fields and woods minister is the suggestion of an occult relation between man and the vegetable. I am not alone and unacknowledged. They nod to me, and I to them. The waving of the boughs in the storm is new to me and old. It takes me by surprise, and yet is not unknown. . . .

Yet it is certain that the power to produce this delight does not reside in nature, but in man, or in a harmony of both. . . .

Nature in its ministry to man, is not only the material, but is also the process and the result. All the parts incessantly work into each other's hands for the profit of man. The wind sows the seed; the sun evaporates the sea; the wind blows the vapor to the field . . . the rain feeds the plant; the plant feeds the animal; and thus the endless circulations of the divine charity nourish man.

The useful arts are reproductions or new combinations by the wit of man, of the same natural benefactors. He no longer waits for favoring gales, but by means of steam, he realizes the fable of Aeolus's bag, and carries the two and thirty winds in the boiler of his boat. To diminish friction, he paves the road with iron bars, and, mounting a coach with a ship-load of men, animals, and merchandise behind him, he darts through the country, from town to town, like an eagle or a swallow through the air. By the aggregate of these aids, how is the face of the world changed, from the era of Noah to that of Napoleon!

RALPH WALDO EMERSON, Nature

*What values underlie the
American response to nature?*

Writing, then, as a man whose primary concern was not social justice but individual freedom, not society but himself, Thoreau remarked, "I came into this world, not chiefly to make this a good place to live in, but to live in it, be it good or bad." As Santmire notes, Thoreau was a man of deep moral feeling, particularly hostile to the institution of slavery. Thoreau agitated against slavery, writing and lecturing, but he was at best "a reluctant crusader." Santmire is not unjustified in charging that Thoreau's ethic was basically "predicated on the idea of a *renunciation of sustained political involvement*—that kind of involvement which was the prior condition for the abolition of slavery and the resolution of other social ills."

Thoreau's response to industrialization was not typical of his times; his thought owes much of its interest and power precisely to his refusal to go along with the way his neighbors lived. That refusal meant, however, that he had to get out of the way of progress. As he put it, he had to "get off the track and let the cars go by." Popular thought in the nineteenth century greeted the introduction of machinery and the consequent development of industrial society with more enthusiasm. Leo Marx comments that the railroad was "becoming a kind of national obsession," that it was "the embodiment of the age" and "a testament to the will of man rising over natural obstacles." And, the literary historian notes, writers in the most popular periodicals cited "the power of machines (steam engines, factories, railroads, and, after 1844, the telegraph) as the conclusive sanction for faith in the unceasing progress of mankind. . . . Armed with this new power, mankind is now able, for the first time, to realize the dream of abundance." While Thoreau expressed his doubts and his disaffection, many others expressed their faith in technical progress. Science and free enterprise, ingenuity and hard work, would make the world a better place for everybody.

To return to Santmire's thesis, then, what we've inherited from the nineteenth century are two mutually exclusive or contradictory sets of attitudes toward the environment. The "cult of rustic simplicity" coexists uneasily with the "cult of manipulation." The first glorifies unspoiled nature; the second glorifies civilization, especially in its technological aspects and achievements. "The American approach to nature," Santmire maintains, "apparently has consistently been a contradiction in terms."

Thoreau's thinking about the individual and nature and about political action is relevant today. It leads us to consider what we should do about our "schizophrenia." People are concerned with ecology, with trying to protect the environment. But many political activists, concerned with social inequities, have called this movement a middle-class evasion of responsibility. They say that allotting land for parks, picking up trash, and regulating the drilling for oil will not solve the real problems. Concerted political action is necessary, and it should be aimed at changing the social structure responsible for ecological problems. In their view it might be necessary, for example, to break down large corporations such as the oil and the strip-mining companies, which not only spoil the environment but also exploit the people who work for them. No individual rebellion or retreat will alter the effect of such institutions. Whether or not such drastic measures are necessary, these individuals point to the need to harmonize our feelings for nature and our need for social justice.

Given the terrific environmental and social problems confronting us and given too that these problems can't be resolved by technical means alone but demand that we change our way of thinking and living, what's the answer? What will the future world be like, and what can we do about it? In reviewing the cultural patterns and the modes of thought that have partially shaped our current ways of "being there" in the world, we've entertained some philosophical suggestions. Lynn White, Jr., has argued, for instance, that we have to "find a new religion, or rethink our old one." H. Paul Santmire has argued, in effect, that what we need in this country is a consistent environmental ethic—and one, moreover, that does not slight social concerns. Now let's consider some pragmatic possibilities.

Some Personal and Societal Options

What will the world be like in the future? Estimates of the nature and the extent of the changes in store for us vary, but many physical and social scientists agree that the prospects for continued growth are bleak. Heilbroner writes in *An Inquiry into the Human Prospect* that

> whether we are unable to sustain growth or unable to tolerate it, *there can be no doubt that a radically different future beckons. In either eventuality it seems beyond dispute that the present orientation of society must change. In place of the long-established encouragement of industrial production must come its careful restriction and long-term diminution within society. In place of prodigalities of consumption must come new frugal attitudes.*

In a popular phrase, the future will be an "age of scarcity." As the world's growing population makes increasing demands on diminishing and non-renewable resources, critical shortages (including food and energy shortages) will place tremendous strains not only on the economy but also on the domestic and international political orders. They'll also have a direct impact on the way we live. We can reasonably anticipate, then, that our life styles will be radically affected by these developments even before the second millennium, the year 2000, arrives. And if we do manage somehow to limit further population growth and to avoid war, our children will still inherit a world very different from ours.

Rather than speaking of the coming time as an age of scarcity, though, we might somewhat more positively look forward to it as an age of fundamentals. We might see it as a time in which we learn as individuals to expect less of the world and more of ourselves. And we might look forward to a time when society as a whole will respond creatively to the changing situation. For Americans, a people of plenty whose attitudes have largely been shaped by the long experience of abundance, this will not be an easy adjustment; more than just consuming less, it will mean critically distinguishing between luxuries and necessities, wants and needs. In effect, it will mean new value systems and new ways of living. Anticipated conditions of relative scarcity will dictate these profound changes in our received attitudes, expectations, and valuations. The crises we're evidently facing may be postponed and lessened by the development of alternative technologies; for instance, the green revolution may provide new food sources, and solar power may provide safe, clean energy. But it's unrealistic to place our trust entirely in technological solutions. There are limits to growth, and the ecosystem simply cannot meet steadily increasing demands. In a world that is, for all practical purposes, finite, and whose population continues to increase while its capacity to sustain ever greater numbers diminishes, our survival—and the quality of our lives—will ultimately depend on our value choices.

What are society's alternatives?

For society, the alternatives are as clear as they are complex: It can attempt to maximize the number of people or it can attempt to maximize the standard of living each individual enjoys. It can't do both, however. "The greatest good for the greatest number"—the utilitarian calculus—may help society make decisions among competing goods, but it can't be a goal in itself. Heilbroner insists with good reason that "the societal view of production and consumption must stress parsimonious, not prodigal, attitudes."

In his article "The Tragedy of the Commons," Garrett Hardin presents a scenario that may serve to illustrate the situation many economists and environmentalists envision. This is the tragedy of the commons:

Imagine a pasture limited in size but open to everyone. It's to be expected that each local herdsman will try to keep as many head of cattle as possible on this common pastureland. This cooperative arrangement may work very well too as long as minor disputes, poaching, and disease keep the numbers of herdsmen and cattle below the land's carrying capacity; but once the dream of social stability has become a reality, "the inherent logic of the commons remorselessly generates tragedy."

Acting in his own interest as a rational being, each herdsman still seeks to maximize his gain. When he wonders "What is the utility to me of adding one more animal to the herd?" he sees that although everybody will share the increased cost (namely, the negative effects of overgrazing, including skinnier cattle), he alone will profit from the animal's eventual sale. Obviously, the only sensible course for him to follow is to go ahead and add another animal to the herd. And another. But every herdsman "rationally" acting in his own rather narrow self-interest will reach the same conclusion! "Therein," Hardin writes, "is the tragedy. Each man is locked into a system that compels him to increase his herd without limit—in a world that is limited. Ruin is the destination toward which all men rush, each pursuing his own best interest in a society that believes in the freedom of the commons."

Can the tragedy be avoided? How, and at what cost? Political theorists have given their attention to problems like this, and so have economists. Some would maintain that the system will correct itself; others would contend that only a strong central authority could control the situation. In the present hypothetical case, the herdsmen may recognize in good time that if they continue to pursue their individual interests this way they'll end up destroying themselves by exhausting the commons and starving their cattle. It is to be hoped, although maybe this can't be done realistically, that they might then decide, each one for himself, not to add any more cattle to the overburdened commons. More likely, they might resort, each one, to violence in an effort to relieve the competition for grazing space. Or, they might get together and decide that their best bet is to establish limits so that

Viewpoint

The way to solve the conflict between human values and technological needs is not to run away from technology. That's impossible. The way to resolve the conflict is to break down the barriers of dualistic thought that prevent a real understanding of what technology is—not an exploitation of nature, but a fusion of nature and the human spirit into a new kind of creation that transcends both. When this transcendence occurs in such events as the first airplane flight across the ocean or the first footstep on the moon, a kind of public recognition of the transcendent nature of technology occurs. But this transcendence should also occur at the individual level, on a personal basis, in one's own life, in a less dramatic way.

ROBERT M. PIRSIG, Zen and the Art of Motorcycle Maintenance

the size of the collective herd doesn't exceed the pasture's carrying capacity; they might further decide to form or appoint a governing body to police them. In this event, though, they're voluntarily surrendering, or at least limiting, their own economic freedom—their freedom of the commons.

The world situation today is much more complex and much more serious than that, but Hardin's scenario does illustrate the central problem: the logical and very real impossibility of infinite growth in a finite world.

What are the individual's options?

In practical terms, rather than simply allowing events to overcome us, what can we do to govern our own lives and to shape our future? As we've repeatedly stressed, the question involves value choices (as well as political and economic perceptions), and it's up to each one of us individually to formulate his or her own answer. Paul R. Ehrlich and Anne H. Ehrlich remark in *The End of Affluence* that "each of us must decide how much effort to put into trying to save society, how much into personally preparing for the crises ahead, and how much into doing things that are pleasant while they still can be done." We'd like very briefly to consider some possibilities.

First, if we may distinguish them, both training and education will surely prove essential to human happiness. Training will help us to define and assume new jobs in a changing economy as our society adjusts to new

---

Viewpoint

I should like to give some intimation of how a measure of independence can be achieved in philosophical thought today:

Let us not pledge ourselves to any philosophical school or take formulable truth as such for the one and exclusive truth; let us be masters of our thoughts;

let us not heap up philosophical possessions, but apprehend philosophical thought as movement and seek to deepen it;

let us battle for truth and humanity in unconditional communication;

let us acquire the power to learn from all the past by making it our own; let us listen to our contemporaries and remain open to all possibilities;

let each of us as an individual immerse himself in his own historicity, in his origin, in what he has done; let him possess himself of what he was, of what he has become, and of what has been given to him;

let us not cease to grow through our own historicity into the historicity of man as a whole and thus make ourselves into citizens of the world.

KARL JASPERS, Way to Wisdom

realities. Education in the natural and the social sciences will help us to understand ourselves, others, and the world in which we live. It will also help us to develop alternative technical arrangements. In addition, the humanities will help us to think critically, to recognize excellence, and to realize our own creative potential. Vocational training and a liberal arts education are both immediately relevant to the quality of the lives we lead. In an age of fundamentals—when we can expect more hardships and fewer diversions—we may well discover in ourselves responsive capacities and talents we'd never suspected.

Second, as Thoreau's example shows, self-reliance and an appreciative attitude toward nature are American national traits no less than the conformism and materialism so many contemporary social critics have identified. Accordingly, growing numbers of people in this country are turning to alternative social and economic arrangements, such as communal and cooperative living, homesteading, and subsistence farming. Although these experiments in simpler life styles are clearly not for everyone, they may lead some to develop a renewed sense not only of their personal identity but also of their relatedness to one another and nature. Obviously, most people will legitimately prefer not to change their life styles so radically; obviously, too, such experiments carry risks. However, some seem to be finding these alternatives workable despite the privations they involve.

Finally, there needn't be a conflict between critically reviewing our own values and working for political changes to foster both environmental consciousness and social justice. Heilbroner asserts, "The resolution of the crises thrust upon us by the social and natural environment can only be found through political action." To this we'd add that what's good for the individual may also be good for society. As Amitai Etzioni writes in *The Active Society,* "no man can set himself free without extending the same liberty to his fellow men, and the transformation of self is deeply rooted in the joint act of a community transforming itself."

Summary

Toward the Twenty-First Century: Given a rising world population, and the consequent threat of resource scarcities and environmental pollution, the global prospects are not encouraging. Although philosophy can't solve the problems now arising, critical reflection may help us to see our times more clearly and to make intelligent valuations.

Religion and Science in the West: Generally, the Judeo-Christian tradition sets man apart from nature; the scientific understanding of man sees him as a part of nature. These conflicting views both have ecological implications. Some writers have suggested that we rethink our religion; others, that we review the values underlying technology.

Nature and Civilization in American Life: In this country, the popular cults of rustic simplicity, on the one hand, and of environmental manipulation, on the other, emerged from earlier national experience. Motivated by his dissatisfaction with life in an industrialized society driven by the work ethic, Henry David Thoreau's nineteenth century Walden experiment illustrates one response to that experience.

Some Personal and Societal Options: The coming age of scarcity might more optimistically be anticipated as an age of fundamentals. Hardin's "Tragedy of the Commons" illustrates that there can't be unlimited growth in a limited world. Education, alternative life styles, and political action may allow us both as individuals and as a society to repond creatively to present and future problems.

Suggestions for Further Reading

For an historical understanding of the intellectual currents that continue to influence Western life, the finest study widely available is Crane Brinton's perceptive and readable volume *The Shaping of Modern Thought* (Englewood Cliffs, NJ: Prentice-Hall, 1950). Focusing on American thought about nature and civilization, Leo Marx's seminal literary history, *The Machine in the Garden: Technology and the Pastoral Ideal in America* (New York: Oxford University Press, 1964) is unparalleled.

In *Western Man and Environmental Ethics: Attitudes toward Nature and Technology* (Reading, MA: Addison-Wesley, 1973), editor Ian T. Barbour has brought together some excellent pieces, including the essays by Lynn White, Jr., René Dubos, and H. Paul Santmire discussed in this chapter.

Philip Slater remarks in his recent insightful study of American life *Earthwalk* (Garden City, NY: Doubleday, 1974), "Political leaders merely generalize changes that have arisen elsewhere in the society. . . . Change in America has come from technologists, businessmen, scientists, inventors, artists, musicians, blacks, street people, the media, and from day-to-day decisions made by millions of completely faceless individuals."

Joseph Wood Krutch, the American drama critic whom Arthur A. Ekirch, Jr., describes in his interesting history *Man and Nature in America* (New York: Columbia, 1963) as one of "the most persuasive modern exponents of an equilibrium between the forces of man and nature" and "an ardent defender of the individual and critic of the machine," wrote two noteworthy philosophical studies. One is *The Modern Temper* (New York: Harcourt, 1929); the other is *The Measure of Man* (Indianapolis: Bobbs-Merrill, 1954). Both repay study.

Aldo Leopold's *A Sand County Almanac* (New York: Oxford University Press, 1949) and *Round River* (New York: Oxford University Press, 1953) have been released in an enlarged and slightly revised paperback edition by Sierra Club/Ballantine Books (1970). Leopold's essays are the product of sensitive and intelligent reflection on the effects of human action in the natural world. In "The Land Ethic," Leopold wrote, "No important change in ethics was ever accomplished without an internal change in our intellectual emphasis, loyalties, affections, and convictions. The proof that conservation has not yet touched these foundations of conduct lies in the fact that philosophy and religion have not yet heard of it. In our attempt to make conservation easy, we have made it trivial."

Finally, the British economist and philosopher E. F. Schumacher argues cogently for the development of "intermediate technology" in *Small Is Beautiful: Economics As If People Mattered,* a thoughtful, realistic, and well-written study of "the economics of permanence" (New York: Harper & Row, 1975).

Inquiry

Looking Ahead:
The Future in
Fiction

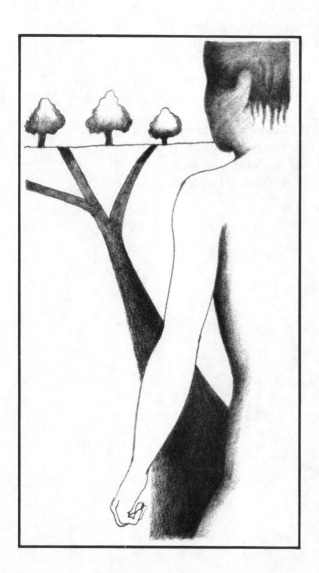

"That you should be startled by what I shall tell you," the stranger said, "is to be expected; but I am confident that you will not permit it to affect your equanimity unduly. Your appearance is that of a young man of barely thirty, and your bodily condition seems not greatly different from that of one just roused from a somewhat too long and profound sleep, and yet this is the tenth day of September in the year 2000, and you have slept exactly one hundred and thirteen years, three months, and eleven days."

Written in 1888, Edward Bellamy's utopian novel *Looking Backward* caused a sensation when it first appeared. Shortly after its publication, enthusiastic readers founded The Boston Bellamy Club to discuss and disseminate the American novelist's social doctrines, and within a few years more than 100 groups had formed for the same purposes. What was Edward Bellamy's vision of the future? To what sort of world did Julian West awaken?

In the year 2000, as the novelist optimistically imagined it and as his narrator described it, Americans have already had about a century to reform society after the Great Revolution, which Bellamy postulated as occurring nonviolently in the 1890s. Americans lived in a world in which mechanization had not only liberated them from the more arduous and tedious forms of labor, but had also added to their enjoyment of the higher life. As his host, Dr. Leete, explained to the dazzled time traveler, "the labor we have to render as our part in securing for the nation the means of a comfortable physical existence is by no means regarded as the most important, the most interesting, or the most dignified employment of our powers. We look upon it as a necessary duty to be discharged before we can fully devote ourselves to the higher exercise of our faculties, the intellectual and spiritual enjoyments and pursuits which alone mean life." While everyone is not equally gifted, he later remarks, "All have some inkling of the humanities, some appreciation of the things of the mind. . . . They have become capable of receiving and imparting, in various degrees, but all in some measure, the pleasures and inspirations of a refined social life."

In this ideal society, of course, new political and economic arrangements have been instituted along the lines that we'd now identify as authoritarian socialism. In the complex governmental system he imagined, Bellamy provided only for the most limited popular participation: Men could run for the presidency, for example, only after having served in a series of lesser offices—a sort of *cursus honoris* ("course of honor") designed to ensure competent leadership—and only those who had already retired from eco-

nomic life were eligible to vote. The "industrial army," in which every citizen served for twenty years, couldn't vote for presidential candidates because that "would be perilous to its discipline." The state directed all the society's economic activities—the production and the distribution of its goods—and it had succeeded, Julian reports, in multiplying the national wealth by eliminating the wasted efforts free, competitive enterprise had previously involved.

As a social theorist, then, Bellamy felt compelled to sacrifice universal, democratic participation in government to the societal need for economic security, which his utopian state guaranteed. "No man any more," Dr. Leete confirmed, "has any care for the morrow, either for himself or his children, for the nation guarantees the nurture, education, and comfortable maintenance of every citizen from the cradle to the grave."

In the light of the recent history of totalitarian states with organized economies, it is, of course, doubtful that central planning is more efficient (or for that matter more human) than the free-market system. The price paid for economic stability is the individual's freedom, surrendered to the state in the interest of the society's collective goals. Friedrich A. Von Hayek, the conservative economist, argues in *The Road to Serfdom* that democracy and central planning are simply incompatible with one another: "planning leads to dictatorship," he writes, "because dictatorship is the most effective instrument of coercion and the enforcement of ideals and, as such, essential if central planning on a large scale is to be possible."

In *Looking Backward*, however, when Julian protests against this extension of the government's functions and powers, Dr. Leete reproves him. This is their exchange:

> "In my day," I replied, "it was considered that the proper functions of government, strictly speaking, were limited to keeping the peace and defending the people against the public enemy. . . ."
>
> "And, in heaven's name, who are the public enemies?" exclaimed Doctor Leete. "Are they France, England, Germany, or hunger, cold, and nakedness? [Because of increased international economic and political cooperation] we have no wars now, and our governments no war powers, but in order to protect every citizen against hunger, cold, and nakedness, and provide for all his physical and mental needs, the function is assumed of directing his industry for a number of years."

The key to the good life enjoyed by all the members of this utopian society was the elimina-

tion of competition. "It is not necessary," Dr. Leete told Julian,

> to suppose a moral new birth of humanity, or a wholesale destruction of the wicked and survival of the good, to account for the fact before us. It finds its simple and obvious explanation in the reaction of a changed environment upon human nature. It means merely that a form of society which was founded on the pseudo-self-interest of selfishness, and appealed solely to the antisocial and brutal side of human nature, has been replaced by institutions based on the true self-interest of a rational unselfishness, and appealing to the social and generous instincts of man.

This new society, then, had, for the first time in history, corrected the "hideous, ghastly mistake," the "colossal world-darkening blunder," that had made life so harsh in earlier societies: the principle of individualistic competition for survival and prosperity. Dr. Leete said,

> If I were to give you, in one sentence, a key to what may seem the mysteries of our civilization as compared with that of your age, I should say that it is the fact that the solidarity of the race and the brotherhood of man, which to you were but fine phrases, are, to our thinking and feeling, ties as real and as vital as physical fraternity.

This sense of everyone's interdependence and relatedness both rests on and leads to the moral principle of equality and the political decision that everyone should have the same income. Again, as Dr. Leete explained, "the title of every man, woman, and child to the means of existence rests on no basis less plain, broad, and simple than the fact that they are fellows of one race—members of one human family." When Julian inquired about the distribution of wealth, Dr. Leete confirmed that the basis of the individual's claim to his equal share was not his contribution to society, but the simple fact that he or she is a person: "all who do their best are equally deserving, whether the best be great or small."

Reflecting on his work, Edward Bellamy wrote, "All thoughtful men agree that the present aspect of society is portentous of great changes. . . . *Looking Backward* was written in the belief that the Golden Age lies before us and not behind us, and is not far away." Today, thoughtful people still agree that changes are coming, but few share Bellamy's optimism. Arthur Koestler's *Darkness at Noon,* George Orwell's *1984,* Aldous Huxley's *Brave New World,* and Evgenii Zamyatin's *We* figure prominently among the antiutopian novels more proper to our own times. All the same, the humanistic, egalitarian ideals that animated Bellamy's work still speak to many people, as does the notion of the solidarity of all persons. Here are some questions you might consider:

At the end of the nineteenth century, Bellamy's view of technology was optimistic: Technology would free people from tedious work and so allow them to use their minds. Moreover, increased leisure would mean that everyone could participate actively in cultural affairs: They could, for instance, enjoy art, music, and philosophy. Since Bellamy wrote *Looking Backward,* technological and social advances in the West have indeed made more leisure time and more formal education available to most people. However, many contemporary writers hold that these advances have also had negative effects, among them, increased conformism, materialism, and a cultural leveling that tends to reduce art to entertainment. Others fear that the electronic media, along with new surveillance devices, may someday be used to maintain social control. In your view, what are technology's positive contributions to American cultural and political life? What are its drawbacks, and what dangers might it pose? How can it be controlled?

Bellamy contended that although human nature is essentially noble, it can flourish only when social institutions promote its growth. Do you agree? What importance does the social environment have in shaping individual character and life? Can social institutions be engineered to improve human nature?

"The equal wealth and equal opportunities of culture, which all persons now enjoy," Dr. Leete said, "have simply made us all members of one class. . . . Until this equality of condition had come to pass, the idea of the solidarity of humanity, the brotherhood of all men, could never have become the real conviction and practical principle of action it is nowadays." Some modern political analysts, however, among them Milovan Djilas in *The New Class* and Herbert Marcuse in *Soviet Marxism,* have focused on the formation of a new managerial class enjoying special privileges in communistic societies. Marcuse writes,

Neither the rise of the Soviet intelligentsia as a new ruling group, nor its composition and its privileges are any longer disputed facts—least so in the USSR. The recruitment and training of highly qualified specialists, technicians, managers, etc., is continually emphasized and their privileges are advertised. . . . Obviously the bureaucracy has a vital interest in maintaining and enhancing its privileged position.

Can equality, an ethical ideal, become a political reality? If so, under what conditions? If not, why not? What is the difference between equal opportunity and equality of condition?

Inquiry

The Universal Declaration of Human Rights: Ethical Ideals and Political Realities

In December 1948, the General Assembly of the United Nations proclaimed the Universal Declaration of Human Rights, which affirmed "the inherent dignity . . . of all members of the human family" and purported to define their "equal and inalienable rights." Though the product of an international commission, the Universal Declaration of Human Rights has been a source of diplomatic disagreement and philosophical controversy ever since it was issued, and its protocols have not yet been ratified by all the UN's member states. Do human beings have any "inalienable rights?" If so, what are they?

The Roman Catholic philosopher Jacques Maritain argued in *The Rights of Man and Natural Law* that they do:

> The human person possesses rights because of the very fact *that it is a person, a whole, master of itself and of its acts, and which consequently is not merely a means to an end, but an end, an end which must be treated as such. The dignity of the human person? The expression means nothing if it does not signify that by virtue of natural law, the human person has the right to be respected, is the subject of rights, possesses rights. These are things which are owed to man because of the very fact that he is man.*

Citing Maritain's remarks, Maurice Cranston notes that "whether one can accept his argu-

ment or not depends on one's attitude to the crucial concept he invokes: that of Natural Law." What, then, is "natural law"?

The notion rests on the distinction between the natural order and the human order or between nature and convention. Natural, moral law is commonly contrasted with positive, conventional law. "Positive law," Cranston notes in his study, *What Are Human Rights?*, "is a collection of specific enactments, with definite sanctions attached to many. Natural law is not written down and carries no specific sanctions." He further remarks, "Each kind of law has its own authority: positive law the authority of force, natural law the authority of conscience or morality; and when positive law coincides with natural law it has the authority both of force and of conscience."

Some examples might clarify the fundamental distinction between these two sorts of law. In your town, positive law (as defined in local statutes) might prohibit your parking your car on certain streets, and it might specify that if you do park your car improperly, you'll have to pay a fine. Natural law, to take a very clear case, would rule out your casually killing someone, not in self-defense, but just because you're bored. In itself, natural law doesn't carry any sanctions; it's simply contrary to conscience, that is, intuitively unjust. It may, however,

coincide with positive law, in which case you'd ordinarily have to pay if you were convicted of a transgression.

If there is such a thing, natural law (which is normative) clearly differs too from natural laws (which are descriptive). Most modern philosophers would agree with Sir Karl Popper that the distinction between physical laws (statements describing regularities of nature) and moral laws (commandments or prohibitions) is a fundamental one: "these two kinds of law," he comments, "have hardly more in common than a name."

Is there a natural law? And do human beings have natural rights, as Maritain argued, by virtue of such a law, or equivalently by virtue of the simple fact that they are human beings? Although legal positivists deny that there's any law but positive law, others experience what Carl Joachim Friedrich calls "a strong sense of the need . . . for a standard of justice by which to evaluate the positive law." There can be, and there certainly have been, unjust laws, and it would seem that people can refuse to obey them only if they can appeal to conscience, morality, or a higher law, one universally binding in principle if not in fact.

The Universal Declaration of Human Rights, which we've reprinted as an end to this chapter, asserts that all people do have certain rights and proceeds to define them. In general, Articles 3 through 20 define civil or political rights. They include the person's right to life, liberty, and security, the right to equality before the law, the right to be counted innocent until proved guilty in a fair trial, the right to own property, and the right to privacy. They also include such rights as freedom from arbitrary arrest and imprisonment, freedom of movement, thought and expression, and freedom of peaceful assembly. In addition, they specifically include prohibitions against slavery and torture.

For the most part, the remaining articles define social and economic rights. As described in the declaration, these include one's "right to take part in the government of his country, directly or through freely chosen representatives" and the corollary right to "periodic and genuine elections . . . by universal and equal suffrage." They also include the right to social security, the right to work, the right to protection against unemployment, and "the right to rest and leisure, including . . . periodic holidays with pay."

In your view, do human beings—"endowed," in the declaration's words, "with reason and conscience"—have natural rights? If so, which of the "rights" detailed in the declaration are truly *rights?* How would you decide? Could you list them in some order? How does the list you draw up reflect your own values, that is, your own social and political philosophy?

Text of the Universal Declaration of Human Rights approved by Resolution 217(III)A of the General Assembly of the United Nations, December 10, 1948:

Preamble

Whereas recognition of the inherent dignity and of the equal and inalienable rights of all members of the human family is the foundation of freedom, justice and peace in the world,

Whereas disregard and contempt for human rights have resulted in barbarous acts which have outraged the conscience of mankind, and the advent of a world in which human beings shall enjoy freedom of speech and belief and freedom from fear and want has been proclaimed as the highest aspiration of the common people,

Whereas it is essential, if man is not to be compelled to have recourse, as a last resort, to rebellion against tyranny and oppression, that human rights should be protected by the rule of the law,

Whereas it is essential to promote the development of friendly relations between nations,

Whereas the peoples of the United Nations have in the Charter reaffirmed their faith in fundamental human rights, in the dignity and worth of the human person and in the equal rights of men and women and have determined to promote social progress and better standards of life in larger freedom,

Whereas Member States have pledged themselves to achieve, in co-operation with the United Nations, the promotion of universal respect for and observation of human rights and fundamental freedoms,

Whereas a common understanding of these rights and freedoms is of the greatest importance for the full realisation of this pledge,

NOW, THEREFORE, THE GENERAL ASSEMBLY proclaims

THIS UNIVERSAL DECLARATION OF HUMAN RIGHTS as a common standard of achievement for all peoples and all nations, to the end that every individual and every organ of society, keeping this Declaration constantly in mind, shall strive by teaching and education to promote respect for these rights and freedoms and by progressive measures, national and international, to secure their universal and effective recognition and observance, both among the peoples of Member States themselves and among the peoples of territories under their jurisdiction.

Article 1. All human beings are born free and equal in dignity and rights. They are endowed with reason and conscience and should act towards one another in a spirit of brotherhood.

Article 2. Everyone is entitled to all the rights and freedoms set forth in this Declaration, without distinction of any kind, such as race, colour, sex, language, religion, political or other opinion, national or social origin, property, birth, or other status.

Furthermore, no distinction shall be made on the basis of the political, jurisdictional or international status of the country or territory to which a person belongs, whether it be independent, trust, non-self-governing or under any other limitation of sovereignty.

Article 3. Everyone has the right to life, liberty, and security of person.

Article 4. No one shall be held in slavery or servitude; slavery and the slave trade shall be prohibited in all their forms.

Article 5. No one shall be subjected to torture or to cruel, inhuman or degrading treatment or punishment.

Article 6. Everyone has the right to recognition everywhere as a person before the law.

Article 7. All are equal before the law and are entitled without any discrimination to equal protection of the law. All are entitled to equal protection against any discrimination in violation of this Declaration and against any incitement to such discrimination.

Article 8. Everyone has the right to an effective remedy by the competent national tribunals for acts violating the fundamental rights granted him by the constitution or by law.

Article 9. No one shall be subject to arbitrary arrest, detention or exile.

Article 10. Everyone is entitled in full equality to a fair and public hearing by an independent and impartial tribunal, in the determination of his rights and obligations and of any criminal charge against him.

Article 11. (1) Everyone charged with a penal offence has the right to be presumed innocent until proved guilty according to law in a public trial at which he has had all the guarantees necessary for his defence.

(2) No one shall be held guilty of any penal offence on account of any act or omission which did not constitute a penal offence, under national or international law, at the time when it was committed. Nor shall a heavier penalty be imposed than the one that was applicable at the time the penal offence was committed.

Article 12. No one shall be subjected to arbitrary interference with his privacy, family, home or correspondence, nor to attacks upon his honour and reputation. Everyone has the right to the protection of the law against such interference or attacks.

Article 13. (1) Everyone has the right to freedom of movement and residence within the borders of each State.

(2) Everyone has the right to leave any country, including his own, and to return to his country.

Article 14. (1) Everyone has the right to seek and to enjoy another country's asylum from persecution.

(2) This right may not be invoked in the case of prosecutions genuinely arising from non-political crimes or from acts contrary to the purposes and principles of the United Nations.

Article 15. (1) Everyone has the right to a nationality.

(2) No one shall be arbitrarily deprived of his nationality nor denied the right to change his nationality.

Article 16. (1) Men and women of full age, without any limitation due to race, nationality or religion, have the right to marry and to found a family. They are entitled to equal rights as to marriage, during marriage and at its dissolution.

(2) Marriage shall be entered into only with the free and full consent of the intending spouses.

(3) The family is the natural and fundamental group unit of society and is entitled to protection by society and the State.

Article 17. (1) Everyone has the right to own property alone as well as in association with others.

(2) No one shall be arbitrarily deprived of his property.

Article 18. Everyone has the right to freedom of thought, conscience, and religion; this right includes freedom to change his religion or belief, and freedom, either alone or in community with others, and in public or private, to manifest his religion or belief in teaching, practice, worship and observance.

Article 19. Everyone has the right to freedom of opinion and expression; this right includes freedom to hold opinions without interference and to seek, receive, and impart information and ideas through any media and regardless of frontiers.

Article 20. (1) Everyone has the right to freedom of peaceful assembly and association.

(2) No one may be compelled to belong to an association.

Article 21. (1) Everyone has the right to take part in the government of his country, directly or through freely chosen representatives.

(2) The will of the people shall be the basis of the authority of government; this will shall be expressed in periodic and genuine elections which shall be by universal and equal suffrage and shall be held by secret vote or by equivalent free voting procedures.

Article 22. Everyone, as a member of society, has the right to social security and is entitled to realisation, through national effort and international cooperation and in accordance with the organisation and resources of each State, of the economic, social and cultural rights indispensable for his dignity and the free development of his personality.

Article 23. (1) Everyone has the right to work, to free choice of employment, to just and favorable conditions of work, and to protection against unemployment.

(2) Everyone, without any discrimination, has the right to equal pay for equal work.

(3) Everyone who works has the right to just and favorable remuneration ensuring for himself and his family an existence worthy of human dignity, and supplemented, if necessary, by other means of social protection.

(4) Everyone has the right to form and to join trade unions for the protection of his interests.

Article 24. Everyone has the right to rest and leisure, including reasonable limitation of working hours and periodic holidays with pay.

Article 25. (1) Everyone has the right to a standard of living adequate for the health and well-being of himself and of his family, including food, clothing, housing and medical care and necessary social services, and the right to security in the event of unemployment, sickness, disability, widowhood, old age or other lack of livelihood in circumstances beyond his control.

(2) Motherhood and childhood are entitled to special care and assistance. All children, whether born in or out of wedlock, shall enjoy the same social protection.

Article 26. (1) Everyone has the right to education. Education shall be free, at least in the elementary and fundamental stages. Elementary education shall be compulsory. Technical and professional education shall be made generally available and higher education shall be equally accessible to all on the basis of merit.

(2) Education shall be directed to the full development of the human personality and to the strengthening of respect for human rights and fundamental freedoms. It shall promote understanding, tolerance and friendship among all nations, racial or religious groups, and shall further the activities of the United Nations for the maintenance of peace.

(3) Parents have a prior right to choose the kind of education that shall be given to their children.

Article 27. (1) Everyone has the right to freely participate in the cultural life of the community, to enjoy the arts and to share in scientific advancement and its benefits.

(2) Everyone has the right to the protection of the moral and material interests resulting from any scientific, literary or artistic production of which he is the author.

Article 28. Everyone is entitled to a social and international order in which the rights and freedoms set forth in this Declaration can be fully realized.

Article 29. (1) Everyone has duties to the community in which alone the free and full development of his personality is possible.

(2) In the exercise of his rights and freedoms, everyone shall be subject only to such limitations as are determined by law solely for the purpose of securing due recognition and respect for the rights and freedoms of others and of meeting the just requirements of morality, public order and the general welfare in a democratic society.

(3) These rights and freedoms may in no case be exercised contrary to the purposes and principles of the United Nations.

Article 30. Nothing in this Declaration may be interpreted as implying for any State, group or person any right to engage in any activity or to perform any act aimed at the destruction of any of the rights and freedoms set forth herein.

EASTERN THOUGHT

INTRODUCTION

The cause of all the miseries we have in the world is that men foolishly think pleasure to be the ideal to strive for. After a time man finds that it is not happiness, but knowledge, towards which he is going, and that both pleasure and pain are great teachers, and that he learns as much from evil as from good.[1]

Many Eastern thinkers maintain that the search for pleasure influences our whole world of experience in addition to many of our actions. We continually pursue what we think we lack and need. We act as if our human needs could be satisfied solely by externals—things like social status, relationships with others, luxurious cars, and fashionable clothes. From the Eastern point of view, even going after knowledge this way is a mistake. When Eastern thinkers say that knowledge is the true goal, they don't mean factual information; rather, they mean knowledge of our true identity.

But where does true identity reside? In our body? Soul? How do we acquire this knowledge? We'll consider these questions in this appendix. But for now let's say that Easterners seek a knowledge that dispels the human ignorance leading us to seek unsatisfying pleasures. True knowledge will lead to serenity or to what we in the West might call salvation or authentic existence.

There are parallels between Eastern and Western thought, and we'll mention a few of them as we go along. But this view of ignorance and knowledge differs markedly from our traditional ideas. It's not that Eastern thinkers never tried to construct critically founded philosophical systems like those we've elaborated in the West. They have done this, especially in India. But their philosophy has for the most part remained inseparable from

[1] Swami Vivekananda, *The Complete Works of Swami Vivekananda*, 14th ed., vol. 1, Calcutta: Advaita Ashrama, 1972, p. 27.

religious concerns, and, as a result, Eastern thinkers emphasize personal transformation more than we do.

Eastern philosophy may be called religious not only because of its fundamental concerns, which we'll consider here, but also because much of it is found in scriptures or is stimulated by religious traditions. For example, studying India's philosophical tradition necessarily involves investigating the *Vedas* and *Upaniṣads*. These are religious texts whose status is comparable to that of our Bible, but we do not necessarily refer to the Bible when we study Western philosophy. Similarly, looking at Chinese thought involves examining the writings of the legendary Lao Tzu, whose mystical religious thought is expressed in deceptively simple poetic language. And Confucius, who does not on the surface appear to be a religious thinker, is deeply and primarily concerned with correct personal conduct. Along with the Taoists, Confucius also provided commentary on religious texts such as the *I Ching*.

Another reason Eastern thought remained religious while ours did not has to do with their answer to the question "Who am I?", which we considered earlier in the context of modern and contemporary Western thought. In the East, generally, human beings have been seen as part of the cosmic whole or as part of nature. Thus the problem has been "How do I live in harmony with what is?" Nature was never seen, as it has been since the Renaissance in the West, as a force or an object to subdue. The cosmos demands reverence; it is deeply mysterious and curiously personal.

Because Eastern thought is more "person-oriented," it reveals a subtle understanding of human psychology. And because it is religious, it is more often than not clothed in parable and myth. However, this point of view, which sees the individual primarily as an arena in the battle against ignorance and explains the world and the human condition in terms of parable and myth, is not without parallel in the West.

For example, Plato, the Greek philosopher of the fourth century B.C., told a story describing the human situation. Human beings live in a dark cave, where all they see are the shadows cast on the wall by passing figures. They never see reality itself, only illusory representations of it. The philosopher's task is to turn people's eyes away from the shadows and toward the blinding light outside the cave, to accustom them to the truth. Similarly, in the East, the student is involved in a rigorous spiritual discipline in close relationship with a master who provides guidance. Yet ultimately the student and all of us in the cave are on our own. "A Master can only be he who opens the door; it is for the disciple to be capable of seeing 'what lies beyond.' "[2] The goal of Eastern philosophy is a knowing as direct and unquestionable as seeing what is before one's eyes.

[2] Alexandra David-Neel and Lama Yongden, *The Secret Oral Teachings in Tibetan Buddhist Sects*, H. N. M. Hardy (trans.), San Francisco: City Lights Books, 1967, p. 3.

Thinkers in the East seek release from ignorance and with it release from the experience of the world's wearisomeness. This stance did not allow science as we know it to develop, at least not until this century. In the Eastern tradition, knowledge is thus not directed toward objective data that can be analyzed and classified in accordance with explanatory theories. Rather, it focuses on human beings, who are seen primarily as desiring, willing, and feeling creatures. They are enmeshed in moral and religious predicaments. Should I go to battle? Should I marry? Should I undertake a certain religious practice? What do my feelings and thoughts tell me? Do they obscure the truth? In the language of Western existentialism, "How can I lead an authentic life?"

All Eastern traditions assert that in some way the individual can directly see who he or she is and what his or her place in the cosmic scheme is. Science in the Western sense will not provide an answer to these questions. (The exception to this, according to some thinkers, may be psychoanalysis in some of its forms.[3]) To understand this assertion, though, we'll have to see how human beings and the world are conceptualized in the East. We'll look at some representative traditions—which do differ significantly from one another—to try to capture the spirit of Eastern thinking.

The first section of this appendix will be concerned with Hinduism and Buddhism. We'll recount the story of Nachiketa, a fictional Hindu youth. By examining his gradual acquisition of knowledge and his relation to a master, we'll introduce some basic themes of Hinduism. We will also see how myth expresses metaphysical speculation. Our examination of Buddhism will begin with the historical figure Gautama Sakyamuni, born Prince Siddhartha, who reached his goal without a teacher. His insight into the cause and meaning of human suffering generated an entire religious and philosophical tradition, which also spread, in various forms, to China and Japan.

The second section will introduce Confucianism and Taoism. We'll discuss how Eastern thinkers have approached the idea of community as well as social issues like morality and work.

Finally, in the third section, we'll explore the theory and practice of art as a means of communicating the central ideas of a religious, philosophical tradition.

SUFFERING AND RELEASE: HINDUISM AND BUDDHISM

The story of Nachiketa comes from the *Katha Upaniṣad,* a sacred text written about 600 B.C. But before looking at Nachiketa's spiritual transformation,

[3]Erich Fromm, D. T. Suzuki, and Richard de Martino, *Zen Buddhism and Psychoanalysis,* New York: Harper & Row, 1960.

we'll look briefly at a major force in the development of Upanishadic thought, the *Vedas*.

The *Vedas—veda* means "sacred knowledge"—are religious texts originating in the third millennium B.C. They reflect a world similar to Homer's. Brimming with speculation about the animate forces (gods, spirits, and principles) behind all things, they are a colorful, polytheistic hymn to nature. Two examples may convey the atmosphere of the *Vedas*. Agni, the god of fire, is the source not only of the sun but also of bodily warmth, cell metabolism, and ordinary fire. Agni represents the heat and light needed to sustain life. The early Hindus also said that "food" is the source and essence of the world. Creatures and plants become food to sustain other creatures in the never ceasing round of birth and death. This metaphor of food reminds us of the pre-Socratic philosophers' attempts to understand water or air as the basic stuff of the universe. Both the Hindus and the pre-Socratics tried to find a name for the substance that never diminished through all its continuous transformations. In time the Hindus came to call this principle Brahman. Immaterial, it is identified as a world-soul or self, and it is seen as the source of all creation.

Upanishadic thought carries this monistic idea further but becomes more instrospective. It asks how the individual self, the microcosm that the *Upaniṣads* call *atman,* is related to Brahman. In other words, they ask "Who am I?" and "Where do I fit into the scheme of things?" Their holistic, nondual view of the cosmos prompts them to identify Brahman and *atman.* "My essence is the same as the essence of the universe." *Atman* is not the same as my empirical ego or physical self that comes to be and passessaway. This realization comes slowly and requires years of religious practice by the individual. This is because the individual is only too ready to identify his or her essence with something mundane. In the story of Nachiketa and again later in this section, we will discuss the way to this realization which, according to Hinduism, will bring tranquillity.

The Story of Nachiketa

As the story[4] opens, Nachiketa is watching his father perform a traditional religious sacrifice when *ṣradda,* or faith, enters him. But the twelve- or

---

[4]The story of Nachiketa is adapted from versions found in *The Principal Upaniṣads,* edited with introduction, text, translation, and notes by Sarvepalli Radhakrishnan, London: Allen and Unwin, and New York: Humanities Press, 1969, pp. 595–648, and in A. K. Coomaraswamy and Sister Nivedita, *Myths of the Hindus and Buddhists,* New York: Dover, 1967, pp. 332–335. We have adopted the spelling "Nachiketa" rather than "Naciketas" as more pleasing to the American reader.

thirteen-year-old boy realizes that the cows being sacrificed can no longer give milk and so are worthless for the sacrifice. He knows that only things of value should be given away in this ritual. Hoping to purify his father's sacrifice by offering himself, Nachiketa asks, "To whom will you give me?" The third time he asks, his exasperated father tells him that he will be given to Yama, the god of death. Nachiketa is not afraid, however, because he knows all must die and be reborn in an endless cycle.

Nachiketa waits in Yama's abode for three days. When the god of death finally returns, he fails to perform the sacred duty of hospitality. Realizing this, he endeavors to escape the consequences of his neglect by offering Nachiketa three wishes. Nachiketa's first wish is to be received back into his father's home after being released from death. Through this wish, Nachiketa acknowledges that he knows who he is as a human being and where he belongs in the social order.

Nachiketa's second wish is to be taught "that fire sacrifice which is the aid to Heaven." Yama teaches him to concentrate properly so that this sacrifice is successful. Yama is pleased, and Nachiketa now knows himself in a cosmic sense because he has correctly performed an important religious function.

Nachiketa's third request is release from attachment to the wheel of birth and death. Yama hesitates to reveal this secret; he tests Nachiketa by offering him many worldly pleasures. Nachiketa turns down all his offers, saying they are transient and cause suffering. Pleasures satisfy for a moment and then craving starts all over again. Wyen Nachiketa reveals that he is concerned only with the transcendent, with what is real, Yama begins his instruction.

Yama tells Nachiketa about his true self (*atman*), which is not limited by earthly or cosmic attachments. The self is described in paradoxical ways because no characterization can capture its essence.

Sitting, he moves far; lying he goes everywhere.
Smaller than the small, greater than the great,
the self is set in the heart of every creature.[5]

After long instruction Nachiketa knows the highest truth: "Thou art That." The self that is Nachiketa's true identity is the same as Brahman. By this knowledge, Nachiketa is freed from attachment to the wheel of birth and death.

But why did Nachiketa need the first two wishes if the last one would do? Generally, Hinduism sees the need for gradual release. Each insight becomes the basis for a new insight and thus for further development. Analogously,

[5] *The Principal Upaniṣads,* pp. 617–618.

children do not learn arithmetic by starting with multiplication and division; first they learn to count and then to add and to subtract. The truth the story of Nachiketa demonstrates is that one must begin where one is.

Nachiketa first asked for a proper ordering of that aspect of life which includes normal worldly aims in a family and community. But he must have religious training. Accordingly, the second wish enabled him to perform duties through which he acknowledged a cosmic dimension to existence. Gradually he acquired tranquillity through meditation. At the final stage, the third wish, Nachiketa attained a sort of "knowledge" that is unattainable by senses or intellect; he had direct insight into the oneness of all things.

Here, East parts company with West dramatically. Western philosophy, for the most part, does not recognize a power or faculty higher than the intellect. And Western religion, except in its mystical tradition, does not believe we can have a direct insight into or union with a divinity. But in the story of Nachiketa, we see the Hindu ideal: vision of the reality beyond all opposites and transient things. The oppositions between life and death, male and female, subject and object, pleasure and pain—and all the attachments and troubles connected with them—are not what is really real. Once this is seen human beings do not fear old age and death or the loss of other people and things. Loss and death are seen as part of the cosmic process; and death never means total cessation.

The Early Life of Prince Siddhartha

Buddhism agrees with Hinduism that the goal for human beings is release from ignorance and worldly attachments. However, Buddhism rejects speculation about cosmic and individual souls; the identity of Brahman and *atman,* from the Buddhist point of view, is mere speculation and no more. It will not lead to release. Speculation and its mythical garb are all part of the dream of life from which we must awaken. We'll look more carefully at this idea as we examine the early life of Prince Siddhartha[6] and the concept of the Buddha.

Unlike Nachiketa, Prince Siddhartha is an historical figure. He was born in the middle of the sixth century B.C. When he was young it was predicted that he would become either the world's greatest emperor or an ascetic. Hoping that his son would not renounce the world to become an ascetic, the king built a fabulous palace. His purpose was to prevent Siddhartha from

[6]The story of the early life of the Buddha is adapted from the version given by A. K. Coomaraswamy and Sister Nivedita in *Myths of the Hindus and Buddhists,* pp. 260–285.

seeing the cares of the world. The prince was content to be surrounded by pleasures and beauty. But in time he began to desire to leave the palace.

Once outside, Siddhartha saw an old man and learned that all people become old. He returned to the palace. On his next three trips outside he saw sickness, death, and finally a hermit who had renounced the world as a means to spiritual growth. These four incidents convinced Siddhartha that he must find a way to deal with human suffering. His search for the cause and the meaning of human suffering marked the beginning of Buddhism.

Siddhartha came to see transitoriness as the root of sorrow, pain, and fear. We suffer if we don't get what we want; we suffer from fear of sickness and death; we even suffer from pleasure because sooner or later it must give way to pain. To have the correct relation to the transitory things through which we cause our suffering, it is necessary to see that they are all unreal, part of the dream of life, the shadows that Plato's cave dwellers see.

Siddhartha left his family and became a wandering ascetic, but nowhere did he find the release he sought. Even fasts and austerities that brought him close to death were to no avail. At last he resolved to rely on no one and to meditate beneath the Bo tree (the *bodhi* tree or the tree of awakening) until he reached enlightenment.

There Siddhartha was tempted by Mara, the evil one. Mara told the prince that evil things had befallen his family, but Siddhartha saw this as yet another reason to seek enlightenment. Mara's beautiful daughters tempted the prince, but they were not successful. Mara then gathered his army together, but none of their weapons had power over the prince. All devices failed, and Mara finally accepted the prince's supremacy.

Enlightenment slowly rose in Siddhartha's heart. He understood the exact condition of things, that everything far or near appears close at hand. He realized the conditions for remaining on this wheel of birth and death. Finally, he recognized the Four Noble Truths, which tell of the nature of suffering, its origins, cessation, and the Eightfold Path that leads out of it. (We will discuss these ideas later.) At dawn he became the Supreme Buddha. Thus the historical figure of Prince Siddhartha fades into the concept of Buddha, which represents a *way* to enlightenment. A "buddha" is a "perfectly awakened one."

On one level, Hinduism and Buddhism go in different directions. Hinduism looks for the source of reality behind appearances; Buddhism seeks the removal of suffering in this world. But both point to the possibility of a relationship to the world not based on the transitoriness of things. This new relationship can only come about through an understanding of who we are. And it takes the personal courage and knowledge of a Nachiketa or a Buddha to see through our cares and attachments while remaining compassionate toward other beings.

The World

In Hinduism the phenomenal world is not primarily the world Western science "sees." Rather, it is the world of human experience. Life here and now is the means to liberation so it makes no sense to discuss a world apart from human purpose. But the world as we perceive it in all its multiplicity and sorrow is illusory, and therefore it's also the barrier to our liberation. The Hindus explain this paradox through the concept of *maya. Maya* is the veil worn by Brahman; it is our transient existence in space and time in contrast to the timeless reality. Thus, for us, it both conceals and reveals that reality, depending on our spiritual state.

The concept of *maya* is illustrated by many stories. In one of them, the god Vishnu—creator of the world—agrees to show the secret of the *maya* he uses to create and maintain the world. Vishnu and his disciple Narada walk by a small village. Vishnu asks Narada to go and get water while he waits. Narada knocks at the door of a house where he meets a maiden so enchanting that he forgets his purpose. Narada marries her, fathers three children, and becomes absorbed in his family responsibilities. Twelve years later a flood forces him to flee with his family, but they are swept away by the waters. Coming to himself again, Narada recognizes the voice of the god: "Where is the water you went to fetch for me? I have been waiting half an hour." Then Vishnu asked him, "Do you comprehend now the secret of my maya?" [7] Vishnu's drink of water has no meaning for the person caught up in daily cares; those cares have no meaning for the person who sees the god once again.

Maya, in the form of worldly things and cares, leads Narada to forget his relation to the divinity. But *maya* is not simply illusion. It appears to be a form of deception, but on another level it is a form of revelation. Only after Narada experiences worldly cares is he ready to know about Vishnu. *Maya,* as the condition of the world, means that no matter where we are we can be led from a limited understanding to a more inclusive understanding.

Had Vishnu offered his disciple an explanation to accept without question, Narada would only have replaced ignorance with the illusion of understanding. Interpretation is always suited to a particular level of comprehension. Whatever interpretation Narada could have at a lower level would be guaranteed false because it would be partial and exclude the higher level. Narada could not know the meaning of his experience with Vishnu as long as he remained enmeshed within it, as long as he remained

[7] Adapted from the version given by Heinrich Zimmer in *Myths and Symbols in Indian Art and Civilization,* Joseph Campbell (ed.), Princeton, NJ: Princeton University Press, 1972, pp. 32–34.

on that level. The secret of *maya* concerns the gap that both separates and relates different levels of reality and understanding.

In Buddhism the world is also human-centered, at least to begin with. In order to describe the world, or the human condition, Buddhism propounds the Four Noble Truths. First, life is suffering. Second, the cause of suffering is ignorance. In other words, because we don't know any better—a natural condition—we are determined by convention, feelings, and attitudes that lead to mundane attachments. We crave things that will cause us pain. We think we cannot do without a certain relationship, an article of clothing, a hot fudge sundae. We think about the sundae; our mouth waters; we *must* have it. The memory of its taste is etched in our experience, only too ready to surface. We create our own style, our own self, through our cravings for various things, and we condition ourselves for further cravings. Buddhism says that the ego is nothing but these cravings. We are continually being "reborn" by our desires.

This brings us to the third noble truth: Suffering can be stopped. And the fourth has it that the way to stop suffering is the Eightfold Path. We should develop right view, right aspiration, right speech, right conduct, right means of livelihood, right endeavor, right mindfulness, and right contemplation. Before discussing the way to the cessation of suffering, and the Buddhist answer to the question "Who am I?", we'll recount a story that illustrates the condition of attachment and its renunciation.

When Kisa Gotami's son died, she searched for someone to revive him. At last she asked the Buddha. He replied that if she could bring him a mustard seed from a family where no one had died, he would be able to bring her son back to life. Finding the task impossible, she realized there is suffering everywhere and in everything. She became a disciple of the Buddha. She had seen that all beings must die and that those who remain will feel sorrow. Any attachment must end in separation. None of the things that bring us pleasure or pain are lasting, just as we are not. But until one has directly perceived the all-encompassing nature of suffering, as Kisa Gotami did, one is not likely to look for a way out. Buddhism does not say we shouldn't love others, or that we shouldn't be grieved when we lose them; rather, it says that if we really understand the transitoriness of things we will grow as a result of our suffering.[8]

Paradoxically, Buddhism answers the question "Who am I?" with the doctrine of "no-self," or *anatta*. Suffering comes from attachment to "I" and "mine." We are deluded into thinking we have "selves," that is, permanent

[8]The story of Kisa Gotami is adapted from the version given in *The Wisdom of China and India*, Lin Yutang (ed.), New York: Modern Library, 1955, pp. 367–369.

identities. Like the eighteenth century British philosopher David Hume, Buddhist thinkers say that what we call the self is merely the aggregates of form, feelings, perceptions, impulses, and consciousness. Anything that we think of as a self can be reduced to one of these five aggregates, called the five *skandhas* ("groups," or "heaps"). Since there is no self-nature in any of these *skandhas* and there is nothing left of our identity without these five, there must not be a self at all. Human beings infer a self-nature and therefore expect and hope for certain things. This leads to attachments, which in turn reinforce the illusion of self.

Both Hinduism and Buddhism assert that freedom can come only when we have moved from the compulsions of the world to a new and deeper understanding. For Hinduism this means seeing that our true nature is beyond the limits of time, space, and causality. For Buddhism this means realizing there is no self-nature.

Freedom

For both the Hindu and Buddhist traditions liberation is the source of all real value. Their ideas of freedom are not often encountered in the West. For example, Western people often think freedom means being able to act without restraint—external or internal. For Easterners, this would be impulsive pleasure-seeking. In the East freedom does not simply refer to actions an individual can perform with impunity; it means primarily the power to choose either to act or not to act.

The important Hindu work *Bhagavad-Gita (The Song of God)* presents conflicts generated by human freedom. Arjuna is a warrior on the battlefield. If he fights he will kill those he loves; if he does not fight, he will abandon a just cause and be a coward in the eyes of the world. The problem is within him; there is no one to tell him the proper course of action. Just like all of us, Arjuna must make a choice about his actions; even choosing not to act is choice and action. And all action has consequences. Arjuna himself is the battlefield of conflicting desires that have him completely trapped.

> *I do not see anything to remove this sorrow which blasts my senses, even were I to obtain unrivalled and flourishing dominion over the earth, and mastery over the gods.*[9]

Such conflicts confront people as long as they look for freedom only in the world, in fulfillment of their desires. Thus, the first possibility of freedom,

[9] *Shrimad Bhagavad Gita,* Swami Swarupananda (trans.), 11th rev. ed., Calcutta: Sharada Press, 1972, p. 32.

freedom to execute one's desires, only looks like freedom. As soon as we have conflicting desires we realize that this is not true freedom at all. Freedom cannot come simply from choosing a particular thing; choosing a particular thing leads to conflicts because every choice necessarily excludes something else.

Once he has recognized his situation, Arjuna receives the beginning of the teaching. He is told that he is not any of his actions or desires; he is *atman* and therefore not determined by the causal world in which he must operate. *Atman* transcends the world of opposites: pleasure and pain, good and evil. Knowing this by direct experiential awareness, a person can make free choices in the world. Only when we see that determination and limitation are merely the sphere of our actions and not our real nature can we be free from the compulsion of desire. Then we are able to choose our actions.

The way of Buddhism, roughly like that of the fourth century B.C. Greek philosopher Aristotle, is called a "middle" way. Both Aristotle and the Buddha advocate the avoidance of extremes. The Buddhism we've been considering avoids pursuing worldly things and also avoids severe ascetic practices, which could lead to the death of the physical body. Although he didn't discuss asceticism, Aristotle did believe virtue was a mean between two extremes. For example, courage is a disposition or balance somewhere between feelings of fear on the one hand and overconfidence on the other. One produces cowardice, and the other produces rashness. Courage enables us—or those following the Buddha's way—to face the inevitable pain of life. Freedom is not possible for the Buddha unless we follow a middle way. Both asceticism and freedom from restraint are forms of bondage. Restraint must be self-imposed; then it generates freedom.

Both Hinduism and Buddhism discuss the possibility of freedom in connection with the concept of *karma. Karma* is the psychological and moral counterpart to the law of universal causation. Every psychological event has its cause in our disposition. This means that our pleasures, pains, joys, and sorrows are caused by our actions or feeling in this life or some previous life. In other words, we are born into bondage; we are born with a certain mental and physical constitution, family, circle of relatives. These things condition us, lead us to have certain unconscious expectations and feelings. Our pleasures, pains, joys, and sorrows are caused by our feelings and actions in this life or in some previous life—unless we learn to see through the mechanism of causation.

The Importance of Religious Practice

The Buddha attained the goal of freedom without a teacher. At first he was afraid that no other person would benefit from *his* teaching. "Of what use to reveal to men that which I have discovered at the price of laborious effort? Why should I do so?—This doctrine cannot be understood by those filled by desire and hatred." [10]

The high god Brahma (not the same as Brahman, creator of the universe) prevailed on the Buddha, saying that some people can learn. The Buddha looked through his third eye and realized that Brahma spoke the truth. He declared, " 'Let the Gate of the Eternal be open to all! Let him who has ears to hear, hear!' " [11]

Thus Buddhism began. But, as in all religious traditions, the problem of how to communicate the experiences of one individual to another arises. The reality that the Buddha experienced, like the reality that Yama revealed to Nachiketa, cannot be taught by words or found in books. There must be a method to lead the individual from his or her present condition to a new awareness.

Buddhism and Hinduism are both ways of describing individuals' present conditions. But both also point to the goal of release from this condition. Once a person has truly heard the teaching, he or she begins to doubt commonly held beliefs because the teaching has led to a new perspective. The individual becomes more independent.

Knowledge and religious practice are two aspects of the same reality. What one knows and what one does must be in harmony if growth is to be possible. For this reason, both traditions rely on meditation, renunciation, yoga, and *mantras*. These practices, as well as the individual methods given by the master, aim at focusing the attention of the religious aspirant in the proper direction to allow for psychological change. This is not unlike the function of prayer in the Western world.

Both traditions, the Hindu and the Buddhist, emphasize the importance of the master-disciple relationship. The master already knows the truth and can show the disciple how to look for it, but ultimately success depends on the disciple's sensitivity. Even after Yama tested Nachiketa to make sure the teaching wouldn't be totally wasted on him, he still had no guarantee that Nachiketa would understand or have the courage to persevere. The master-disciple relationship, which may be a tie stronger than that of the family, is considered the best method of transmitting the subtle doctrines of Hinduism and Buddhism.

In many systems of Eastern thought, including Hinduism and Buddhism, practice is not only an individual but also a social responsibility. The individual has certain obligations to others while he is involved in the religious quest, and society can support the individual seeker if it is structured according to religious truth.

[10] Alexandra David-Neel and Lama Yongden, op. cit., p. 4.
[11] Ibid., p. 6.

SOCIETY AND THE INDIVIDUAL: CONFUCIANISM AND TAOISM

So far we've discussed philosophies originating in India. Traditions vary considerably in the East, though, and we find a completely different world view in China. To introduce Chinese thought, we'll investigate Confucianism and Taoism, to which we'll compare Hindu and Buddhist thinking on some issues.

Born about 551 B.C., Confucius was roughly the contemporary of Prince Siddhartha. However, Confucius was primarily concerned with social reform on a large scale; he saw in tradition ideals, such as piety and courtesy, that could be reinterpreted and revitalized for his contemporaries. An idea essential to Confucianism is that of the golden mean. "It is the discovery that the gentleman can do nothing exciting or out of the way to distinguish himself except by his indistinguishability from other gentlemen." [12] As with Aristotle's mean, virtue is the balance between extremes.

To investigate Taoism, we'll look at the *Tao Te, Ching,* a book filled with terse, mystical speculation about the nature of the universe and human beings' place in it. The legendary author of the *Tao Te Ching* is Lao Tzu, supposedly a near contemporary of Confucius. The work appears, however, to have had many authors. In any case, the philosophy of Taoism is concerned with individual spiritual growth, which is to be achieved by acting in harmony with the forces of nature. Taoism, unlike Confucianism, is not concerned with political reform. A central idea of Taoism, expressed by Lin Yutang in *The Wisdom of China and India,* is that "it teaches the wisdom of appearing foolish, the success of appearing to fail, the strength of weakness and the advantage of lying low, the benefit of yielding to your adversary and the futility of contention for power." [13] Confucianism and Taoism have existed alongside one another in China for centuries, even though on many issues they advocate opposing positions.

Before examining Chinese views of society, the individual, and morality, we'll look at an idea that permeates all Chinese culture and thinking. It is central to both Taoism and Confucianism, although its meaning differs from one tradition to the other.

The Way

Tao means "a road" or "a way." But it also refers to a correctness about the way a thing is done: the way water flows, the way a good government is run,

[12] *The Wisdom of China and India,* p. 813.
[13] Ibid., p. 579.

the orderly way nature changes. For Confucius, *Tao* refers primarily to personal conduct and morality as the way a society is held together. A society that conforms to *Tao* will be a good society, and its members will be happy. Especially does *Tao* mean the way of the ancients that should be cultivated and respected if we are to have proper relationships between persons and governments. In the *Analects,* Confucius outlines methods for acting in harmony with the way.

For the Taoist, *Tao* acquired a mystical, supernatural cast. It was still a way, but one by which an individual sought to align him or herself with the laws of nature. The Taoist thought that rather than following social rules the individual should learn to see directly or intuitively the correct way to be. *Tao* also became a metaphysical principle; it was identified as the source of the universe.

There was something undifferentiated and yet complete,
Which existed before heaven and earth.
Soundless and formless, it depends on nothing and does not change.
It operates everywhere and is free from danger.
It may be called the mother of the universe.
I do not know its name; I call it Tao. [14]

By contrast, Confucius preferred not to speak of the ways of the universe, the ways of unseen powers, or the will of Heaven.

Tzu-kung said, Our Master's views concerning culture and the outward
[manifestations of an inward] goodness, we are permitted to hear; but about
Man's nature and the ways of Heaven he will not tell us anything at all. [15]

In a common sense way, Confucius would speak only of the duties of one person to another. However, both Confucius and the Taoists found in *Tao* something to guide human beings through the vicissitudes of life, whether the idea of the way is given a worldly, social meaning or a spiritual, individual meaning.

Society

Attitudes toward society vary within the different Eastern traditions. For Confucians, the question "Who am I?" makes no sense apart from a

[14] *The Way of Lao Tzu,* Wing-Tsit Chan (trans.), Indianapolis: Bobbs-Merrill, The Library of Liberal Arts, 1963, no. 25, p. 144.
[15] *The Analects of Confucius,* Arthur Waley (trans.), London: Allen and Unwin, 1938, p. 110.

consideration of the social order. Not unlike Plato, Confucius saw the ideal or best state as emerging with the advent of the ideal person or, in Confucius' words, the "superior man" or "gentleman." This person will rule by example, not by force.

Because the superior person is in control of his actions, he is able to treat people fairly and to show by example how they should conduct their lives. Ideally, his government is not run according to the dictates of greed and personal power, but with an understanding of the people's needs. Confucius realized that such a person rarely appears; but it is just such an extraordinary man who is needed in order to have a properly functioning society. In the ideal society, everyone's conduct would be governed by knowledge of the Five Relationships: "father and son, elder and junior brother, husband and wife, elder friend and junior friend, and ruler and subject." [16] By knowing how to act in these various relationships and by acting accordingly, one becomes a total human being. Political status should be based on merit rather than birth. But if a person usurps the power or authority rightfully belonging to another, he invites chaos.

Taoism conflicts with Confucianism on the question of how to establish an ideal society. In fact, for the Taoist the question itself is a symptom of man's estrangement from the rhythm of nature. Confucianism envisioned a unified social order, and Taoism rejected any attempt on man's part to make his own world. The Confucian ideal can be compared to a great walled city. Unimpressed by its inner workings, Taoists saw the city in the context of the surrounding countryside and laughed at its walls. Historically, Taoist criticism of the dominant philosophy may have counteracted the tendency for Confucian orderliness to become static and stifling.

Hinduism promoted a caste structure in society. In theory, each person is where he or she belongs according to natural inclinations and abilities. However, the caste system became very rigid. A person may live and die in the caste to which he or she is born. This seems to us a complete suppression of personal growth and freedom, but the principle behind it points to complete freedom in the Hindu sense—mastering the duties of one's particular caste and acting in accordance with them. Also, living in a religiously structured society allows one to live in accord with the cosmic order. Today the caste system has eased considerably.

In place of a well-ordered hierarchy, such as Hinduism and Confucianism suggest, Buddhism emphasizes the monastic life as proper for a community of seekers. This life is the middle path between the householder

---

[16] Huston Smith, *The Religions of Man,* New York, Harper & Row, 1958. Excerpt reprinted under the title "The Way of Deliberate Tradition," in *The Ways of Religion,* Roger Eastman (ed.), San Francisco: Canfield Press, 1975, p. 201.

and the *sannyasin* ("the person who renounces all worldly relations and attachments"). The monastery or convent is seen as the structure in which renunciation is most easily accomplished. Its orderly life is a constant, freely chosen reminder that one is working for release from bondage.

A social structure like those promoted by Confucianism and Hinduism is concerned with the well-being of the majority. It is intended to help most people come to a better understanding of themselves through the guidance of social convention. But the early Buddhists, the Taoists, and the Hindu *sannyasin* seek a sudden release from the bondage of the world; they try to understand their role in the cosmos in a new way. This kind of radical separation from the ways of the world and social organization is not the road of the many. This is probably why, as a later development, Buddhism included a way for the householder to follow the path.

Morality

What is the good for human beings? How must one act to achieve it? Philosophers, both Eastern and Western, have been considering such questions for centuries. Many have formulated entire philosophical systems in order to find or to justify an ethical standard such as the golden rule. Questions of right action usually involve an appeal to a conception of the nature of human beings and a principle higher than the sanctions of ordinary everyday life. For instance, Confucius and the Taoists believe we must act in accord with the *Tao*. However, as we've seen, their understandings of this idea differ significantly. Accordingly, their views of what is right for human beings to do also differ.

Western thought is influenced by Christianity, which holds that human beings are born into sin and so are basically evil. In contrast, Eastern thought generally believes that people may become either good or bad but are neither at birth. What is needed is some method by which people can develop their natural potential for good. Although people are not naturally evil, they do not become "naturally" or spontaneously good without effort and forethought.

The goal of Confucianism, as we mentioned, is to produce the superior man. This person will embody the quality of *jen,* or "human-heartedness." A moral quality or perfection, *jen* is difficult to define. It includes such attributes as benevolence, compassion, and altruism. The human-hearted person recognizes an obligation not to act for selfish personal gain. Rather, one should act in such a way as to benefit society. These actions will be righteous, and they will be of most benefit to the individual as well. The truly superior person will automatically desire for him or herself what is good for all.

Thus the *jen*-person must know the meaning of *jen;* he or she must be able to know consciously and purposefully how to act with a view to goodness. It is only after a great deal of reflection and long practice in following precepts that this kind of action becomes spontaneous and agrees with the *Tao* for human beings. To help the individual learn, Confucius placed great reliance on etiquette. However, he did not simply mean artificial good manners. It is through correct conduct in relation to others—family, friends, and strangers—that we may show both our respect and our humility. Rules of conduct provide a standard that represents the golden mean we mentioned earlier. Before we really know what is right, these examples of conduct such as filial piety provide a way to learn correct behavior. According to Confucius, filial piety is one of the most important duties. By observing the duties one has to one's parents, children ensure both a smoothly running society and the proper development of *jen* in the individual. Morality is a distinctively human achievement.

The Taoists also wanted to live in harmony with *Tao*. They criticized the Confucians for holding that society was the highest good; they thought the Confucians did not believe there was a moral principle or good transcending the social order. But Confucius, like the eighteenth century German philosopher Immanuel Kant, refused to speculate about realities beyond the human sphere; he believed he found in the doctrine of the golden mean—similar to Aristotle's idea of the mean—a principle to guide human action. He did not think it was necessary to seeksmoral sanctions in a transcendent realm.

The Taoists believed they had to conceive of *Tao* as a metaphysical or cosmological principle for it to function as a proper guide for human action. In so doing they reflect the Eastern tendency to reduce or to overcome dualities. *Tao*—nature or the way—is beyond opposites like good and evil. The Taoist sage attempts to live simply and spontaneously in accord with nature. He does not *try* to be virtuous. That would be only apparent virtue. Rather, he sees that one should move with the ever-changing flow of things.

A primary symbol of this way of action is the movement of water.

There is nothing weaker than water
But none is superior to it in overcoming the hard. [17]

Water is without form. It is pliable and yet does not lose its essence in meeting with obstacles. Water does not resist things; it envelops them and can move with them. Thus human beings should learn to move through the world without violence. If a person is not pliable in this way, that person will be broken by his or her own resistance.

[17] *The Wisdom of China and India*, p. 622.

And this is true in the moral realm. Chuang Tzu, a disciple of Lao Tzu, expressed the Taoist understanding of a person's place and right action in society this way:

> Conscious of my own deficiencies in regard to Tao, I do not venture to practice the principles of charity and duty on the one hand, nor to lead the life of extravagance on the other. [18]

Thus for Taoists too the individual should act according to a mean and should be willing to be passive, weak, or humble if the situation calls for it.

For the Hindu, correct morality means knowing one's *dharma*. *Dharma* means, essentially, "law," or "duty." And so one should fulfill one's duty, meet one's obligations, or realize one's potential in life. For example, to be born into a holy caste involves duties to become a holy person. In any case, one must follow one's own *dharma, not* someone else's. This theme is reflected in many of the Hindu epics. The people who are considered heroic or saintly are those who have discovered what right action is for them. Regardless of the consequences, they follow that path for the rest of their lives.

Man is not all that has a *dharma* or inner law to follow; so does the whole cosmos. If each being follows its *dharma,* the whole will function in a proper manner. If people live in accordance with their *dharma,* they will be aided by other beings and supported in their tasks.

The concept of *dharma* involves both an external and an internal law. Morality is a part of *dharma,* for it gives human beings the proper range within which to work and search for their own personal understanding. The social and moral realm is part of a greater structure that has the function of teaching the individual his or her right place in the whole cosmic scheme. By choosing the good, people move in accordance with this order and can grow in awareness of their individual functions.

Buddhism places a great deal of emphasis on the ethical life. All sentient beings are trapped in the world of ignorance. Because of the shared condition of ignorance, one has a responsibility toward all other beings. One is not free to harm another in any way. Rather, one is responsible to others. This idea can be seen in the Eightfold Path, one formulation of the way to put Buddhism into practice. All aspects of the Eightfold Path must be developed if one is to move from ignorance to freedom.

Acting in accord with precepts that in the West would be called "moral" or "ethical" has a central position in Buddhism. To do so is to acknowledge that one has understood what it means to see the world as suffering. One acts morally in order not to cause more suffering either for oneself or for others.

[18]Ibid., p. 669.

However, the ethical life is not an end in itself. It is a means to become and to remain aware of one's true condition. One's selfish desires are part of the world of suffering and hence must be curbed if one is to be free from suffering.

In general, Eastern thinkers see morality as performing an important function. In each tradition, acting correctly is considered a means of seeing oneself more clearly as part of a whole rather than as an isolated individual entity. As we remarked earlier, freedom for Hinduism and Buddhism is beyond the world of opposites. But one cannot start from the goal; rather one must acknowledge his or her place in the world to be able to transcend it. Morality is a means of breaking down the feeling of "I" and "mine" because it directs attention away from the ego to others and the greater structure of the world. One acts morally, not from fear of retribution, but in acknowledgement of a higher reality.

Work

Work, too, is a means for knowledge and growth. Work is not merely an economic necessity; it is a religious duty. Performing work with the right intention and attention is a way of using one's energy and the tools that are available in a productive instead of a destructive manner. A story by Chuang Tzu points out clearly the possibilities of work as a spiritual method.

Prince Huei watched his cook cutting up a bull. The cook had a phenomenal rhythm to his work, and the prince questioned him about his skill.

"Sire," replied the cook laying down his chopper, "I have always devoted myself to Tao, which is higher than mere skill. When I first began to cut up bullocks, I saw before me whole animals. And now I work with my mind and not with my eye. My mind works along without the control of the senses. Falling back upon eternal principles, I glide through such great joints or cavities as there may be, according to the natural constitution of the animal. I do not even touch the convolutions of muscle and tendon, still less attempt to cut through large bones.

He goes on to say that "a good cook changes his chopper once a year" while the ordinary cook needs a new one every month. But because he did his work through devotion to the *Tao,* he had used the same chopper for nineteen years, and it was still just like new. At the end of the tale, the prince exclaimed, "Bravo. . . . From the words of this cook I have learnt how to take care of my life." [19]

[19] Ibid., pp. 643–644.

Although the cook is not a great man in society, he is able to apprehend the natural order of things and to work with it instead of against it. Because of this he is an inspiration to those above him in station. All work, no matter how insignificant by worldly standards, can be the means to achieve harmony with *Tao.* And one also sees that his understanding has made the cook's job easier because he is not fighting his work but learning from it.

Hinduism expresses this same view. Members of the various castes can all learn about their true nature through a proper attitude toward work. As long as we fulfill our own *dharma,* it is not what we do but our attitude toward our work that gives it a constructive or destructive quality. Although work fulfills a similar function in Buddhism, the great variety of roles that can be an aid to development in Hinduism and Taoism is not open to the Buddhist. Right livelihood, as a part of the Eightfold Path, must always be considered. Any job that will cause injury to another sentient being cannot be undertaken. One could not be a soldier or a butcher, for example, because these jobs involve injury to others, which Buddhism prohibits. When Buddhism came to China, work was integrated into the monastic way of life that in India had been exclusively dedicated to religious and scholarly activities.

In Confucianism, work is considered part of one's social responsibility. In his work the superior man will put his moral principles into practice. They will guide not only his way of acting but also his choice of actions. For example, he must not try to isolate himself in the midst of a corrupt society. Confucius himself longed for an opportunity to make practical reforms, and many of his followers held governmental posts.

Transmission of the Teaching

Traditional Eastern societies see religious practice as the most fundamental part of one's life. All aspects of life are subsumed under the "teaching." Society is seen to have a higher purpose than just keeping the peace and making it possible for individuals to secure material well-being. The value of society is determined by its capacity to encourage spiritual development.

One function of a religiously structured society is to serve as a means for transmitting the teaching. Ideally, a person growing up in such a society always has the teaching in view. However, a tension exists between keeping its truths intact and making those truths available in new circumstances. The teaching must be adapted without losing its essential character or its true meaning. One way this has been accomplished in the East is through the master-disciple relationship.

Gauging their disciples' level of awareness, teachers commonly reserve the careful explanation of certain doctrines for those whom they judge able to penetrate them. This method not only safeguards the teaching from misinterpretation, but it also allows the master to lead each particular student in the direction best suited to that student's needs and abilities.

It is tken to be as impartial and immutable as a natural law that only a person's own understanding can qualify him to receive the truth. Confucius said: "I point out the way only to the student who has first looked for it himself. . . . If, when I give the student one corner of the subject, he cannot find the other three for himself, I do not repeat my lesson." [20] Traditionally, a pupil must demonstrate his readiness by asking the right questions. Even if nothing is deliberately withheld, an esoteric teaching is said to preserve its secrecy and integrity since only those who are able to "hear with the spirit" will understand its meaning.

In this way, "Reading for a man devoid of prior understanding is like a blind man's looking in a mirror." [21] In the *Lankavatara Sutra,* the Buddha says, "Meaning is entered into by words as things are revealed by a lamp. . . . So, I, making use of various forms and images of things, instruct my sons; but the summit of Reality can only be realized within oneself." [22] The lamp or the mirror is only of use to one who can see and knows where to look.

Since these traditions are experiential, there must be a form or a path that will transmit not only the ideas but also the quality of experience from the knower to the followers. Each aspirant's investigation of religious truth can help to develop the teaching in a new way and revitalize old ideas. There is, however, the chance that the new aspirant will misinterpret the teaching and lead others further from the truth. That is why certain social structures have been seen as the best means to allow the individual to come in contact with spiritual truth.

Another means for preserving the teaching and, at the same time, adapting it to the needs of the individual in a particular time and place is sacred art. It too is seen as a means through which the individual seeker can come to understand the heart of the teaching because its expression of the truth is timeless.

EASTERN ART

So closely bound to the life style and values of Eastern people is their practice of art that this practice becomes one more avenue for us to

---

[20] *Analects* 7.8, quoted by H. G. Creel in *Chinese Thought: From Confucius to Mao Tse-Tung,* Chicago: University of Chicago Press, 1953, p. 29.

[21] Quoted from *Garuda Purana,* vol. 16, no. 82, by Ananda K. Coomaraswamy, *Am I My Brother's Keeper?,* Freeport, NY: Books for Libraries Press, 1967, p. 32.

[22] Quoted by Sri Krishna Prem, *The Yoga of the Bhagavat Gita,* Baltimore: Penguin, 1958, p. xiv.

understand Eastern thought. Particular works become visible, tangible representations of ideas. One "feels" what Hinduism or Buddhism is all about simply by experiencing a statue of the Buddha or of a Hindu deity. In fact, since study of the written teaching was in many ways restricted—by membership in a caste, by formal initiation, or simply by illiteracy and the scarcity of texts—ritual and art were essential in making traditional wisdom accessible to the majority of people.

Representation of the Ideal

The characteristically Hindu appreciation for the relationship between different orders of reality is expressed with extraordinary power and beauty in the images of Shiva, Lord of the Dance. The rhythm of the god's dance marks time for the creation and destruction of the world. Yet the feeling it conveys is one of joy and peace. The statue represents a moment of the dance. Every gesture and ornament is significant. But the symbols are not mere artistic conventions; they are a precisely defined "body language" that can speak to the untutored viewer. For example, Shiva's raised foot invites whoever has had enough of the passing pleasures of this world to enjoy release from its compulsions. We may experience ourselves walking on the path of attachment to the phenomenal world. We may come to identify with Shiva's manifold activity, continually moving the world while he himself is unmoved by it; so, instead of chaos there is order and rightness even in this world. As Mai-Mai Sze points out in another context, these lines from T. S. Eliot's "Burnt Norton" might express such Eastern modes of thought and experience:

> *At the still point of the turning world. Neither flesh nor fleshless;*
> *Neither from nor towards; at the still point, there the dance is,*
> *But neither arrest nor movement. And do not call it fixity,*
> *Where past and future are gathered. Neither movement from nor towards,*
> *Neither ascent nor decline. Except for the point, the still point,*
> *There would be no dance, and there is only the dance.*
> *I can only say,* there *we have been: but I cannot say where.*
> *And I cannot say, how long, for that is to place it in time.*[23]

In the midst of creation and destruction, Shiva's quiet and untroubled expression exemplifies the Hindu ideal of life, the same ideal Krishna taught

[23] T. S. Eliot, "Burnt Norton," in *Four Quartets,* New York: Harcourt, 1943, p. 5. Quoted by Mai-Mai Sze in *The Way of Chinese Painting: Its Ideas and Techniques,* New York: Random House (Modern Library), 1959, p. 32. Reprinted by Harcourt Brace Jovanovich, Inc., New York.

Arjuna on the battlefield: "He who sees inaction in action, and action in inaction is intelligent among men, he is a Yogi and a doer of all action."[24]

And standing before the statue of the Buddha, we are drawn into the Buddha's boundless compassion and serenity; we are aware of the possibility of existing without individual, binding attachments. Reading Buddhist texts might lead to a misunderstanding of the idea of no-self or void, to thinking it is a pessimistic rejection of all value. But this mistake could not be made after experiencing the statue of the Buddha.

Although the statues depict particular individuals, they represent the ideal of Buddhahood, or enlightenment, with which no personal characteristics are associated. The figure of a monk meditating or making the ritual gesture that signifies teaching the *dharma* is not intended as a likeness of a particular individual. The same is true of earlier depictions of the Buddha. Indeed, he was sometimes shown not as a human figure at all but as the wheel of life or simply as footprints pointing out the path to *nirvana,* that is, to selflessness and so to release from suffering and desire.

Theory and Practice of Art

In the East, a work of art is a vehicle of understanding for both the artist and the viewer. Only secondarily can it be considered the communication of the artist's personal experience. This contrasts with a contemporary Western notion of art, namely, "art for art's sake." It also differs from our idea that art is substantially self-expression.

The practice of art is a spiritual discipline in which the artist seeks a degree of concentrated awareness such that he becomes one with his subject. Thus, as the Chinese philosopher Chuang Tzu says, "The mind of the sage, being in repose, becomes the mirror of the universe."[25]

The artist, too, is a vehicle through which "seeing" occurs. However, this seeing and the ability to respond to it with words, sounds, or lines do not become spontaneous without years of rigorous discipline. The artist must learn to work within the confines of a medium. The seventeenth century Chinese *Mustard Seed Garden Manual of Painting* contains the rules for holding a brush and for painting a tree, a rock, a person. Only when those basic skills, and others, are mastered can the artist freely respond to his or her "seeing." It is also true that through drawing and painting and mastering techniques, the artist learns to see more deeply into the nature of things. But for this the *Manual* requires more: "He who is learning to paint must first

[24] *Shrimad Bhagavad Gita,* p. 106.
[25] Quoted by Ananda Coomaraswamy in *The Dance of Shiva: Fourteen Indian Essays,* rev. ed., New Delhi: Sagar, 1968, p. 28.

learn to still his heart, thus to clarify his understanding and increase his wisdom."[26]

The Hindu artist begins by visualizing an image or theme. The artist assumes a ritual attitude by repeating the *bija mantra,* or "seed syllable;"[27] which expresses its essence in sound vibration. Focusing awareness on this *mantra* helps the artist achieve a state of emptiness from which the "seed" of an external representation may flow. In meditation and creation the artist imitates divine cosmogony, the generation of the universe.

Eastern art is not at all naturalistic in the sense of trying to imitate objects. In India, portraits, the most notable exception to this generalization, are paintings of a person's essential type. They are not likenesses of actual physical appearance. Outer form must reveal hidden essence. For example, a mark of artistic greatness would be the successful portrayal of the difference between a sleeping man and a corpse.

Formal Restrictions

Traditionally the artist remained anonymous and worked within strictly defined canons of proportion and composition. Particular objects, postures, gestures, and colors carry definite symbolic meanings. The established Hindu and Buddhist iconography guarantees the precise translation of ideas and qualities into visible images. Rather than inhibiting the artist, they were designed to guide his awareness. Such formal restrictions tend to discourage novelty. However, the aim of artistic communication is not primarily to say something new or even to say something in a new way. To the Eastern mind, originality depends on the artist's having, by his power of concentrated awareness, perceived the original of which the work is an image. Once the artist has realized the essence of what he is to communicate, the act of expression is theoretically spontaneous and egoless.

This is especially true in Japan, where the arts, and culture in general, have been deeply influenced by Zen, a sect of Buddhism. Painting, drama, and poetry, as well as tea ceremonies, gardening, flower arranging, swordsmanship, and archery reveal the spiritual simplicity and natural elegance of the Zen mood. The artist seeks to express an immediate intuition of "the object in its original unity with ourselves."

This idea, the original unity of subject and object, is the key to understanding Zen. For Zen all the diversity of nature is merely what is

[26] Mai-Mai Sze, op. cit., p. 133.
[27] Ibid., p. 118.

perceived; in truth, all is one. The seventeenth century Dutch philosopher Baruch Spinoza is spiritually akin to Zen, although he was probably never directly influenced by it. For both Zen masters and Spinoza, each blade of grass, each person, each thought is a perspective of the universe, of what is. These things are not separate realities. Each of us is a point through which the universe is seen rather than a subject over against an unrelated object. According to Zen, insight into this basic truth—whether it occurs in a monastery during meditation or with a brush over a sheet of rice paper—will help human beings overcome suffering. (This is the same idea we encountered earlier when we discussed Buddhism in general.)

Let's look at a feature of Japanese painting that will illustrate our point. An art of brushwork has been developed in which the materials themselves demand that the artist work spontaneously, that the artist, materials, and painting become "one." Using fragile paper, ink that dries on contact, and a brush that responds to every change of tension in the hand, the artist is permitted no revision or hesitation. Before beginning, the artist must sense the natural rhythm of his subject and the inner tensions that give it its peculiar quality. Then, to be effective and not to betray the directness of true insight, the artist's expression of his understanding must be unmediated and uninterrupted. "Each brushstroke should be a living idea."

Japan has also produced a unique poetry called *haiku;* it is heavily influenced by Zen. Each poem is composed of seventeen syllables, a length considered most suitable for expressing the direct seeing we have been discussing. But don't expect of *haiku* something singularly exalted or profound! Far from it. Consider this poem by Basho, founder of the modern school of *haiku:*

Along the mountain road,
Somehow it tugs at my heart:
A wild violet.[28]

Nothing could be simpler. We do not know what Basho thought or felt on seeing a wild violet. Was he preoccupied or thoughtful as he climbed the mountain road? We know only that there was a moment of meeting, perhaps an intuition of meaning in which nothing other than the wild violet was meant. Or we may think that the mountain path is the lonely path we travel through life; the flower may be a momentary interruption of the loneliness. Another example:

[28]Translated by Makoto Ueda in *Matsuo Bashō,* Boston: Twayne Publishers, 1970, p. 49. Reprinted with the permission of Twayne Publishers, A Division of G. K. Hall & Co., Boston.

How admirable,
He who thinks not "life is fleeting"
When he sees the lightning! [29]

Once one labels experience as if to secure it, to nail it down, the rightness of the moment has disappeared. A Westerner might think that something had been understood in the moment when one was able to interpret the experience, to extract its meaning and name it—"Life is fleeting!" According to Zen, however, nothing could be less truly his or her own than a person's program of associations that automatically analyzes and classifies the data of experience. Only before that happens—in a moment as brief as a flash of lightning—is there any real understanding.

Aesthetic Experience

The work of art thus offers a kind of experience in which something can be understood directly. For a moment, the viewer or listener forgets himself and realizes something that cannot be understood from the ordinary viewpoint of personal advantage. Egoistic concerns subtly and constantly influence our way of interpreting experience, our way of "taking" things. *Haiku* poetry, D. T. Suzuki writes, presents ordinary objects and situations as coming "out of an unknown abyss of mystery, and through every one of them we can have a peep into the abyss." [30]

To appreciate the *haiku,* the reader must discover in himself the same emptiness that awakened the poet's intuition. The outer form of the poem or painting is only the provisional means of communicating an insight that depends directly on a condition of receptivity. These words of Chuang Tzu might be addressed to the person who reads *haiku:*

> *Do not listen with the mind, but with the spirit. . . . The function of the ears ends with hearing; that of the mind with symbols of ideas. But the spirit is an emptiness ready to receive all things.* [31]

Much depends, then, on the quality of listening or seeing. According to the Hindu view of art, "it is the spectator's own energy that is the cause of aesthetic experience." [32] Artistic communication serves a power of under-

[29] Basho, *Haiku,* R. H. Blythe (trans.), from *Silent Flowers* © 1967 by Hallmark Cards, Inc. and Hokuseido Press. Reprinted by permission.
[30] D. T. Suzuki, *Zen Buddhism: Selected Writings of D. T. Suzuki,* William Barrett (ed.), Garden City, NY: Doubleday (Anchor Books), 1956, p. 287.
[31] Mai-Mai Sze, op. cit., p. 110.
[32] Dhanamjaya, *The Dasarupa; A Treatise on Hindu Dramaturgy,* vol. 6, George C. O. Haas (trans.), New York: Columbia University Press, 1912, p. 47.

standing already present. No elaboration of the message can eliminate the need for a special kind of listening or looking.

The Function of Sacred Art

Art in general—both Eastern and Western—makes us aware of something more than our limited range of everyday preoccupations; or it enhances their meaning. And art in the East tries to uncover a spark of awareness that is not ego-bound and then to fan the flame. In the Thanka art of Vajrayana Buddhism, the objects represented—deities, *bodhisattvas,* demons—are meant to be understood subjectively as kinds of awareness. They are not symbolic in the sense of pointing beyond themselves; "they only point beyond our initial comprehension of them." [33] According to this view, art doesn't just represent an idea visually. Its teaching is effective if it heals the separation between subject and object that conditions ordinary knowledge. The art object can be the catalyst urging the viewer out of his limited and confused way of interpreting the world. "This art meets us at our own level and grows in significance as we grow in penetrating clarity of mind." [34]

When the mind itself is affected, the work of art is not the only thing that appears more meaningful. This discussion began with the view that nothing could be further from the Eastern idea of art than the notion of "art for art's sake." It now appears that the phrase would serve if it were taken in a truly radical sense. What do we usually understand the phrase to mean? Does it mean that art is a luxury, a separate domain as yet unaffected by the demand that everything prove its worth in a measurable way, as a commodity? Does it mean that the artist is not accountable to anyone? Does it mean that art is apolitical? Is it simply a justification of meaningless products of individual "creativity" that people don't know how to take seriously and are afraid to criticize? If it is taken this way, nothing could be further from the Eastern view of art.

Yet one might interpret "art for art's sake" to mean that any attempt to describe or interpret the meaning of an art object falsifies its significance as an attempt at direct communication. In the Eastern view, art can be thought of as a bridge of communication, but one that only serves those who actually cross it and come to stand on the other side.

According to the Vajrayana view, the idea that a thing's meaning is its being does not just apply to particular products that are labeled works of art. If one begins by approaching art in this way, the work of art itself can

---

[33] Tibetan Nyigma Meditation Center, "Introduction to Tibetan Sacred Art," *Sacred Art of Tibet,* 2 ed., Berkeley: Dharma, 1974.
[34] Ibid.

revolutionize the way one approaches everything else. For the person "who has fully mastered the Vajrayana path, nothing could be more obvious or more profound than the discovery that everything *is* art, and is art for no other reason than that everything is what it is . . . that is enough." [35]

Suggestions for Further Reading

Two valuable surveys of Eastern thought are Heinrich Zimmer's *Philosophies of India* (New York: Meridian Books, Inc., 1964) and Fung Yu-Lan's *The Spirit of Chinese Philosophy,* trans. E. R. Hughes (Boston: Beacon Press, 1967). Many fine anthologies are available; among them, we would signal *The Wisdom of China and India,* edited by Lin Yutang (New York: Modern Library, 1955) and *A Sourcebook in Indian Philosophy,* edited by Sarvepalli Radhakrishnan and Charles A. Moore (Princeton, NJ: Princeton University Press, Princeton Paperbacks, 1967). In *The New Religions* (rev. ed., New York: Pocket Books, 1972), Jacob Needleman, a perceptive American philosopher, investigates the California-centered spiritual movements inspired by the teachings of such Eastern thinkers as Meher Baba, Maharish Mahesh Yogi, and J. Krishnamurti.

In *The Hindu View of Life* (New York: Macmillan, 1927), Sarvepalli Radhakrishnan offers an overview of Hindu philosophy. R. C. Zaehner's *Hinduism* (New York: Oxford University Press, 1966) is an excellent introduction.

Christmas Humphrey's *Buddhism,* 2d ed. (Baltimore: Penguin, Pelican Books, 1955) comes highly recommended as a general introduction. In this country, Zen Buddhism has had the greatest impact, largely due to the writings of D. T. Suzuki and Alan Watts. *Zen Buddhism: Selected Writings of D. T. Suzuki,* edited by William Barrett (Garden City, NY: Doubleday, 1956) and *The Way of Zen* by Alan W. Watts (New York: Pantheon, 1957) are especially valuable. Paul Reps compiled *Zen Flesh, Zen Bones; A Collection of Zen and Pre-Zen Writings* (Garden City, NY: Doubleday, Anchor Books, n.d.); few collections convey the spirit of Zen as successfully as his. Also focusing on Zen, several Catholic scholars have investigated points of contact between Eastern and Western thought from a religious perspective; see especially Dom Aelred Graham's *Zen Catholicism; A Suggestion* (New York: Harcourt, Harvest Books, 1963) and the essays by Thomas Merton collected in his *Mystics and Zen Masters* (New York: Dell, Delta Books, 1967).

[35] Ibid.

Lin Yutang edited *The Wisdom of Confucius* (New York: Random House, 1938); Arthur Waley translated *The Analects of Confucius* (London: Allen and Unwin, 1938), a traditional collection of Confucius' teachings as remembered and recorded by his followers. H. G. Creel's *Chinese Thought: From Confucius to Mao Tse-Tung* (Chicago: University of Chicago Press, 1953) offers an informative and readable survey.

In *The Parting of the Way: Lao Tzu and the Taoist Movement* (Boston: Beacon Press, 1957), Holmes Welch gives a concise and comprehensible exposition of the major aspects of Taoism, and presents the philosophy of Lao Tzu in contemporary terms. Lao Tzu's *Tao Te Ching* is available in many translations; in writing this essay, we consulted Wing-Tsit Chan's *The Way of Lao Tzu* (Indianapolis: Bobbs-Merrill, The Library of Liberal Arts, 1963), but Arthur Waley's *The Way and Its Power* (London: Allen and Unwin, 1934) is also excellent. Finally, Burton Watson has translated *The Complete Works of Chuang Tzu* (New York: Columbia University Press, 1968).

Selected Bibliography

Note: Space limitations prohibit our citing all the books and articles we have consulted; only our principal sources figure in this selected bibliography. Furthermore, works acknowledged on the copyright page are not mentioned here.

Arendt, Hannah: *The Human Condition,* Garden City, NY: Doubleday, 1959.

Aristotle: *Nichomachean Ethics,* W. D. Ross (trans.), in *The Works of Aristotle,* Oxford: Clarendon Press, 1925, rep. in Ethel M. Albert, Theodore Denise, and Sheldon Peterfreund (eds.), *Great Traditions in Ethics,* 3d ed., New York: Van Nostrand, 1975, pp. 40–58.

Austin, J. L.: *How to Do Things with Words,* Cambridge, MA: Harvard University Press, 1962.

——: "A Plea for Excuses," *Proceedings of the Aristotelian Society,* Vol. LVII (1956–1957), rep. in Donald F. Gustafson (ed.), *Essays in Philosophical Psychology,* Garden City, NY: Doubleday, 1964, pp. 1–29.

Ayer, A. J.: *The Concept of a Person and Other Essays,* London: Macmillan, 1968.

——: "The Vienna Circle," in *The Revolution in Philosophy,* New York: St. Martin's Press, 1965, pp. 70–87.

Bambrough, Renford: "Universals and Family Resemblances," *Proceedings of the Aristotelian Society,* vol. LXI (1960–1961), rep. in George Pitcher (ed.), *Wittgenstein: The Philosophical Investigations,* Garden City, NY: Doubleday, 1966, pp. 186–204.

Barbour, Ian G.: *Myths, Models, and Paradigms: A Comparative Study in Science and Religion,* New York: Harper & Row, 1974.

—— (ed.): *Western Man and Environmental Ethics: Attitudes toward Nature and Technology,* Reading, MA: Addison-Wesley, 1973.

Barnes, Hazel: *An Existentialist Ethic,* New York: Knopf, 1967.

Beardsley, Monroe C.: *Aesthetics from Classical Greece to the Present: A Short History,* New York: Macmillan, 1966.

Becker, Theodore: *The Impact of Supreme Court Decisions,* New York: Oxford University Press, 1969.

Bellah, Robert N.: *Beyond Belief: Essays on Religion in a Post-Traditional World,* New York: Harper & Row, 1970.

Bellamy, Edward, *Looking Backward: 2000–1887,* New York: New American Library, Signet Classics, 1960.

Berdyaev, Nicolas: *The Fate of Man in the Modern World,* Ann Arbor: University of Michigan Press, 1963.

Billington, Ray Allen: *America's Frontier Heritage,* New York: Holt, Rinehart & Winston, 1966.

Bonifazi, Conrad: *A Theology of Things: A Study of Man in his Physical Environment,* Philadelphia: Lippincott, 1967.

Brandt, Richard B.: "The Morality and Rationality of Suicide," in Seymour Perlin (ed.), *A Handbook for the Study of Suicide,* New York: Oxford University Press,

1975, rep. in James Rachels (ed.), *Moral Problems: A Collection of Philosophical Essays,* 2d ed., New York: Harper & Row, 1975, pp. 363–387.

Britton, Karl: *Philosophy and the Meaning of Life,* Cambridge, Cambridge University Press, 1969.

Broad, C. D.: *Five Types of Ethical Theory,* New York: Harcourt, 1930.

Bronowski, Jacob: *Science and Human Values,* rev. ed., New York: Harper & Row, 1965.

Buber, Martin: *I and Thou,* Walter Kaufmann (trans.), New York: Scribner, 1970.

———: *Two Types of Faith,* Norman Goldhawk (trans.), New York: Harper & Row, 1961.

Burtt, E. A.: *The Metaphysical Foundations of Modern Science,* Garden City, NY: Doubleday, 1954.

Caillois, Roger: *Man and the Sacred,* Meyer Barash (trans.), New York: Free Press, 1959.

Campbell, Charles A.: *On Selfhood and Godhood,* London: Allen and Unwin, 1957.

Camus, Albert: *The Myth of Sisyphus and Other Essays,* Justin O'Brien (trans.), New York: Vintage, 1955.

———: *The Rebel: An Essay on Man in Revolt,* Anthony Bower (trans.), New York: Vintage, 1956.

———: "Reflections on the Guillotine," *Resistance, Rebellion,*

and Death, Justin O'Brien (trans.), New York: Vintage, 1974, pp. 173–234.

Cassirer, Ernst: *An Essay on Man: An Introduction to a Philosophy of Human Culture,* New Haven: Yale University Press, 1974.

Choron, Jacques: *Death and Western Thought,* New York: Macmillan, 1963.

———: *Death and Modern Man,* New York: Macmillan, 1964.

Cranston, Maurice: *What Are Human Rights?,* New York: Basic Books, 1962.

Descartes, René: *The Philosophical Works of Descartes,* E. S. Haldane and G. R. T. Ross (trans.), Cambridge, Cambridge University Press, 1931.

Dewey, John: *The Philosophy of John Dewey,* vols. 1 and 2, John J. McDermott (ed.), New York: Putnam, 1973.

Dubos, René: "A Theology of the Earth," in Ian T. Barbour (ed.), *Western Man and Environmental Ethics: Attitudes toward Nature and Technology,* op. cit., pp. 43–54.

Durkheim, Émile: *Suicide: A Study in Sociology,* John A. Spaulding and George Simpson (trans.), New York: Free Press, 1951.

Eddington, Sir Arthur: *The Nature of the Physical World,* Ann Arbor: University of Michigan Press, 1974.

Edwards, Paul: "The Meaning and Value of Life," in Paul Edwards (ed.), *The Encyclopedia of Philosophy,* vol. 4, New

York: Macmillan and Free Press, 1967, pp. 467–477.

Ehrlich, Paul R. and Anne H. Ehrlich: *The End of Affluence,* New York: Ballantine, 1974.

Eliade, Mircea: *The Sacred and the Profane: The Nature of Religion,* Willard R. Trask (trans.), New York: Harper & Row, 1961.

Evans, Donald D.: *The Logic of Self-Involvement: A Philosophical Study of Everyday Language with Special Reference to the Christian Use of Language about God as Creator,* London: SCM Press, 1963.

Faulkner, William: "Address Upon Receiving the Nobel Prize for Literature," in James B. Meriwether (ed.), *Essays, Speeches and Public Letters,* New York: Random House, 1965, pp. 119–121.

Feuer, Lewis (ed.): *Marx and Engels,* Garden City, NY: Doubleday, 1959.

Feuerbach, Ludwig: *The Fiery Brook: Selected Writings of Ludwig Feuerbach,* introduction by Zawar Hanfi (trans.), Garden City, NY: Doubleday, 1972.

Fletcher, Joseph: *Situation Ethics: The New Morality,* Philadelphia: Westminster Press, 1966.

Flew, Anthony: "Theology and Falsification," in Anthony Flew and Alasdair MacIntyre (eds.), *New Essays in Philosophical Theology,* London: SCM Press, 1955, pp. 96–99.

Frankena, William: *Ethics,* 2d ed., Englewood Cliffs, NJ:

Prentice-Hall, 1973.

Freud, Sigmund: *A General Introduction to Psychoanalysis,* Joan Riviere (trans.), New York: Washington Square Press, 1960.

——: *Civilization and Its Discontents,* Joan Riviere (trans.), Garden City, NY: Doubleday, 1957.

Fromm, Erich: *Escape from Freedom,* New York: Holt, Rinehart and Winston, 1961.

——: *The Forgotten Language: An Introduction to the Understanding of Dreams, Fairy Tales and Myths,* New York: Grove Press, 1951.

Frondizi, Risieri: *What Is Value?,* LaSalle, IL: Open Court Publishing Co., 1971.

Gabriel, Ralph Henry: *The Course of American Democratic Thought: An Intellectual History Since 1815,* New York: Ronald Press, 1940.

Golding, William: *Lord of the Flies,* New York: Coward-McCann, 1962.

Gordon, David Cole: *Overcoming the Fear of Death,* Baltimore: Penguin, 1972.

——: *Self-Love,* Baltimore: Penguin, 1972.

Hall, A. R.: *The Scientific Revolution,* Boston: Beacon Press, 1960.

Hampshire, Stuart (ed.): *Philosophy of Mind,* New York:

Harper & Row, 1966.

Hanson, Norwood Russell: *Observation and Explanation: A Guide to Philosophy of Science,* London: Allen and Unwin, 1972.

Hardin, Garrett: "The Tragedy of the Commons," *Science,* 162, Dec. 13, 1968, pp. 1243–1248.

Heidegger, Martin: *Being and Time,* John Macquarrie and Edward Robinson (trans.), New York: Harper & Row, 1962.

Heilbroner, Robert L.: *An Inquiry into the Human Prospect,* New York: Norton, 1974.

Heisenberg, Werner: *Physics and Philosophy: The Revolution in Modern Science,* New York: Harper & Row, Harper Torchbooks, 1962.

Hempel, Carl: *Aspects of Scientific Explanation and Other Essays in the Philosophy of Science,* New York: Free Press, 1965.

Hick, John: *Faith and Knowledge: A Modern Introduction to the Problem of Religious Knowledge,* Ithaca, NY: Cornell University Press, 1957.

Hobbes, Thomas: *Leviathan: Or the Matter, Forme and Power of a Commonwealth Ecclesiasticall and Civil,* Michael Oakeshott (ed.), New York: Collier, 1962.

Huizinga, Johan: *Homo Ludens: A Study of the Play Element in Culture,* trans. anon., Boston: Beacon Press, 1955.

Hume, David: *The Philosophy of David Hume,* introduction

by V. C. Chappell (ed.), New York: Modern Library, 1963.

Husserl, Edmund: *Ideas: General Introduction to Pure Phenomenology,* W. R. Boyce Gibson (trans.), New York: Collier, 1962.

——: "Philosophy as Rigorous Science," in *Phenomenology and the Crisis of Philosophy: Philosophy as Rigorous Science and Philosophy and the Crisis of European Man,* Quentin Lauer (trans.), New York: Harper & Row, 1965, pp. 71–147.

Hyland, Drew A.: *The Origins of Philosophy: Its Rise in Myth and the Pre-Socratics,* New York: Putnam's, Capricorn Books, 1973.

Ibsen, Henrik: *A Doll's House,* in *Three Plays by Ibsen,* New York: Dell, 1959, pp. 113–203.

James, William: *The Principles of Psychology,* New York: Dover, 1950.

——: *The Varieties of Religious Experience: A Study in Human Nature,* New York: Collier, 1961.

——: *Pragmatism and Other Essays,* New York: Washington Square Press, 1963.

Jaspers, Karl: *The Future of Mankind,* E. B. Ashton (trans.), Chicago: University of Chicago Press, 1961.

——: *Man in the Modern Age,* Eden Paul and Cedar Paul (trans.), Garden City, NY: Doubleday, 1957.

Jörgensen, Johannes: *Saint Francis of Assisi: A Biography,* T.

O'Conor Sloane (trans.), New York: Image, 1955.

Kammen, Michael: *People of Paradox: An Inquiry Concerning the Origins of American Civilization,* New York: Vintage, 1973.

Kant, Immanuel: *Critique of Pure Reason,* F. Max Müller (trans.), Garden City, NY: Doubleday, 1966.

———: *Fundamental Principles of the Metaphysic of Morals,* Thomas K. Abbott (trans.), from *Kant's Critique of Practical Reason and Other Works on the Theory of Ethics,* London: Longmans, Green, and Co., 1898, rep. in Ethel M. Albert, Theodore Denise, and Sheldon Peterfreund (eds.), *Great Traditions in Ethics,* 3d ed., New York: Van Nostrand, 1975, pp. 206–224.

———: *Critique of Practical Reason,* introduction by Lewis White Beck (trans.), Indianapolis: Bobbs-Merrill, Library of Liberal Arts, 1956.

Keen, Sam: *Apology for Wonder,* New York: Harper & Row, 1969.

Kierkegaard, Søren: *Fear and Trembling and The Sickness Unto Death,* introductions and notes by Walter Lowrie (trans.), Princeton, NJ: Princeton University Press, 1973.

———: *Either/Or,* vol. 1, David F. Swenson and Lillian Marvin Swenson (trans.), with revisions and foreword by Howard A. Johnson, and vol. 2, Walter Lowrie (trans.), with revisions and foreword by Howard A. Johnson, Princeton, NJ: Princeton University Press, 1971.

Koyré, Alexandre: *From the Closed World to the Infinite Universe,* New York: Harper & Row, Harper Torchbooks, 1958.

Kramer, Samuel Noah (ed.): *Mythologies of the Ancient World,* Garden City, NY: Doubleday, 1961.

Kübler-Ross, Elisabeth: *On Death and Dying,* New York: Macmillan, 1969.

Kwant, Remy C.: *Philosophy of Labor,* Pittsburgh: Duquesne University Press, 1960.

Langer, Susanne K.: *Philosophy in a New Key: A Study in the Symbolism of Reason, Rite, and Art,* Cambridge, MA: Harvard University Press, 1942.

———: *Feeling and Form: A Theory of Art,* New York: Scribner's, 1953.

———: *Philosophical Sketches,* New York: Mentor, 1964.

Locke, John: *Two Treatises of Government,* a critical edition with introduction and apparatus criticus by Peter Laslett, New York: Mentor, 1965.

Loew, Cornelius: *Myth, Sacred History and Philosophy: The Pre-Christian Religious Heritage of the West,* New York: Harcourt, 1967.

MacGregor, Geddes: *Philosophical Issues in Religious Thought,* Boston: Houghton Mifflin, 1973.

Macquarrie, John: *Principles of Christian Theology,* New York: Scribner, 1966.

Malcolm, Norman: *Knowledge and Certainty: Essays and Lectures,* Englewood Cliffs, NJ: Prentice-Hall, 1963.

Marcel, Gabriel: *Being and Having,* New York: Harper & Row, Harper Torchbooks, 1965.

Marcuse, Herbert: *Reason and Revolution: Hegel and the Rise of Social Theory,* Boston: Beacon Press, 1941.

——: *One-Dimensional Man,* Boston: Beacon Press, 1964.

Maritain, Jacques: *Man's Destiny in Eternity,* Boston: Beacon Press, 1949.

Marx, Karl and Friedrich Engels: *The Communist Manifesto,* Samuel Moore (trans.), Baltimore: Penguin, 1967.

Marx, Leo: *The Machine in the Garden: Technology and the Pastoral Ideal in America,* New York: Oxford University Press, 1964.

McGill, Vivian Jerauld: *The Idea of Happiness,* New York: Praeger, 1968.

Merleau-Ponty, Maurice: *The Essential Writings of Merleau-Ponty,* Alden L. Fisher (ed.), New York: Harcourt, 1969.

Mill, John Stuart: *The Essential Works of John Stuart Mill,* Max Lerner (ed.), New York: Bantam Books, 1961.

Murchland, Bernard (ed.): *The Meaning of the Death of God,* New York: Random House, 1967.

Nietzsche, Friedrich: *Thus Spoke Zarathustra,* Walter Kaufmann (trans.), in *The Portable Nietzsche,* Walter Kaufmann (ed.), New York: Viking, 1954, pp. 103–440.

——: *The Will to Power,* Walter Kaufmann and R. J. Hollingdale (trans.), New York: Vintage, 1968.

O'Briant, Walter H.: "Man, Nature, and the History of Philosophy," in William T. Blackstone (ed.), *Philosophy and Environmental Crisis,* Athens: University of Georgia Press, 1974, pp. 79–89.

Ortega y Gasset, José: "The Dehumanization of Art," Helene Weyl (trans.), in *The Dehumanization of Art and Other Essays on Art, Culture, and Literature,* Princeton, NJ: Princeton University Press, 1968, pp. 3–54.

——: *The Revolt of the Masses,* New York: Norton, 1932.

Otto, Rudolph: *The Idea of the Holy,* 2d ed., John Harvey (trans.), London: Oxford University Press, 1957.

Parker, DeWitt Henry: *Human Values,* New York: Harper & Row, 1931.

Paton, H. J.: *The Categorical Imperative: A Study in Kant's Moral Philosophy,* New York: Harper & Row, Harper Torchbooks, 1967.

Plato: *Apology,* Benjamin Jowett (trans.), in *The Works of Plato,* Irwin Edman (ed.), New York: Modern Library, 1956, pp. 59–88.

——: *The Laws,* Trevor J. Saunders (trans.), Baltimore: Penguin, 1970.

Pepper, Stephen: *The Sources of Value,* Berkeley: University of California Press, 1958.

Popper, Sir Karl R.: "Of Clouds and Clocks: An Approach to the Problem of Rationality and the Freedom of Man," St. Louis, MO: Washington University Press, 1965.

——: *The Logic of Scientific Discovery,* New York: Harper & Row, Harper Torchbooks, 1965.

Quine, Willard Van Orman: "Two Dogmas of Empiricism," *From a Logical Point of View: Nine Logico-Philosophical Essays,* 2d rev. ed., Cambridge, MA: Harvard University Press, 1961, pp. 20–46.

Rawls, John: *A Theory of Justice,* Cambridge, MA: Harvard University Press, 1971.

Rhinelander, Philip: *Is Man Incomprehensible to Man?,* Stanford, CA: Stanford Alumni Association, 1973.

Rousseau, Jean Jacques: *The Social Contract and Discourses,* G. D. H. Cole (trans.), New York: Dutton, 1950.

Russell, Bertrand: "A Free Man's Worship," *Mysticism and Logic: And Other Essays,* London: Allen and Unwin, 1959.

Ryle, Gilbert: *The Concept of Mind,* New York: Barnes & Noble, 1949.

Sabine, George: *A History of Political Theory,* 3d ed., New York: Holt, Rinehart and Winston, 1937.

Santmire, H. Paul: "Historical Dimensions of the American Crisis," *Dialog,* Summer 1970, rep. in Ian T. Barbour (ed.), *Western Man and Environmental Ethics: Attitudes toward Nature and Technology,* op. cit., pp. 66–92.

Sartre, Jean-Paul: "Existentialism," *Existentialism and Human Emotions,* Bernard Frechtman (trans.), New York: Philosophical Library, 1957, pp. 9–51.

Scheler, Max: *Man's Place in Nature,* Hans Meyerhoff (trans.), New York: Noonday Press, 1971.

——: *The Nature of Sympathy,* Peter Heath (trans.), New Haven: Yale University Press, 1954.

Schopenhauer, Arthur: *The Works of Schopenhauer,* Will Durant (ed.), introduction by Thomas Mann, New York: Frederick Ungar, 1955.

Schuck, Peter H.: "Why Regulation Fails," *Harper's,* September 1975, p. 16 ff.

Schütz, Alfred: *On Phenomenology and Social Relations,* introduction by Helmut R. Wagner (ed.), Chicago: University of Chicago Press, 1970.

Scott, Andrew: *Political Thought in America,* New York: Holt, Rinehart and Winston, 1964.

Searle, John R.: *Speech Acts: An Essay in the Philosophy of Language,* Cambridge, Cambridge University Press, 1969.

Shaw, George Bernard: *Man and Superman: A Comedy and a Philosophy,* New York: Bantam, 1959.

Shorter, J. M.: "Other Minds," in Paul Edwards (ed.), *The*

Encyclopedia of Philosophy, vol. 7, New York: Macmillan and Free Press, 1967, pp. 7–13.

Slater, Philip: *The Pursuit of Loneliness: American Culture at the Breaking Point,* Boston: Beacon Press, 1970.

——: *Earthwalk,* Garden City, NY: Doubleday, 1974.

Smart, Ninian: *Philosophers and Religious Truth,* London: SCM Press, 1964.

Smith, John E.: "The Experience of the Holy and the Idea of God," in James M. Edie (ed.), *Phenomenology in America,* New York: Quadrangle, 1967, rep. in Paula Rothenberg Struhl and Karsten J. Struhl (eds.), *Philosophy Now: An Introductory Reader,* 2d ed., New York: Random House, 1975, pp. 203–211.

Skinner, B. F.: *Science and Human Behavior,* New York: Free Press, 1965.

——: *Beyond Freedom and Dignity,* New York: Knopf, 1971.

Stevenson, C. L.: *Ethics and Language,* New Haven: Yale University Press, 1972.

Strauss, Leo: *The Political Philosophy of Hobbes: Its Basis and Its Genesis,* Elsa M. Sinclair (trans.), Chicago: University of Chicago Press, Phoenix Books, 1963.

Strawson, P. F.: *Freedom and Resentment and Other Essays,* London: Methuen, 1974.

——: *Individuals: An Essay in Descriptive Metaphysics,* London: Methuen, 1965.

Tawney, R. H.: *Religion and the Rise of Capitalism,* Gloucester: Peter Smith, 1962.

Thoreau, Henry David: *The Writings of Henry David Thoreau,* vols. 1 to 4, New York: AMS Press, 1968.

Tillich, Paul: *Systematic Theology,* vols. 1 to 3, Chicago: University of Chicago Press, vol. 1, 1951, vol. 2, 1957, vol. 3, 1963.

Tocqueville, Alexis de: *Democracy in America,* abr. ed., Richard Heffner (ed.), New York: Mentor, 1956.

Tolstoy, Leo: *What Is Art?,* Aylmer Maude (trans.), Indianapolis: Bobbs-Merrill, Library of Liberal Arts, 1960.

Weber, Max: *The Protestant Ethic and the Spirit of Capitalism,* New York: Scribner, 1930.

Weitz, Morris: "The Role of Theory in Aesthetics," *Journal of Aesthetics and Art Criticism,* vol. XV, no. 1, September 1956, rep. in Morris Weitz (ed.), *Problems in Aesthetics: An Introductory Book of Readings,* New York: Macmillan, 1959, pp. 145–156.

Wellman, Carl: "The Ethical Implications of Cultural Relativity," *The Journal of Philosophy,* vol. LX, no. 7, Mar. 28, 1963, pp. 169–184.

White, Jr., Lynn: "The Historical Roots of Our Ecologic Crisis," *Science,* 155, Mar. 10, 1967, rep. in Ian T. Barbour (ed.), *Western Man and Environmental Ethics: Attitudes toward Nature and Technology,* op. cit., pp. 18–30.

Wilson, Edmund: *I Thought of Daisy,* New York: Avon, 1968.

Winch, Peter: *The Idea of a Social Science and Its Relation to Philosophy,* London: Routledge & Kegan Paul, 1958.

Wisdom, John: "Gods," *Philosophy and Psychoanalysis,* Oxford: Blackwell, 1953, pp. 149–168.

Wittgenstein, Ludwig: *Tractatus Logico-Philosophicus,* D. F. Pears and B. F. McGuinness (trans.), London: Routledge & Kegan Paul, 1961.

——: *The Blue and Brown Books,* Oxford: Blackwell, 1964.

——: *Philosophical Investigations,* G. E. M. Anscombe (trans.), New York: Macmillan, 1953.

Index

Index

Terms defined in context are in **boldface.** Viewpoint selections, listed by author and title, are indicated by *v* after the page number.